COSMIC ASCENSION PATHWAYS

Inner Guidance for Cosmic Ascension

AMERISSIS KUMARA

BALBOA
PRESS

A DIVISION OF HAY HOUSE

Balboa Press books may be ordered through booksellers or by contacting:

Balboa Press
A Division of Hay House
1663 Liberty Drive
Bloomington, IN 47403
www.balboapress.com.au
1 (877) 407-4847

Because of the dynamic nature of the Internet, any web addresses or links contained in this book may have changed since publication and may no longer be valid. The views expressed in this work are solely those of the author and do not necessarily reflect the views of the publisher, and the publisher hereby disclaims any responsibility for them.

The author of this book does not dispense medical advice or prescribe the use of any technique as a form of treatment for physical, emotional, or medical problems without the advice of a physician, either directly or indirectly. The intent of the author is only to offer information of a general nature to help you in your quest for emotional and spiritual well-being. In the event you use any of the information in this book for yourself, which is your constitutional right, the author and the publisher assume no responsibility for your actions.

Any people depicted in stock imagery provided by Getty Images are models, and such images are being used for illustrative purposes only.
Certain stock imagery © Getty Images.

Print information available on the last page.

ISBN: 978-1-5043-1275-2 (sc)
ISBN: 978-1-5043-1276-9 (e)

Balboa Press rev. date: 03/28/2018

Contents

PART 1: INNER GUIDANCE KEY PRAYERS FOR THE SACRED
FLAMES AND RAYS

PART 2: INNER GUIDANCE AFFIRMATION/THEMES/ISSUES/
PROBLEMS SACRED FLAMES HEALING SOLUTIONS

PART 3: INNER GUIDANCE
MEDITATIONS THE SACRED FLAMES AND RAYS
CRYSTALS, GEMSTONES AND SINGING BOWLS

PART 4: INNER GUIDANCE HEALING AND PURIFICATION
     CLEARINGS AND CHARTS

Introduction

As I walked within the shadows, I felt a presence within my soul and I wondered, what is this feeling, that I feel coming from inside of my being? Where do these thoughts come from that ask questions for which I have no answers? Why do I have these painful emotions that stir my being to have me feel so alone, lonely and unloved?

What are the reasons for the stirrings that come forth un-beckoned?

The Spirit of the Christed Light Consciousness had stirred within me and as persistent whispers and tendrils of Light, reached out across all the dimensions of time and space to touch my Spirit, Heart and Mind and awakened me to the Awareness of my Divinity of Spirit and to the Divinity of all beings in the Cosmic All.

Many eons ago I set forth on a mission, I was to remain asleep for a very long time, through thousands upon thousands of incarnations in Universes and Multiverses too numerous to recall, like the stars in the heavens they are to me now. I being sent by The One, to walk amongst all the beings that existed and exist, in the All That Is, The One, to be one being that would ever remember the Cosmic and Universal Laws of One that these Laws would remain in the Collective Consciousness of all Universes and Multiverses, Eternal and Infinite, as is the All That Is.

This book of Prayers, Meditations and Healing Procedures, is a Key to Cosmic Ascension, and One Unity Christed Light of God Consciousness and comes down through the ages of time, the Keys have been held within this Spirit that is I, for I did say unto The One, The Ultimate and Supreme God of All Creations, the All That Is, that I would come down through all the dimensions and walk with all of the Children of Creation, with the understanding that I would always remember the Truth of the Oneness of All Kingdoms and Realms, the Oneness of All Universes, Multiverses and the Omniverses, the Oneness that is the Cosmic All, and that I would be always in Service to the One.

I ask that you honor this book of prayers, meditations and the techniques held within the prayers, for the truth that it contains, and take these prayers, meditations and healing processes into the Sacred Chambers of Your Heart and Feel the Love of The One, the All That Is.

Your Mighty I AM Presence will guide you to the Prayers, Meditations and Healing Processes that will best serve you, in your Cosmic Ascension to the energy of the 5th Dimension and beyond.

I AM That I AM!

Blessings to You,
Amerissis Kumara
Member, Elohim Council of Elders
Channel, for Cosmic Christed Light Consciousness

Acknowledgements

To the Beloved Reader, and all Lightworkers who are in Service to the
All That Is, The One, the Ultimate and Supreme God of All Creation.
I Desire in the following few words to acknowledge the Planetary
Hierarchy: The Planetary Logos: Lord Gautama Buddha.
Planetary Hierarchy: Lord Sanat Kumara and Lady Venus. The
Planetary Logos: Lord Maitreya. The Universal Logos: Lord
Melchizedek. The Great Divine Director: Master Ragoczy. The
Maha Chohan: and the Chohans of the Twelve Sacred Flames
and Rays. All Great Light beings who Overlight the Cosmic Rays.
The Universal Judge: The Masters and Lady Masters of Love and
Light, All the Archangels, their Divine Complements and the
Legions of Angels who serve the Sacred Flames and Rays.

I pay tribute to them for their great truth, wisdom, unconditional
love, compassion, understanding, purification, mercy, dedication and
perseverance.

In keeping the Sacred Flames and Rays alive, they are the saviours of
Humanity and Planet Earth (our Glorious and Precious Mother), who
in the words of this book is Greatly Loved and Honored with Heartfelt
Gratitude.

I AM in Gratitude from the very depths of the Sacred Chambers of My
Heart for Your Service to Humanity, Planet Earth and All the Kingdoms
and Realms of Planet Earth.

I especially wish to acknowledge, Master Adama, of Telos and the
Heart of Lemuria, and the Council of Elders of Telos, for bringing the
teachings of Lemuria to Humanity through the beloved channel and
medium, Aurelia Louise Jones.

I Thank Aurelia for the Blessing of Her Life and dedication to bringing the teachings of Master Adama of Telos and the Heart of Lemuria, and the Masters and Lady Masters of the Seven Sacred Flames to the Conscious Awareness of Humanity.

I acknowledge The One, the Ultimate and Supreme God Creator of All and my Mighty I AM Presence for the precious words of Christed Light of God Consciousness. They have become the voice of the many Prayers, Meditations, Healing Processes and Wisdom contained within the teachings of this book.

Blessings to You,
Amerissis Kumara

The Purpose of This Book

The Purpose of this Book is to inform and assist you on your pathway to Healing and Ascension, through the frequency and vibration of the Prayers, Meditations and Healing processes. They are designed to access your inner belief systems and bring to your conscious awareness - from your cellular memory and unconscious and subconscious mind - the negative mental and emotional patterns and programs that are affecting your life in detrimental ways.

This Book is called –
Cosmic Ascension Pathways
Inner Guidance for Cosmic Ascension

The Prayers, Affirmations and Meditations are Keys, in that they are stated in the positive. This is so that the lower mind, the ego, will respond with negative thoughts or feelings. From this you will gain insights into what beliefs, patterns and programs you have running from your unconscious mind.

The Prayers, Affirmations and Meditations are the Keys that will help you open the doorways to access your hidden unconscious memories. There are affirmations for each Prayer that are also Keys that will bring forth beliefs that show the reverse of the affirmation.

The Sacred Flames and Rays each have Key attributes that they enhance and amplify on certain days of the week. Also, if you have an issue or problem with a particular Sacred Flame or Ray attribute, the energy and vibration of the Sacred Flame of that Ray will help you heal the issue or problem, and reframe to a positive outcome by your having received its Wisdom and understanding.

The information about the day in which each of the Rays is amplified on is found on the Cover for each of the Rays and within the section for Affirmation/Themes/Issues and Problems.

Foreword

The Prayers for the Twelve Sacred Flames and Rays are <u>powerful</u>, and are designed to help you to Access your Unconscious Mind. They are <u>not</u> comfort prayers, or prayers to create energy, but prayers that help you gain Access to the Energy created by the hidden beliefs within you, which prevent you from seeing beyond the Veils, to the Truth of who you really are, thus clearing away the illusions, so that you are able to be the in reality.

<u>The Prayers can be used in many ways:</u>

Prayers for Ascension

These help you see beyond the Veils of Forgetfulness to the Truth, by having cleared from the Unconscious Mind, the beliefs, patterns and programs that have kept you tied to the cycles of reincarnation.

Prayers to Heal in One's lifetime the Causes
of what you are at the Effects of

The Prayers help you eliminate the causes through the healing gained from the Sacred Flames and Rays, coupled with the releasing, relinquishing and handing over of old negative beliefs, to your Mighty I Am Presence or the Sacred Flames and Rays of Christed Light of God Consciousness, thus changing the negative causes to positive causes.

The transformation of the old negative belief patterns to new positive belief patterns is very important for your inner growth and Ascension to Ever - Higher Levels of Consciousness. This will happen once you have the Wisdom and Understanding of your old negative beliefs, and changed them into positive ones.

Prayers to the Twelve Sacred Flames and Rays

These are able to cancel out negative energy and bring in positive energy to all areas of the Mind, Body and Physical Heart. The Positive Energy of the Sacred Flames and Rays remove the Negative Energy, eliminating it from your Mind, Body and Physical Heart. <u>The Sacred Heart</u>, which your Divine-Self, (True-Self) resides, is All Knowing, Eternally Free, Forgiving and Unconditional Love, because your True-Self is the God -Self within.

Prayers for Enlightenment

Held within these prayers are many Wisdoms, Understandings and Information coming to you from the Ascended Masters, and the Sacred Flames and Rays of Christed Light Consciousness.

Prayers for Healing

There are special healing prayers in this book that are meant to be used for Self-Healing, both in private and group situations. These prayers are processing prayers. When you work with them, feel the energy of your Divine-Self within you and working through you. If you cannot feel the energy, trust that the process in happening. Know; that the more you trust, the more likely it is that you will begin to feel the energy.

<u>There can be resistance to the Prayers coming from one's Ego,</u> (False Self).

For your continued Healing and Growth, you are to research any thoughts and feeling of resistance within yourself, these can be blocks caused and created and by the Ego, they stem from egoism, arrogance and control of you (the person), in an effort to prevent your evolution and growth to enlightenment, self-awareness and healing.

<u>Nothing is outside of self, all is within you</u>.

Because the energy of the Universe is all in Oneness, there is always energy. If you are unable to feel that energy or even be aware of it, then something within yourself is blocking you from feeling, knowing and accessing the energy that emanates from the Divine True-Self and the Universe around you. You need to be aware of the many avenues that the Ego is prepared to use in its efforts to be in control and prevent you from being your True-Self and connected to the Universal Mind of God, which is The One, the Ultimate and Supreme God of All Creations, the All That Is.

Prayers for Shifting Consciousness

These Prayers can help you shift to higher levels of Consciousness. This happens when a person reads and studies the Prayers silently. And then ponders the messages contained within the prayers. You can select paragraphs, phrases and words from the Prayers that resonate for you as something you need to use as an affirmation.

The Prayers are not so much about creating energy, as about accessing the energy of your Mind or Heart, as it is now, and bringing about a change in consciousness which takes you up to ever - higher levels of consciousness. There can be great resistance to these changes in consciousness, because the Ego, does not want to relinquish control. This resistance can happen at any level, even to those in the higher levels of consciousness, who have already ascended to the 5th Dimension and beyond. They still have to be on alert to this energy coming from the Ego, as there are many levels of consciousness that need to be experienced, learned from, cleared, etc., before one can attain the level of God Consciousness found at the Godhead.

While we are in the physical body, we have the Ego, even though we also have the True-Self, our Divine I AM Presence within us, the Ego (personality) is still present and is learning from the True-Self, our Divine

I AM Presence how to be the truth of who we are. We still have to keep the Ego from being in control and allow the True-Self our Divine I AM Presence within us, to guide our actions and reactions to be Unconditional Love.

We are all being challenged to grow to ever higher levels of Consciousness. The way is different for each one. In the development of these Prayers, many different types of messages had to be conveyed, to many different types of Mind Consciousness.

As the developer of these Prayers, which have been designed to aid the consciousness of Humanity to evolve to Cosmic Ascension, the task has been a delight and also an amazing experience. As such, I feel honored to have been of service in this manner during this incarnation.

The Prayers are meant to Challenge you. As you go higher in consciousness, you will find that you have become the Prayers, and the information contained within the Prayers is within you, within your Consciousness, within your Soul, within your Physical Body, Body Elemental and Inner Child.

With this understanding, you will no longer feel compelled to read the prayers as often, or feel any energy from the prayers, as the emotional charges that were negative, have either been changed to positive energy or have disappeared. As you dealt with the energy's density, and cleared enough of the negative energy, you are able to relax and be still. Or if the negative energy is still there, the energy charge in any given situation is greatly decreased.

The energy is not created by the Prayers; so much as the Prayers access the energy that is within you. With your connection to the Key Prayers for Cosmic Ascension, you have become one with them, and you are that. You are the Prayers, and the Prayers in consciousness have become part of you.

In achieving the Higher Consciousness that is at the higher end of the 4th Dimension and into the 5th Dimension, the Prayers help you shift to the Consciousness necessary for entry into the 5th Dimension. They aid you in the clearance, clarity, enlightenment, and acceptance of the Divine Perfection that you are.

In the attainment of the 5th Dimensional energies and beyond, the Prayers can help you deal with the challenges and changes that are happening for you.

Continued use of the Prayers, Affirmations, or select Paragraphs or Phrases from the Prayers will assist you as situations arise and in the maintenance of the Higher Consciousness that you have achieved. These Prayers etc. will be ones that appeal to your Mind and Heart. You have within you the format, techniques and skills necessary to formulate prayers that suit the level of consciousness that you are at now in your evolution.

How to Use This Book

There are many ways in which you may wish to use this book:

Read the Prayer slowly and feel the Prayer from your Heart Energy. Read the Prayer, speaking it aloud, begin slowly and repeat the prayer while gradually speeding up the tempo a bit; so that the energy, vibration and frequency are uplifted.

When Reading Prayers as a group participant; be certain that you read them aloud and at the same pitch of voice and tempo as others in the group.

Be Mindful and Heartfelt at what thoughts and feelings come up for you when you are saying the Prayers; or after having said the Prayers, notice what thoughts and feelings come through to your conscious awareness during the day.

Observe what thoughts and feelings come through for you during the weeks that follow, especially if you are saying the same Prayers consistently, as in each morning or evening.

Read, Speak and Write an affirmation three times and then repeat it three more times during the day for 28 days; this is a powerful exercise.

Notice what issues and problems you desire to have healed, and choose the Prayers, Affirmations and the Sacred Flame of Healing that has the attributes for the healing.

Whenever you have an issue or problem occurring during your day, bring in the Sacred Flame of Healing that would cover that issue or problem, and ask your Mighty I AM Presence to remove the negative energy from that issue or problem, and to ensure that you attain the level of Wisdom and Understanding needed that can clear this issue or problem from your Mind and Emotions.

You must consciously change a Negative Belief to a Positive Belief in order to achieve the Positive Cause that leads to the Positive Effects. Your Mighty I AM Presence can help you choose the new Positive belief that brings about the desired change.

The Sacred Flames of Healing Solution is a combination of Sacred Flames and Rays that can help you heal a situation, issue or problem, in that the Sacred Flames will show you the negative thoughts, feelings, emotions and belief system that you are to consciously change; this will affect the unconscious mind which contains the negative program, changing the program and thus creating positive thoughts, feelings, emotions and beliefs.

The Sacred Flames and Rays can help you achieve the necessary Wisdom and Understanding that will clear the limiting beliefs from you; be sure to ask your Mighty I AM Presence to remove the negative energy from your four body systems. The four body systems consists of; The Physical Body, Etheric Body, Mental and Emotional Body and the Spirit/ Soul.

Ask your Mighty I AM Presence to receive the negative energy from you, so that it can then be transmuted, transformed and transfigured to positive energy that will benefit you, the Planet Earth and Humanity.

When you read the Prayers to yourself, listen into your thought processes and your feelings, and notice what comes up for you. Your mind may wander - this being avoidance of some part of the Prayer. It may be a word or a sentence that contains something that the mind does not want to think about - because of the triggers contained within the unconscious mind that lead to belief systems that are out of consciousness, and therefore of the unconscious.

Be aware of any physical charge of energy - no matter how large or small that charge of energy may be - and what thoughts or emotions preceded that charge. The charge of energy is a trigger to what is occurring within your unconscious mind, an indicator that there is something here for you to investigate.

Notice any mental or emotional distractions that occur for you when reading the Prayers, such as, loss of focus or lack of comprehension. These distractions represent issues that need to be addressed. In so doing you will develop a greater understanding of what is happening within your unconscious mind.

Realize that we manifest in our lives the dis-ease of our mental and emotional state, which thus creates our physical disease or wellness. The dis-ease of the Mind, (mental and emotions), creates the diseases within our physical body.

<u>Say each prayer once, three, six or nine times, in accordance with your inner guidance.</u>

(Repeat the Prayer in a series of three.) Followed by the prayer - Prayer to the Subconscious Mind, (page 46)

Each time you repeat a prayer, you build a momentum of Light encoded in the prayer.

This enables the Prayer to change the Subconscious Mind

Speak your Prayers from your Heart, because your Heart is connected to your Higher-Mind, your Higher-Self, which in turn connects you to your I AM Presence, the Lord God essence of your being.

The Mind is connected to the Left Brain, the consciousness of the lower mind. The Heart is connected to the Right Brain, the consciousness of the higher mind, enabling access to the All-Knowing of Higher Consciousness and your I AM Presence.

Observe your thoughts and feelings, your belief systems, patterns and programs. Apply the Sacred Flames and Rays that can help you achieve the necessary Wisdom and Understanding that will help clear these limiting beliefs from you. Be sure to ask your mighty I AM Presence to remove the negative energy from your four body system.

Ask your Mighty I AM Presence to receive the negative energy from you so, that it can then be transmuted, transformed and transfigured to positive energy that will then benefit the Planet and Humanity.

<u>Questions to ask one's self when you have an emotional reaction.</u>

What is the emotion that I am feeling?

What is the cause of this emotion? What thoughts and feelings preceded this emotional reaction?

What is the reason for the emotion?

What is behind the emotion? And is there anything else, anything more?

When thinking back over my life, when was the first time I felt this emotion, this feeling of...?

What was happening to or for me at the time?

What was being said to me then?

What did I make this event or what happened, mean about me?

What prevents me from being or achieving ...?

<u>Next ask yourself these questions:</u>

Am I ready to heal this emotion?

Is there any part of me that does not want to heal this emotion?

If so, what is the positive reason for this part of me holding onto this emotion?

Have a conversation with this part of you, and explain to it, that you are okay, that it is time to heal and let go, to release the old negative programs and their energy, and rewrite their meanings to new positive and heartfelt ones; manifesting new programs that will enhance your life and expand your consciousness, creating a joyful and successful experience.

Ask these additional questions:

Have I achieved the Understanding and Wisdom needed about these emotions and reactions?

What Understanding and Wisdom do I still need in order to be able to move on?

What belief about myself is blocking me from achieving my desires?

What prevents me from being ...?

Write an affirmation that changes the meaning from a negative causal belief to a positive causal belief.

Examples: I am unworthy, to I AM Worthy. I am a bad person, to I AM a Good person. If possible, keep your affirmation simple and easy to remember, so that you can instantly reframe the negative thoughts and emotions to positive thoughts and emotions, as they come into your awareness of your mind's consciousness.

Ask your Mighty I AM Presence to receive all the negative energies contained within your Soul Being, on all levels of your four Body Systems that relate to the negative thoughts and emotions. Then have the Sacred Violet Flame transmuted and transform this negative energy into Freedom, Forgiveness and Unconditional Love.

Always ask your Mighty I AM Presence, for the Wisdom and

Understanding in any situation, And that all of this information is for your highest good, and the highest good of all.

Beloved One, as you read these prayers, feel their messages, and observe how you are touched within your Heart-Mind by their power and magical healing:

I ask that you envisage yourself contained within a circle of fire, formed by the Sacred Flame. To feel the Flame surround you, encapsulating your entire being within its vibrant energy, and as these energies entwine and merge around you, permeating every particle of your being, feel and know from your Heart-Mind that the attributes and qualities of these Flames are healing you and are creating changes into your life, along with the greater Understanding and Wisdom that you require.

Surrender to the possibilities and they become actualities. Allow the Sacred Flames to permeate and saturate you entirely. Simply be in their energy and trust.

The Sacred Flames and Rays are energized from the Source that is The One, the Ultimate and Supreme God of All Creations, the All That Is. They are one of the greatest gifts that have been bestowed upon Humanity in our lifetime. They are for the healing of all Humanity, all Kingdoms and Realms of Planet Earth, this Universe the Multiverses and the Omniverse.

Know that when you call upon the Sacred Flames and Rays of Christed Light of God Consciousness, they come to your aid instantly and begin their wondrous healing and guidance immediately.

Surrender your doubts to your Mighty I AM Presence and Invoke the Sacred Flames and Rays of the Will of God and Illumination. This will enable you to surrender, let go and receive the Wisdom and Understanding needed for you Inner Growth.

Ask for and allow the Sacred Flames and Rays to be with you, in you and surround your life with Healing, Guidance, Wisdom and Understanding, and then all in your life will be Divine Perfection.

If you discover any resistance to the idea of the Sacred Flames and Rays being within you and around your auric field, call in your Mighty I AM Presence, and request that you receive the Wisdom and Understanding about this resistance. What it is all about? What part of you is rejecting the aid of the Sacred Flames and Rays? What is the purpose of this resistance?

Work with this part of you and explain the Positive Benefits of the Sacred Flames and Rays. In that they can bring healing for your Mental, Emotional and Physical Well-being, as well as Spiritual Growth. They can help to resurrect you to the New Encodement of Divine Perfection, as decreed by The One, the Ultimate and Supreme God of All Creations.

The Sacred Flames and Rays have the Power to help you, but you are the one that has to make the decision on what help you desire.

The Sacred Flames and Rays do not make the choices for you. It is all done in accordance with your Divine Will for this incarnation. The Divine Will of your Spiritual God-Self that is your True-Self, has the plan for your lifestream and evolution, and ensures that everything needed for your life is manifested as required.

The Sacred Flames and Rays: further information

Ray 7, the Violet Flame of Transmutation:

The Synthesis energy: Blue, Yellow and Pink Rays, (Rays, 1, 2 and 3).
The Masculine and Feminine Principles of the Will, Mind and Heart of God:
a) The Blue Ray = Will of God.
b) The Yellow Ray = Mind of God.
c) The Pink Ray = Heart of God.

The Violet Flame of Transmutation transmutes all negativity to Freedom, Forgiveness and Unconditional Love.
Freedom: Coming from the Surrender to God's Will, and going into the Acceptance of the Flow of Life.

Forgiveness: Being without Blame or Shame.

Within the Mind of God all things are illuminated; all is accepted as Divine Perfection.

Unconditional Love: Living from the Heart as the Heart of God, all things are God; we are that, we are all things, therefore we all are God.

The Three-Fold Flame within the Sacred Chambers of the Heart

When you combine the colors of the Will, Mind and Heart of God Flames within each Soul, you have Violet.

Ray 9, the Magenta Flame of Highest Potentials

The Synthesis Energy: Rays 1 to 7 manifests all the attributes of the first seven Rays within the Spirit/Soul, Mind and Emotions, Etheric and the Physical Body. This creates the Highest Potentials for each Spirit/Soul in their journey.

As the Veils of Forgetfulness are cleared and the belief system is returned to Balance, Harmony and Unconditional Self Love, the gifts of each one's Highest Potentials, held within the Spirit/Soul, are released by the Sacred Flames and Rays, Activated, Actualized and Amplified.

Ray 12, the Golden Ray of One Unity Consciousness

The Synthesis Energy: Rays 1 to 12, combining the attributes of all the Sacred Flames and Rays create One Unity Consciousness. It transfigures all programs, positive and negative to Oneness and Union with Self, Others and the Universe.

United Integrated Twelve Sacred Flames and Rays

A Vortex of Energy is created by the forming of a Grid, which connect it to the Gravity Grid, Electromagnetic Grid, and the Crystalline Grids of Planet Earth.

The Combined Colors form a Clear Prism with Rainbow flashes of the Twelve Sacred Flames and Rays of Christed Light of God Consciousness.

Cosmic Rays and the United Twelve Flames and Rays of Christed Light Consciousness

A Vortex Energy Grid – connecting the Gravity Grid, Electromagnetic Grid, Crystalline Grids and the Cosmic Rays for Planet Earth – Is made up of Rays 1 through to 24.

Swirling Vortex Energies, formed by the Planetary Flames and Rays, combine with the Cosmic Rays, to give support and source energy to the Planetary Flames and Rays.

Planetary Chakra Connection

The Chakra System for Planet Earth and Humanity consists of 1 to 50 major Chakras. The Chakras for the 4th Dimensional Individual include 1 to 12 with access to the higher Chakras of 13 to 24, which are available upon ascension to the 5th Dimensional Levels of Consciousness.

The Sixth Initiations occurs when one has achieved one's Ascension to the 5th Dimension; then one can begin to bring in the 6th Dimensional Chakras of 24 to 30.

The Seventh Initiation is the highest that can be taken on this plane and it is referred to as the Resurrection, then one can begin to bring in the 7th Dimensional Chakras of 30 to 36.

Cosmic Logos: Avatar of Synthesis, the Mahatma energy encompasses all the Chakra Levels: 1 to 352 up to the 49th Dimension

The Mahatma is available to assist the Soul's Journey through Evolution; calling on the help of the Mahatma enables the Spirit/Soul to receive whatever assistance is required energetically to advance with ease and grace, to the next level of consciousness.

As one works with the Twelve Sacred Flames and Rays that represent the Twelve Major Chakras of our physical and metaphysical being, we clear and cleanse the blueprints contained within each of these Chakras. And resurrect them, to the New Encodements of Divine Perfection from the Christed Light of God Consciousness of The One, the Ultimate and Supreme God of All Creation, the All That Is.

The Twelve Sacred Flames and Rays, along with the Cosmic Rays, heal the Human Code, the Genetic Code and resurrect the Twelve - Strand DNA to - the New Encodements of Divine Perfection, the Christed Light of God Consciousness.

The Twelve Sacred Flames receive their energy from the Cosmic Rays of God Consciousness, the Cosmic Rays of Christed Light Consciousness, coming from the God-head

The Source of the Cosmic Rays energy is the Christed Light of God Consciousness of The One, the Ultimate, and Supreme God of All Creations. The Cosmic Rays bring the energy from the Source that is The One, to the Cosmic All, Omniverses, Multiverses, and to all the Universes.

The Energy comes to all the Omniverses, Multiverses, and Universes, and then to this Universe, being the Source of the Rays for this Universe, Solar System and Galaxy. And then the energy frequency is lowered gradually down in power levels, to create the Planetary Rays which are the energetic source of the Planetary Twelve Sacred Flames.

The Cosmic Rays are the Source from which all the Sacred Flames gain their Life Force

There can be NO Flames without the Rays. The Rays provide the Life Force Energy that brings forth the Cosmic Christed Light and Cosmic Christed Love of The One, the Ultimate and Supreme God of All Creations to the Flames.

<u>The Sacred Flames express individually the voice of God.</u>

This Happens through the Sacred Flames Divine Principles and Attributes. When they are integrated within the Golden Flame of Oneness, they become the Voice of One Unity Consciousness that is the God Consciousness Energy.

<u>The United Integrated Vortex is formed by the Connection to the Planetary Grids.</u>

The Sub-Grids of Gravity, Electromagnetic and Crystalline – connect the energies back to the Great Central Sun, and then on up to the Godhead at the Center of the Cosmic All.

In the Silence within the Sacred Chambers of the Heart, we hear the Voice of God.

In the Silence of the Cosmic Rays and the Twelve Sacred Flames of Christed Light Consciousness, we see God in Action. In the Silence of our Mind, we hear the Voice of God. In the Silence within our Heart, we feel the Love of God. In Silence within our True Self, we are One with God, we are our God-Self.

The Power of Surrender

<u>What does surrender mean?</u>

Surrender means: Relinquishing, Handing over, Releasing, Letting Go and the Giving to, a Power Source - such as one's Mighty I AM Presence, to Mother/Father God, or to the Sacred Flames and Rays, - an Issue, Problem, Belief System, Pattern, Program, Negative Energy etc. that you desire to cleanse, clear, balance and harmonize, and to receive the Clarity, Wisdom and Understanding you require as you go forward in your evolution.

The Self-Empowerment comes from the Feeling of Freedom, Forgiveness and Unconditional Love that Surrender brings to your Soul, Heart, Mind/Emotions and Physical Body. As such you release, handover or relinquish all that which no longer serves you.

In the Power of Surrender, be in Gratitude for all the Learnings you have received and Experiences you have endured, because of your belief systems, patterns, programs and past-life Akashic records that have been held within your cellular memory, having given you great Wisdom and Understanding, these are an important part of who you are and why you are here on Planet Earth at this point in time. Also they will give you the directions for where you are to go next in your journey.

Prayer to Release and Relinquish
to the Divine Light of Source

I Release and Relinquish to the Divine Light of Source, the All That Is, all the negative energies contained within my being, my Spirit energy, my four Body Systems of Spirit/Soul, Mind/Emotion, Etheric and Physical Body - that have kept me in fear.

I Surrender and Relinquish to the Divine Light of Source, the All That Is, the Akashic Records of all my Past Lives that I have ever lived, including this current life incarnation. All the negative energies that stem from events and incidence of the past are restored to Peace, Balance, Harmony, Unconditional Love, Freedom and Forgiveness.

I Surrender and Relinquish to the Divine Light of Source, the All That Is, All the Drama and Stories that are held within my Subconscious Mind, I AM Living Free and I AM Forgiven for all the beliefs of transgressions against myself and toward others that I have held energetically within my beingness.

I Invoke the Sacred Flames and Rays to transmute and transform all meanings, beliefs, patterns and programs contained within my Mind/ Emotions, to the Balance and Harmony of the Divine Perfection that is the Holy Spirit of God.

"Love Is All That Is! And ... So It Is!"

Part 1

Inner Guidance
Key Prayers for the Sacred Flames and Rays

Sacred Flame of the Will of God – Image yourself within a Circle of Radiant Blue Flames at the core center of the Sacred Flame and Ray of the Will of God Surrender to the Divine Principles of The One, the Supreme Creator God.

Ray 1 – The Blue Ray

The Sacred Flame of the Will of God

Elohim: Hercules and Amazonia

Chohan: Master El Morya

Archangel: Michael

Divine Complement: Lady Faith

Key Attributes:

Courage, Faith, Initiative, Dependability, Divine Power, Omnipotence, the Will of God, Self-reliance, Surrender, Focus, Protection and Certainty

Sacred Flame Energy Amplified on Monday

Divine Principles of The One, the Ultimate and Supreme God of All Creations

The Will of God!

Prayer to the Chohan:
Master El Morya for Guidance

Beloved Master El Morya, Chohan of the Blue Ray and the Sacred Flame of the Will of God, Great Spiritual Hierarch of the Brotherhood of the Diamond Heart, and Hierarch of the Temple of Good Will.

I Call upon you to assist me in my desire to Surrender to the Will of God, and to hold within my being the Divine attributes of the Blue Ray – which are courage, faith, initiative, dependability, divine power, self-reliance and certainty. These are the qualities of the Divine Principle of The One, the Ultimate, Supreme God of All Creation, the All That Is.

I Invoke the Holy Spirit of the Christed Light of God Consciousness; that I AM the embodiment of these attributes. I AM spiritually focused and disciplined in applying to my life the Divine teachings of the Blue Ray, and I Request the aid of the Blue Flame Angels to protect and guard me in my journey of exploration within myself.

I AM One with the Heart of God and I AM aware that I AM held within the embrace of the Unconditional Love of All That Is.

Beloved Master El Morya, I Thank You for your service and life in guarding and protecting the spiritual heart centers of the world, in all areas of movement and spiritual growth that will bring into manifestation the changes that will restore the human race to peace and harmony, and advance the evolution of Humanity.

Thy Will IS Done, Thy Will IS Done, and Thy Will IS Done, in this Now Moment. Thank you, Beloved Master El Morya.

"And… So It Is!"

Prayer of Surrender to My I Am Presence

I Surrender all my fear – related thoughts, feelings and emotions that are held within me on all levels of my being – my Soul, Spirit, Mind and Body, Etheric Body, All Subtle Bodies, Body Elemental and Inner Child – to my Beloved Mighty I AM Presence, the Lord God essence of my being.

All Belief Systems, Patterns and Programs relating to Fear and the creation of negative energies are removed from me Now!

I Surrender these Belief Systems, Patterns and Programs to my Mighty I AM Presence, to be transmuted and transformed to the Divine Perfection and Unconditional Love Energy of The One, the Ultimate and Supreme God of all Creations, in the knowledge that these energies are used for my Highest Good and the Highest Good of All.

I AM Healed of all negative fear – based programs, they are resolved, and there is Divine Love, Harmony, Balance and Peace within my Heart, Soul, Spirit, my four Body Systems, All Subtle Bodies, Body Elemental and Inner Child.

Beloved I AM! "And... So It Is!"

Prayer for Protection

I AM protected always by the Will of God.
I AM protected by my Mighty I AM Presence.
I Call upon the Sacred Flame and Ray of the Will of God to
Saturate my beingness with waves upon waves of Blue Flame Fire.
I AM positive in all situations and I speak my truth. I AM
calm and in discernment no matter what is said to me.
I AM in my Power and Empowered by my Divinity.
I Stay true to my inner self and my inner guidance.
I Remain peaceful, tranquil and compassionate in the now moment.
I Embrace the Energy of the Blue Flame Angels of Protection.
The Blue Flame Angels protect and guard my beingness, as I go
forth in life; I AM courageous, faithful, in control of my Destiny.
I AM strong and I AM my Spiritual God-Self State. I AM the
Love of my Holy Christed Light Self. Beloved Archangel Michael
and the Divine Complement Lady Faith: I Thank You for your
Guidance and Wisdom. I AM in Gratitude for Your Protection and
the Protection of the Sacred Blue Flames and Rays of God's Will.
I AM protected in all areas of my life. Protected I AM!

"And... So Is It!"

Prayer to Archangel Michael and the Divine Complement Lady Faith

Beloved Archangel Michael and the Divine Complement Lady Faith, I AM in Gratitude for your dedication to the Evolution of Humanity. I Honor you for your involvement in the Protection of Humanity and All the Kingdoms and Realms of Planet Earth throughout eons of time.

I Call upon you, in this period of Planet Earth's Cosmic Ascension to the 5th Dimension and Beyond, to be my Mentor, Guide and Guardian in how I AM in Christed Light of God Consciousness, best able to be of Divine Service to The One, the Ultimate, Supreme God of All Creation, the All That Is, as a Protector and Keeper of the Sacred Flames and Rays of God's Will upon the surface of Planet Earth.

I AM in Gratitude and Thank you for all that you have done and Continue to do for our Beloved Planet Earth.

Blessings of Divine Love and Cosmic Light are with you always.
"And... So It Is!"

> Sacred Flame of Illumination – Image yourself within a Circle of Illuminating Yellow Flame at the core center of the Sacred Flame and Ray of Illumination Experience the Expansion of Wisdom and Understanding that is the Mind of God.

<u>Ray 2 – The Yellow Ray</u>

<u>The Sacred Flame of Illumination</u>

<u>Elohim:</u> Apollo and Lumina

<u>Chohans:</u> Lord Lanto and Master Kuthumi

<u>Archangel:</u> Jophiel

<u>Divine Complement:</u> Christine

<u>Key Attributes:</u>

Illumination, Wisdom, Understanding through Love, Truth, Integrity, Omniscience, Transparency, Perceptions, Precipitations, Discrimination, Discernment and the Activation of the Mind of God

<u>Sacred Flame Energy Amplified on Sunday</u>

<u>The Expansion of Wisdom and Understanding through</u>

<u>the Unconditional Love of Self and Others</u>

<u>The Mind of God!</u>

Prayer to the Chohan:
Lord Lanto and Master Kuthumi

Beloved Lord Lanto, Master Kuthumi and the Beloved Masters and Lady Masters of the Sacred Flame and Ray of Illumination; as I Reflect and be in the quiet times of my life, I Wonder at the magnitude of the Will of God. I Ask myself the questions: Who am I? What am I here in this Life to learn? And how do I go about this learning? I Recall and Remember in my mind and heart that you, the Chohan and Master Teachers, have held the Sacred Flame and Ray of Illumination alive for Humanity and Planet Earth for eons of time. I AM in deepest Gratitude for your Fortitude and Great Love for us All.

I Request your Guidance, as I seek the answers to my questions and go forth on my quest for greater understanding of myself – to experience, to see, to feel and to hear, and thereby gain the Wisdom and Understanding that I require from my learning. From which I then move forward and Let Go and Let God receive from me all energies that no longer serve me. I AM the Wisdom and understanding and I AM able to attain, sustain and maintain the Illumination Energy within my being, from the Sacred Flame and Ray of Illumination.

I Call upon you to advise me in all matters of Communication, within myself to my Inner Child and Body Elemental, with my Beloved Mighty I AM Presence, with All Humankind and All the Kingdoms and Realms of Planet Earth.

I AM pledged to be of Service to The One, the Ultimate and Supreme God of All Creations. I Request that I be counselled by you in all matters pertaining to my communication with the Holy Spirit. I AM in Gratitude for my Wisdom and Understanding. I Give Thanks for the wise counsel that I AM receiving in this now moment of time. I AM in Gratitude for ALL the Guidance and Light bestowed upon me, from you, Beloved Lord Lanto, Master Kuthumi, All the Masters and Lady Masters and the Archangels of the Sacred Flame and Ray of Illumination. Beloved I AM! "And... So It Is!"

Prayer for the Illumination of Planet Earth

Beloved Cosmic Logos: Avatar of Synthesis: the Mahatma. Beloved Universal Logos: Lord Melchizedek. The Universal Hierarchy; Beloved Planetary Logos: Lord Gautama Buddha. The Planetary Hierarchy: Lord Sanat Kumara and Lady Venus. Beloved Planetary Christ: Lord Maitreya. The Great Divine Director: Master Ragoczy. The Universal Judge; the Maha Chohan: Master St. Germain. The Chohan: Master Kuthumi and Lord Lanto of the Sacred Flame and Ray of illumination – and the Archangel Jophiel and Lady Christine.

I Call upon you to encapsulate Planet Earth within a circle of Illumination Fire, the Sacred Flame and Ray of Illumination, so that every particle, atom, molecule, cell, proton, electron and DNA that forms Planet Earth and its inhabitants are immersed within the Illumination Fire of Wisdom, Understanding and Truth.

All Humankind and All the Kingdoms and Realms that live on or within Planet Earth, down to the very Core of Planet Earth, are immersed in the Light of Illumination. The Truth is revealed to All about this Great and Beautiful Planet – Our Home, that it is a Living entity and a wonderful, benevolent Goddess and Mother to us all.

The Earth, the Air, the Fire and the Water Elements of Planet Earth, are cleansed and cleared of all negative toxins and beliefs systems that are not of the Illumination Ray of Truth. The Sacred Flame and Ray of Ascension and Purification, along with the Sacred Flame and Ray of Healing and Manifestation, aid Planet Earth in this Healing process – as they bring in the Divine Energy of God Consciousness, through the Sacred Flames and Rays, to Rejuvenate and Connect Planet Earth to the New Encodements of Divine Perfection. The Holy Spirit of Christed Light of God Consciousness encapsulates and permeates all of Planet Earth, and All the Kingdom and Realms of Planet Earth, within the Cosmic Christed Light Energies of The One, the All That Is. "And... So It Is!"

9

Invocation of the Sacred Flame
and Ray of Illumination

I AM my Beloved Mighty I AM. I Hereby Invoke the Sacred Flame and Ray of Illumination to enhance my focus upon the Mind of God daily, and in all matters – in my thought processes, perceptions, comprehension, precipitation and discernment. Expand my Wisdom to the higher perspectives and consciousness of the Holy Spirit, the Mind of God.

The Mind of God within me is Activated, and All my Decisions and the manner in which I Conduct my Life, are always in ways that bring me Wisdom, Understanding and Unconditional Love, with ease and grace.

Elohim: Apollo and Lumina. Lord Lanto, Master Kuthumi and Lord Gautama Buddha of the Sacred Flame and Ray of Illumination, Invoke and Amplify the Mind of God within my Mind.

I AM the Mind of God. In the Sacred Chambers of my Heart, I know and feel that this is for my Highest Good and the Highest Good of All.

I AM in Gratitude for the Amplification of the Sacred Flame and Ray of Illumination; I AM One with the Holy Spirit, the Mind of God.

I AM Illumination blazing Now!
"And... So It Is!"

Prayer to Archangel Jophiel and the Divine Complement Lady Christine

My Beloved Mighty I AM Presence, Lord God essence of my being, be within me now. I Request the presence of the Archangel Jophiel and the Divine Complement Lady Christine, to be with me in this now moment of time, to help me understand with Love the many problems that beset me, and lower my thoughts and feelings into energy that is the opposite of Love.

I Ask of you in this time of Depressed Emotions, for the Comprehension and Perceptions that will best assist me in attaining; Clarity, Wisdom and Understanding.

I AM Open to receive from you the Wisdom and Knowledge that will be for my Highest Good and the Highest Good of all in these situations. Then I AM Free and Ready to be of Service to The Holy Spirit, the Mind of God. The All That Is!

I AM That I AM!
"And… So It Is!"

> Sacred Flame of Cosmic Love — Sacred Crystal-Rose Flame of Cosmic Love: Image yourself within a Circle of Pulsating Pink Flame at the core center of the Sacred Flame and Ray of Cosmic Love, Connect with the Sacred Chambers of your Heart and Be Love.

Ray 3: The Pink Ray

The Sacred Flame of Cosmic Love

The Crystal Rose Quartz

Elohim: Heros and Amora

Chohan: Master Paul the Venetian

Archangel: Chamuel

Divine Complement: Lady Charity

Key Attributes:

Divine Self-Love, Unconditional Cosmic Love: the Key to Multiplication, Love of Others, Compassion, Mercy, Charity, True Brotherhood of the Spirit, Wisdom of the Heart of All Knowing, Open Heartedness, and Living from the Heart: the Sacred Chambers of the Heart.

Sacred Flame Energy Amplified on Tuesday

The Three-fold Flame within the Heart

The Heart of God!

Prayer to the Chohan: Master Paul the Venetian

Beloved Master Paul the Venetian, Chohan for the Sacred Flame and Ray of Cosmic Love. With the Grace of the Holy Spirit, I welcome you into my Heart and Feelings, to reside within me on all levels of my being, across all dimensions, time and space.

I Desire of you, the Master of Divine Love, to teach me the pathways to Divine Self-Love that I AM as you are, a Divine expression of Love in ALL that I AM in my Life.

I Request your Guidance and Wisdom in that I AM able to stay within my Truth and Live from my Divine Heart, at all times and during all situations. I AM in need of the Knowledge, Wisdom and Understanding of what prevents me from Living in and from my Divine Heart of Self Love.

I Request of you Beloved One that all the negative energy, pain and trauma that are in my Heart, be revealed unto me, so that I AM able to Release these Energies, to the Sacred Flame and Ray of Cosmic Love. With the Learning and Wisdom attained, I AM the Divine Love that is the Divine Heart of Lemuria.

I Affirm that Master Paul the Venetian, and the Sacred Flame and Ray of Cosmic Love, surround me with waves upon waves of the Crystal Rose Fire. I AM the Divine Love of Self in this now moment of time.

In the name of my Beloved I AM Presence, from the very Heart of God, I Breathe in the Love Energy of the Heart of Lemuria, to encapsulate my Heart, and merge with the Sacred Flame and Ray of Cosmic Love, that is the KEY to the Power of Multiplication and all the Good things that my Heart desires.

I AM a Temple of Divine Love. I AM in Gratitude to my Mighty I AM Presence for this Divine Love. I AM Blessed by the Divine Love of All That Is. "And... So It Is!"

Prayer: I AM My Heart

I AM My Heart: I AM Love Loved Unconditionally.
I AM My Heart: I AM Light; I AM Enlightened, Wise,
All Knowing and Understanding.
I AM My Heart: I AM Illumine Truth, Just, Honest and True.
I AM My Heart: I AM Abundant, Endowed with
Limitless Supply and Good Fortune;
I AM My Heart: I AM Trusting My I AM Presence.
I AM My Heart: I AM Infinite, Immortal and Harmonious.
I AM My Heart: I AM My Divine Spiritual I AM Presence.
I AM My Heart: I AM that I AM and All That IS, IS "I AM."
I AM My Heart: I AM in Oneness; I AM One and United with
My Divine Spiritual God-Self:
I AM My Heart: I AM Manifesting my Heart's
Desires, Oneness with All That Is.
I AM My Heart Always. "And... So It Is!"

Invocation to the Sacred Flame and Ray of Cosmic Love

I Call upon the Beloved Elohim: Heros and Amora; Beloved Maha Chohan: Master St. Germain. Beloved Chohan: Master Paul the Venetian of the Sacred Flame and Ray of Cosmic Love, All the Masters and Lady Masters of the Temple of Divine Love, the Archangel; Chamuel and Divine Complement Lady Charity, and All the Angels of Cosmic Love to be with me in this now moment of time.

My Beloved Mighty I AM Presence, Lord God essence of my being, be within me as I Invoke the Sacred Flame and Ray of Cosmic Love to saturate, permeate and infuse every man, woman and child on Planet Earth, with the Cosmic Love from the Heart of God.

I Decree that the glorious Pink Flame and Ray of Cosmic Love encapsulate All Humanity, to restore the Wisdom of the Heart, which encompasses the Wisdom Principles and the Holy Christ Love Principles of the Holy Spirit of the Christed Light of God Consciousness. I acknowledge with the Deepest Love, Respect and Gratitude the Immortal Three-fold Flame of Life cradled within the Sacred Chambers of my Heart. Through the Divine Love that I AM, I direct my Heart Flames to manifest the Divine Plan for my Life.

I AM Pure Divine Love, the True Nature of the Heart of God, the Divine Cosmic Love that is the Power of Creation. I AM the Higher Consciousness of Divine Love. I AM a magnet for Divine Love. I AM radiant with Divine Love. I radiate this Love to All Life Forms and All Force energy.

I AM in Gratitude to my Mighty I AM Presence, my Holy Christ-Self, to my Spirit, Soul and to all aspects of my four Body Systems, my Body Elemental and Inner Child and to all the Elementals of Life.

I Give Thanks to the Elohim: Heros and Amora; to Master Paul the Venetian, to the Archangel Chamuel and the Divine Complement Lady Charity, and to the Legions of Divine Love Angels – for your great Unconditional Love, Compassion, True Brotherhood and Charity.

I AM Divine Love. Therefore, I think feel and respond with Love, I AM Rejuvenated to Divine Cosmic Love and Connected to the New Encodement of Divine Perfection, Beauty, Harmony and Inner Peace.

I AM Cosmic Love! "And... So It Is!"

Prayer to Archangel Chamuel and the Divine Complement Lady Charity

As I have walked through the days of my life, in this incarnation and lifestream, Archangel Chamuel and the Divine Complement Lady Charity, have shown me the Beauty of my Life. I AM in Appreciation of the Beauty and Artistry of the Mother, Lady Gaia/Virgo and in her creation of all that I experience of this world through my senses of sight, hearing, feeling, touch and the olfactory senses – which are all part of my physical experience of this wonderful world upon which I live and do dwell.

I Love what I see, hear and feel of her that brings to me a sense of Wonderment and Awe at her Power and Majesty.

I AM a Custodian and Guardian for this wonderful world. I pledge to be of Service and light the way so that others will know from their Hearts the Living Life Force that is Mother Earth, Lady Gaia/Virgo.

I hear her Music, the sounds, vibrations and frequencies in which she surrounds us on all levels of our lives.

I hear her Voice and I feel her need of me to be the Truth of Unconditional Love, toward her and All of her Kingdoms and Realms, who are the Children of her Heart.

I AM in Gratitude to the Archangel Chamuel and the Divine Complement Lady Charity, and all the Angels of the Angelic Realms for the Sacred Flame and Ray of Cosmic Love, for their Compassion, Charity and Caring for us all, and in their being the keepers of the Sacred Flame and Ray of Cosmic Love.

I thank you from the Sacred Chambers of my Heart, for keeping this Sacred Flame and Ray of Cosmic Love alive and activated for Mother Earth, "And... So It Is!"

> <u>Sacred Flame of Purification and Ascension</u> – Image yourself within the vibrant Dazzling White Flame at the core center of the Sacred Flame and Ray of Purification and Ascension; Be in Acceptance of What Is, as Divine Perfection.

<u>Ray 4: The White Ray,</u>

<u>The Sacred Flame of Purification and Ascension</u>

<u>Elohim:</u> Purity and Astrea

<u>Chohan:</u> Lord Serapis Bey

<u>Archangel:</u> Gabriel

<u>Divine Complement:</u> Lady Hope

<u>Key Attributes:</u>

Ascended State of Self-Mastery-Wisdom, Peace and Tranquillity,

Acceptance, Balance, Harmony and Perfection of
Health, Christed Light Consciousness,

Self-Discipline and Access to Unlimited and Ever – present Supply
from The One, the Ultimate and Supreme God of All Creation.

Purification: Purity of Spirit, Mind and Body. Immortality: Of the Soul.

<u>Sacred Flame Energy Amplified on Friday</u>

<u>Acceptance of what is, as Divine Perfection</u>

<u>Cosmic Ascension!</u>

Prayer to the Chohan: Lord Serapis Bey, the Lord of Purification

Beloved Lord Serapis Bey, Lord of Purification, and the Beloved Ascension Brotherhood of Luxor, I AM here before you requesting, your guidance and assistance in my attainment of the Ascended State of Self-Mastery, Wisdom, Peace, Balance, Harmony, Perfect Health, Self-Discipline, and with Unlimited and Ever – present Supply.

I AM as you are, the Embodiment of Discipline on my Pathway of Ascension to the 5th Dimension and Beyond, to the many Dimensions of this Universe. I AM totally reliant upon my Mighty I AM Presence, the Lord God essence of my being within the Sacred Chambers of my Heart for the teachings and disciplines of the Ascension Brotherhood, which will allow me to shift my Conscious Awareness from outer – world concerns to the inner realms of my Heart Center, the seat of my Spiritual Divinity, the Sacred Chambers of my Heart, to my God-Self State, in order to manifest my Divine Spiritual Essence, my Mighty I AM Presence in physical manifestation.

I Call upon the white dazzling Sacred Ascension Flame and Ray of Purification and Immortality, to purify and transform all that is hindering my Transfiguration, Resurrection and Ascension into the arms of God's Unconditional Love; and the Restoration of all that I AM, of my Spiritual God-Self and the memories of All That Is.

I AM Resurrected, and Living as a Divine Child of The One, the Ultimate and Supreme God of All Creations, and Residing in the World of Christed Light of God Consciousness. I AM in Gratitude to you Lord Serapis Bey, and to the Ascension Brotherhood of Luxor, for your dedication in ensuring that I pass through the Fires of Purification and in supporting me to maintain Perseverance in my quest for Ascension, so that I AM indeed victorious.

I AM Transformed to Purity and Light in this now moment of time, And... So It Is!

Prayer for Personal Ascension

Beloved Lord Serapis Bey, Lord of Love, the Ascension Brotherhood, the Office of the Christed Light of God Consciousness, Archangel Gabriel and the Divine Complement Lady Hope and the Ascension Angels from the Temple of Ascension.

I Desire from the Sacred Chambers of my Heart for the Grace of Ascension in this incarnation. I AM dedicated to be firm and vigilant in my commitment to my Cosmic Ascension, until that Glorious Victory becomes my Reality.

I have your Guidance and Support, as I Let Go of the Lower Dimensional Consciousness of separation, duality, polarity and drama, in all its many guises and forms. I Let Go of Judgements and Expectations about myself and others, and in how life should unfold for me.

I have Fully Embraced my holy vows, the holy vows that are held within my cellular memory, cellular structure and DNA, and also found residing in the Sacred Chambers of my Heart. I AM Conscious and I AM Connected and United in Oneness with my Mighty I AM Presence. I AM Totally Determined to fulfil the Divine Plan for my life – the Ascension, Unification and Merger into the magnificence that is my Mighty I AM Presence.

I AM Love, harmlessness and the truth of my Spiritual Divinity. I AM the Consciousness of Harmony. I honor the sanctity of all life and All the Kingdoms and Realms sharing Planet Earth with me. I AM living from my Heart, talking and behaving like an Ascended Master as a way of being in the world. The Master that I AM is awake and alert. I Recognize the Master within my Heart as my Mighty I AM Presence.

I Release and Relinquish into the Sacred Fires of Purification all old beliefs, patterns and programs, all negative emotions stored in my conscious, unconscious, and super-consciousness memories, including all the beliefs about the balancing of all karmic debts incurred toward life.

I AM the Attitude of Love for All of Humanity, for Mother Earth and All the Kingdoms and Realms of Earth. I AM in the Attitude of Gratitude for All of Creation and for All that I AM. I AM in Gratitude and Give Thanks to Lord Serapis Bey, to the Ascension Brotherhood of Luxor, to Archangel Gabriel, and the Divine Complement Lady Hope, and the Ascension Flame Angels. For all your guidance, love and support for my heartfelt desire for my Ascension to Immortality in this Lifetime.

Beloved I AM! "And... So It Is!"

Prayer for the Purification of Mind, Body, Spirit and Soul

I Call upon Lord Serapis Bey to aid me in my Journey, bringing to me the Purification of my Mind, Body, Spirit and Soul. With this Purification I move forward and manifest for myself greater discipline in my life, on all levels of my beingness. Also, for me to be ready for Ascension, and thereby be of greater service to Humanity, Mother Earth and All the Kingdoms and Realms of Planer Earth.

I Hereby Surrender all resistance that is part of me to my Mighty I AM Presence and to the Sacred Flame and Ray of Ascension, Purification and Immortality, receiving in return all the Healing that I require.

I AM my Mighty I AM Presence and I State that I AM willing to Release all negative energy within my being, and from all levels of my being, my Spiritual, Soul, Mental, Emotional, Body Elemental, Inner Child and all Subtle Energy Bodies – to bring in the effects of Purity and the Divine Perfection of Health to my Mind, Body, Spirit and Soul.

I thank you and accept this as being done for my Highest Good and the Highest Good of All, in accordance with the Divine Will and the Divine Perfection of The One, the Ultimate and Supreme God of All Creations. The All That Is!

"And... So It Is!"

Prayer to the Archangel Gabriel and the Divine Complement Lady Hope

Beloved Archangel Gabriel and Lady Hope, in all the days of my incarnations, I have Desired from the depths of my Spirit and Soul to Ascend to higher levels of Christed Light of God Consciousness. To Ascend to the 5th Dimension and Beyond, and transcend the need to reincarnate into lifestreams, in which I have endured the pain of separation from The One, the Ultimate and Supreme God of All Creations, the All That Is.

In this Journey, I have been lost and I have been in pain and torment. From my Spirit and Soul, I Reach out to find the Keys to Inner Peace, Purity and Immortality, and to be made whole again, healed and ready to return to the Truth of Who I AM.

I Hold a Memory of a place that is all of Inner Peace, Purity and Immortality, a memory of a time when I knew the Truth of Who I AM.

I AM this day Releasing to the Sacred Flame and Ray of Ascension, and to the Ascension Flame Angels all that which is within me that requires purification.

I Release it all so that I AM Free, Purified on all levels of my being, and made ready to receive All the Initiations required for my Ascension to the 5th Dimension and Beyond. Wisdom and Understanding comes to me with ease and grace.

I AM in Gratitude to the Archangel Gabriel and the Divine Complement Lady Hope for keeping the Sacred Flame and Ray of Ascension, Purification and Immortality alive in my Heart and the Memory of Home within my Mind, Body, Spirit and Soul. I Remember the Truth of Who I AM. I AM Living from my Heart. I AM One with myself, others and The One, the Ultimate and Supreme God of All Creation, the All That Is! "I AM Forever Grateful, And... So It Is!"

Sacred Emerald Flame of Healing and Manifestation – Image yourself within the Living Life energy the Green Flame at the core center of the Sacred Emerald Flame and Ray of Healing and Manifestation. Connect with the Healing and Manifestation energy of your Mighty I AM Presence.

Ray 5: The Green Ray,

The Sacred Emerald Flame of Healing and Manifestation

Elohim: Cyclopea and Virginia

Chohan: Master Hilarion

Archangel: Raphael

Divine Complement: Lady Regina

Key Attributes:

Divine Healing of Physical Pain and Dis-ease, Poverty Thinking, Mental/Emotional Confusion, Critical Thinking about Self and Others, Healing at All Levels, Constancy, Creation through Manifestation, God's Abundance through the Immaculate Sacred Heart of I AM.

Sacred Flame Energy Amplified on Wednesday

Divine Abundance of Perfect Health in Mind, Body and Soul

The Divine Healing Power of God!

Prayer to the Chohan: Master Hilarion for Guidance

I Call upon Beloved Master Hilarion, all the Masters and Lady Masters of the Sacred Emerald Flame and Ray of Healing and Manifestation.

I Request of you in this period of my life, your guidance – to counsel and guide me in the ways best suited for me to achieve the Healing of my Physical, Mental and Emotional Being, on all levels of my Auric Fields. So that my body is free and full of the Divine Healing Power of the Sacred Flame and Ray of Healing.

I Desire your Wisdom and Understanding so that I too may be as you are, and walk as you walk, in Perfect Health, Balance and Harmony in every now moment.

I Desire from my Heart and Mind to talk as you talk in all manner of communication; that I Express myself in the ways that you express yourselves, in that like you, my Mind, Emotions and Heart will be free and full of the Divine Abundance of Perfect Health in Mind, Body, Spirit and Soul.

I AM Living my Life in service to the Divine Holy Spirit of the All That Is, in accordance with the desires of my Beloved Mighty I AM Presence.

I Invoke the Laws of Manifestation that the life I lead during this incarnation is a Life of Total Abundance in Prosperity, Health and with Loving, Harmonious Relationships. I Believe that all that which is made manifest in my Life is for my Highest Good and the Highest Good of All.

For this I AM Grateful. "And... So It Is!"

Prayer for Health and Wellbeing

Beloved Chohan: Master Hilarion of the Sacred Flame and Ray of Healing and Manifestation. Beloved Masters and Lady Masters of the Sacred Flame and Ray and the Beloved Archangel: Raphael and the Divine Complement Lady Regina, and the Green Ray Angels of the Sacred Flame and Ray of Healing and Manifestation.

My Beloved Mighty I AM Presence, Lord God essence of my being. My entire being – my Spirit, Soul, Mental, Emotional, Physical Body and Elemental Body, are encapsulated and immersed within waves upon waves of the Sacred Emerald Flames of Healing.

I AM received at the Great Jade Temple of Healing, my Health and Wellbeing are Restored to the Divine Perfection of Eternal Youth and Beauty.

I AM Rejuvenated and Revivified to the Optimum Healing that I AM able to attain; sustain and maintain at this point in time.

I know these Healing Procedures are for my Highest Good and for the Highest Good of All, and take place when I AM asleep, resting and relaxed.

I AM Grateful – I Give Thanks to all those concerned in my Healing Procedures.

Perfection in Health I AM! "And... So It Is!"

Prayer for the Abundance of God

Beloved One, the Ultimate and Supreme God of All Creations, the All That Is,

I AM that I AM, and in the name of my Beloved Mighty I AM Presence, and the Beloved Holy Spirit that I AM, I AM my Sacred Heart. I Call upon the Lords of Manifestation, the Angels of Prosperity, Goddess Fortuna and the Lord of Gold.

I AM my Sacred Heart. I Call upon the Holy Spirit of the Great White Brotherhood, to Release Abundance of Wealth from your Unlimited Supply of Prosperity to me Now!

I AM my Mighty I AM Presence. I AM manifesting a continuous Flow of Wealth, in order to become the Divine Perfection required to manifest my Life Plan, in this now moment of time.

I AM my Mighty I AM Presence, directing and manifesting Great Abundance, including all the Prosperity of Money that I will ever need, from The One, the Ultimate and Supreme God of All Creations, the All That Is.

I Praise God. In the Silence of my Heart and Mind, within the Sacred Chambers of my Heart, I AM in Gratitude that I have it now. As I speak these words from the Silence that is Golden, my prayers are manifested and I AM Prosperity.

Prosperity I AM! "And So It Is!"

Prayer to Archangel Raphael and the Divine Complement Lady Regina

Beloved Archangel Raphael and the Divine Complement Lady Regina,

I AM in Gratitude for the Healing that I AM receiving from you in this now moment of time. I Ask for Healing and Guidance regarding the Cause of my Physical, Mental and Emotional Pain, so that I AM able to Heal and Purify the many levels of my being that are in need of healing, through the Wisdom and Understanding of the Negative Causes, that are creating the Negative Effects in my Life.

I Desire counselling from you and the Angelic Realm in the many ways of healing all my beliefs, patterns and programs that have caused and kept me in pain. I AM prepared to be guided by you in the manifestation of my Abundance in Health and Wellness, for all the levels of my four Body Systems, my Spirit, Soul, Body Elemental and Inner Child.

I accept that all is Divine Perfection and I know I AM ready to be the truth of Who I AM, I Desire from my Heart to clear and cleanse the Veils of Forgetfulness, and to Release to the Emerald Angels of Healing All that which serves me not. All the negative energy that had been attached to me at any and all levels, is now transformed by the magnificence of the Emerald Green Fire to the manifestations of Abundance in Health, Prosperity and Loving, Caring Relationships with Myself, Others and the Universe.

I Give Thanks to you, Archangel Raphael and Lady Regina. I know that all will be done with Divine ease and grace.

In the Acceptance from my Heart of my Pain, I See it and accept it as; it is what it is, Divine Perfection.

I AM therefore Free of my pain. "And... So It Is!"

Sacred Flame of Resurrection and Immortality – Image yourself within the Vibrant energy of the Ruby/Golden Flame, at the core center of the Sacred Flame and Ray of Resurrection and Immortality, in Selfless Service, Ministration and One Unity Consciousness.

Ray 6: The Ruby/Golden Ray,

The Sacred Flame of Resurrection and Immortality

Elohim: Peace and Aloha

Chohan: Lord Sananda

Archangel: Uriel

Divine Complement: Lady Aurora

Key Attributes:

Immortality, Mortality, Perfectionism, Planetary Service, and Time Related issues, Resurrection, Restoration, Revivification, Regeneration to the New Encodements of Divine Perfection and Spiritual Worship and Reverence.

Sacred Flame Energy Amplified on Thursday

Selfless Service and Ministration

The Resurrection to Immortality!

Prayer to Chohan: Lord Sananda, for the Resurrection of My Life

Beloved Lord Sananda, in Reverence to you and the Eternal Sacred Flame and Ray of Resurrection, I Decree that I AM as you are in Service and Ministration to The One, the Ultimate and Supreme God of All Creations.

In my Spiritual True God-Self State, I AM That I AM:

I AM That I AM, I AM my Higher Self. I AM That I AM, I AM my Mighty I AM Presence. I AM That I AM, I AM my Spiritual Divinity, and I AM One with All Creation.

I AM the Resurrection of my Life; I AM Rejuvenated and Restored to the New Encodements of Divine Perfection.

I AM the Resurrection of my Life; I AM Healed Completely of All Pain and Trauma.

I AM the Resurrection of my Life; I AM Living in the Now! I AM the Resurrection of my Life; I AM Living in the Unconditional Love and Light of the Cosmic Love and Light of Source, the All That Is.

I AM the Resurrection of my Life; I AM a Christed Light of God Consciousness Spiritual Soul. I AM the Resurrection of my Life; I AM in my Ascension to the 5th Dimension and Beyond.

I AM the Resurrection of my Life; I AM in Oneness and Unity, with The One, the Ultimate and Supreme God of All Creations, the ALL That Is.

Resurrected to Oneness I AM! "And... So It Is!"

31

Prayer to the Sacred Flame and
Ray of Resurrection

I Call upon the Sacred Flame and Ray of Resurrection to enter my Physical Heart and lifestream, and Restore my Spirit, my Soul, my Heart, and my four Body Systems to the normal, natural Spiritual God-Self State of Divine Perfection and Immortality.

I Decree that I AM the Resurrection of my Life.

I AM the Resurrection of my Lightbody in this now moment of time and space.

I AM the Resurrection of the New Encodements of Divine Perfection.

I AM the Resurrection of my True God-Self State. As an infinite being of God Consciousness my entire consciousness, being and world are immersed within this wondrous Sacred Flame and Ray of Resurrection. I AM the Embodiment of Selfless Service and Ministration to the All That Is. Thy Will is done on Earth Now, as it is in Heaven, in Accordance with the Divine Heart, Mind and Will of The One, the All That Is.

The Sacred Flame and Ray of Resurrection Blesses All with Eternal Life!

"And... So It Is!"

Prayer for the Resurrection of Planet Earth

Beloved Lord Sananda, Chohan of the Sacred Flame and Ray of Resurrection, and the Beloved Archangel Uriel and the Divine Complement Lady Aurora.

I Invoke the Sacred Flame and Ray of Resurrection, to send waves upon waves of wondrous Ruby/Golden Fire Energy to surround Planet Earth in a Golden Halo of Christed Light – that will restore this beautiful Planet to her True God-Self State of Perfection. And to prepare her to receive the full Transformation of the Ascension Flame and Ray, and the energies that will assist her in moving into the 5th Dimension and beyond.

I Decree that the Sacred Flame and Ray of Resurrection has Purified the Electrons of Planet Earth which have been misused and restored them to Health, Harmony and Tranquillity.

I Invoke the Sacred Flame and Ray of Resurrection to Restore and Rejuvenate Planet Earth to Harmony and Peace, healing all issues that caused the separation of Humanity from their True God-Self State, and so bring to all, the Oneness and Unity Consciousness of The One, the Ultimate and Supreme God of All Creations, the All That Is.

In this now moment of time, Thy Will Is Done, Thy Will Is Done, Thy Will Is Done.

Beloved We Are! "And... So It Is!"

Prayer to Archangel Uriel and the Divine Complement Lady Aurora

I Call upon the Beloved Archangel Uriel and the Divine Complement Lady Aurora. Greetings to you and Thank You for all that you are and have been for the Christed Light of God Consciousness in the World and for Planet Earth.

I AM in Gratitude to the Sacred Flame and Ray of Resurrection for the Life Changes that they bring forth for me from the Sacred Chambers of my Heart.

I Believe in the Powers of the Sacred Flame and Ray of Resurrection. I Feel the influence of the Resurrection Angels in all areas of my Life. The Resurrection of my Life is in the Acceptance of the Sacred Flame and Ray of Resurrection and the Resurrection Angels – as my Life is changed, Resurrected, Restored and Rejuvenated, in accordance to my Heart's Desire and the Divine Plan for my Life in this incarnation.

I AM the Resurrection of my Life, I AM the Resurrection
of my Life, I AM the Resurrection of my Life of Oneness
with the Archangel Uriel and Lady Aurora.

I Give Thanks for your Presence in the World and for All that you do, for the Resurrection of Humanity to Eternal Life, and the Resurrection of Planet Earth to the 5th Dimension and the Resurrection of the Christed Light of God Consciousness of The One, the Ultimate and Supreme God of All Creation, the All That Is.

Resurrected to Eternal Life I AM!
"And... So It Is!"

> The Sacred Flame of Transmutation and Freedom – Image yourself within a Circle of Violet Fire, at the central core of the Violet Flame of The Sacred Flame of Transmutation, Feel the Energy of Freedom, Forgiveness and Unconditional Love.

Ray 7: The Violet Ray

The Sacred Flame of Transmutation and Freedom

Elohim: Arcturus and Victoria

Chohan: Lady Portia

Archangel: Zadkiel

Divine Complement: Lady Amethyst

Key Attributes:

Transmutation: to Freedom, Forgiveness and Unconditional Love. Transformation: Change, Acceptance of God's Will, Tact and Diplomacy. Ceremony and the Application of the Science of True Alchemy;

Sacred Flame Energy Amplified on Saturday.

Transmutation to Freedom, Forgiveness and Unconditional Love –

Violet Flame of Omri Tas from The Violet Planet!

Prayer to Chohan: Lady Portia for Justice and Opportunity

Beloved Lady Portia, Goddess of Justice and Opportunity, Chohan of the Sacred Violet Flame and Ray of Transmutation, Freedom and Forgiveness. Beloved Master St. Germain, Beloved Archangel Zadkiel and the Divine Complement Lady Amethyst, and the Violet Flame Angels from the Great Violet Flame Temple.

Beloved Masters and Lady Masters of the Violet Flame and Ray, in the name and authority of my Beloved Mighty I AM Presence, I Come before you in humbleness and gratitude. I thank You for holding the vibration and frequency of the 7th Ray, the Sacred Violet Flame of Transmutation.

I AM seeking the way to Justice and Freedom of Opportunity, for all levels of my being. I Desire from my Heart to be Just and Fair, Merciful, Compassionate and Caring toward myself and others. I Ask for your guidance, Lady Portia, in delivering unto myself True Acceptance and Forgiveness that comes from my Heart of All-Knowing, so that I completely understand myself and my fellow Humanity, and thereby I AM Justice and Truth.

I Ask for your counselling to recall all of Who I AM, and to know my Divine Authority and Heritage. I AM Unconditional Love, for in embracing Justice and Truth, I see, hear and know through the Divine Truth of All-Knowing, the complete Journey of every Spiritual being. Therefore, I Judge not the Journey of another. For in truth we are All One and share the same Journey, the Journey of Spirit, and the Journey Home.

I AM in Gratitude and Give in Gracefully to the Universal Laws of Justice.

I Judge not; for in the eyes of God, I AM Love.
"And... So It Is!"

Invocation to the Sacred Violet Flame and Ray of Transmutation

I Call upon the Beloved Elohim: Arcturus and Victoria; Beloved Universal Logos: Lord Melchizedek; Beloved Planetary Logos: Lord Gautama Buddha; Planetary Hierarchy: Lord Sanat Kumara and Lady Venus; The Planetary Christ: Lord Maitreya; Maha Chohan: Master St. Germain; and Chohan: Lady Portia, and all the Masters and Lady Masters of the Violet Flame and Ray of Transmutation.

I Call upon Omri Tas from the Violet Planet, and Beloved Archangel Zadkiel and the Divine Complement Lady Amethyst, as witness to this invocation.

I Invoke the Sacred Violet Flame and Ray of Transmutation, Freedom and Forgiveness to permeate and saturate every Particle, Cell, Atom, Proton and Electron of my Spirit, Soul, and my four Body Systems, to replenish my entire being with the Violet Fire to my Divine Spiritual authority, Heritage and Truth.

I Request that I receive energy attunements to Higher Levels of Consciousness, and I Call upon Lady Portia to bring forth the Amplified Energetic frequencies that are designed to raise one's awareness to the Higher Dimensions of Consciousness.

I Ask Lady Portia for the Enlightenment that will allow me to be of greater assistance in bringing in the Cosmic Light Rays of Justice, Freedom of Opportunity, Forgiveness and Unconditional Love to Humanity. In turn this will Release the Veils of Forgetfulness from Humanity – revealing unto them the Truth of Who they really are as Children of God and to the Knowledge of their Divine Spiritual Heritage.

I Invoke in the name and authority of my Mighty I AM Presence into the World, the Divine Justice and Divine Truth of the Violet Fires of Freedom, Forgiveness, Unconditional Love, Compassion and Mercy. Planet Earth is Restored to the Divine Principles of the Violet Flame from the Violet Planet of Omri Tas.

Omri Tas, Lord of the Violet Planet from whence the Violet Flame originated and is generated, aides me and the Light Realms of Planet Earth, in the best way of using the Violet Flame and Ray of Transmutation, for the Highest Good of Planet Earth and the Highest Good of the Universe in accordance with the Divine Will of the Universal Logos: Lord Melchizedek.

My Feelings of Gratitude flood my world with waves upon waves of the Sacred Violet Flame and Ray of Transmutation, so that I AM quickly able to manifest the Divine Perfection of the New Golden Age in this now moment of time.

I AM Freedom, I AM Forgiveness and I AM Unconditional Love!
"And... So It Is!"

Prayer to Lord Omri Tas of the Violet Planet

Lord Omri Tas of the Violet Planet, to you we of Humanity and Planet Earth are in deepest gratitude. For in your great Wisdom, Understanding, Compassion, Unconditional Love, Forgiveness and Freedom Energy, you saw a great need of the Sacred Violet Flame to be with us here on Planet Earth, to aid Planet Earth and All the Kingdoms and Realms of Earth.

I AM in Gratitude for your bestowing onto Humanity through the Maha Chohan, Master St. Germain, the Sacred Violet Flame and Ray of Transmutation. Thus Humanity has then been able to be embraced by the Violet Fire of the Flames of Transmutation to be in Forgiveness of Self and Others, Freedom and Unconditional Love.

Because of your Generosity of Spirit, and Your Great Love for The One, the Ultimate and Supreme God of All Creations, and in your Service to All That Is, we are able to raise our Consciousness to be in the Light and become Awakened, Enlightened and in Oneness with our God-Self and with others – and therefore in Oneness with All of Creation.

I AM Honored by the example that you have set before all to emulate as beings of Christed Light of God Consciousness.

I AM One with the Violet Flame of Transmutation.
I AM Free. "And... So It Is!"

Prayer to Archangel Zadkiel and the Divine Complement Lady Amethyst

Beloved Angels of Freedom and Unconditional Love, In the Light of Love I AM, I Call upon the Beloved Archangel of Freedom and Unconditional Love to be with me in this now moment.

Herald my return to Awareness, Peace and Acceptance for all my past and present misdemeanours.

I AM in the Embrace of Love Unconditional, for I Know that you, Archangel Zadkiel and the Divine Lady Amethyst, are here with me. Lost I have been in the shadows of my mind, returned I AM now; I AM to my Heart sublime. In the Christed Light of Love I AM.

Forever Freedom surrounds me as I Surrender to the All-Knowing of My Heart. In Gratitude and Grace, I AM before you, Beloved Angels of Freedom and Unconditional Love. I Thank You, Archangel Zadkiel and the Divine Complement Lady Amethyst, for your Guidance and the Unconditional Love that you bestow upon me.

From my Heart I emulate that Love to myself, others and all who are likewise in the heavenly fields of Mother/Father God, to be in One Unity Consciousness with myself, others and All the Kingdoms and Realms of Creation.

I AM Freedom and I AM Unconditional Love.
I AM Forever One with God! "And... So It Is!"

Sacred Flame of Transcendence – Image yourself within a Circle of Swirling Aqua and Sea Green Flame, at the core center of the Sacred Flame and Ray of Transcendence, Feel yourself taken beyond confusion to Certainty and Clarity.

Ray 8: The Aqua and Sea Green Ray

The Sacred Flame of Transcendence

Overlighted by: Helios & Vesta

Solar Council of Twelve

Chohan: Lady Nada

Archangel: Aquariel

Divine Complement: Lady Clarity

Key Attributes:

The Following: Certainty, Courage, Justice, Clarity, Integrity, Wisdom, Understanding, Stability, Equilibrium, Unconditional Love, Unity and Infinite Expansiveness. Sacred Flame Energy Amplified on Wednesday

Transcendence beyond Confusion

to Certainty and Clarity

The Sea of Clarity!

Prayer to the Chohan: Lady Nada of the Sacred Flame and Ray of Transcendence

In the name and authority of my Beloved Mighty I AM Presence, Lord God essence of my being, I Call upon the Beloved Lady Nada, Chohan of the Sacred Flame and Ray of Transcendence, Beloved Lord Chietal, Archangel Aquariel and the Divine Complement Lady Clarity, All the Masters and Lady Masters of the Sacred Flame and Ray of Transcendence, and Beloved Lady Nada, blessings to you, beautiful Lady of Light.

I Ask that this Sacred Flame and Ray of Transcendence, Anchors and Activates my higher light energies, and Assists me in becoming the self-actualization of my truth as a Master of Light and Love and thereby create and manifest the qualities and sonic vibrations of certainty and clarity of purpose in my Life and on all levels of my being.

Blessings of the Sacred Flame and Ray of Transcendence – Certainty and Clarity – are with me and All of Humanity Now!

Thy Will Is Done, Thy Will is Done, Thy Will is Done.
Beloved I AM! "And... So It Is!"

Prayer of Gratitude for the World

Beloved Chohan: Lady Nada. Masters and Lady Masters of the Sacred Flame and Ray of Transcendence, Archangel Aquariel and the Divine Complement Lady Clarity, and your Legions of Aqua/Sea Green Ray Angels.

I AM in Gratitude for your Presence and for your Blessings as they are made manifest into the world at this time.

I Ask that Planet Earth be surrounded and immersed into this amazing sonic vibration of transcendence, so that all beings of Planet Earth are awakened to the Certainty and Clarity of who they are and what they are as Spiritual beings of higher light vibrations and frequency from the Source of the All That Is.

I Invoke the Sacred Flame and Ray of Transcendence to be Anchored, Activated, Actualized and Amplified, for Humanity and All the Kingdoms and Realms of Planet Earth in this now moment of time.

I Ask that this be for the Highest Good of All
and the Highest Good for the Universe.
Thy Will Is Done, in and through me now. "And... So It Is!"

Invocation to the Sacred Flame and Ray of Transcendence

In the name and authority of my Mighty I AM Presence, I Invoke the Sacred Flame and Ray of Transcendence to encapsulate my entire being with the Sacred Fires of Aqua/Sea Green Light Energy, as I Embrace my Service role in Love, Integrity, Equilibrium and Balance.

I Trust and Surrender to my Mighty I AM Presence. I AM a Co-creator with the Company of Heaven and a Divine Keeper of the Cosmic Light, manifesting all that I Desire through my Service in Love and Light to the Glory of The One, the Ultimate and Supreme God of All Creations.

As I Embrace the Energy of Transcendence, I Expand and Deepen my Love of the Creator. I AM Living my Life in Truth, Harmony and Balance. I Let Go and Let God Heal all old memories, beliefs, patterns and programs that are irrelevant to my experience and ascension to the Light of Christ Consciousness, the Holy Spirit of my Being the True God-Self State that I AM.

I AM Embraced by the Energy of Transcendence,
I AM the Light of Christed Consciousness.
"And... So It Is!"

Prayer to Archangel Aquariel and Lady Clarity for Mother Earth

Beloved Archangel Aquariel, and the Divine Complement Lady Clarity, Divine Lady Nada, Lord Chietal and all the Masters and Lady Masters of the Sacred Flame and Ray of Transcendence.

I Ask you to encircle Mother Earth with the Sonic Vibrations of the Sacred Flame and Ray of Transcendence and Anchor, Activate, Actualize and Amplify these Energies into the Awareness of All Humanity, and thereby Awaken All to the Responsibility of being the Keepers of the Light and Love for this Sacred Planet, our Beloved Mother Earth.

Beloved Archangel Aquariel, Lady Clarity and the Pleiadian Emissaries of Light and Peace, Bless us all with the qualities of Courage, Justice, Integrity, Wisdom, Stability, Equilibrium, Unconditional Love, Understanding, Unity and Infinite Expansiveness, these are the attributes of the Sacred Fire of Transcendence, thus enabling us to be the Masters of the Sacred Flame and Ray of Transcendence, Clarity and Certainty for Mother Earth.

Thank You in Gratitude I AM!
"And... So It Is!"

> Sacred Flame and Ray of Highest Potentials – Image yourself within a Circle of the Vibrant Magenta Flame, and at the central core of this beautiful Sacred Flame and Ray of Highest Potentials, You receive Divine Guidance in achieving your Highest Potentials.

Ray 9: Magenta Ray

The Sacred Flame of Highest Potentials

Synthesis of Rays 1 to 7

Overlighted by: Lord Goyana

Sirian Archangelic League of Light

Chohan: Lady Mother Mary

Archangel: Anthriel

Divine Complement: Lady Harmony

Key Attributes:

The Synthesis of Flames and Rays 1 to 7. Guidance in achieving one's Highest Potentials and in manifesting in life the Gifts that will assist in the Cosmic Ascension of One's Soul and Divine Guidance, Compassion, Unity, Justice, Peace, Order, Wisdom, Creativity, Mercy, Unconditional Love and Splendour.

Sacred Flame Energy Amplified on Tuesday

The Cradle of Love, Compassion

Divine Guidance to Highest Potentials

Prayer to the Chohan: Lady Mother Mary. Archangel Anthriel and Lady Harmony

Beloved Lady Mother Mary, Beloved Archangel Anthriel and the Divine Complement Lady Harmony of the Synthesis of Rays 1 to 7, and my Beloved Mighty I AM Presence, Lord God essence of my being.

I Invoke the Sacred Flame and Ray of Highest Potentials for the Synthesis of Rays 1 to 7 to Clear and Cleanse my Spirit, Soul, four Body Systems, Body Elemental, Inner Child and all Subtle Bodies.

I Ask that the elements and attributes that form this Synthesis transmute, transform and transfigure all negative aspects to the positive aspects of Surrender, Discipline, Illumination, Wisdom and Understanding, Unconditional Love, Compassion, Mercy, Purity, Perfect Health, Abundance, Resurrection and Restoration of the Divine Perfection of my Lightbody, Freedom and Forgiveness, to be the Divine Light and Divine Love That I AM.

I Invoke the Sacred Flame and Rays of Highest Potentials to manifest in my Life the Gifts that have been bestowed upon me by Mother/Father God through my Beloved Mighty I AM Presence, and for this to be done with ease and grace and for the Highest Good of All.

I AM committed to be of Service to Humanity and Mother Earth. And to fulfilling my Life Purpose in this incarnation by using the Gifts within me to achieve my Highest Potentials and to assist others to achieve their Highest Potentials and thereby bring Healing to Mother Earth.

Beloved Lady Mother Mary, Archangel Anthriel, and the Divine Complement Lady Harmony, I AM in Gratitude and I Thank You for Your Unconditional Love, Inner Peace and Harmony,

Blessings of Love, "And... So It Is!"

Prayer to be the Cradle of Love

Beloved Chohans of Unconditional Love, Lady Mother Mary, Lady Portia, Lady Nada, Lady Vessa Andromeda, Lady Quan Yin and Lady Pallas Athena. Beloved Sisterhood of Lemuria, Galatia, Angelina and Celeste,

I Open my Heart to Thee and ask that I AM taken within your most Holy Retreat of Love. I Desire with all my Heart to be embraced by your Love Essence – the Essence of the Divine Mother.

I AM Eternally Grateful for all the Love that I AM receiving from you. I Ask to BE the Love and Joy that you are. I Pledge, from my Heart to your Hearts, to BE Compassionate, Merciful, Unconditional Love, Harmonious and Peaceful. To BE as you and portray Love and Compassion to the world,

As I Walk through the World, wherever I dwell, I AM as You. As I AM as You, and All That Is, We are One Heart, the Cradle of Love.

The Cradle of Love I AM.
"And... So It Is!"

Prayer for My Highest Potentials

In the name of my Beloved Mighty I AM Presence, I Call upon Beloved Lady Mother Mary, Chohan of the Sacred Flame and Ray of Highest Potentials.

I Attract to me, my Fullest Potentials Now! I Call for a great Cosmic Beam of the Sacred Flame and Ray to attract to me my Crystalline Lightbody and Integrate my Crystalline Lightbody to all levels of my being Now!

I AM the Creative Extension of the Higher Mind of my Mighty I AM Presence. I Connect to the Realms of Illumined Truth in Wisdom, Joy, Splendor and Mercy.

I Experience my Highest Potentials through the merger and integration of my Higher God-Self of the Light and the Holy Christed I AM Presence of the Light.

I AM Love and Compassion in Physical Embodiment, I Manifest Creations of Light and Love, in accordance with the Divine Will of The One, the Ultimate, and Supreme God of All Creation.

Forever, I AM Love.
"And... So It Is!"

Prayer to Lord Goyana and the
Sirian Archangelic League

I Call upon Lord Goyana, the Sirian Archangelic League of Light; Lady Mother Mary, Chohan of the Sacred Flame and Ray of Highest Potentials; and the Archangel Anthriel and the Divine Complement Lady Harmony, to assist Mother Earth and Humanity in achieving their Highest Potentials in this now moment of time.

I Invoke the Cosmic Flames and Rays of Light and the United, Integrated Twelve Sacred Flames and Rays to be of assistance to Mother Earth in her Ascension.

I Request that a great Cosmic Beam of the Sacred Flame and Rays of Highest Potentials attracts to Mother Earth her Crystalline Lightbody and to Anchor, Activate, Actualize and Amplify her Crystalline Lightbody to All levels of her being Now!.

I Ask that this be for the Highest Good of Mother Earth and the Highest Good of All.

I Thank You, Beloved Lady Mother Mary, Beloved Lord Goyana and the Sirian Archangel League of Light and the Archangel Anthriel and Lady Harmony, for helping us all to achieve our Highest Potentials.

So be it now. "And... So It Is!"

Sacred Flame and Ray of Divinity – Image yourself within a Circle of Pearlescent Fire. Feel yourself at the core center of the Sacred Pearlescent Flame and Ray surrounded and embraced by the Shimmering energy of Inner Divinity and Peace.

Ray 10: The Pearlescent Ray.

The Sacred Flame and Ray of Divinity

Overlighted by: Lord Huertal

Andromedan Intergalactic Beings of Light

Chohan: Lady Vessa Andromeda

Archangel: Valoel

Divine Complement: Lady Peace

Key Attributes:

Peace, Balance, Equilibrium, Justice, Power, Infinite Wisdom,

Detachment, Attainment, Responsibility, Self-Mastery, Opulence, Divinity and Transcendence to the God-Self State of The One, the Ultimate and Supreme God of All Creations.

Sacred Flame Energy Amplified on Friday

The Shimmering Sacred Pearlescent Flame of Peace

Divine Inner Peace

Prayer to the Chohan: Lady Vessa Andromeda. Archangel Valoel and Lady Peace

Beloved Chohan: Lady Vessa Andromeda. Beloved Archangel Valoel and the Divine Complement Lady Peace, Master Allah Gobi and the Andromeda Council of Elders, the Intergalactic Emissaries of Light.

I Know the Truth of my Spiritual Divinity that I AM as you are. As I Feel the Christed Light of God Consciousness Energy within me, I AM Living in the Light of my Divinity and in Divine Opulence.

I AM shown the way to recognize the Spiritual Divinity that I AM. And to see, feel and hear the Divine Energy of the Christed Light of God Consciousness as it releases from my being, all that is not of the Divine Light and Inner Peace; and that this be for my Highest Good and the Highest Good of All.

I Embrace the Sacred Flame and Ray of Divinity. I AM in Gratitude to this vibrant Pearlescent Flame and Ray, as it blazes forth sending its powerful Rays of Divinity to Encapsulate my entire being and lift my consciousness to be in Balance, Inner Peace and Harmony. And to be the Wisdom and Understanding of the All-Knowing of my Mighty I AM Presence.

Divine Inner Peace I AM!
"And... So It Is!"

Prayer to the Pearlescent Fire

I Embrace the Pearlescent Fire, as its Shimmering Pearlescent Light transforms the negativity that is present here on Mother Earth, into the Divinity of the Christed Light of God Consciousness.

The Sacred Flames and Rays of Pearlescent Fire in their Opulence are raised high into the atmosphere, and Surround All Humanity and Mother Earth with waves upon waves of Sacred Pearlescent Flames and Rays of Divinity, Opulence and Inner Peace. The Divine Light of Inner Peace and the Sacred Flames and Rays of Divinity enter into All the Kingdoms and Realms of Mother Earth.

Oh Gracious Lady Vessa Andromeda, Chohan of the Sacred Shimmering Pearlescent Fire that is the Sacred Flame and Ray of Divinity, I AM Grateful for your Presence, in your being here for Mother Earth.

I Give Thanks to Master Allah Gobi and the Andromeda Council; Intergalactic Emissaries of the Light, for their aid in awakening Humanity to the Truth of their Divinity in this now moment of all Time and Space.

In Gratitude, I Thank You All. Awakened to My Divinity I AM!
"And... So It Is!"

Prayer to Anchor the Crystalline Lightbody

My Beloved Mighty I AM Presence, Lord God essence of my being. The Chohan: Lady Vessa Andromeda, of the Sacred Flame and Ray of Divinity. I AM the Divine embodiment of the Sacred Flame and Ray of Divinity. I AM the Divine Expression of Inner Peace and Opulence. I AM Power, Love, and Light, in Balance and Harmony. I AM Infinite Wisdom and Detachment as I Experience the Higher Mind of The One, the Ultimate and Supreme God of All Creations, through the integration of my Mighty I AM Presence, my Higher Light.

All levels of forgetfulness are lifted; I now experience the Immortal Aspect of my True Nature. I AM in my Self-Mastery and Spiritual Divinity Now!

The Power and Divinity of the Sacred Flame and Ray have changed my four Body Systems to be Crystalline. I AM merged with my Spirit and Soul.

The programs of Spiritual Divinity, Inner Peace and Opulence have been encoded into my Mental, Emotional, Physical Body and Body Elemental.

I Anchor my Crystalline Lightbody fully into my being. I integrate my Crystalline Lightbody at all levels, as this is integral to my achieving my Cosmic Ascension in this lifetime.

I Call upon Lady Vessa Andromeda, Lord Huertal and the Andromeda Intergalactic Emissaries of Light, to assist me in the attainment of my Spiritual Divinity, Opulence and Inner Peace, and in the Mastery of the Cosmic Christed Light of God Consciousness Energy that is my God-Self State – by the full Activation and Amplification of my Crystalline Lightbody in this Life incarnation.

I AM That I AM, I AM my Crystalline Lightbody. "And... So It Is!"

Invocation to Lord Huertal and the Andromedan Intergalactic Beings of Light

Beloved Lord Huertal and the Andromedan Intergalactic Beings of Light; Beloved Lady Vessa Andromeda, Chohan of the Sacred Flame of Divinity, and the Beloved Archangel Valoel and the Divine Complement Lady Peace.

As I Embrace my Divinity, I Invoke the Sacred Flame and Ray of Divinity, Peace and Opulence to permeate my entire being – my Spirit and Soul, my Chakra System, every Particle, Cell, Atom, Proton, Electron and Neutron, with waves upon waves of powerful Pearlescent Fire, the Shimmering Flame of Peace, surging through me and bringing to me Inner Peace and Opulence.

I Command that the Sacred Flame and Ray of Divinity encapsulates every particle of my Etheric and Auric Fields, my Spirit and Soul, passing upwards through the higher levels of my Chakra System to the Universal, Solar and Multidimensional levels of my Christed Divine God-Self State, bringing me back to the Oneness of my Holy God-Self.

I AM in Deepest Gratitude to Lord Huertal and the Andromedan Intergalactic Beings of Light, and Lady Vessa Andromeda, for being the embodiment of the Sacred Flame and Ray of Divinity.

I Reclaim my Divinity and I Live in Inner Peace and Opulence Now!

I AM my Divine God-Self State.
"And... So It Is!"

> Sacred Flame and Ray of Illumined Truth – Image yourself within a Circle of Peach Flame and at the core center of the Sacred Flame and Ray of Divine Illuminated Truth, View before you the Truth of Who you are and See the Truth of what you are here in this incarnation to learn.

Ray 11: The Peach Ray.

The Sacred Flame of Illumined Truth

Overlighted by: Lord Semveta

Brotherhood of Light

Chohan: Lady Quan Yin

Archangel: Perpetiel

Divine Complement: Lady Joy

Key Attributes:

Illumine Truth, Joy, Serenity, and Activation, Awakened and Awareness of Their Truth, Compassion and Mercy, Rebirth and Rejuvenation, Understanding, Strength, Stability, Loving Kindness, Wisdom, Generosity, Abundance, Compassion, Balance, Organization and Discernment.

Sacred Flame Energy Amplified on Thursday

Seeker of the Illumine Truth of my Life

Divine Truth Illuminated!

Prayer to the Chohan: Lady Quan Yin for Illumined Truth

Beloved Lady Quan Yin, Chohan of the Sacred Flame and Ray of Illumine Truth, Beloved Lord Semveta and the Brotherhood of Light.

I AM a Seeker of the Illumine Truth of my Life. I Ask for the Wisdom and Understanding of the Sacred Flame and Ray, as I become more awakened and aware of the truth of Who I AM and what my purpose is for being in this incarnation.

I Pray to you, Beloved Lady Quan Yin for Humanity, that all who are Seekers of the Truth of who they are, be granted their desires and become Activated, Awakened and Aware of the Oneness of all things. And that they learn to dwell within the Heart Flame of their Heart and know the Love and Light of their Divine I AM Presence, the God-Self within.

I AM my Divine I AM Presence.
"And... So It Is!"

Prayer for Joy and Serenity

Beloved Archangel Perpetiel and the Divine Complement Lady Joy, I AM in Deepest Gratitude for the Boundless Joy that is in my Life.

I Feel the Serenity and the Peace which that brings, filling up my entire being with the Love of Archangel Perpetiel and Lady Joy. I AM in the Balance and Harmony that is Joy and Serenity.

I Know that you are with me in all areas of my Life, helping me to see, feel and hear the Joyfulness that emanates from my family, my friends and from my fellow Humanity.

I See the Hidden Joyfulness within me now. I AM that JOY, I AM that JOY in all things, and thereby know and feel the Deepest Serenity within my Spirit and Soul.

In Gratitude I AM for your Service to ALL.
Thank you, Beloved Archangel Perpetiel and Lady Joy.
"And... So It Is!"

Prayer to Awaken Humanity to the Illumine Truth of Planet Earth

Beloved Lord Semveta and the Great White Brotherhood of Light; As Humanity and All the Kingdoms and Realms of Planet Earth, sit upon the brink of great changes coming from the Universal Logos: Lord Melchizedek. Solar System of Helios and Vesta and the Galactic Logos: Lord Melchior, Let there be Peace, Harmony and Balance in their Awakening.

I Call upon Lord Semveta and the Great White Brotherhood of Light to Awaken Humanity to the Illumine Truth of the Mother, Virgo/Gaia the sentient being that inhabits Planet Earth, and who they are as custodians and guardians of her Wellbeing and Perfect Health.

The Cosmic Rays, Anchor, Activate, Actualize and Amplify the energies of Illumine Truth into Humanity, to Awaken Humanity to the Illumine Truth of the Planet, and expand this Awareness throughout the many levels of Consciousness that are present here on Earth and in All the Kingdoms and Realms of Planet Earth.

Humanity Awakens to the Truth of who they are and what they need to do, in order to be in the Flow of Life and in Oneness within themselves and with each other and All the Kingdoms and Realms of this great Planet, which is Home to Mother, Virgo/Gaia, many different beings, and of many different species and life streams.

The Sacred Flame and Ray of Illumine Truth send waves upon waves of the Sacred Fire, to Planet Earth, surrounding Planet Earth, and All that dwell therein – with the Joy and Serenity that comes with the Awakening to the Truth of the Oneness of All Things.

Illumine Truth brings Joy and Serenity!
"And... So It Is!"

Prayer to Archangel Perpetiel and the Divine Complement Lady Joy

My Beloved I AM Presence, Lord God essence of my being, as I Call upon the Beloved Archangel Perpetiel and the Divine Complement Lady Joy, and the Beloved Lady Quan Yin, I Embrace the Joy and Serenity of this Sacred Flame and Ray of Illumine Truth to my Heart, Mind, Body and Soul.

I Honor you with the Truth of my Heart, I AM surrounded in the Sacred Flame and Ray of Illumine Truth, which allows me to express my Spiritual Reality in increased discernment and Abundance in Health.

The Sacred Flame and Ray of Illumine Truth heals my lower bodies and Rejuvenates and Regenerates my organs and physical body to the New Encodements of Divine Perfection.

The Sounds that Emanate from my Organs, my Physical Body and my Skin are the Sounds of Health and Vitality. I AM in Wellness of Mind, Body, Spirit and Soul.

I experience Rebirth and Rejuvenation through the Cosmic Heart, Mind and Will of God. I AM Reborn into the Divinity of the Creator, the All That Is.

I AM thankful to Archangel Perpetiel and the Divine Complement Lady Joy for bringing Serenity and Joy into my Life.

I AM Eternally Grateful, Beloved Lady Quan Yin. I Honor You for your Compassion and Mercy. I AM in Gratitude to my Mighty I AM Presence for I AM Joyous and in Serenity.

Merciful and Compassionate I AM!
"And... So It Is!"

> Sacred Flame and Ray of One Unity Consciousness – Image yourself within a Circle of Golden Fire, and at the core center of the Sacred Golden Opalescent Flames and Rays of One Unity Consciousness with Self and Others, Feel in Oneness with All things and the Oneness you have with The One, the Ultimate and Supreme Creator God of All That Is.

Ray 12: The Golden Opalescent Ray.

The Sacred Flame of One Unity Consciousness

Overlighted by: Lord Ardal

Cosmic Logos: The Avatar of Synthesis: the Mahatma and Lord Melchizedek

Chohan: Lady Pallas Athena

Archangel: Omniel

Divine Complement: Lady Opalescence

Key Attributes:

Acceptance of what is – as Divine Perfection, Oneness with All Things, Transfiguration, Balance and Harmony, Connection to All That Is, Inner Peace and Tranquillity.

Divine Qualities: Wisdom, Devotion, Illuminating Intelligence, Love, Power, Harmony, Peace, Equilibrium, Creativity, Inspiration, Magnetism, Enlightenment and One Unity Consciousness.

Sacred Flame Energy Amplified on Sunday

One Unity Consciousness with Self

Transfiguration to Divine Oneness!

Prayer to the Chohan: Lady Pallas Athena, Archangel Omniel and Lady Opalescence

Beloved One, the Ultimate and Supreme God of All Creations, the All That Is, the Beloved Chohan: Lady Pallas Athena, the Archangel Omniel and the Divine Complement, Lady Opalescence, Lord Ardal and the Cosmic Logos: the Avatar of Synthesis: the Mahatma; and the Universal Logos: Lord Melchizedek.

I Call upon Lady Pallas Athena, the Masters and Lady Masters of the Sacred Flame and Ray of One Unity Consciousness and the Archangel: Omniel and Lady Opalescence.to assist me, as I Call forth the Twelfth Sacred Flame and Ray of One Unity Consciousness.

I Invoke the Sacred Flame and Ray of One Unity Consciousness in order to create the New Golden Age of Oneness, Peace and Harmony. I AM a Christed Light Conscious Being in service to All Life, to Humanity and All the Kingdoms and Realms of Planet Earth.

I AM Free of the veils of forgetfulness, revealed unto me are the gifts that have been bestowed upon me by the Holy Spirit of All That Is, which will enable me to be of greater service to Humanity, and for All the Kingdoms and Realms Planet Earth.

I Now access the Hidden Knowledge that is held within my being, which will enable me to fulfil my Life Purpose, and be of One Unity Consciousness. I Experience the Sacred Flame and Ray of One Unity Consciousness, within my Immortal Nature and the Cosmic Embrace of The One, the All That Is. .

I AM Connected and in Total Oneness and Complete Remembrance, with the Source of All Life, the All That Is. I AM incorporated within the Divine Mission of the Planetary Hierarchy to actively create and manifest the New Golden Age of One Unity Consciousness, through the Unconditional Love and Christed Light of The One, the Ultimate and Supreme God of All Creations, the All That Is! "And... So It Is!"

Prayer: I Surrender to the Heart of God

I Surrender to the Heart of God – I AM the Heart of God, I Love all beings of the Cosmic All as from the Heart Consciousness of God, Love Unconditional. I AM One with God.   I AM All That Is.

I Surrender to the Heart of God – All the negative energies held within my four Body Systems, All Subtle Bodies, Body Elemental and Inner Child, I Receive the Wisdom and Understanding of these negative energies with ease and grace.

I Surrender to the Heart of God – All Old Beliefs, Patterns and Programs held within my being, that have still to be Resolved, Balanced and Harmonized; in order for my Cosmic Ascension to the 5th Dimension and Beyond to occur. I Receive the Wisdom and Understanding of these Old Beliefs, Patterns and Programs with ease and grace.

I Surrender to the Heart of God – All my Pain and Grief from my beingness – that has been with me since the beginning of my Spiritual Journey.

From the Sacred Chambers of my Heart, I Pledge my Service to the Heart, Mind and Will of God. I Affirm that all is and has been for the Highest Good of All and in accordance with the Divine Will of The One, the Ultimate and Supreme God of All Creations.

Beloved I AM! "And... So It Is!"

Prayer for I AM One Unity Consciousness

Beloved Chohan: Lady Pallas Athena of the Sacred Flame and Ray of One Unity Consciousness. Archangel: Omniel and the Divine Complement Lady Opalescence, and the Golden Angels of One Unity Consciousness. Beloved Universal Logos: Lord Melchizedek.

I AM One Unity Consciousness. I AM as you are, and as I AM One Unity Consciousness All Limitations fall away. I AM held within the essence of the Creator that is only Cosmic Love and Enlightenment. I AM Limitless and I AM Strong. I Feel the Strength within me that encourages me to go forth and allows me to be a pure vessel for the Sacred Light that is the Cosmic Light and Cosmic Love of The One, the Ultimate and Supreme God of All Creations, the All That Is.

I AM Accepting the Light and Love Information from the All That Is, with every Breath That I AM. As I fulfil my Cosmic Ascension pathway, I Feel the Limiting Beliefs falling away from me. I AM holding this Light Energy of Love and All-Knowing. I AM creating within me the Sacred Humble Loving Strength that comes from the Wisdom and Understanding of my Beloved Mighty I AM Presence. I AM Pure of Heart. I AM Clear in Mind.

I AM Devoted to Being of Service to The One, the Ultimate, Supreme God of All Creation, the All That Is, and to the Return of the Remembrance of Who I AM in Truth, therefore, I AM Free from the attachments to the physical realms of Planet Earth.

I AM Totally Healed. My Divine Connection to the Holy Spirit of The One, is Enhanced, and in so being Enables me to Create the Healing for Humanity, All the Kingdoms and Realms of Earth, Planet Earth and the Universe.

I AM One Unity Consciousness.
"I AM All That Is, And... So It Is!"

Invocation to Lord Ardal and the Cosmic Logo:
the Avatar of Synthesis: the Mahatma.

In the name and authority of my Beloved Mighty I AM Presence, Lord God Essence of my Spirit, I Reach Out to you Lord Ardal and to the Cosmic Logos: Avatar of Synthesis, the Mahatma; to Anchor and Activate within me the Consciousness that is of the Mahatma energy for One Unity Consciousness.

I Invoke the Presence of Lord Ardal and the Mahatma Energy to dissolve the crystallized and fixed meanings, beliefs, patterns and programs that are locked into my Spirit, Soul, my four Body Systems, my Inner Child and Body Elemental.

I Call forth the frequency and vibration energy of Lord Ardal and the Mahatma Energy, so that the higher frequency and vibration of their energy will enable and facilitate my attaining the Higher Levels of Consciousness that are necessary for my Cosmic Ascension to my Spiritual God-Self State of the Holy Spirit of One Unity Consciousness.

The Over-lighting Energy of Lord Ardal and the Mahatma Energy blazes forth throughout all levels of my being, bringing me to the ultimate goal of raising my Spirit, Soul, all my four Body Systems, Auric Fields, Universal, Solar and Multidimensional Systems into the frequency of light and into the integrated energies of the Sacred Flame and Ray of One Unity Consciousness and, therefore, into the energy of the Cosmic Rays of Service.

I AM in Gratitude to Lord Ardal for Over-lighting the Sacred Flame and Ray of One Unity Consciousness and to the Cosmic Logos: Avatar of Synthesis: the Mahatma.

Thank you, Beloved Ones. "And... So It Is!"

The United Sacred Flames and Rays of Christed Light Consciousness – Image yourself within the core center of the Sacred Flames and Rays of Christed Light of God Consciousness, in Unity with Helios and Vesta of the Great Central Sun.

The United Twelve Sacred Flames and Rays –

The Sacred Flames of Christ Light Consciousness

Overlighted by: Helios and Vesta

Solar Council of Twelve

Lord Zohar of Shamballa

Cosmic Logos: Avatar of Synthesis: The Mahatma

Chohans: Maha Chohan and All Twelve Chohans of the Flames and Rays

Archangel: Lord Metatron

Angelic Realm: Legions of Angels that Service the Flames and Rays

Key Attributes:

Solar Service: Solar Christ Consciousness, and the Reunion with Helios and Vesta. The Combined Attributes of All the Sacred Flames and Rays of Christed Light Consciousness lead to Unification, and Oneness with the Christed Light Consciousness of the Holy Spirit.

Reunion with Helios and Vesta

Solar Service in Unification to Be All That Is;

Cosmic Logos: Avatar of Synthesis; the Mahatma.

66

Prayer to the Cosmic Logos: Avatar of Synthesis: the Mahatma

Beloved Holy One, the Ultimate and Supreme God of All Creations, the All That Is! The Beloved Cosmic Logos: Avatar of Synthesis, the Mahatma; the Maha Chohan and the Chohans of the Twelve Sacred Flames and Rays; the Archangels and the Divine Complements of the Twelve Sacred Flames and my Mighty I AM Presence to be present in this now moment.

I Feel the Sacred Flames and Rays Unite as One and enter into my Spirit, my Soul, my Heart, and all four Body Systems, Subtle Bodies, Body Elemental and Inner Child, to bring Healing, Love, Light, Inner Peace, Balance and Harmony to all levels of my being.

From the Sacred Chambers of my Heart, the United Sacred Flames and Rays connect me to the Christed Light of God Consciousness, the All That Is. I AM One, with the Heart, Mind and Will of God.

The United Sacred Flames and Rays connect All Humanity, All Kingdoms and Realms in and of the Earth to the Heart, Mind, and Will of God, The United Sacred Flames and Rays surround Mother Earth and Assist her in Ascending to the 5th Dimension and Beyond, with ease and grace.

The Integrated Sacred Flames and Rays assist All on Planet Earth to Ascend to the 5th Dimension and Beyond at this time, if they have chosen to do so.

I AM in Service to The One, the Ultimate and Supreme God of All Creations, and therefore know that this is for the Highest Good of All and for the Highest Good of the Universe.

I AM In Unity and Oneness, with the Heart, Mind and Will of God.
"And So It Is!"

Prayer to the United Integrated Twelve Sacred Flames and Rays

O Sacred Flames of Life on Earth, I AM in Gratitude and Love for your unending work in keeping our precious Mother Earth Alive.

I AM a Child of Earth and I AM Home to Rejoice in your Love. I AM once again united with the Children of the Inner Realms and the Inner Earth Cities of Infinite Wisdom and Love.

In Oneness and Unity with The One, the Ultimate and Supreme God of All Creations, the All That Is; In Oneness and Unity from my Heart, our Hearts become One Heart, Beating to the Rhythm of our Mother's Heart, The Hearts once broken and rendered apart are Now Rejuvenated, Revivified and Resurrected to their normal God-Self State.

Rejoice, Rejoice and Rejoice in Love and Light for Beloved Ones, I AM once again Free, and Restored to Divine Oneness and Unity with the Creator, The One, the Ultimate and Supreme God of All Creations, the All That Is.

My Journey of Cosmic Ascension continues United I AM and One with my God-Self State, Others and The One, the All That Is.

"And... So It Is!"

Prayer: I AM the Master of My Destiny

My Beloved Mighty I AM Presence, Lord God essence of my being; I AM in the Mastery of my Destiny. I Rejoice, Rejoice, Rejoice in my abilities to resolve and dissolve all negative energies, thought forms and emotions, as they appear to me and as shown by Spirit and from my Soul – the Holy Spirit God-Self State that I AM.

As the Master of my Destiny, I Choose to remove all negativity from my four Body Systems. I Send all negativity to the Light of Source, which is at the central core of my Sacred Heart, for resolution and to be dissolve by the Transmutation, Transformation and Transfiguration Flames and Rays of the Sacred Christed Light of God Consciousness, which are within the Sacred Gateways and Portals of my Heart, connecting me to the Truth of Who I AM as a Master of Light and Love.

All my Past Life Akashic Records have been Cleared and Cleansed of any and all Imbalances, and Restored to the Divine Perfection of Balance and Harmony.

All Memories and Records that are held in my Subconscious Mind have been Cleared and Cleansed, and Restored to the Perfection of the Christed Light of God Consciousness.

All Beliefs, Patterns and Programs contained within my Conscious Mind, my Subconscious Mind, and my Super Conscious Mind are Reframed, Restored and Resurrected to the Light and Love of the Cosmic Heart and Mind of God.

I AM Living from the Sacred Chambers of my
Heart, as the Master That I AM.
"And... So It Is!"

Prayer to Archangel Lord Metatron
of the Angelic Realm

Beloved Archangel Lord Metatron of the Angelic Realm, in all that you do and in all that you hold,

I AM in Gratitude to you from the very depths of my Soul. I Honor you and your beingness with all that I AM.

I See, Hear and Feel in all that surrounds me the Light Energy that is you. I Feel Blessed in the knowing that the All That Is also is you.

I know with every fibre of my being that we are One. As a child of The One, I emulate you in my Breath, in my Thoughts and Emotions, and in my Soul.

I AM Grateful for all that you are in my Life; As you walk with me throughout my Life, I Feel your Presence within me. You Guide me and show me by your example, the way home to be in Unity with my God-Self, to be in Unity with others, and to be in Unity with The One, the Ultimate and Supreme God of All Creations, the All That Is;

I AM One with my God-Self. I AM One with Others. I AM One with You Archangel Metatron.

I AM One with the One, I AM All That Is.
"And... So It Is!"

The Sacred Cosmic Rays of Light – Image yourself within a Circle of Cosmic Light Rays and at the core center of the Sacred Rays, feel immersed with them and traverse these Rays to the Portals and the Gateways to all Dimensions of Time and Space.

Cosmic Prayers

Prayer of the Portal of Diamonds

I have no other journey Only the One within myself;

As I Pass through the Portal of Diamonds,

And bathe in the Splendor of My Glorious Mighty I AM Presence,

I know that the Cosmic Heart of The One, the All That Is,

Blesses me with Unconditional Love and Christed Light,

And with the Blessings from the Cosmic Heart,

Coming through me as a sparkling River of Diamonds,

Bringing Peace, Love and Harmony to All,

I AM That I AM,

I AM the Diamond Heart, the All That Is!

I AM my True Self, the Holy God-Self of my Diamond Heart!

"And... So It Is!"

Prayer to the Cosmic Rays of Light

O Cosmic Rays of Light, Surround my Heart and Mind with
Enlightenment, Awareness and Harmony. Light up the Sacred
Chambers of My Heart and Mind with your Crystal Clear Diamond
Fire of All-Knowing and Cosmic Understanding of All That Is.
O Cosmic Rays of Light, the Diamond Fire that is your
Portal, the Gateway to all Dimensions of Time and Space,
Embrace me with your Enlightenment and Acceptance that
I AM Worthy to pass through your Cosmic Gateways. I AM
Purity in One United Consciousness with All That Is.
I AM One with the Cosmic Rays.
I AM that I AM!

"And... So It Is!"

Prayer to the Cosmic Rays for Peace and Harmony

Oh Beloved One, the Ultimate and Supreme God of All Creations. Manifest for this World, Planet Earth, in this Very Moment of the Now, The Wondrous Peace, Harmony and Unconditional Love, that is the birth right of All the Children of God.

Send forth the Cosmic Rays to impart unto All the Kingdoms and Realms of Planet Earth, the Knowledge that you are Unconditional Love. Your Love is Eternal and Bestowed upon All of your Children – regardless of Religion, Race, Creed or Species – and includes All the Kingdoms and Realms of Planet Earth.

Beloved One, the Ultimate and Supreme God of All Creations, I Claim my birth right as a Child of your Creation, the Peace, Harmony, Love, Compassion and Mercy, the Love and Light of the Christed Light of God Consciousness, that you ordained was for all of your Children. As in Heaven... so it is on Earth.

O Beloved One, the Ultimate and Supreme God of All Creations, the All That Is, Create in this very Now moment of time, Heaven on Planet Earth, Surrounding and Permeating All with the Holy Spirit, the Cosmic Rays of the Christed Light of God Consciousness.

Peace and Harmony I AM!
"And... So It Is!"

Prayer to the Cosmic Platinum Ray of Purification, Light and Love

Cosmic Platinum Ray of Purification, Light and Love, Come in with your Ray of Purification, and Restore All the Land and Water Regions of Planet Earth to Optimum Health and Well-being.

Cosmic Platinum Ray of Purification, Light and Love, Rejuvenate the arid drought-affected lands of the World. Restore and Regenerate the water ways to vibrant Life Force Energy. Manifest the removal of all that which is harmful and Detrimental to their Rebirth and Regenerative growth; Restore and Rejuvenate All the Lands and Waterways of Planet Earth to Optimum Health and Well-being.

Cosmic Platinum Ray of Purification, Light and Love, awaken All of Humanity to their responsibilities as Caretakers of Planet Earth and the awareness of the Goddess Gaia/Virgo, our Beloved Mother of Earth and to our Duty as Custodians of her Well-being.

Cosmic Platinum Ray of Purification, Light and Love, Restore to the Heart, Mind and Will of Humanity the knowledge that they are to be in Oneness with Mother Nature, All Life Forms and All Life Force Energy, that dwells here on Planet Earth. And to Command the respect of Humanity toward Mother Earth in order that All Life forms and All Life Force Energy, All the Kingdoms and Realms of Earth Is sustained and maintained in accordance with the Universal Laws of Purification and Ascension; Peace and Harmony I AM. I AM in Self-responsibility, therefore, upon the completion of my healing and the manifestation of my Purification, Self- Love and Enlightenment. I Let Go and Release the Cosmic Platinum Ray back to the Source of All That Is.

I Request that all Restoration and Rejuvenation is done in Ease and Grace, and be for the Highest Good of Planet Earth and the Highest Good of the Universe.

"I AM in Gratitude and I AM Thankful." "And ... So It Is!"

Prayer to the Platinum Ray

Beloved Platinum Ray; I Feel you in my life, and I Embrace the many influences that you bring. I AM in Gratitude for your coming. I embody all that you are teaching me in my Journey of Cosmic Ascension to the 5th Dimension and beyond. My Mighty I AM Presence and you the Platinum Ray are One within me, and as you enter my being; all my thoughts and feelings are Purified to Balance and Harmony, Love and Light, Truth and Integrity, and the All-Knowing that I AM the Master of My Destiny, and a Master in My Ascension.

I AM at Peace; my Mind, Body, Spirit and Soul, Embody the Purification energy of the Platinum Ray within the Sacred Chambers of My Heart. I Feel the Integrity and the Truth of the Platinum Ray as it touches my Core Issues and Problems. I Accept the Truth as being my True-Self my God-Self, expressing its Truth, the Truth of who I AM, through the Power of the Platinum Ray.

I Feel the Regenerative Power of the Platinum Ray as it restores my Physical and Etheric Bodies to Perfect Health, reactivating the Crystalline Body of my Self Mastery. My Twelve Strand DNA is reactivated. My Physical and Etheric Bodies experience a complete transformation and regeneration as is appropriate for my evolution.

I Release all Struggle and Resistance of this Truth to the Platinum Ray and in so doing, know the Inner Peace and Harmony of The One, the Ultimate and Supreme Mind of God. I Surrender my Limiting Beliefs of how I Believe things ought to be for my life, and for the lives of others, to the Sword of the Platinum Ray – to be converted to the Truth, Integrity and Purity of the Christed Light of God Consciousness contained within the Sword.

I AM in Acceptance of the Purification and the Truth as they are shown to me and thus I AM Freedom, I AM Purity, I AM Truth, I AM Integrity and I AM Peaceful in All Situations. As I feel the God-Power Spirit within me; and I AM in Acceptance of God's Plan for my Life; I Let Go and Let God Control my Life. And as I Go with the Flow, All is in Ease and Grace. I AM Grateful to the Universal Logos: Lord Melchizedek, and the Order of Melchizedek for the manifestation of the magnificent Platinum Ray to Planet Earth.

I AM in Self-responsibility; therefore, upon the completion of my healing, the manifestation of my optimum health, I Let Go and Release the Platinum Ray back to the Source of All That Is.

"I AM in Gratitude and I AM Thankful. And ... So It Is!"

Invocation to the Twin Rays of the Divine Feminine and the Divine Masculine – (for Justice, Equality, Support and Abundance for All)

Beloved One, the Ultimate and Supreme God of All Creation, the All That Is! Beloved Cosmic Logos: the Avatar of Synthesis; the Mahatma. Beloved Universal Logos: Lord Melchizedek and the Beloved Planetary Logos: Lord Gautama Buddha.

The Divine Feminine and the Divine Masculine Principles within me are joined in Oneness of Spirit, Harmony and Unconditional Love; we are God-Power in Action. I AM in Oneness with my Divine Twin Flame, my Divine I AM Presence is in Oneness with my Divine Twin Flame.

My Twin Flame and I are United and in Oneness with each other in Spirit, and our mighty Monads are within us now. My Twin Flame and I have One Heart, One Mind and One Will, The One, the Ultimate and Supreme God of All Creation is within us now.

I AM that I AM a Child of God and I AM One with the All That Is. I AM Supported and Abundant in All things and in All areas of my Life. I AM Supported by The One, the Ultimate and Supreme God of All Creation, in All that I Do.

I AM Living my Life in the Truth, Justice and Transparency. I Trust in the Support and Fairness of The One, the Ultimate and Supreme God of All That Is.

I Hereby affirm that the Cosmic Laws of Justice apply to All Life Forms and All Life Force energies within this Cosmic All.

The vibrations and frequencies of Transparency and Integrity in All things – Respect and Responsibility toward others, the Support and Fair distribution of God's Abundance to All – flowing through to Unconditional Love, Fairness, Equality; Compassion, Mercy, Metaphysical and Physical

Laws are Distributed to All Life Forms and All Life Force energies, in accordance with the New Encodements for the Cosmic All.

The New Encodements of Divine Perfection in All things, as per the Holy-Spirit Consciousness of The One, the Ultimate and Supreme God of All Creations.

The Divine Feminine and The Divine Masculine Principles are United and in Oneness. The Twin Flame energies are United and in Oneness with each other.

Balance, Harmony and Equilibrium are Cosmic Laws, applied to All Levels of Creation, whatsoever their Life Source energy – be they of the Light or the Dark.

All Energies that reside in the Cosmic All shall abide by the Cosmic Laws of Justice, Truth, Equality of Support and Freedom in Evolution, secure from any interference whatsoever from the Metaphysical and Physical Realms.

By Cosmic Law and Decree; All Life Forms and All Life Force energies forthwith, are to Respect and not interfere in the Spiritual/Soul or Physical Growth of others, another Life Form or Life Force energy.

It is stated herein, that the development and evolution of All Life Forms and All Life Force energies, in this Cosmic All, are the Jurisdiction of the Elohim Council of Elders and the Cosmic Logos: the Avatar of Synthesis; the Mahatma, and are done in accordance with the Holy Writ for the New Encodements of Divine Perfection as declared by The One, the Ultimate and Supreme God of All Creations.

I AM in Gratitude for the Wisdom, Justice and Unconditional Love for All Life, irrespective of the Life Form or Life Force energies as shown by the Divine Feminine and the Divine Masculine Principles.

I AM Eternally Grateful for the Unconditional Love and Dispensations from The One, the All That Is.

I AM Humble and I AM One with All.
"And... So It Is!"

Prayer to Master Adama of Telos

Beloved Master Adama, High Priest of Telos and the Telosian Council of Elders; Beloved Masters and Lady Masters of the Temples for the Sacred Flames in Telos; the Archangels and their Divine Complements; and all members of the Galactic Federation residing in Telos, in this now moment.

I AM here this day in the Temple of my Heart, the Sacred Chambers of my Heart. I AM Open to receive from you the Blessings of Love and Harmony that are the energies of Telos, and all my Brothers and Sisters who are in Telos and within the Telos Communities, around the World.

I AM in Deepest Gratitude for your Unconditional Love and the Light of Harmony that you are in bringing to me this day, the wonders of your Wisdom, Understanding and Truth. I AM in Deepest Gratitude for the Teachings that you have personally delivered to us – your family upon the surface of this Beautiful Planet, our Home; Mother Earth.

I AM in Deepest Gratitude for your Presence in the Earth – for Mother Earth, Humanity and All the Kingdoms of Earth. I thank you from the Sacred Chambers of my Heart to your Hearts, for the Divine Service that you have been to The One, the Ultimate and Supreme God of All Creations.

I AM Open to be with you and for you to be with me in this now moment. I Kneel before the Alter of my Heart in Worship to the Cosmic Light of Christ. I Receive an Infusion of Light from the Great Central Sun. With this Infusion of Light I AM in my own reunification. I AM connected with the Divinity That I AM, and the Great Plan of Light that is my Beloved I AM Presence.

I AM Open in the Sacred Chambers of my Heart to Embrace the Massive Energies of Transformation as they come to me, with ease and grace. I Feel your Embrace and my Entire beingness is Encapsulated with the Energies of Unconditional Love and Harmony – that is Lemurian, the Heart of Lemuria.

I AM in profound humbleness, as I AM in awareness of the Service that you are and image to us all, and I AM as you are, a devoted servant to the All That Is, The One, the Ultimate and Supreme God of All Creations.

"I AM in One Unity Consciousness Now! And So It Is!"

Prayer for Harmony

My Beloved Might I AM Presence, Lord God of my being, I Ask for the Blessings of the Flame of Harmony to be within me always.

I Strive to Remain in the State of Harmony at all times. As I do so, I AM Living in Harmony with All of Creation and All of Nature.

I AM Harmony in All Situations, blessing all beings that come into my life as I Go Forth with what is my own Truth, the truth of my Mighty I AM Presence.

I Remain where Harmony reigns at all times in the NOW moment. I Surround myself in the Total Acceptance of what is.

I AM a Seeker of Illumine Truth and Harmony. I Embrace the new energies that are Flooding the Earth with all of my Heart, Mind, Body and Soul.

I AM in Total Acceptance of Who I AM and what I have been. I Strive always to improve myself. I AM in Deepest Gratitude for all the Assistance that I AM Receiving in this now moment.

I AM Harmony and Harmony is the number one quality in my Life that I Embody. As I Live in Harmony, it paves the way for my admittance to the "Hall of Ascension."

I AM in my Heart always. I AM in Gratitude and I AM Happy with All of Creation. In Total Acceptance of What Is, I See the Perfection in All Things and in All Situations.

I AM Receiving the Blessings of the Flame of Harmony Now! I AM in Gratitude for the Sacred Flame of Harmony. I AM in Deepest Gratitude to Lord Zohar, Lord of the Sacred Flame and Ray of Harmony

Blessed I AM! "And... So It Is!"

Prayer for Peace on Earth, Good Will toward All Humanity

Beloved One, the Ultimate and Supreme God of All Creations, the All That Is! Beloved Cosmic Logos: Avatar of Synthesis: the Mahatma. The Universal Logos: Lord Melchizedek. The Universal Judge; Galactic Logos: Lord Melchior. Helios and Vesta of the Great Central Sun. Beloved Planetary Logos: Lord Gautama Buddha. Beloved Lord Sanat Kumara and Lady Venus: Lord Zohar of Shamballa, and the Beloved Spiritual Hierarchy for Planet Earth: Lord Maitreya.

I Desire with all of my Sacred Heart, Spirit, Soul, Mind and Might for Peace on Earth and Good Will toward all Humanity through and from the Cosmic Heart, Mind and Will of God.

The Full Divine Intervention of the Godforce has been called forth, to manifest Peace and Harmony through the Energy of the Cosmic Christed Light of God Consciousness and Cosmic Love, Wisdom and Understanding of The One, the Ultimate and Supreme God of All Creations, into the troubled Regions of Planet Earth, in this now moment of time.

I Decree with all my Sacred Heart, Spirit, Soul, Mind and Might, that God's Divine Plan of Peace and Harmony for Planet Earth is now manifested, Anchored, Activated, Actualized and Amplified; Into all Governments of all Nations on Planet Earth, All World and United Nations Corporations and Into the Earth, Air and Water Areas and Regions of Planet Earth.

I thank you and I accept this as being done for the Highest Good of All and in Accordance with Divine Will of God, in the Divine Perfection of All That Is,

"And... So It Is!"

Prayer for Planet Earth's Cosmic Ascension

I Call upon the Beloved One, the Ultimate and Supreme God of All Creations. Beloved Elohim Council of Co-Creator Gods; the Beloved Cosmic Hierarchy and Cosmic Logos: Avatar of Synthesis; the Mahatma. The Universal Hierarchy and Universal Logos: Lord Melchizedek. Planetary Logos: Lord Gautama Buddha. Beloved Planetary Hierarchy and the Planetary Christ: Lord Maitreya.

The Great White Brotherhood and the Company of Heaven that are the Christed Light of God Consciousness of this Universe and the Cosmic All to Anchor, Activate, Actualize and Amplify all the points of the Planetary Crystalline Grid of Planet Earth, to connect with the corresponding points of the Crystalline Grid of the Great Central Sun of this Universe.

I Decree that Planet Earth is Resurrected to the New Encodements of Divine Perfection as per the Universal Laws of One Unity Consciousness. I Decree that Planet Earth is lifted through the Veils of Consciousness, Resurrected and Aligned within the Universe, and Embodies the Universal Laws of Christed Light of God Consciousness.

I Decree that this Universe is lifted through the Higher Levels of Consciousness and Resurrected and Aligned to the Cosmic Laws and to the Cosmic Light of Christed Light of God Consciousness. I Decree that this is God's Will for Planet Earth and for the Universe. God's Will is done, God's Will is done, God's Will is done. And So It Is!

Planet Earth is Resurrected to her Rightful Place in space, Finite and Infinite, Oneness and Unity, Light and Love. The Universe is Resurrected to its Rightful Place in space, Finite and Infinite, Oneness and Unity, Cosmic Light and Cosmic Love.

God's Grace is upon Planet Earth, and with all beings that dwell therein forever.

Beloved I AM! Thank You! Thank You! Thank You! "And... So It Is!"

Prayer for Guiding Light and Love

Guiding Light of my Beloved Mighty I AM Presence, bring forth the Cosmic Light and Cosmic Love of the Christed Light of God Consciousness, to change all the vibrations and frequencies energies held within my being, across all levels and dimensions of time and space, to be Cleansed and Cleared of all that is not Purity.

All the Energy that I have been, as part of my Evolutional Journey, has been Restored to Unconditional Love, Wisdom and Understanding, Balance, Harmony, Peace and Oneness.

All the hurt and harm that I have caused to myself and to others has been Healed by the Cosmic Light and Cosmic Love of the Christed Light of God Consciousness.

All the hurt and harm that I have received from others, has been healed by the Cosmic Light and Cosmic Love of the Christed Light of God Consciousness.

Guiding Light and Love of my Beloved Mighty I AM Presence, brings forth the Unconditional Love of the Holy God Energy, the Christed Light of God Consciousness, so that my broken Heart is Healed, and Restore to Optimum Health.

The energies held within my being, across all levels and dimensions of time and space are Purified, Healed and blessed by the Unconditional Love of God.

I AM Light! I AM Love! I AM All That Is! I AM That I AM!

Thank You, Thank You, Thank You. I AM This I AM.

"And... So It Is!"

Prayer for the Miracle of Manifestation

My Beloved Mighty I AM Presence, please take me each night to the Temples of the Twelve Sacred Flames and Rays of Christed Light of God Consciousness, so that I AM prepared for the initiations I AM to Receive. I Ask to be prepared fully for the Dimensional Gateways that are Open to me. I Ask the Mother Earth Energy to receive and balance my Energy Fields and prepare my Physical, Spiritual, Mental and Emotional being for my ascending the Mountain within, with ease and grace.

I Ask the Inner Mountain Energy to embrace me and carry me in my Journey to the Pinnacle of the Mount. I Call upon my Beloved Mighty I AM Presence to take me to the Temple of the Whales, so that I may Communicate with the Ancient Ones and be blessed by their Wisdom

I Request that my Spirit, Soul and my four Body Systems are prepared for this greater wisdom and the Opening of my Higher Heart and Thymus, my Pineal and Pituitary Glands of the Brain. Beloved Mighty I AM Presence, I Request the Miracle of my Ascension to the 5th Dimension and Beyond to be in my Life as soon as I meet all requirements. I Ask for all initiation procedures to take place and be for my highest good and the highest good of the Planet Earth and the Universe.

The Miracle of Prosperity and Financial Freedom is to be made Manifest in my Life Now! The Miracle of Unconditional Love in all my Relationships – with Self, Others and the Universe – is made Manifest in my Life, and also that which is for my Highest Good and the Highest Good of all.

The Miracle of Perfect Health to be made Manifest in my Life and is in accordance with the Divine Plan for my Life and Life Purpose, being for my Highest Good and the Highest Good of All. The Miracle of the

Violet Flame resides within me and around me on all levels of my being, across all dimensions of time and space, 24 hours a day, 7 days a week. The Miracles of my Life are made Manifest Now! I AM Eternally Grateful for the Miracle of Manifestation. "And... So It Is!"

Prayer to the Holy Spirit of Cosmic Christed Light Consciousness

My Beloved Mighty I AM Presence, Lord God Essence of my being, through you I Call upon the Beloved Planetary Logos: Lord Gautama Buddha. Planetary Hierarchy: Lord Sanat Kumara and Lady Venus. The Planetary Christ: Lord Maitreya. Universal Logos: Lord Melchizedek. Beloved Maha Chohan: Master St. Germain and the Chohans of the Twelve Sacred Flames and Rays of Christed Light of God Consciousness.

I Call upon you to witness my request to the Holy Spirit of the Cosmic Christed Light of God Consciousness. I AM my Mighty I AM Presence and I Invoke the Holy Spirit of the Cosmic Christed Light of God Consciousness to enter my Spirit and Soul, and all levels of my beingness – to come down through the Layers of my Multiverses Self, my Universal Self and my Multi-dimensional Self, God-Self, entering my Auric Fields, all levels of my Auric Sheathes, through the Etheric Field, my Chakra System, Meridian System and into my Physical Body and Body Elemental, connecting with the Crystalline Mother Lode energy of Mother Earth.

I AM my Mighty I AM Presence and I Invoke the Holy Spirit of the Cosmic Christed Light of God Consciousness to enter my Physical Being, my Body Elemental, the Cellular Structure of my Body, to encapsulate every Atom, Proton, Electron and Neutron of my Body with the Healing Powers of the Cosmic Christed Light of The Holy Spirit. Healing with Unconditional Love and Light, all levels of my being, across all dimensions, Universes and Multiverses.

I AM my Mighty I AM Presence. I Invoke the Holy Spirit of the Cosmic Christed Light of God Consciousness to pass through and around every Neutron, Electron, Proton, Atom and the Cellular Structure of my Body, with the Healing Powers of the Cosmic Christed Light of The Holy Spirit, moving through my Body Elemental, embracing my Body Elemental with Unconditional Love and Light, passing out through my Chakra System, Meridian System, Etheric Field and all the Auric Sheathes that surround my Body, my Spiritual God-Self, my Soul, returning to the Cosmos, through my Multi-dimensional Self, Universal Self and Multiverses Self. To finally return to the One Unity Consciousness of the Holy Spirit of the Cosmic Christed Light of God Consciousness.

I AM my Mighty I AM Presence. I Command that this is done in accordance with the Holy Writ for my Life, and that this is for my Highest Good and the Highest Good of all.

Thy Will is Done, Thy Will is Done, Thy Will is Done Now!
Beloved Holy Spirit that I AM! "And... So It Is!"

Prayer for the Restoration of the
Genetic Codes and DNA

I Invoke the Presence of the Elohim Council of Elders; the Co-Creator God's to be present in this now moment of time. I AM That I AM, in the image of Divine Perfection that is my Beloved Mighty I AM Presence.

I Claim my Genetic Codes and DNA to be Restored, Rejuvenated and Revivified to the New Divine Encodements of Perfection that is the Crystalline Lightbody, in accordance with the Divine Will of God, The One, the Ultimate and Supreme God of All Creations, the All That Is.

The Genetic Codes and DNA are Restored by the Elohim Council of Elders: Co- Creator God's to the Divine Perfection of the Crystalline Lightbody Encodements, for every man, woman and child on Planet Earth and throughout All the Kingdoms and Realms of Earth.

The Elohim Council of Elders and Co-Creator God's, configure the updates to the Genetic Codes and DNA Encodements that are the Crystalline Lightbody requirements for the Cosmic Ascension to the 5th Dimension and beyond, for All the Kingdoms and Realms of Planet Earth and for the Universe.

The Christed Light of God Consciousness permeates All Life Forms and All Life Force energy on Planet Earth and in the Universe, creating the Crystalline Lightbody within All Life Forms and All Life Force energy, finite and infinite.

Resurrecting in all, the Crystalline Lightbody as required for Cosmic Ascension to the 5th Dimension and Beyond. All Life Forms and All Life Force energy now have the New Encodements of the Crystalline Lightbody, elevated and Anchored, Activated, Actualized and Amplified, to be in the Awakened and Aware State of the Higher Level Consciousness of the 5th Dimension and Beyond.

God's Love Is All That Is. "And… So It Is!"

Part 2

Inner Guidance Affirmation/
Themes/Issues/Problems
Sacred Flames Healing Solutions

Affirmations/Themes/Issues/Problems and Sacred Flames and Rays Solutions

Ray 1: Blue Ray – Sacred Flame and Ray of the Will of God. Amplified on Monday

1. <u>Prayer to the Chohan: Master El Morya for Guidance</u> **Affirmation:** I AM the Embodiment of_____.
   "And... So It Is!"
   Affirmation: I and the Will of God are One. Humanity is One with God's Will. "And... So It Is!"
   Affirmation: I Surrender to the Will of God all my _____ _____. "And... So It Is!"

2. <u>Prayer of Surrender to My I AM Presence</u> Affirmation: I AM One with My I AM Presence. "And... So It Is!"

3. <u>Prayer for Protection</u>   Affirmation: I AM Protected Always by the Will of God. "And... So It Is!"
   Affirmation: I AM the Resurrection and the Life of the Encodement Blueprint of Divine Spiritual Perfection for Planet Earth. "And... So It Is!"

4. <u>Prayer to Archangel Michael and to the Divine Complement Lady Faith</u>
   Affirmation: I AM a Protector and Keeper of the Sacred Flame and Ray of God's Will for Planet Earth. "And... So It Is!"
   Affirmation: I AM in Oneness with my Spiritual God-Self; the Will of God is within me. "And... So It Is!"
   Affirmation: I AM the Embodiment of the Sword of Archangel Michael. "And... So It Is!"
   Affirmation: I AM Living in accordance with God's Will already, because through the Sacred Flame and Ray of God's Will. I have surrendered to the Will of God. "And... So It Is!"

Affirmation: I AM Protected already, because the Protective energy of the Sacred Flame and Ray of God's Will, that protects all things, surrounds me and resides within me. "And... So It Is!"

Affirmation: I AM Courageous in all situations already, because I have the Courage of the Sacred Flame and Ray of the Will of God within me. "And... So It Is!"

Affirmation: I AM the Will of God already, because the Will of God I AM. "And... So It Is!"

Themes/Issues/Problems: Surrender. Trust, Truth, Focus, Protection, Courage, Faith, Initiative, Stealing, Demeaning yourself or others, Dependability, Omnipotence, the Will of God, Divine Power, Self-reliance and Certainty.

Sacred Flames to Invoke for Healing:
Sacred Flame of the Will of God, Sacred Flame of Ascension, Purification and Immortality, Sacred Flame of Illumination and Wisdom, and the Sacred Flame of Transmutation

----

Ray 2: Yellow, the Sacred Flame and Ray of Illumination and Wisdom. Amplified: Sunday

1. Prayer to the Chohan: Lord Lanto and Master Kuthumi
   Affirmation: I AM Wisdom and Understanding. I AM able to sustain and maintain the illumination Energy within my being from the Sacred Flame of Illumination. "And... So It Is!"
   Affirmation: I Transform all that is not of the Divine Light from my being to the Wisdom, Understanding and the Unconditional Love of the Illumination of Truth. "And... So It Is!"

2. Prayer for Illumination of Planet Earth
   Affirmation: I Call upon the Sacred Flame of Illumination to encapsulate Planet Earth within a Circle of Illumination Fire. So

that Planet Earth and all its inhabitants are immersed within the Illumination Fire of Wisdom, Understanding and Truth. "And... So It Is!"

3. Invocation of the Sacred Flame and Ray of Illumination
   Affirmation: I AM One with the Holy Spirit, the Heart, Mind and Will of God. "And... So It Is!"

   Affirmation: My Subconscious Mind is in Awareness and Connected to the Source of my being. "And... So It Is!"

4. Prayer to Archangel Jophiel and the Divine Complement Lady Christine **Affirmation:** I understand and Love the many problems that beset me. I Accept the Divine Perfection of what they are as being for my Highest Good and learning experience. "And... So It Is!"

   Affirmation: I AM Perceptive, and show Discernment and Compassion in All Areas of my Life. "And... So It Is!"

   Affirmation: I AM Wise and Understanding in All Situations. "And... So It Is!"

   Affirmation: I AM transformed by the Light of the Mind of God to be the Divine illumination of the Light of Wisdom, Understanding and Love. "And... So It Is!"

   Affirmation: I AM Illuminated with the Wisdom and Understanding of God Consciousness already, because I AM Connected to the Source, my I AM Presence, the Mind of God is within me. "And... So It Is!'

   Affirmation: I have the Perceptiveness and Precipitation abilities of God Consciousness already, because the Sacred Flame and Ray of Illumination encompass all levels of my being. "And... So It Is!"

   Affirmation: I AM the energy of Discernment and Discrimination already, because these attributes are held within the God Consciousness of the Sacred Flame and Ray of Illumination. "And... So It Is!"

Themes/Issues/Problems: Clarity of Thinking and Feeling, Comprehension, Communicating Clearly, Wisdom, Understanding, Truth, Integrity, Transparency, Unconditional Love, Perceptions, Precipitations, Omniscience, Discrimination, Discernment and the Anchoring, Activation and Amplification of the Mind of God.

Sacred Flames to Invoke for Healing: Sacred Flame of Illumination and Wisdom, Sacred Flame of Cosmic Love, Sacred Flame of Illumine Truth, and the Sacred Flame of Healing and Manifestation;

Ray 3: Pink, the Sacred Flame and Ray of Cosmic Love. Amplified on Tuesday

1. Prayer to the Chohan: Paul the Venetian for Self-Love
    Affirmation: I Love myself completely. I Accept myself as Divine Love. "And... So It Is!"
2. Prayer: I Am My Heart
    Affirmation: I AM Living in My Heart. I AM Heart Centered in My Life. "And... So It Is!"
    Affirmation: I Open my Heart to Love. I AM the Love of God's Heart. "And... So It Is
3. Invocation of the Sacred Flame and Ray of Cosmic Love
    Affirmation: I AM Compassionate and Merciful. "And... So It Is!"
    Affirmation: I AM in Love with my life and from the Sacred Chambers of my Heart, the center of my Soul, I Love myself completely. "And... So It Is!"
    Affirmation: I AM Living within my Sacred Heart. "And... So It Is!"
    Affirmation: The Hearts of Humanity and the Heart of God are One. "And... So It Is!"

Affirmation: I AM the Divine Unconditional Love and Compassion of my Mighty I AM Presence. "And... So It Is!"

Affirmation: I AM Love and I Invoke the Radiant Light of Cosmic Love to encapsulate all of Humanity and All the Kingdoms and Realms of Mother Earth. "And... So It Is!"

4. <u>Prayer to Archangel Chamuel and the Divine Complement Lady Charity</u>

Affirmation: I AM in appreciation of the Beauty and Artistry of the Mother, Lady Gaia. "And... So It Is!"

Affirmation: I AM Eternally Grateful to the Angelic Kingdom, for bringing me back to the Pathway of Love. "And... So It Is!"

Affirmation: I Love what I see, hear and feel of Mother Earth that brings to me a sense of wonder and awe at her power, majesty and magnificence. "And... So It Is!"

Affirmation: I AM Connected to my Higher Mind already, because I AM One with the Higher Mind of God within me. "And... So It Is!"

Affirmation: I AM Divine Self-Love already, because I have the Divine Sacred Flame and Ray of God's Love within me. "And... So It Is!"

Affirmation: I AM Living from my Heart already, because the Heart of God is within me. "And... So It Is!"

Affirmation: I AM Unconditional Cosmic Love already, because this is the Key to the Multiplication of ALL things in and of God's Creation. "And... So It Is!"

Themes/Issues/Problems: Heart Centeredness, Divine Self-Love, Unconditional Cosmic Love: that is the Key to Multiplication, Love of Others, Compassion, Mercy, Charity, True Brotherhood of the Spirit, Wisdom of the Heart, Open Heartedness and Living from the Heart: the Sacred Chamber of the Heart. The Three-fold Flame within the Heart.

<u>**Sacred Flames to Invoke for Healing:**</u>
Sacred Flame of Cosmic Love,
Sacred Flame of Highest Potentials,
Sacred Flame of Illumine Truth, and the
Sacred Flame of Ascension and Purification;

<u>Ray 4 White, the Sacred Ascension Flame and Ray of Purification: Amplified on Friday</u>

1. <u>Prayer to the Chohan: Lord Serapis Bey, the Lord of Purification</u>
   Affirmation: I AM Purified; I AM the Holy Spirit on All Levels of My four Body Systems.
   "And... So It Is!"
   Affirmation: I AM in Gratitude for my life. I Release all energies that serve me not, to the Holy Spirit of Cosmic Christed Consciousness. "And... So It Is!"
   Affirmation: Planet Earth has ascended to the 5th Dimensional Consciousness of Harmony. "And... So It Is!"
2. <u>Prayer for Personal Ascension</u>
   Affirmation: I Accept myself as I AM. I AM Pure Divine Perfection and Worthy of my Ascension. "And... So It Is!"
   "And... So It Is!"
   Affirmation: I AM That I AM. As I stand before you this day of my Cosmic Ascension, I AM Humble and I Choose to be of Service to Humanity and Planet Earth. "And... So It Is!"
   Affirmation: I AM within the vibration and frequency of my I AM Presence. "And... So It Is!"
   Affirmation: I AM whole and I AM immortal. "And... So It Is!"
3. <u>Prayer for the Purification of Mind, Body, Spirit and Soul</u>
   Affirmation: I AM the Purification of my Mind, Body and Soul. "And... So It Is!"

Affirmation: I have the Purity of Heart, Mind and Soul to see my I AM Presence and Holy Christ Self. "And... So It Is!"

Affirmation: I AM Purified and Whole already, because I AM the Purity and Wholeness of the Ascension Flame and Ray. "And... So It Is!"

4. <u>Prayer to Archangel Gabriel and the Divine Complement Lady Hope</u>

   Affirmation: I Release to the Sacred Flame of Ascension and to the Ascension Angels, all that which is within me, that requires purification. "And... So It Is!"

   Affirmation: I AM Eternally Grateful for having achieved my Self-Mastery, Inner Peace and Tranquillity. "And... So It Is!"

   Affirmation: I AM Ascended already, because the Sacred Flame and Ray of Ascension has immersed me into the Christed Light Consciousness of The One, the Supreme Creator God. "And... So It Is!"

Themes/Issues/Problems: Divine Perfection, Whole and Complete, Separation, Ascension, Self-Mastery, Self-Acceptance, Self-Worth, Wisdom, Peace and Tranquillity, Christed Light Consciousness, Balance, Harmony and Perfection of Health: Be Self-Disciplined, and with Access to Unlimited and Ever-present Supply from Father/Mother God. Purification: Purity of Spirit, Mind and Body. Immortality: Immortality of the Soul.

<u>**Sacred Flames to Invoke for Healing:**</u>
Sacred Flame of Ascension and Purification, Sacred Flame of Healing and Manifestation, Sacred Flame of the Will of God and the Sacred Flame of Resurrection

---

<u>**Ray 5: Green, the Sacred Flame and Ray of Healing ad Manifestation: Amplified on Wednesday**</u>

1. <u>Prayer to the Chohan: Master Hilarion for Guidance</u>
   Affirmation: I AM Healthy and Abundant on all levels of my being. "And... So It Is!"
2. <u>Prayer for Health and Well being</u>
   Affirmation: I AM in Perfect Health and Wellness. "And... So It Is!"
3. <u>Prayer for the Abundance of God</u>
   Affirmation: I AM Totally Abundant and Prosperous. "And... So It Is!"
4. <u>Prayer to Archangel Raphael and the Divine Complement Lady Regina</u>
   Affirmation: I AM in Acceptance of my Pain, as it was Divine Perfection. I AM therefore Free of my Pain, and it is no more. "And... So It Is!"
   Affirmation: The Waterways of Planet Earth are Healed and Purified by the Great Sacred Flame of Healing and the Cosmic Rays. "And... So It Is!"
   Affirmation: I Let Go and Release to the Sacred Flame of Healing all the negative energies held within my Mind, Body and Soul. "And... So It Is!"
   Affirmation: I AM the Loving Vibration that Radiates Love, Inner Peace, Wealth and Abundance.
   "And... So It Is!"
   Affirmation: I AM All That Is. I AM Totally Wealthy, Healthy and Happy in my Life. "And... So It Is!"

Affirmation: Divine Perfection and Restoration of All the Kingdoms and Realms of Planet Earth to Christed Light Consciousness is happening Now! "And... So It Is!"

Affirmation: I AM Healthy and Wealthy already, because the Divine Healing and Manifestation Powers of the Sacred Flame and Ray of Healing and Manifestation surround me and permeate every atom, cell and electron of my being. "And... So It Is!"

Affirmation: I Manifest ALL that I need in my life already, because the Sacred Flame and Ray of Healing and Manifestation, is the God-Power within my Mind, Body and Soul. "And... So It Is!"

<u>**Themes/Issues/Problems:**</u> Physical Pain and Dis-ease, Poverty thinking, Mental/Emotional Confusion, Critical Thinking about Self or Others, Healing at All Levels, Constancy, Creation through Manifestation, God's Abundance through the Immaculate Sacred Heart of I AM. Divine Abundance: Perfect Health in Mind, Body and Soul.

<u>**Sacred Flames to Invoke Healing:**</u>
Sacred Flame of Healing and Manifestation,
Sacred Flame of Purification,
Sacred Flame of Resurrection, and the
Sacred Flame of Transmutation;

<u>**Ray 6, Ruby/Gold, the Sacred Flame and Ray of Resurrection: Amplified on Thursday**</u>

1. <u>Prayer to the Chohan: Lord Sananda for the Resurrection of My Life</u>
   Affirmation: I AM the Resurrection of my Life. I AM restored to my Original Blueprint of Divine Perfection. "And... So It Is!"

2. <u>Prayer to the Sacred Resurrection Flame and Ray of Resurrection</u>

Affirmation: I AM in Devotion to the Sacred Flame of Resurrection. "And... So It Is!"

Affirmation: I AM the Resurrection of my Life. I AM One with the Resurrection Flame. I AM Resurrected to Eternal Life. "And... So It Is!"

3. <u>Prayer for the Resurrection of Planet Earth</u>

   Affirmation: I AM in Selfless Service of God, Humanity and Planet Earth. "And... So It Is!"

4. <u>Prayer to Archangel Uriel and the Divine complement Lady Aurora</u>

   Affirmation: I AM the Resurrection of my Life, I AM the Resurrection of my Life, I AM the Resurrection of my Life of Oneness with the Archangel Uriel and Lady Aurora. "And... So It Is!"

   Affirmation:

   I AM Born to the Spiritual Worship of the Divine Heart of God. "And... So It Is!"

   Affirmation: I AM Restored to Perfect Health and Harmony. My Electrons have been Purified and Restored to Divine Perfection of Health and Harmony. "And... So It Is!"

   Affirmation: I AM the Resurrection of my Life. My Body Elemental and I are One. "And... So It Is!"

   Affirmation: The Resurrection Flame, Rejuvenate and Restore the Elemental Kingdom to Divine Perfection, Peace and Harmony. "And... So It Is!"

   Affirmation: I Invoke the Energy of Peace and Aloha into the World. "And... So It Is!"

   Affirmation: I AM my Personal Power already, because I have the God-Power of the Sacred Resurrection Flame and Ray within me. "And... So It Is!"

   Affirmation: I AM Rejuvenated, and Revivified in every cell of my mental, emotional and physical body already, because the Sacred

Flame and Ray of Resurrection, has rejuvenated and revitalized me. "And... So It Is!"

Themes/Issues/Problems: Immortality, Mortality, Perfectionism, Planetary Service, Time-related Issues. The Resurrection, Restoration, Revivification, Regeneration to the Original Blueprint of Divine Perfection, Selfless Service and Ministration, Spiritual Worship and Reverence.

Sacred Flames to Invoke for Healing:

Sacred Flame of Resurrection,
Sacred Flame of Transcendence,
Sacred Flame of Divinity, and the
Sacred Flame of One Unity Consciousness;

Ray 7, The Violet Ray, The Sacred Flame and Ray of Transmutation: Amplified on Saturday

1. Prayer to the Chohan: Lady Portia for Justice and Opportunity
    Affirmation: I AM Just and Fair, Merciful, Compassionate and Caring toward myself and others. "And... So It Is!"

2. Invocation of the Sacred Flame and Ray of Transmutation
    Affirmation: I Invoke the Divine Justice and Divine Truth of the Violet Fires of Freedom, Forgiveness, Unconditional Love, Compassion and Mercy, restoring all that which is within Mother Earth, to the Divine Principles of the Violet Flame. "And... So It Is!"

    Affirmation: I AM the Freedom that Gives Opportunity for Growth. "And... So It Is!"

    Affirmation: I AM the Temple of Grace; I AM Divine Love, Compassion and Gratitude. "And... So It Is!"

Affirmation: I Release unto the Light Source within the Sacred Chambers of my Heart, all Family Constellation beliefs, patterns and programs that have controlled my Life. "And... So It Is!"

Affirmation: I AM FREE to be the Truth of Who I AM! "And... So It Is!"

3. Prayer for Lord Omri Tas of the Purple Planet

   Affirmation: In the Violet Flame of Transmutation, I AM Free and I AM Love.
   "And... So It Is!"

   Affirmation: I AM the Embodiment of the Divine Principles of Dimplomacy and Alchemy. "And... So It Is!"

4. Prayer to Archangel Zadkiel and the Divine Complement Lady Amethyst

   Affirmation: I AM Freedom, I AM Forgiveness, I AM Uncondition Love and I AM Forever One with God "And... So It Is!"

   Affirmation: I AM the Violet Flame of Transmutation already, because I AM One with the Sacred Flame and Ray of Transmutation. "And... So It Is!"

   Affirmation: I Live my Life in Freedom and Forgiveness already, because the God Consciousness energy of the Sacred Flame and Ray of Transmutation has directed my Life Force to the Christed Light Consciousness of God. "And... So It Is!"

   Affirmation: I Love everything with the Unconditional Love of God already, because I AM One with the God-Mind of my God-Self within me. "And... So It Is!"

   Affirmation: I AM Diplomatic already, because the Diplomatic energy of the Sacred Flame and Ray of Transmutation is within me. "And... So It Is!"

Themes/Issues/Problems: Freedom, Forgiveness, Unconditional Love, Transmutation, Transformation, Changes, Tact and Diplomacy, Ceremony and the Application of the Science of True Alchemy.

Sacred Flames to Invoke for Healing

Sacred Flame of Transmutation,

Sacred Flame of God's Will,

Sacred Flame of Illumination,

and the Sacred Flame of Cosmic Love.

Ray 8, Aqua Ray, the Sacred Flame and Ray of Transcendence: Amplified on Wednesday

1. Prayer to the Chohan: Lady Nada of the Sacred Flame of Transcendence

   Affirmation: I AM the Self-actualization of my Truth as a Master of Light and Love. "And... So It Is!"

   Affirmation: I Have Clarity of thinking in all things, I AM Clear and I AM Certain of my Ascension into the Light of the 5th Dimension and Beyond in this incarnation. "And... So It Is!"

2. Prayer of Gratitude for the World

   Affirmation: All of Humanity on Planet Earth is awakened to the certainty with the clarity of who they are and what they are as beings of higher light vibrations and frequencies from the Source of the Great Central Sun. "And... So It Is!"

3. Invocation to the Sacred Flame and Ray of Transcendence

   Affirmation: I AM living my Life in Truth, Harmony and Balance. "And... So It Is!"

   Affirmation: I Let Go and Let God heal all old memories, beliefs and programs that are irrelevant to my experience and ascension to the Light of Higher Consciousness. "And... So It Is!"

   Affirmation: I AM Cleansed and Cleared, of all my old false belief patterns and judgements. "And... So It Is!"

Affirmation: I AM Balanced and Harmonized within my Mind. "And... So It Is!"

Affirmation: My Overly Active Mind is Balanced and in Harmony with my Heart. "And... So It Is!"

Affirmation: I Invoke the Sacred Flame and Ray of Transcendence to bring Certainty and Clarity of thoughts and emotions, to Humanity in these times of confusion. "And... So It Is!"

4. Prayer to Archangel Aquariel and Lady Clarity for Mother Earth

   Affirmation: I AM a Keeper of the Light and Love for this Sacred Planet, our Beloved Mother Earth. "And... So It Is!"

   Affirmation: I have Transcended all my issues and problems already, because the God-Power of the Sacred Flame and Ray of Transcendence is greater than any problem that I may have. "And... So It Is!"

   Affirmation: I AM full of Certainty, Clarity and Confidence already, because the Sacred Flame and Ray of Transcendence transform all my concerns to Wisdom and Understanding. "And... So It Is!"

   Affirmation: I have Stability and Equilibrium in all areas of my life already, because the Sacred Flame and Ray of Transcendence, brings balance and harmony into my life-stream. "And... So It Is!"

Themes/Issues/Problems: Certainty, Courage, Justice, Clarity Integrity, Wisdom, Understanding, Stability, Equilibrium, Unconditional Love, Unity and Infinite Expansiveness.

<u>**Sacred Flames to Invoke for Healing:**</u>
Sacred Flame of Transcendence,
Sacred Flame of the Will of God,
Sacred Flame of Illumination,
and the Sacred Flame of Purification.

<u>Ray 9. Magenta Ray, the Sacred Flame of Highest Potentials: Amplified on Tuesday</u>

1. <u>Prayer to Chohan: Lady Mother Mary. Archangel Anthriel and Lady Harmony</u>
   Affirmation: I AM my Original Blueprint of Divine Perfection of my Light Body, Freedom and Forgiveness to be the Divine Light and Divine Love that I AM. "And... So It Is!"

2. <u>Prayer to be the Cradle of Love Prayer</u>
   Affirmation: I AM the Love and Joy, the Essence of the Divine Mother, Lady Mother Mary. "And... So It Is!"

3. <u>Prayer for My Highest Potentials</u>
   Affirmation: I AM the Creative Extension of the Higher Mind of my Mighty I AM Presence; I AM living my Highest Potentials Now. "And... So It Is!"

4. <u>Prayer to Lord Goyana and the Sirian Angelic League</u>
   Affirmation: I Invoke the Sirian Archangelic League of Light to Assist Mother Earth and Humanity in Achieving their Light Body and Highest Potentials Now. "And... So It Is!"
   Affirmation: I AM Grateful for the Unfailing Unconditional Love and Compassion of my Divine Heart, the Essence of Lady Mother Mary. "And... So It Is!"
   Affirmation: I AM the Rose, the beautiful flower in the Crown of Heaven.
   "And... So It Is!"

Affirmation: I have achieved my Highest Potentials already, because the Sacred Flame and Ray of Highest Potentials is within me and aides me to achieve success in my life. "And... So It Is!"

Affirmation: All my Gifts and Abilities are within me already, because I have the Sacred Flame and Ray of Highest Potentials within me, and therefore achieve my Life Purpose. "And... So It Is!"

Affirmation: I AM my Higher Mind already, because the Mind of God, my God-Self is within me. "And... So It Is!"

Themes/Issues/Problems: The Synthesis of Flames and Rays 1 to 7, Guidance in Achieving one's Highest Potentials and manifesting in life the Gifts that will Assist in the Cosmic Ascension of One's Soul, Divine Guidance, Compassion, Unity, Justice, Peace, Order, Wisdom, Creativity, Mercy, Unconditional Love and Splendor.

Sacred Flames to Invoke for Healing
Sacred Flame of Highest Potentials,
Sacred Flame of Cosmic Love,
Sacred Flame of Purification,
and the Sacred Flame of Transmutation.

Ray 10. Pearlescent Ray, the Sacred Flame and Ray of Divinity: Amplified on Friday

1. Prayer to the Chohan: Lady Vessa Andromeda. Archangel Valoel and Lady Peace
   Affirmation: I AM the Truth of my Divinity, I AM my Divine Holy Christ Self.
   "And... So It Is!"

2. Prayer to the Pearlescent Fire

   Affirmation: I AM completely Awakened to the Truth of my Divinity in this NOW moment across all dimensions of Time and Space. "And... So It Is!"

3. Prayer to Anchor the Crystalline Light Body

   Affirmation: I AM my Light Body NOW, I AM Power, Love, and Light, in Balance and Equilibrium. "And... So It Is!"

   Affirmation: I Choose to Crystalline my Physical Body; I Bring my Physical Body into Crystallization Now! "And... So It Is!"

   Affirmation: I AM Building my Crystalline Light Body. "And... So It Is!"

   Affirmation: I AM Feeling your Divine Love; I AM at Peace with myself as I discover within myself, my Divinity and Oneness with my I AM Presence. "And... So It Is!"

   Affirmation: God's Divine Plan for Peace and Harmony is made manifest into Planet Earth Now! God's Will IS Done! "And... So It Is!"

4. Invocation to Lord Huertal and the Andromedan Intergalactic Beings of Light

   Affirmation: With the aid of Lord Huertal, and the Andromedan Intergalactic Beings of Light, I Invoke the Sacred Flame of Divinity to encapsulate and permeate my entire four Body Systems, Now! "And... So It Is!"

   Affirmation: I AM my Divinity already, because I AM encompassed within the Sacred Pearlescent Flame and Ray of Divinity. "And... So It Is!"

   Affirmation: I have attained Inner Peace already, because the Calm Inner Peace of the Sacred Flame and Ray of Divinity is within me. "And... So It Is!"

Affirmation: I AM Opulent already, because the Opulence of God the Creator, through the Sacred Flame and Ray of Divinity is within me. "And... So It Is".

Affirmation: I AM in my Divine God-Self State already, because the God-Self is the Truth of Who I AM. "And... So It Is!"

Themes/Issues/Problems: Divinity, Immortality, Light Body, Peace, Balance, Equilibrium, Justice, Power, Infinite Wisdom, Detachment, Attainment, Responsibility, Self-Mastery and Transcendence to Divinity, the Divine God Self State.

Sacred Flames to Invoke for Healing:
Sacred Flame of Divinity,
Sacred Flame of Ascension, Purification and Immortality,
Sacred Flame of One Unity Consciousness,
and the Sacred Flames of Christed Light Consciousness.

Ray 11, Peach Ray, the Sacred Flame and Ray of Illumine Truth: Amplified on Thursday

1. Prayer to the Chohan: Lady Quan Yin for Illumined Truth
   Affirmation: I AM Activated, Awakened and Aware of the Illumined Truth of my Life. "And... So It Is!"

2. Prayer for Serenity and Joy
   Affirmation: I AM that JOY in all things, and thereby know and feel the deepest Serenity within my Soul. "And... So It Is!"
   Affirmation: I AM Truly Blessed by the Truth of my Past Life Recall. "And... So It Is!"
   Affirmation: I AM the Representation of the Illumine Truth of my Life and I Live in Awakened Awareness of All That I AM! "And... So It Is!"

3. <u>Prayer to Awaken Humanity to the Illumine Truth of Planet Earth</u>

   Affirmation: I, and Humanity are Awakened to the Illumine Truth of Planet Earth Now! "And... So It Is!"

4. <u>Prayer to Archangel Perpetiel and Lady Joy for Rebirth & Rejuvenation</u>

   Affirmation: I AM in Wellness of Mind, Body and Soul; I AM Reborn and Rejuvenated to Perfect Health. "And... So It Is!"

   Affirmation: I AM Living a Life of Illumine Truth already, because the Sacred Flame and Ray of Illumine Truth reveal the Truth to me. "And... So It Is!"

   Affirmation: I AM Joyful in every moment already, because the Sacred Flame and Ray of Illumine Truth reveal to me the Joy in the Truth that God is everything. "And... So It Is!"

   Affirmation: My Life is a Life of Serenity and Joy already, because I accept the Illumine Truth of God's Plan for my Life. "And... So It Is!"

   Affirmation: I AM Reborn already, because the Sacred Flame and Ray of Illumine Truth has Rejuvenated, my Physical Body to Perfect Health. "And... So It Is!"

<u>Themes/Issues/Problems:</u> Truth, Rebirth and Rejuvenation, Joyfulness and Being in Serenity, Illumine Truth, Joy, Serenity, and Activation, Awakened and Aware of their Truth, Compassion and Mercy, Understanding, Strength, Stability, Loving Kindness, Wisdom, Generosity, Abundance, Compassion, Equilibrium, and Balance, Organization and Discernment.

<u>**Sacred Flames to Invoke for Healing:**</u>
Sacred Flame of Illumine Truth,
Sacred Flame of Cosmic Love,
Sacred Flame of Resurrection,
and the Sacred Flame of Illumination.

<u>Ray 12. Golden Opalescent Ray the Sacred Flame and Ray of One Unity Consciousness; Amplified Sunday</u>

1. <u>Prayer to the Chohan: Lady Pallas Athena for One Unity Consciousness</u>
   Affirmation: I AM in Total Oneness and Complete Remembrance with the Source of All Life, the All That Is. "And... So It Is!"
   Affirmation: I AM Totally Surrendered to The One, the Supreme God of Creation. "And... So It Is!"

2. <u>Prayer of Surrender to the Heart of God</u>
   Affirmation: I AM the Heart of God. I Have Surrendered to The One, the Supreme God of All Creation. "And... So It Is!"

3. <u>Prayer: I AM One Unity Consciousness</u>
   Affirmation: I AM the Sacred, Humble and Loving Strength that comes from the Wisdom and Understanding of my Beloved Mighty I AM. I AM One with my Beloved I AM Presence. "And... So It Is!"
   Affirmation: I AM Creating Abundance through One Unity Consciousness.
   "And... So It Is!"

4. <u>Invocation to Lord Ardal and the Avatar of Synthesis: the Mahatma</u>
   Affirmation: I Invoke the Presence of Lord Ardal and the Mahatma Energy to Dissolve the Crystallized and Fixed Meanings, Beliefs, Patterns and Programs that are locked within my Soul, my four

Body Systems, my Inner Child and Body Elemental. "And... So It Is!"

Affirmation: I AM One with myself already, because I AM One with the Golden Sacred Flame and Ray of Transfiguration and Oneness. "And... So It Is!"

Affirmation: I AM Living in the Consciousness of Unity already, because the Sacred Flame and Ray of Transfiguration, has changed all programs held within my Unconscious Mind to One Unity Consciousness. "And... So It Is!"

Affirmation: All Patterns and Programs held within my Unconscious Mind are Transfigured and Transformed, to Balance, Harmony and Oneness already, because the God Consciousness energy of the Golden Sacred Flame and Ray of Oneness is within me. "And... So It Is!"

<u>**Themes/Issues/Problems**</u>: Acceptance of what is as Divine Perfection, Oneness with All Things, Transfiguration, Balance and Harmony, Connection to All That Is. Inner Peace and Tranquillity, Divine Qualities, Wisdom, Devotion, Illuminating Intelligence, Love, Power, Harmony, Peace, Equilibrium, Creativity, Inspiration, Magnetism, Enlightenment and One Unity Consciousness.

Sacred Flames to Invoke for Healing:

Sacred Flame of One Unity Consciousness,

Sacred Flame of Illumination,

Sacred Flame of Divinity,

and the Sacred Flame of Harmony.

The United Twelve Sacred Flames and Rays of Christed Light Consciousness

The Avatar of Synthesis: Mahatma; Rays 1 to 12: Amplified Daily

1. Prayer to Cosmic Logos: the Avatar of Synthesis: the Mahatma
   Affirmation: I AM Healed Completely by the United Sacred Flames of Healing. "And... So It Is!"
   Affirmation: I AM the Embodiment of The One, the Supreme God of All. "And... So It Is!"

2. Prayer to the United Integrated Twelve Sacred Flames
   Affirmation: I AM One within myself; my four Body Systems are United and Integrated into Oneness. "And... So It Is!"
   Affirmation: I AM One with the United Sacred Flame of Christed Light Consciousness. "And... So It Is!"

3. Prayer: I AM the Master of My Destiny
   Affirmation: I AM the Master of my Destiny. "And... So It Is!"

4. Prayer to Archangel Lord Metatron and the Angelic Realm
   Affirmation: I AM One with myself, I AM One with Others, I AM One with Lord Metatron, and I AM One with God. "And... So It Is!"
   Affirmation: The Sacred United Flames and Rays within me are united already, because the energies of the Sacred United Flames and Rays are the energies of the Holy-Self of The One, the Supreme Creator God of the Cosmic All. "And... So It Is!"

<u>**Themes/Issues/Problems**</u>: Acceptance of What Is as Divine Perfection, Oneness with All Things, Transfiguration, Balance and Harmony, Connection to All That Is, Inner peace and Tranquillity. Divine Qualities: Wisdom, Devotion, Illuminating Intelligence, Love, Power, Harmony, Peace, Equilibrium, Creativity, Inspiration, Magnetism, Enlightenment and One Unity Consciousness.

<u>Sacred Flames to Invoke for Healing:</u>
Sacred Flame of One Unity Consciousness,
Sacred Flame of Illumination,
Sacred Flame of Divinity and the Sacred Flame of Harmony

<u>Cosmic Prayers of Light</u>

**<u>Rays 13 to 22. Silver, Platinum, Gold and Clear
Rays - Cosmic Light Rays; Amplified daily</u>**

1. <u>Prayer of the Portal of Diamonds</u>
   Affirmation: I AM the Gateway to the Stars. "And... So It Is!"
2. <u>Prayer to the Cosmic Rays of Light</u>
   Affirmation: I AM the Cosmic Light that shines upon the Earth, bringing Peace, Harmony and Unconditional Love. "And... So It Is!"
   Affirmation: I AM the Cosmic Christed Light Consciousness already, because the Cosmic Christed Light Ray of God Consciousness is within me. "And... So It Is!"
   Affirmation: I AM That I AM; I Reach into the Hearts and Minds of all who are connected with the Heart Energy of the Crystalline Grid. "And... So It Is!"
3. <u>Prayer to the Cosmic Rays of Peace and Harmony.</u>

Affirmation: I Manifest for this World, Planet Earth in this very Moment of the Now, the Wondrous Peace, Harmony and Unconditional Love that is the birth right of All the Children of God. "And... So It Is!"

Affirmation: I AM the energy of Peace, Balance and Harmony already, because the energy for Peace, Balance and Harmony from the Cosmic Heart, Mind and Will of God, dwells within the Sacred Chambers of my Heart. "And... So It Is!"

4. Prayer to the Cosmic Platinum Ray of Purification, Light and Love

   Affirmation: I AM purity in One United Consciousness with All That Is. I and the Cosmic Platinum Ray of Purification, Light and Love are in Oneness. "And... So It Is!"

   Affirmation: I AM the Cosmic Light already, because the Cosmic Light energy of The One, Supreme God of Light is within me. "And... So It Is!"

   Affirmation: I AM Cosmic Love already, because the Cosmic Love energy of The One, Supreme God of Love is within me. "And... So It Is!"

5. Prayer to the Platinum **Affirmation:** I AM Purified by the Platinum Ray to the Mastery of my Ascension.
   "And... So It Is!"

6. Invocation to the Twin Rays of the Divine Feminine and Masculine Principles

   Affirmation: I AM the Embodiment of the Divine Feminine and Masculine Principles. "And So It Is!"

Themes/Issues/Problems: Unification, Oneness, Christed Light Consciousness, Purification, Responsibility, Love, Enlightenment, Solar Service, Solar Christ Consciousness and the Reunion with Helios and Vesta, The Combine Attributes of All the Sacred Flames and Rays of Christed Light of God Consciousness.

Sacred Flames to Invoke for Healing:

The United Twelve Sacred Flames - Sacred
Flame of One Unity Consciousness,
Sacred Flames of the Cosmic Rays of Light, Peace and Harmony,
and the Sacred Cosmic Platinum Ray of Purification and Responsibility.

Special Holistic Prayers

1. Prayer to Master Adama of Telos

   Affirmation: I AM Open in the Sacred Chambers of my Heart to encompass the massive energies of transformation, as they come to me with ease and grace. "And... So It Is!"

   Affirmation: I Choose to be in Acceptance of who I AM, and to be in Acceptance of ALL others and who they are, as we are all Divine Perfection in One Unity Consciousness, with our Holy Christed Self. "And... So It Is!"

2. Prayer for Harmony

   Affirmation: I AM in my Heart always; I AM in Gratitude and I AM Happy with All of Creation and in Total Acceptance of What Is. I See the Perfection in all things and in all situations. "And... So It Is!"

3. Prayer for Peace on Earth, Good Will toward All Humanity

   Affirmation: I hereby Ask and humbly Pray with all of my Sacred Heart, Soul, Mind and Might for Peace on Earth and Good Will toward all Humanity through and from the Cosmic Heart, Mind and Will of God. "And... So It Is!"

   Affirmation: Mount Shasta, Mountain of Wonder, Master of Mystery, impart unto me the Mysteries within thee, I AM in the Wonder of the Mystery within me. "And... So It Is!"

4. Prayer for Planet Earth's Cosmic Ascension

   Affirmation: I hereby Decree that Planet Earth is restored to the Original Blueprint of Divine Perfection as per the Universal Laws of One Unity Consciousness. "And... So It Is!"

   Affirmation: I AM Empowered on all levels of my being; I therefore, fulfil all tasks that are asked of me, in accordance with God's Heart, Mind and Will. "And... So It Is!"

5. Prayer for Guiding Light and Love

   Affirmation: I AM Light, I AM Love, I AM All That Is, I AM that I AM. "And... So It Is!"

6. Prayer for the Miracle of Manifestation

   Affirmation: I Manifest the Miracle of Prosperity and Financial Freedom into my life Now! "And... So It Is!"

7. Prayer to the Holy Spirit of Cosmic Christed Light Consciousness (Long Prayer for Healing)

   Affirmation: I AM my Holy God-Self. "And... So It Is!"

   Affirmation: I Invoke the Sacred Flames and Rays of Christed Light Consciousness to come into my life in this now moment of time, across all dimension of time and space. "And... So It Is!"

8. Prayer for the Restoration of the Genetic Codes and DNA

   Affirmation: The Genetic Codes and DNA are Restored to the Divine Perfection of the Crystalline Lightbody Encodements, for every man, woman and child on Planet Earth. "And... So It Is!"

   Affirmation: I have Released and Relinquished to the Light Source within the Sacred Chambers of my Heart the following issues/problems/beliefs (make a list). "And... So It Is!"

   Affirmation: I Affirm that my Genetic Codes and DNA are Restored, Rejuvenated and Revivified, to the Divine Perfection of the Light body Encodements for my Ascension to the 5th Dimension and beyond. "And... So It Is!"

Affirmation: I have Released all Akashic Records of my past lives and current life here on Earth and elsewhere in this Universe to my Mighty I AM Presence, they are Cleared and Cleansed of all energies and beliefs that no longer serve me in this life incarnation. "And... So It Is!"

Affirmation: I AM the Embodiment of my divinely perfected twelve planetary chakras. "And... So It Is!"

Affirmation: I Accept and Surrender to the Protection of the Ashtar Command of the Galactic Federation, the Universal Council of Elders and the Elohim Council of Elders for All of Humanity, for Mother Earth and for the Universes, Multiverses and Omniverses, from the influence of the Dark-Force Energies of Fear and Hatred. "And... So It Is!"

Affirmation: I Hereby call forth the Full Divine Intervention of the Godforce to Now fully end All Wars, bringing Peace and Harmony through the energy of the Christed Light Consciousness and Cosmic Love, Wisdom and Understanding of The One, the Ultimate, Supreme God of All Creation, to All troubled Regions of the World on Planet Earth, in this Now Moment. "And... So It Is!"

Affirmation: The Seven Seals have been Cast Aside, by the Christed Light of God Consciousness of the Holy Spirit, to reveal the Divine Eternal Truth contained within my Soul. "And... So It Is!"

Affirmation: I AM the Resurrection and the Life of my Restored, Revitalized and Rejuvenated Crystalline Light Body that is NOW energized by the Integrated Breath throughout my Physical Body. "And... So It Is!"

Affirmation: I AM your Brethren; I Embrace your Journey and Thank You for being part of my Journey, the Journey of Ascension to One Unity Consciousness, Unconditional Love and Light. "And... So It Is!"

Affirmation: I AM Free of All Curses, implants, spell's and negative entities, from all levels of my beingness, physical, mentally, emotionally and spiritually, and restored to my Original Blueprint of Divine Perfection of Christed Light Consciousness. "And... So It Is!"

Part 3

Inner Guidance
Meditations
The Sacred Flames and Rays
Crystals, Gemstones and
Singing Bowls

Crystals and Crystal Singing Bowls

Crystals and Crystal Singing Bowls are wonderful tools for Meditation and Healing, allowing Connection to one's Inner Divinity, Higher Self; I AM Presence and Guides, the Angelic Realm, and the Crystal Elders of the Crystal City above Mt. Shasta in the 8th Dimension.

As you Connect to the Devic and Life Force Energies held within the Crystals, Feel the Energy and Listen from your Heart for a Message to you from the Crystal.

When you listen to the Crystal Bowls Singing Voice, breathe into your lower abdomen and feel centered within your Sacred Heart Center and allow the Sound Waves to Wash over you, lifting you up into the Etheric Realms, and Transporting you to the Crystal City of Light above Mt. Shasta in the 8th Dimension.

Record the Meditations contained herein to a CD or DVD
for accessing your Inner Guidance and Healing.

Crystal Healing Sessions

Procedure 1: Self-Healing Technique (Self, Individual or Group Sessions)

You or your Participants are seated on mats or cushions on the floor, or on chairs placed in a circle around a Central Crystal Generator which is connected to Mother Earth, and the Universal Logos: Lord Melchizedek.

For Self-Healing, you play the Crystal Bowl for at least 10 minutes, until you have reached an altered state of consciousness, feeling connected to yourself at a deeper level. Then you say the meditation, continuing to play the bowl as you speak. Next place the chosen crystals or gemstones in your hands. Finally, go within to silently meditate for 15 minutes, focusing on the Attributes of the Crystals or gemstones and the Sacred Flame and Ray which will help you heal your problems/issues.

Individual or Group Healing Sessions

The Facilitator or Crystal Healer plays the Crystal Quartz Bowl, and speaks the meditation that relates to the Crystal and Sacred Flame and Ray Healing Session.

You may use a Classic Frosted Crystal Bowl or a Clear Quartz Crystal Bowl for the Crystal Bowl Toning, with all the participants holding in their hands the Crystals that are the main focus of the meditation.

Begin by playing the bowl for 2 to 5 minutes, and then say the meditation – continue playing the bowl throughout the session.

Choose the Crystals and Gemstones that relate to the Sacred Flame and Ray Attributes and Chakra being Activated, Aligned, Actualized, Balanced or Healed.

Example: As per the Chart showing the Twelve Sacred Flames and Rays Chakra System and the Key Flame and Ray Attributes (charts are in Part 4 of this book).

Blue Ray 1: The Will of God – Meditation for the Lapis Lazuli – Throat Chakra.

Theme/Issues/Problems: Surrender, Trust, Truth, Focus, Protection, Courage, Faith, Initiative, Stealing, Demeaning Yourself and Others, Dependability, Omnipotence, the Will of God, Divine Power Self-reliance and Certainty.

Sacred Flames to Invoke for Healing:

Themes/Issues/Problems and the Sacred Flames to Invoke for Healing are found within the Affirmations/Themes/Issues/Problems and Sacred Flames Solutions Section of Part 1 for Rays 1 to 6, and Part 2 for Rays 7 to 12, plus the United Integrated Sacred Flames and the Cosmic Rays.

Procedure 2: Group or Individual Healing Technique

The participants are seated, either on mats or cushions on the floor, or chairs placed in a circle around a Central Generator, which is connected to Mother Earth, and Lord Melchizedek: the Universal Logos.

Place four Crystal Bowls in the center of the room, with the facilitator seated in the middle, forming a circle.

These Crystal Bowls can be the Classic Crystal Bowls, Clear Crystal Bowls, or a selection of the Alchemy Crystal Bowls that relate to the Sacred Flames Healing Solutions.

Each one of the Bowls is to represent a Sacred Flame and Ray as stated in the Sacred Flames Healing Solutions. Tap on the side of each bowl four times, and invoke the Sacred Flame that the bowl will represent for this healing session.

The Facilitator/Crystal Healer plays the bowls and speaks the meditation that relates to the Flame and Ray that covers the theme/problem/ issues during the Crystal Bowls Toning Session.

Start by playing the first Bowl for 2 to 5 minutes, next begin to say the Flame and Ray Meditation, and then go on and play the second Bowl for 2 to 5 minutes, Continue saying the meditation during the Crystal Bowl Toning until the process with all the Crystal Bowls have been completed. Keep on playing all the Bowls, thus allowing all the participants to go deeper into the experience of the toning sounds.

The participants are to hold in their hands Crystals or Gemstones that relate to the Sacred Flames and Rays Healing process.

Ideally, the Crystal Bowl Sessions should last at least 30 minutes.

Example: Sacred Flames and Rays to Invoke Healing

Ray 1 Blue Ray, the Sacred Flame and Ray of the Will of God

Blue Ray1: The Will of God – Meditation for the Sacred Flame and Ray of God's Will, and Lapis Lazuli – Throat Chakra.

White Ray 4: Ascension and Purification – Activate a Crystal Bowl to represent the Ascension and Purification Flame and Ray - Lemurian Seed Crystal – Base Chakra.

Yellow Ray2: Illumination and Wisdom – Activate a Crystal Bowl to represent the Illumination and Wisdom Flame and Ray - Citrine Quartz – Crown Chakra.

Violet Ray 7: Transmutation – Activate a Crystal Bowl to represent the Transmutation to Freedom and Forgiveness Flame and Ray – the Amethyst Crystal – Sacral Chakra.

When the session is completed, the participants should remain where they are, in Silent Meditation for a further 15 minutes, reflecting upon hearing, seeing, sensing or feeling the God Presence within their Sacred Heart and Soul.

MEDITATION TREATMENTS

Ray 1 – The Will of God Flame and Ray
Throat Chakra – Lapis Lazuli
The Diamond Heart

Breathing gently into your abdomen and then breathing out, release all tension and listen to_the vibrations and frequencies of The Stone of Truth. As the Crystal Bowl sings into your being... the energy of integrity and prosperity, the vibrations and frequencies of the Lapis Lazuli, and the Diamond Heart of Beloved Master El Morya resonate within you. Feel the energy enhancing your Wisdom, Inner Vision and Mental/Emotional Clarity and Certainty.

Feel the vibrations and frequencies of Serenity and Loving Acceptance of yourself, as they expand within you, encouraging you to express your inner voice, your inner power. And they purify your Spirit, Mental and Emotional thoughts and feelings to Truth, Integrity and Prosperity.

As you Breathe in the Vibrate energy of the Lapis Lazuli to the Throat Chakra, feel the support of the energy as you interact with your Mighty I AM Presence and your Spirit Guardians from the Temple of Good Will. Sense within you, the vibrations of the Security and Safety that is felt there from the Protection of the Mighty I AM Presence.

I invite you to relax and let go of all tensions in your body. Take three deep breaths, each one deeper than the previous one. Release all thoughts and emotions, thus becoming even more relaxed in your Body, Mind and Soul. Focus and connect to the Sacred Chambers of your Heart.

Take several very deep breaths, breathing in slowly and releasing, expelling any feelings of tension and mental, emotional or physical stress from your beingness. Consciously ask your Divine I AM Presence or your Higher Self to take you on a journey within, to the Temple of Good Will. You arrive there in your personal Merkebah, accompanied by one of your guides. Notice a fairly large opalescent blue structure, quite tall,

127

in the form of a six-sided pyramid. As you approach, everything around you resonates with the beautiful Blue Ray energy of Good Will; it is so refreshing and soothing.

Walk up the mother-of-pearl stairway to the main entrance of the Temple, where you will be greeted by the Masters and Lady Masters of the Blue Ray and the Blue Flame Angels. Observe and feel the majestic blue mist emanating from various high fountains situated all around the Temple.

Many varieties of blue flowers are growing in white and gold boxes; all are flourishing in great abundance around the fountains, including sweet forget-me-nots.

Walk now through the entrance with your Guides, and there you will be welcomed by three Blue Flame Angels, who are there to escort you into the main Hall of Good Will.

As you enter into the large hallway, see a transparent chamber in the center containing a huge Blue Flame Diamond, around 15 to 18 feet high, the biggest diamond that you will ever see. Your Guides invite you to enter that Sacred Chamber. The Diamond contains several thousand facets, each one representing a different aspect of the Diamond Heart of the Divine Will.

When you come into the Sacred Chamber of the Divine Will, you are greeted by Master El Morya, a tall being with deep-set eyes. He is wearing a blue robe partially covered with a luminescent white cape, with a turban on his head and a shining Diamond Star at its center.

He greets and welcomes you to his Diamond Heart, and invites you to sit on one of the "blue flame" cushions. He now guides you to focus on the energy of that Diamond Heart and to breathe in the energies, so that you can take back as much of this energy as possible, with you when you return to your physical body.

Take a few deep breaths. Intend for the energies of this huge Diamond to magnetize and absorb your fears, and for them to be released and healed by the Blue Flame of God's Will. As you surrender your fears from your heart, you will receive a tremendous healing of Divine Love. Breathe deeply and exhale, releasing all the tension from your body. Now connect with your Higher Self who is standing there with you.

Your Mighty I AM Presence, the unlimited being that is really who you are, is waiting for all your fears to be released into the Blue Flame and Ray and thus healed. Connect with this Divine Presence. When you feel ready, make your commitment to surrender all the fears that have kept you in so much pain, to your Mighty I AM Presence, so that you can be Resurrected to the New Encodements of Divine Perfection.

Keep breathing in this wonderful Blue Flame energy, as much as you can, right into your Lungs and into your Abdomen and Heart. Do this consciously because you want to bring this energy back into your physical body, so that it is with you from this day forward. Also, know that all of your multi-dimensional aspects and all the beings of the Light Realm are supporting your journey home to Divine Grace.

In ease and grace, your journey home is accomplished in this now moment. You are not alone in your journey, as you have so much love and support available to you. You can do it, if you choose to do so.

Feel the soothing action of the Blue Flame. It has its own way of bringing you comfort and lessening all your pains. Now Master El Morya has a gift for you, as you sit in front of the Diamond in the Temple. He is going to superimpose a smaller etheric Diamond of total perfection, radiating the qualities of the Blue Flame and Ray essence, within the Sacred Chambers of your Heart, right within the energetic center of your own Sacred Heart.

This Diamond will reflect to you the Divine Perfection of that Diamond Heart that you are, within the Sacred Chambers of Your Heart.

With this gift, the perfection of the Diamond Heart will be reflected to you constantly, as long as you choose to work with it.

Ask your Beloved Higher Self to show you which facets of the Diamond are still holding pain, or attitudes that need to be healed and aligned.

The Diamond you have just received will continue to reflect everything you need, and so complete the Opening and Healing of your Heart. It will take you to the path of surrender with joy and grace. It is alive and vibrant; its color reflects a luminous peacock blue.

Keep breathing in its energies, with allowance and surrender to what is. Be resolute in walking this path, and feel free to communicate with your Guides. Stay with this energy for a while, and be thankful for the grace you have just received.

The Diamond Heart also has a vibration of Self-Confidence. Tap into this energy to assist you to release your fears, so that your surrender can be accomplished gracefully.

Call upon the Blue Ray Masters to assist you, as they are available to you at this or any time.

We invite you to return to this healing place often to meditate with us on the Will of God. When you feel that you are complete, return to your body, taking this treasure with you to help you in every way possible to achieve your Life Purpose.

When you are ready, open your eyes, and return to the room, feeling truly refreshed, confident and at ease. "And... So It Is!"

The Temple of Good Will Is Always Open to You.

Ray 2 – The Illumination Flame and Ray
Crown Chakra - Citrine
Wisdom and Understanding

Breathe deeply into your abdomen. As you relax into you beingness, you feel the energy of the Citrine coursing through your meridian system and resonating through your four Body Systems.

Listen to the Sounds of the Citrine Quartz Crystal, and feel the resonance of the Citrine Deva as the energy amplifies its joyful vibrations, passing through your physical body, mental and emotional bodies, and filling your Soul with the Golden Yellow Energy of pure frequencies that align the Base and Solar Plexus Chakras with the Crown Chakra.

Feel the vibration and frequency waves of the Citrine, as it dissolves and transmutes the negative energies while purifying and balancing the etheric and auric fields, cleansing and clearing you to optimum health, vitality, wealth and joy.

Known as the Merchant Stone, Citrine with its beautiful energy expands and maintains the wealth and prosperity of your Soul with waves upon waves of vibrant frequency, acting as a catalyst for enlightened communication, mental strength and new beginnings of enhanced optimism, balance, initiative and personal power.

Breathe in the frequencies of the Citrine and feel the crystalline energy structure within you, resonate and hum in response, responding with Awareness and Joy. Relax and Respond to the Resonance within you. Breathe in deeply and breathe out all that is not of Divine Light. Breathe in again. As you breathe in, inhale the Lightbody Energy that surrounds you. Feel and see this Crystalline Lightbody Energy cleans your many energy fields that are you. Your Lightbody will sparkle with a new vitality and your electromagnetic fields will encompass your being with energy that has a higher light quotient level.

This quotient level will be for your highest good and the highest good of all, raising your vibration and frequency to levels that will enable you to hear your heart singing to you. You will see your I AM Presence and Higher Self and your Guides as they speak with you of your mission here on Planet Earth; that you will assist the Mother Goddess of Earth in her Journey of Ascension.

Settling yourself even deeper into your being, you are totally relaxed now… Totally relaxed, more than you have ever been before go deeper and deeper into your Soul. Breathe into the breath that is the Universal Bliss. Feel the Sacred Flame and Ray of Illumination and Wisdom surround you, saturating your energy fields with wave upon wave of Yellow Fire Flames.

Image yourself within these flames and rays as they embrace you with their powerful light. Feel the presence of Lord Lanto, Master Kuthumi and Lord Maitreya, as they stand beside your Mighty I AM Presence in the Sacred Chambers of your Heart, embrace the Wisdom and Understanding that they are, and become this within your Inner Beingness.

Listen to the Guidance from these Masters of Wisdom and Knowledge. Take the time to ask them any questions that you desire from your heart. Taking a few deep breaths, feel calm and clear in the Certainty of Who You Are and what you need to know in this now moment of time, with all the Understanding and Wisdom that you already are, because the Sacred Flame and Ray of Illumination of Wisdom and Understanding is within you.

In a few moments, taking whatever time you need, be in gratitude to Lord Lanto, Master Kuthumi and Lord Maitreya for all their Wisdom and Understanding. Come back into this space and retain the feelings of Inner Calmness, Peace and Tranquillity that your connection with your Mighty I AM Presence, Higher Self and the Masters of Illumination, Wisdom and Understanding have bought unto you. "And… So It Is!"

Let Go, relax and be the Beacon of Light that you are.

Ray 3 – The Cosmic Love Flame and Ray
Heart Chakra – Crystal Rose Quartz
Self-Love

Breathe into your Heart. As you breathe into the Sacred Chambers of your Heart and the Vibrant Frequency of the Crystal Rose Quartz Energy of Self- Love, you are transformed in your Heart and the Innate Love of Yourself is Activated and Energized.

You are Healed of ALL emotional pain and trauma from your past. You are Calm and you feel the Serenity of Inner Harmony – that is the wondrous energy of the Rose Quartz Crystal as it encompasses your Body, Mind, Spirit and Soul.

You are Relaxed and you are Free. As you Let Go and Release all the tension from your Body to the Rose Crystal Quartz Energy, all your Chakra Centers are Aligned and in Resonance with the Gentle Love Vibration that is the Rose of Self Love.

Feel the Transformational vibrations of Love, as they surround your relationship with yourself and your Divine I AM Presence. You are in Total Acceptance of the Unconditional Love of your Divine I AM.

Breathe in deeply and breathe out all that is not of Divine Love.

Breathe in again. As you breathe in, inhale the Crystalline Energy that surrounds you. Feel and See this Crystalline Energy cleanse your many Energy Fields that are you. Your Crystalline Fields will sparkle with a new vitality, and your Electromagnetic Fields will encompass your being with Energy that is of a Higher Light Quotient Level.

This quotient level will be for your Highest Good and the Highest Good of All. It will raise your vibration and frequency to levels that will enable you to hear your Heart Singing to you. You will see your Mighty I AM Presence, Higher Self and your Guides speak with you of your Mission here on Planet Earth, and how you will assist Planet Earth in her Journey of Cosmic Ascension.

Settle yourself even deeper into your being. You are totally relaxed now… Totally relaxed, more than you have ever been before. You are going deeper and deeper into your Soul.

Feel the Sacred Flame and Ray of Cosmic Love Surround you. Master Paul the Venetian, the Chohan of the Sacred Flame and Ray of Cosmic Love, and all the Masters and Lady Masters of the Cosmic Flame of Love are present with you in this now moment of time.

As you enter the Sacred Chambers of your Heart, the Sacred Chambers that are in the center of your Heart, hear your Heart Sing the Song of Love.

Singing the many Sounds of Creation, you will be in Joy – for you are then One with all things. The Sounds that are emanating from your Heart are the Sounds of the forgotten language, the language of Heart Oneness – which we once were, and knew as the only language, the language of Love. It united us all, human to human, human to all other beings of Nature, and all other Kingdoms and Realms that share this wonderful Planet.

From Your very Heart, your Songs of Life come forth to embrace us all in the Resonance that is Love, Light and Truth. The Sacred Flames and Rays of Cosmic Love embrace you with waves upon waves of Unconditional Love, throughout all levels of your beingness.

From Your Very Heart, the Love Songs of Creation come forth to amplify the Heart of God and Manifest great JOY from within your Heart, which encompasses all living things. As you live from your Heart, you become more and more enlightened, and you move through the many mansions of The One, the Ultimate and Supreme God of All Creations, to become that Oneness of who you really are as a Co-Creator God!

Relax! Relax! Relax! Breathe deeply into your Heart and merge with your Mighty I AM Presence within the Sacred Chambers that are there within your Heart. Feel the Heartbeat of your Body and your Soul. Feel the Heartbeat of the Universe that is within you. And feel the Sacred Fire of Passionate Love and Compassion, encapsulate your entire beingness.

You are One with All That Is. You are All That Is. Be Still and Surrender to the Heart, Mind and Will of God. Know that you are connected with your Mighty I AM Presence within the Sacred Chambers of your Heart.

Prepare yourself to return to the Room and to be in the Present Moment of time. Do whatever you need to do to bring yourself back into the Now.

Be in Gratitude for All that you have received from the Sacred Flame and Ray of Cosmic Love, the Rose Crystal Quartz and Master Paul the Venetian, Chohan of the Sacred Flame and Ray of Cosmic Love. "And... So It Is!"

Divine Love You Are!

Ray 4 – The Flame and Ray of Ascension
Base Chakra – Lemurian Seed Crystal
Ascension and Purification

Beloved One, Breathe into your Body the Divine Energy of the Sacred Flame and Ray of Ascension and Purification. Feel the effects of the Purification Flame as it Cleans, Clears and Balances all Energy within you to be in Acceptance, Harmony and Inner Peace. The Acceptance of all that is, as Divine Perfection. It is what it is, Divine Perfection

Settle yourself even deeper into your being. You are totally relaxed now… Totally relaxed, more than you have ever been before; you are going deeper and deeper into your Soul.

Feel yourself go deep into the Sacred Chambers of your Heart. When you enter your Heart Chambers, feel relaxed and breathe deeply into your Physical Being. As you Journey within your Physical Body, your Body Elemental speaks to you of ages past, when the Crystalline Lightbody was Anchored and Activated within your Physical Form – and you were your Crystalline Lightbody. As you Listen to the Lemurian Seed Crystal Deva and hear the Voice of Lemuria, you are once again transported back in time to the Heart of Lemuria, and into the Peace, Tranquillity and the Unconditional Love that is the Lemurian way of being in Harmony.

Feel the Sound Waves emanating from the Lemurian Seed Crystal Encapsulate every Cell, Atom, Electron and Proton of your being, permeating all with the Harmonic Sounds of Peace. As you breathe these Energies even deeper into your Soul, your Subconscious Mind connects to your Conscious Awareness. Thus you remember the Ancient Days of Lemuria, and you are in the Ascended State of the 5th Dimension and beyond. You are in the Halls of Ascension and you know the Divine Perfection of All Things as being as intended by The One, the Ultimate and Supreme God of All Creations. Breathe in the Lemurian Seed Crystal Energy. Feel the vibration and frequency of the God-Self State of the Truth of who you are. Breathe in the Universal Breath of Purification and

Ascension. As you are that, breathe in to the Lemurian Seed Sound Waves and Know the Christed Light of God Consciousness. Feel the Sacred Flame and Ray of Ascension and Purification surround you. Realize the greater knowing of the truth of who you are, that you are a Blessed Child of God. You are here on Planet Earth in this amazing period of Earth's History and Ascension to the Higher Levels of the 5th Dimension and beyond.

As you breathe deeply, feel the presence of Lord Serapis Bey and the Masters of the Dazzling White Fires of the Ascension Flame, as it surrounds you with its Sacred Purifying Rays. You and your Consciousness are uplifted to ever Higher Levels of Purification and in Completion, sealing in the changes to be made permanent, and bringing you a sense of the Holy Divine Spirit that you are.

Have a sense of the Presence of the Archangel Gabriel, his Divine Complement Lady Hope, and all the Angels of Ascension, and Ask them for whatever insight and assistance you require in your life in this Now moment. Breathe deeply and relax into the Peace and Harmony of Self-Acceptance. Know that you are, in this Now moment, Purified and with the Self-Discipline that the Sacred Flame and Ray of Purification and Ascension bring to you. Thus you are able to go forth in your Life and complete the tasks contained within your Life Purpose.

Be still now and contemplate your Journey, knowing that all is in Divine Perfection. Give Thanks to the Sacred Flame and Ray of Ascension and Purification, to the Lemurian Seed Crystal for the Reconnection to the Heart of Lemuria, and to Lord Serapis Bey and All who have helped you in your Journey to Ascension. When you are ready, return to this Sacred Place and Feel the effects of the Sacred Flame and Ray of Ascension and Purification, and the Lemurian Seed Crystal. Your Victory is assured! "And So It Is!"

Ascension and Purification you become in this Now Moment of Time.

Ray 5 – The Healing and Manifestation Flame and Ray
<u>Brow Chakra – Emerald Crystal</u>
<u>Health and Abundance of Prosperity</u>

Breathe in deeply, breathe into the very Core of your being, and breathe into your Soul. Know that you are the Vibration of the Sacred Emerald Fire. As you breathe in, take within you the Vibrant Alchemy that blends your Heart and Grail Energies with the powerful frequencies and waves of Fire that are radiating through your Heart Chakra from your Divine Realms of Loving Intention and Wholeness.

You are the exquisite vibrant Waves of Frequency that are of flowing Heart Healing. They help you to be in Alignment with your Heart Wisdom and encourage your Higher Self Purpose of Centeredness, Emotional Balance and Courageous Compassion – as you live your Life Core of Oneness. You are the Power of the Emerald as it is packed with Love, opening your Heart to the Universal Grace, the Holy Grail. You are the Loving Vibrations that radiate Love, Inner Peace, Wealth and Abundance. You are the strong spiritual "Heart Medicine" that helps your Physical Heart and Emotional Body to be in Balance and hold the feelings of Worthiness.

You are the Emerald Stone of Healing Fire Flaming in
your Heart. You are All That Is, you are Love.

Beloved One, relax and go deep into your breath, taking deeper and deeper breaths. Breathe into the Sacred Chambers of Your Heart, and Connect with your Higher Self and Mighty I AM Presence. Imagine yourself surrounded by the Sacred Emerald Green Flame of Healing and Manifestation, and seated upon a throne of Emerald Crystal. Feel deeply into your Spirit/Soul. Know that as you persist in your Desires, and visualize their Manifestation, so it is done.

Believe in the Outcomes and it shall be so, Manifested in all its Glory.

Beloved One, you are truly blessed by so many. Trust in your Divine I AM Presence. Believe that Persistence, Perseverance and Patience will bring to you the Power of Peace and Prosperity. Take a few moments to gather your thoughts and feelings. Decide in this Now moment what it is that you wish to Heal within yourself, or Make Manifest in your Life.

Within the Sacred Chambers of your Heart, communicate with your Higher Self and Mighty I AM Presence and discuss what it is that you think and feel about your Life, and what it is that you most desire to manifest in your Life. Ask of your Mighty I AM Presence, 'are these desires in accordance with my Life Purpose'. Be still within and hear or sense your Beloved Higher Self or Mighty I AM Presence Communicating with you, and note in your Mind and Heart what it was that was said unto you.

Visualize and Feel yourself Healed and it is done. Visualize and Image yourself in the manifested Desires from your Heart and so it is manifested.

Trust in your Messages, whatever the form may be, and in Gratitude to your Guides. Give thanks for the wonderful new understandings that you now have of your Life. Imagine – and the Imagined becomes Manifested. Visualize – and the Visualized becomes Reality. Desire – and the Desired becomes your Truth. You are a Co-Creator God. The Power to Heal the Universe is within you. You have the Power to Create the New Golden Age. When you are ready, and only when you are ready, return to the awareness of the Now moment, and reflect upon what you feel, sense or believe was said between you and your Guides. Abundance and Prosperity are your Birthright. "And... So It Is!"

Ray 6 – The Resurrection Flame and Ray
Solar Plexus – Angel White Ajoite
the Angel White Ajoite
I Am the Resurrection and the Life of My Ascension

Make yourself comfortable, either seated or lying down. Take three deep breaths, each breath deeper than the previous breath. Feel yourself relax, relax and relax, even more into your Heart center, count from one to five.

With the number one, you feel connected to your Heart even more; with number two, you enter the throne room of your Heart and relax even more into yourself; and with number three and number four, you feel even more at ease and connected to the Golden Orange Sacred Flame of Resurrection.

Now imagine yourself walking along a track – a track that is winding its way up the slopes of a hill. As you approach the top of this hill, you notice that there is a stone seat; it is placed under the branches of a massive Redwood Tree.

In front of this stone seat there is a massive stone formation, upon which is rested a beautiful white quartz crystal, an Angel White Ajoite. It holds the vibrant Angelic Energies that are the Ascension frequencies of the higher realms. It helps one to maintain a close connection to the Heart during one's incarnation here on Planet Earth.

Upon seeing the Angel White Ajoite, you decide to sit upon this stone seat. You lean back against this tree and feel its wonderful Powerful Energy. Close your eyes and ponder your life. In so doing, you call upon the Sacred Flame and Ray of Resurrection. Just as you are going deeper and deeper into contemplation, there appears before you a beautiful Angel. The Angel introduces himself to you as the Archangel Uriel. Uriel is accompanied by his Divine Complement Lady Aurora. They begin to talk with you, discussing your Life Journey to Ascension and beyond.

You are listening to what the Archangel Uriel and Lady Aurora are saying to you. You ask for the Sacred Flame and Ray of Resurrection to be in your Life, blessing you and your entire beingness with its Golden Orange Fire. Waves upon waves of the Resurrection Flame swirl about you, bringing to you all that you desire, from the Sacred Chambers of your Heart.

The Chohan: Lord Sananda of the Sacred Flame and Ray of Resurrection comes to you in this now moment and you feel his great Love and Compassion embrace you. You relax and become at ease with everything in your life, and Feel Joy and Happiness in your Heart.

The Deva of the Angel White Ajoite speaks to you about your Ascension and blesses your journey with gentle and Harmonious Energies which will enable you to pass through all turbulence – Mental, Emotional and Physical – with ease and grace.

As you are about to take leave of the Lord Sananda and the Angels, you Give Thanks to them for being in your presence. You rise from the stone seat, and begin your Journey back down the track to return to this place in the present.

Upon your return, you feel at peace; a great stillness has come over you, for you are in the Joy of Bliss and All Knowing of the Sacred Flame and Ray of Resurrection in your Life.

When you are ready, counting back from 5, 4, 3, 2 & 1, slowly return to the present and feel calm, relaxed and at peace, and say within the Sacred Chambers of your Heart.

I AM the Resurrection of my Life, I AM the Resurrection of my Life, I AM the Resurrection of my Life of my Ascension to the 5th Dimension and Beyond. "And... So It Is!"

Ray 7 – The Transmutation Flame and Ray
Sacral Chakra – Amethyst Crystal
Temple of Grace

Breathe in deeply, taking three deep breaths, each breathe a little deeper than the previous one. As you prepare yourself for the Journey to the Temple of the Violet Flame, bring into your awareness the wondrous sound waves and frequency of the Violet Flame and Ray of Transmutation and the vibration and frequency of the Amethyst Crystal Deva which supports and spiritually enhances the expansion of your Crown Chakra, creating a personal "Temple of Grace."

Invoke the Vibrant Energy of the Sacred Violet Flame and Ray, the master transmuters and transformers, to be a catalyst that expands and focuses your intention for Cosmic Ascension with a clear connection to the Source of All That Is.

Within the Vibrations of the Sacred Violet Flame and Ray, you become a Chalice of Light. You evoke Freedom and enhanced Unconditional Love into your lifestream.

As you breathe in the vibration and frequency of the Sacred Flame and Ray of Transmutation, you are in Balance and Harmony within your Heart, your Mind and your Soul.

Relaxing into your breath, breathing deeply into your abdomen, move your body to find a more comfortable position. Breathe deeply again, then taking an even deeper breath, go within your being to feel centered, at ease in connecting with your Divine God-Self.

As you go further into your being, have a sense of the Holy Spirit being within you, and feel the presence of your Higher Self and your Mighty I AM Presence.

Breathe into the Sacred Chambers of your Heart. As you pass through the Gateway of the Divine, enter into the Energy of Unconditional Love, Forgiveness, and Freedom. You become even more relaxed, and you call in the Sacred Violet Flame and Ray of Transmutation and the Vibration and Frequency of the Amethyst Crystal.

You Feel the Violet Fire surround your beingness with its Vibrant Transmuting Energy, bringing to you the Transformation to Freedom, Forgiveness and Unconditional Love.

Call upon Lady Portia, the Chohan for the Sacred Violet Flame and Ray, to come to you in this Now moment, to help you with any issues that you may have found difficult to Balance, Harmonize and bring into the Acceptance of all that is in life, as being Divine Perfection.

As you Listen to Lady Portia, Hear the Truth and Love that she is and the expression and emanation of Justice and Growth that is there for you in your journey.

When you are ready, come back into the present moment, feel the energy of Freedom and Be Relaxed. Give Thanks to Lady Portia, to the Sacred Violet Flame and Ray of Transmutation, and to the Amethyst Crystal Deva for their help. Ask for their Continued Guidance in your Life. Be Still and Be Balanced and in Harmony with yourself.

You Are One with the Sacred Violet Flame and Ray.
You know Inner Peace. Blessed You Are. "And... So It Is!"

Ray 8 – The Transcendence Flame and Ray
Causal Chakra (Etheric) – Aqua Quartz Crystal
To Balance and Harmonize the Mind

Relax! Relax! Relax! Take three deep breaths, each breath deeper than the previous one.

Feel comfortable and at ease with yourself. Let go of any tension in your body. Relax your feet, then your legs, moving up into your torso. Feel your lower abdomen relax.

Relax even more, release all tension held within. As your chest area relaxes, breathe into the lungs and feel your breath become easier and more flowing. Feel yourself enter this Altered State of Bliss. Call upon your Higher Self and I AM Presence to be with you, and feel their Presence as they guide you on your inner journey.

You are totally relaxed now. You are prepared to open up your being to the wonders of the Sacred Flame and Ray of Transcendence. Breathe the Vibrate Aqua Quartz Crystal Energy to all levels of your being. As you speak to the Deva of the Crystal, ask her Guidance to bring Balance and Harmony to your Active Mental and Emotional Mind.

As you go even deeper into the breath of Balance and Harmony, ask the Sacred Flame and Ray of Transcendence to help you Balance your overly active Mind, to be in Clarity and Certainty, and also to Transmute all blockages, enabling you to be Open, Balanced and in Harmony.

Feel yourself embrace the Energetic Properties of the wondrous Aqua Sea/Green Flames of the Sacred Flame and Ray of Transcendence, in order to undergo a Metamorphosis that will result in you receiving an entirely new, Elevated Aqua-Crystalline Healing Vibration. You are Connected and Activated by the Sacred Flame. Your Psychic Center is Open and your Yang Energy is in Alignment with your Yin Energy. Your Auric Fields are entrained for Shifting, Cleansing and activating your Upper Chakras.

Breathe in deeply and Feel the Peace that comes from the Yang and Yin Energies and their Colors, as they are activated to help Balance and

Harmonize your Analytical Mind and lift your Spirits to Transcendence. You are uplifted within your Mind and Heart by the Energy of the Aqua Quartz Crystal and the Sacred Flame and Ray of Transcendence to being as one with your Sacred Heart, Mind and Soul. Imagine before you a beautiful Circular Pool of Aqua/Sea Green Fire, so cool and inviting. And you feel the urge to go into this Aqua/Sea Green Fire – that is the emanation of the Sacred Flame and Ray of Transcendence.

You Step forward and pass through and into this Sacred Flame. Feel your Consciousness as it Transcends beyond confusion, and into the Certainty and Clarity that accompany the knowing of Wisdom and Understanding that is from the Sacred Chambers of your Heart.

Lady Nada; Chohan of the Sacred Flame and Ray of Transcendence, and the Deva of the Aqua Quartz Crystal join you there in the circular pool of Aqua/Sea Green Fire. You speak with them about all your concerns regarding where you are at in your Life and what you most desire as a positive outcome in your current incarnation.

They calmly Guide you to receive from your innate Inner Wisdom the Confidence to achieve your Dreams. Feel the blessings of Lady Nada and the Aqua Quartz Deva as the Sacred Flame and Ray of Transcendence and the Aqua Quartz Crystal permeate your being. Be Calm and Confident in the Clarity and Certainty of all that is there for you. In Gratitude, be still and be confident in yourself. Prepare yourself for your return. As you return to this time, bring with you all that you need, in order to go forth and complete your Desired Outcomes for this Life. Relax.

Simply be in the Clarity and Certainty of Your Divine God-Self. "And... So It Is!"

Ray 9 – The Highest Potentials Flame and Ray
Synthesis of Ray 1 to Ray 7
Etheric Heart – Ruby Crystal
To Receive the Gifts of Highest Potentials

Make yourself comfortable, seated or lying prone, being sure to have your back as straight as possible. Take a few deep breaths down into the Etheric Heart and Base Chakra, your power base.

Breathe deeply within, down into your stomach area and feeling everything in your body.

Relax and Release any and all tension and tightness contained within your body through stress and the overload of your body senses because of the frustration of not being all that you can be. Relax in the knowledge that your Highest Potentials and Gifts are available to you now – from the attributes of the Synthesis of the Rays 1 to Ray 7.

Breathe even deeper into your abdomen and feel or see before you an amazing Ruby Pyramid of deep vibrant red. Feel the Radiance of Loving Protection and Spirituality of the Mystical Ruby, the Regal Stone of Royal Nobility, as its vibration and frequency bring you a feeling of Health, Wealth and Happiness.

Enter into the Ruby Pyramid and Feel the Light of the Ruby, as your Inner Planes are alight with the Diamond Heart Energy that is enhancing all your Relationships and Soul Connections. Feel the Spiritual Wisdom of the Ruby as she fills your Energy Fields with the Divine Transformation of Love, unifying all the Chakras and Rays of the Synthesis of Rays 1 to 7 of the Sacred Flame and Ray of Highest Potentials.

In this relaxed state of being, see or sense your Mighty I AM Presence. Hear your Mighty I AM Presence speaking to you. Feel the Sacred Flame and Ray of Highest Potentials manifest before you. Realize that you are able to enter into this Sacred Flame and Ray Energy. In so doing, you access your Highest Potentials – the Gifts that are yours to receive are manifested in your life Now!

Step into the Circle of Magenta Fire, the Flame and Ray of Highest Potentials, and Feel your entire being – every particle of your Physical, Mental, Emotional and Spiritual – saturated by the Energy of this Sacred Flame and Ray.

Now experience the Heightened Energies of the Sacred Flame and Ray as they pass through you and around you. Know the Compassion and Mercy of Lady Mother Mary, the Chohan of this amazing Flame and Ray, as she comes to reassure you of your Gifts and Abilities. You can Feel the Confidence that you require to go forward and explore these newer and much more Expanded Abilities.

As you return to this space, be Calm. Be Confident.
Feel from the Sacred Chambers of your Heart. Be Relaxed and
in Gratitude for all the Gifts and Abilities you have received.

"And... So It Is!"

Ray 10 – The Divinity and Peace Flame and Ray
Soul Star Chakra – Celestite Crystal
Divine Inner Peace

Relax into your breath, breathe deeply into your abdomen, move your body as required into a more comfortable position. Sitting upright or lying prone, with your back straightened; relax even further into your Divinity. Feel the angelic Energy of the Celestite Crystal, as it embraces you and enters into your four Body Systems, bringing to you Divine Guidance and aiding you in your Connections and Communications with the Company of Heaven. This creates a bridge between Heaven and Earth. The Celestial Energy of the Celestite enables your Divinity, the Divine Essence of you, to be in Sacred Communication through your own personal Song with the Universe. As You Sing your message across all dimensions of time and space, you connect to the Holy Spirit Realms of Cosmic Light and Cosmic Love.

Breathe deeply and again take an even deeper breath. Go within your being and Feel centered, at ease in Connecting with your Divine God-Self. As you go into your being, have a sense of the Divine Holy Spirit being with you, and feel the presence of your Beloved Higher Self and your Mighty I AM Presence.

Breathe into the Sacred Chambers of your Heart, and enter there into the Divine Energy of Inner Peace and Unconditional Love.

Beloved One, feel the Energy of the Sacred Flame and Ray of Divinity, Peace and Opulence enter your being. In the Sacred Chambers of your Heart, feel Inner Peace and Opulence expand within you on all levels of your Spiritual, Mental, Emotional and Physical Bodies.

Imagine, Sense or Feel a Circle of Pearlescent Flame before you. As you gaze in wonder at this enormous Flame of Divinity, Feel yourself drawn to enter it. Feel and Experience the Energy of this Flame against your Body.

Step into the Circle of the Pearlescent Flame. Feel the Divinity of the Holy Spirit and the Christed Light Consciousness as it surrounds you and enter your essence – bringing to you great Inner Peace and the Knowing of your Divinity.

Be in this Energy and Feel the Presence of the Divine Lady Vessa Andromeda. She contains the Flower of Life within her Essence and bestows this unto you. Listen to her Guidance, and Feel at Peace.

As you take your leave of the Sacred Flame and Ray of Divinity and from Lady Vessa Andromeda, be in Gratitude for the experience, and Embrace the Divinity that you are into your Heart.

Relax, Relax, Relax and be Inner Peace and Opulence.
"And... So It Is Now!"

Soul Star Chakra – Milky White Calcite
The Heart of the Divine Mother

Make yourself comfortable, seated or lying prone, being sure to have your back as straight as possible. Take a few deep breaths down into Sacred Chambers of your Heart.

Breathe deeply within, down into your stomach area and feel everything in your Body Relax and be at Ease. Relax even more, and be Open to Receive the Blessings of Inner Peace and Love from the Divine Mother.

As you give birth to the Sounds of the Mature Divine that are of the Mother/Gaia Energies within you, you feel the Heart of the Divine Mother.

Breathe in the energy of the Milky White Calcite Crystal, feel yourself carried forth by the Resonances and Peace, to the Comfort of the Energy of the Deva and the Energy of Divinity and Inner Peace.

You Feel the Energy of the Divine Mother and her Divine Love. You are at Peace with yourself. As you surrender to the Nurturing Vibrations of the Crystal Devic Elementals, breathe in and feel the ever-present and fullness of the Spirit of your Divinity.

You feel the Embrace of the Vibration and Frequency of the Milky White Calcite. You are Whole and Complete in your Divinity, with feelings of Peace and Love, for the Universe.

You are Free and Tranquil and at Peace. As the White Calcite Amplifies and Cleanses your emotional issues and they drift away from your Awareness, you discover within yourself that you have risen to a Higher Spiritual State. You are connected to your Inner Divine and Feel as one with your Mighty I AM Presence, the Lord God essence of your being.

The Beloved Mother of Divinity lifts up your Divine Life Force Energy and you Feel yourself borne on the Crest of her Sound Waves, to Higher Levels of Consciousness.

When you are ready to return to this now moment of time, take your leave from the Divine Mother, giving Thanks and Gratitude for the Love, Compassion, Wisdom and Understanding of the Divine Mother that you have received and experienced.

Be in the Energy of Gratitude and Honor to receive the
Divine Mother's blessings of the Sounds of Love and Compassion.
Blessed You Are. "And... So It Is!"

Ray 11 – The Sacred Flame and Ray of Illumine Truth
Stargate Chakra - Green Chrysoprase
Divine Truth Is in My Heart

Be still and breathe into your Heart, the Sacred Chambers of your Heart. Know that you are One with the Universal Breath of God, the Mother/Father God of this Universe, Lord Melchizedek.

Imagine before you a huge Global Sphere of Green Chrysoprase. Reach out and touch the surface of this sphere. As you touch and feel the Vibrant Energy emanating from the sphere, feel the Energy of Truth, the Divine Truth, as it permeates you Soul – revealing unto you the Truth of who you are and embracing you with Feelings of Joy, Serenity and Happiness.

Feel the frequency of the Green Chrysoprase as it Pumps its energy through your Heart, Lifting you up into the Energy of Love, Abundance and Prosperity.

Notice the Energy in your Heart as it Shifts your Awareness to the Vibration of Divine Truth, Joy and Serenity and Promotes more Happiness in your Life.

Breathe deeply and totally relax your Body, Mind and Spirit. Release all concerns that are with you in this now moment, to the Energy of your Mighty I AM Presence. Know that all is well.

As you are Embraced by the Energy of the Green Chrysoprase of Truth, See or Sense before you the Sacred Chambers of your Heart. As you enter into the most Sacred Place within your Heart, before you is the Gateway into the All-Knowing of your Divinity.

Behold the Beloved Chohan Lady Quan Yin, and Hear her special messages for you. Feel her Compassion and Mercy and Know of her great Love for you and your Journey.

Imagine before you an enormous Peach Sacred Flame that is the Sacred Flame and Ray of Illumine Truth. As you Desire Truth to be in your Life, for all that you are and all that you are destined to be, feel the desire to enter this Sacred Flame and Ray of Illumine Truth.

As you enter this Flame, you are met by the mirror of Truth, that shows you where you are at in your Life Journey and Life Purpose, and what it is that you need to do in order to achieve your Life Purpose.

You now Understand in Illumine Truth who you are and what you are, and what you need to do from this day forward. The Truth has been revealed to you. Have Courage and Compassion.

Be Merciful unto yourself. Know that you are in Divine Perfection at all times in your Life, in all that you do and in all that you have done.

In a few moments you will return to this Sacred space and be thankful for all that you have received. In your leave taking from Lady Quan Yin, be in Gratitude for what you have learned and now know about yourself.

Be Peaceful and Tranquil. Be Joyous and Serene in your Life.
"And... So It Is!"

12th Ray – The Sacred Flame and Ray of One Unity Consciousness
Universal Chakra #1 – Golden Topaz
Golden Ray of Oneness

Make yourself comfortable, either seated or lying down. Take three deep breaths, each breath deeper than the previous one. Feel yourself relax, relax and relax even more into your heart center, counting from one to five. With the number one, you Feel even more Connected to your Heart, with number two, you Enter the Throne Room of your Heart and relax even more into yourself; and with, number three and number four, you Feel even more at Ease and Connected to the Golden Sacred Flame and Ray of One Unity Consciousness.

The Golden Flame and Ray of Manifestation, creates Divine Oneness in One's Life. The Golden Topaz Deva is Present with you in your Sacred Heart Center; Feel its Presence as it attunes you to your desires, and brings to you your creative abilities as a Channel to Fruition and Growth.

Feel the Clarity and Clearings occur for you, as you become more amd more Aligned and Enlivened, and a Creator of your Dreams in the Purity of your Intention.

The Golden Topaz helps you to focus your thoughts and emotions on your Vision for your Life. You feel the Acceleration and Big Shifts of Awareness as the Golden Topaz aids you to push through your limitations and into the next level of Awareness.

Now find yourself in a place of Nature and Beauty and either See, Feel or Sense this place in as much detail as you can. As all have our own unique way of Connection, use whatever way best suites you.

Feel the Love that you have for Nature and for the Mother, our Beloved Mother Earth. Let this Love Grow and Expand in your Heart until you Feel that Love throughout your Entire Body, Mind and Soul.

When the time feels right, take your Love and put it into a small round bubble; and with your Intention, send it down deep, through the multiple layers of the Earth, to the very core of our Planet, Mother Earth.

Let the Divine Mother Know how much you Love and Care for her. Let her Feel your Love and Understanding. Then wait for the Divine Mother of Earth to send her Love back to you.

When you See, Feel or Sense the Love of the Divine Mother enter your Energy Fields; Let it move in any way and into any place. Just let it be. Feel and Embrace this Flow of Love between you and the Divine Mother. You can stay here as long as you wish.

When you feel that the time is right, without breaking the flow of Love between you and the Divine Mother, Shift your attention to the Divine Father.

In your Inner Vision, See, Feel or Sense a night sky, the Star Constellations, the very depths of space. Behold the Planets and the Moon glowing in the night sky and Feel the Presence of the Great Central Sun.

Let yourself feel the Love you have for All of Creation and for your Divine Father. When the time feels right, put your Love in a small bubble and send it up into the heavens, with the Intention that it goes directly to your Divine Father. Send it into the grids – the Crystalline Grid and the Electromagnetic Grids - around Planet Earth, and to the Great Central Sun. Let the Divine Father know how you feel.

And wait for the Love of the Divine Father to come to Planet Earth and enter your Body. When it does, let it move in any way and into any place within your being. Do not attempt to control this Love, simply feel it.

At this moment, the Holy Trinity is Alive on Planet Earth. The Divine Mother and the Divine Father and you, the Divine Child – are all joined in pure Cosmic Love, Cosmic Light and One Unity Consciousness.

From this place of Pure Love, open to the Awareness of the Presence of The One, the Supreme God of All Creation, who surrounds you, who encapsulates you and who lives within you.

Simply be aware of and feel this Union of Cosmic Forces. Breathe the breath of life, the breath of Oneness that connects you to All That Is.

When you feel ready, in a few moments more, slowly begin to return to this room. At number five, begin the return to this space; at number four, feel the Energy of the Divine Mother embrace your beingness; at number three, sense the Heart and Mind of the Divine Father that supports you in your Journey to Oneness and Unity,; at number two, feel yourself become Present and in Oneness with your Body; and at number one, know that you are in One Unity Consciousness. And remember everything that you experienced from within yourself of One Unity Consciousness.

In Oneness You Are. "And... So It Is!"

Universal Chakra #1 –
Smokey Citrine Quartz Crystal
The Golden Brown Rainbow

Breathing gently and deeply into the core of your being, feel the Beloved Golden Brown Rainbow Energy that emanates from the Smokey Citrine Quartz Crystal, as it weaves its magic spell of sounds, and creates around you and within you the serene Smokey Citrine Quartz Energies. Feel centered within, and feel the Joy, Cooperation and Clarity that Promotes Positive Mental, Emotional and Spiritual Thinking. Breathe in the Energy of the Smokey Citrine – breathe deeply. Feel the Resonance of the powerful sound vibrations and Frequencies permeating your Solar Plexus, Sacral and Root Chakras. You are now able to stay Balanced and in Harmony.

Be still and breathe with ease. Feel the Energy of the Crystal as it permeates your being.

You are Creative and Well-Grounded within the rich Energetic Vibrations and Frequencies of Beloved Mother Earth.

Breathe into your Thoughts and Emotions, and Feel the Power inside you.

You are now empowered by the Positive Mental, Emotional and Spiritual Thinking Energy that your song creates. You go forth with Confidence to manifest a world of Serenity and Tranquillity. Be Still, Go within and communicate with your Mighty I AM Presence, the Lord God Essence of your being. Feel the Support and Love Energy of your Mighty I AM Presence, surround you in this now moment of time. When you are ready, and only when you feel ready; take one further breath and come back into this time, place and space.

Be in Oneness with the Golden Brown Rainbow Crystal. "And... So It Is!"

Ray 13 – The Sacred United Flames and Rays
Universal Chakra #2 and All Cosmic Chakra Levels
Apophyllite Crystals

Breathe deeply, taking in the Energy of the Light Realm to all areas of your Body. Truly relax into your Divinity and Trust that you are Totally Safe to travel deeply within your Heart, Mind and Soul.

Beloved One, relax and breathe into your Heart, Mind and Soul. Feel the Will of God and all the Energies, Vibrations and Frequencies of the United Twelve Sacred Flames and Rays of Christed Light of God Consciousness.

Breathe in the Energy of the Vortex that has been formed by the combined United Twelve Sacred Flames and Rays and the Matrix Energy of the Apophyllite Crystal.

See before you a Crystal Spire, a tall, clear and frosted Tower structure, formed by the Apophyllite Crystal. You approach this spire and run your hands along the surface of the Apophyllite. Hear it Speak to you through the Electromagnetic Vibrations and Frequencies of the Crystal to your Heart, Mind and Soul.

Feel the Resonance of the Electromagnetic Vibrations and frequencies of the Crystal as they permeate your skeletal structure, telling you the Story of you, the Story of your Evolution.

Feel the Energy permeate and saturate your beingness. Listen to the Story as the Vibrations and Frequencies of the Apophyllite, bathes you in Energy of Liquid Light. This helps you see through the Illusions that surround you, and connect you to the Energy of the Godhead.

Feel the Energy Uplift your Heart, Mind, Body and Soul, to manifest your Crystalline Lightbody, showing you the Road Map to your Divinity.

As the United Twelve Sacred Flames and Rays combined with the Vibrations and Frequencies of the Apophyllite Crystal, feel every particle of your Soul, Mind, Emotions, Physical Body and Body Elemental and all Subtle Body Energies rise up to even Higher Levels of Consciousness.

The Attributes of all the United Twelve Sacred Flames and Rays and the Crystals for all the Rays, combine to bless your Journey and bring to you their Gifts.

Believe and Trust in this now moment, and Release and Relinquish to the United Twelve Sacred Flames and Rays of Christed Light of God Consciousness and to the Crystal Devic Realms, all Negative energies contained within you which do not enhance your experience in this lifestream.

Feel the United Twelve Sacred Flames and Rays and the Apophyllite Crystal Matrix, Restore you to your Crystalline Lightbody and your Personal Energy to Inner Peace, Illumine Truth, Balance, Harmony, Forgiveness, Freedom and Unconditional Love.

When you feel that you have completed the Releasing and Relinquishing of all Negative Energies that no longer serve you, and only when you feel ready, return to the awareness of where you are physically in this now moment of time.

Relax and Feel the Blessings of the United Twelve Sacred Flames and Rays and the Apophyllite Crystal, as they Rain down upon you.
"And... So It Is!"

Cosmic Rays
Universal Chakra's up to and including the Cosmic Chakra's
Phenacite Crystal
Cosmic Rays of Christed Light of God Consciousness

Make yourself comfortably; ensure that your back is straight, either in the sitting or lying position. Move your body and flex your limbs, clearing any feelings of tension and tightness.

Relax, Relax, and Relax. Feel the breath of Christed Light Consciousness taking you deeper and deeper into your Sou. Feel the energy of the Cosmic Rays wash over you, entering your Source Star and Crown Chakra, moving down throughout your Chakra System. This connects you to Mother Earth and All the Kingdoms and Realms of the Mother, Planet Earth.

Imagine, feel or sense a ribbon of Clear Light Phenacite Crystal Energy filling your entire being. As you breathe in the Phenacite Vibrations and Frequencies, feel the energy enter into your Psychic Awareness, enhancing and facilitating the Clearing, cleansing and activating of all the Crystalline Energy Systems of your body, and helping you make contact with your Guides, the Angelic Realm and the Ascended Masters of Light and Love.

Breathe deeply and connect with your Heart Chakra. Enter the Sacred Chambers of Your Heart. As you go through the Sacred Doorway, sense, see or feel an Archway ahead of you with Ancient Writing above the Arch, welcoming you to this Cosmic Gateway to the Sacred Golden Chambers of the Universal Logos: Lord Melchizedek.

Take three deeper breaths of the Cosmic Rays Energy and Feel yourself elevate in Light and Love Consciousness. Step Forward and Go forth, entering the Cosmic Gateway and feel yourself being Transported instantly to an amazing room of Golden Light. Upon your arrival, sense the presence of your Mighty I AM Presence, your Guides and the Angels – who are with you on your Journey in Life.

Behold before you the Energy that is the Universal Logos: Lord Melchizedek. Approach this great energy. As you are greeted, acknowledge this Great God of Light, and receive from him the benediction of the Golden Chamber of Lord Melchizedek, unique unto you, in acknowledgment of your Spiritual Journey, your Acceptance of Self and Others, your Courage, Faith, Trust, Love, Light, Forgiveness and Freedom that come from the Sacred Chambers of your Heart. This allows you to be present in this most Sacred of Places of this Universe in this now moment of time.

The Cosmic Rays of Light and Love have raised your Vibrations and Frequency to the required levels of Higher Consciousness, thus enabling you to be in the presence of the Universal Logos, and to be within the Golden Chambers of Lord Melchizedek.

Be at ease and Feel these Cosmic Rays expand your Awareness. Know that your Consciousness has risen to higher levels within the Cosmic Christed Light Consciousness of The One, the Ultimate and Supreme God of All Creations, the All That Is.

As you prepare yourself to return with the Cosmic Rays to this Sacred Place in this now moment of time; Give Thanks to Lord Melchizedek for the Unique Personal Benediction that you have received. Be in Gratitude to the Cosmic Rays for the Elevation of your vibrations and frequencies that allowed you to be in the Sacred Golden Chambers of Lord Melchizedek.

When you feel ready, and only when you have completed your Journey, breathe in and out, and slowly return to this now moment of time. Be still for a while. Feel the energy of the Cosmic Rays within your being.

Trust that all is as it is meant to be, and be in the Acceptance of Who You Really Are. Be Still within. "And So It Is!"

Holistic Meditations
Holy Spirit of Christed Light Consciousness through
The Mirror Reflecting – The Genius that You Are
Azeztulite Crystal

Take three deep breathes, relaxing, relaxing even more into your breath – breathing deeply into your abdomen. Move your body as required into a more comfortable position, sitting upright or lying prone with your back straightened. Breathe deeply and again take an even deeper breath. Go within your being and feel centered, at ease in connecting with your Inner Divine.

Breathing into your Mighty I AM Energy, feel the presence of the Celestial Connector Crystal, the Azeztulite. As its presence within your being heightens your Consciousness and Understanding, feel the changes occurring for you at a cellular level. This allows your Awareness to grow, expand and become illuminated and attuned to the clear vibrant energy of the Azeztulite.

Feel a connection with the Azeztulite as it activates your Third Eye and Crown Chakras and the Chakras above in the Etheric Body and your Universal Body.

Activate and enter your Merkebah. In your Merkebah, Ascend into the Universe. Pass through the Gateways and Portals into the Multi-dimensions of the Universe. As you do so, hear the sounds of the Universe and the Songs of the Galaxies, as they speak to you in Welcome and Love.

Breathe deeply and relax even more. Have a sense of the Holy Spirit being with you and feel the presence of your Higher Self and your Mighty I AM Presence, the Lord God essence of your being.

Breathe into the Sacred Chambers of your Heart. Enter there into the Divine Energy of Unconditional Love, Harmony and Peace.

Feel secure and safe in the Knowledge that the Holy Spirit is with you. Along with your

Mighty I AM Presence and Higher Self; it is taking you on a Journey of Discovery through the Magic of the Mirrors of Reflections – the Reflections of the Mirrors in your Life.

Breathe in and take your breath into your Heart. Today in this now moment, your Mighty I AM Presence, along with the Holy Spirit, are taking you to a Sacred Place within you, in which you will learn how to recognize the mirrors as they are reflected back at you by Spirit.

Be Open and Listen to the Guidance of your Mighty I AM Presence, as you are shown the Mirrors that Reflect the Energies of your Heart.

Be a witness, as your Spirit and your I AM Presence bring to you people with whom you have had issues with in your life.

Ask your Mighty I AM Presence to assist you in Recognizing the Lessons that you need to learn from this person or situation, so that you attain the Wisdom and Understanding required thereof.

What is the Mirror? What is this person or situation reflecting back at me for me to recognize?

What is there within me that I need to heal?

All is reflected back at you by the Holy Spirit. Your personal world, your life, and the life that you live, are a direct reflection of all that you are Inside of Yourself, in this now moment of time.

All is a Reflection of the Self, which is in Truth, the Real YOU.

In speaking to Spirit, your Mighty I AM Presence or your Beloved Higher Self, ask for the help that you need, that will resolve and dissolve the energy around any problems or issues, mental or emotional, that appears for you, to be Purified and Returned to LOVE.

In this now moment, make a Commitment to yourself to make whatever Changes are required to bring about the Healing and Transformations that will propel you forward in your Evolution.

Breathe in and relax. Breathe out any energy that
you wish to dispel from your body.

Ask your I AM Presence to bring in the Vibrations and Frequencies of the Azeztulite Crystal in order to bring to you Heightened Awareness, Illumination and Understanding of the issues that you need to clear, cleans and resolve.

Ask the United Twelve Sacred Flames and Rays of Christed Light Consciousness to saturate your entire being with waves upon waves of Christed Light and Love. Thus you clear, cleanse and resolve the issues, bringing you to the energies of One Unity Consciousness of The One, the Ultimate and Supreme Creator God of All That Is..

Breathe in the Sacred Flames and Rays of Christed Light. Feel Totally at Peace with yourself.

You are the Reflections in the Mirror. The Mirror reflects back to you the Many Aspects of yourself. What you See, Hear or Feel are the Reflections that come from the Heart of Yourself.

In a few minutes more and when you feel ready, you will
return to the present moment in this room. Affirm within
your memory the messages that you have received from your
Mighty I AM Presence, your Teachers and your Guides. Slowly
return to the room, feel refreshed, relaxed and composed.
You are the Holy Christed Light Consciousness. "And... So It Is!"

Crystal Quartz Singing Bowl
Meditation of Longevity

Be Still and Silent. Take three very deep breaths and as you breathe in the Energy of the Crystal Quartz, you feel uplifted within your Crystalline Lightbody. As you listen to the Sounds and Tones of Vibrations and Frequencies emanating from the Crystal Quartz Bowl, you in this now moment of time and space, manifest the Cosmic Blueprint of Whole Brain Experience. Breathe in these wonderful Sound Waves of Vibrations and Frequencies that communicate to your Body Elemental.

They assist your Body Elemental, in manifesting the Crystalline Lightbody and in the morphing of your Body to an anti-aging, balanced God-Self State. Absorb into your Body the elements and sine waves contained within the Crystal, to promote Longevity and expand you Spirituality.

You have Perfection of Health; your flow of Chi Energy is balanced and your Diet is Perfection. They enhance your lifestream and mobility. Your Third Eye Chakra is activated by the wondrous Sounds and Tones emanating from the Crystal Singing Bowl. You are Spiritually Aligned with the Masculine and Feminine Energies contained within your Body, and you are Balanced and Harmonized on all levels of your Mind, Body and Soul.

Breathe into your Heart Center. Be Still and Silent within. When you feel ready and only when you are ready – return to the room feeling relaxed, refreshed and revitalized. Breathe In the Divine Crystalline Light, and Breathe Out the Divine Crystalline Light. Say this Affirmation: I AM Cleared and Cleansed already, because my Body is Crystalline on all Levels of my being.

"And So It Is!"

Part 4

Inner Guidance
Healing and Purification
Clearings and Charts

The Twelve Sacred Flames and
Rays Clearing – Part 1

28 - Day Clearing, Using the Affirmations and the Sacred Flames and Rays of Christed Light Consciousness for Flames and Rays 1 to 6

<u>Instructions</u>: Before beginning your clearing process, make a photocopy of this original document. File your original and use the copy. You can then redo the whole clearing process again at a future date by simply doing another photocopy of the original.

When you finish the whole clearing process, destroy the photocopy to complete the cleansing. In order for the process to be most effective do the full 28 days of the clearing consecutively without a break.

The unconscious mind clears progressively and frees you up at each stage. Say the affirmations below at least once a day, preferably three times a day.

The Sacred Flames for Healing will lessen the reactions that may occur and bring the Wisdom and Understanding required for Complete Healing to your Conscious Awareness.

To help you deal with any emotional feelings that may arise during work hours, or at any other time, use the affirmation below.

- Whatever happens as a result of this clearing, I release and let go of during my rest and relaxation periods.

Day	Affirmations	Invocations	Date
Day 1 Ray 1	I Surrender to the Will of God; I and the Will of God are One. I AM my True Spiritual God-Self. "And... So It Is!"	I Invoke the Sacred Flame and Ray of the Will of God – to Be with me now; bringing me the Wisdom of the Will of God.	Date:
Day 2	I AM One with my Mighty I AM Presence, Lord God essence of my being Now. "And... So It Is!"	I Invoke the Sacred Flame and Ray of Ascension, Purification and Immortality – to Encapsulate me now, so that I AM One with the Spirit of my Mighty I AM Presence.	Date:
Day 3	I AM the Embodiment of Trust. I Trust The One, the Ultimate, Supreme God of All Creation. "And... So It Is!"	I AM the Sacred Flame and Ray of Illumination and Wisdom in all I say and do – as I Trust in the Will of God.	Date:
Day 4	I AM Focused in all my Endeavors. I AM Disciplined and Calm in my thoughts and emotions in all situations. "And... So It Is!"	I Invoke the Violet Sacred Flame and Ray of Transmutation – to Help me transform and discipline my thoughts and emotions to be focused in All my endeavors.	Date:
Day 5 Ray 2	I AM Wisdom and Understanding. I AM able to sustain and maintain the Illumination Energy within my being. "And... So It Is!"	I Invoke the Sacred Flame and Ray of Illumination and Wisdom to permeate my entire being now with the Energy of Wisdom and Understanding, with ease and grace.	Date:
Day 6	I Have Transformed all that is not of the Divine Light from my being to the Wisdom, Understanding and Unconditional Love that is the Illumination of Truth. "And... So It Is!"	I Invoke the Sacred Healing Flames and Rays of Illumination and Cosmic Love - to Encapsulate and Saturate my entire beingness now, so that I AM Divine Light and Divine Love.	Date:

Day 7	I AM One with the Holy Spirit, the Heart, Mind and Will of God. "And... So It Is!"	I Invoke the Sacred Flames and Rays of Illumine Truth and Divinity – to Be One with me now and expand the Holy God-Self within me to be One with the Holy Spirit of God.	Date:
Day 8	I Communicate Clearly and with Clarity, all my thinking and emotions in a compassionate and comprehensive manner. "And... So It Is!"	I Invoke the Sacred Flame and Ray of Illumination and the Sacred Flame of Healing – to Be with me now – in order that I AM a Compassionate Communicator of Love and Light.	Date:
Day 9 Ray 3	I Love myself Completely; I Accept myself as Divine Love. "And... So It Is!"	I Invoke the Sacred Flame and Ray of Cosmic Love – to Immerse my being in the Fire of Unconditional Self Love, the Love of my Divine.	Date:
Day 10	I Have Opened my Heart to Love. I AM the Love of God's Heart already, because I AM my True Spiritual God-Self. "And... So It Is!"	I Invoke the Sacred Flame and Ray of Cosmic Love and the Sacred Flame of Illumine Truth – to Be in the Sacred Chambers of my Heart Now.	Date:
Day 11	I AM Living in my Heart; I AM Heart Centered in my Life. "And... So It Is!"	I Invoke the Sacred Flame and Ray of Cosmic Love – to Encapsulate my entire being with Unconditional Love, Compassion, Mercy, Creativity, Freedom and Forgiveness..	Date:
Day 12	I AM Compassionate and Merciful toward me in this Life Incarnation and others at all times. "And... So It Is!"	I Invoke the Sacred Fires of Cosmic Love and the Sacred Ascension Flame and Ray of Purification – to Swamp me in waves of Cosmic Love and Purification Energy Now.	Date:

Day 13 Ray 4	I AM Purified; I AM the Holy Spirit on all levels of my four Body Systems. "And... So It Is!"	I Invoke the Sacred Flame and Ray of Purification and Immortality – to Immerse me in their Fiery Flames and bring me back to the Oneness of All That Is. To be my True Spiritual God-Self..	Date:
Day 14	I AM in Gratitude for my Life; I Release all Energies that serve me not – to the Holy Spirit of Cosmic Christed Light of God Consciousness. "And... So It Is!"	I Invoke the Sacred Flame and Ray of Purification and Immortality and the Sacred Flame of Healing and Manifestation – to purify me now and release all negativity from my being unto the Holy Spirit of Cosmic Christed Light of God Consciousness.	Date:
Day 15	I AM Ascended to the 5th Dimension and Beyond. "And... So It Is!"	I Invoke the Sacred Flame and Ray of Ascension and Purification to Purify my beingness of all that which prevents my Ascension to the 5th Dimension and Beyond.	Date:
Day 16	I Accept myself as I AM; I AM Pure Divine Spiritual Perfection and Worthy of Ascension Now. "And... So It Is!"	I Invoke the Sacred Flame and Ray of Ascension and Purification – to Be with me now as I AM Spiritually Purified and made ready for my Ascension within the "Hall of Ascension", to the 5th Dimension and Beyond.	Date:
Day 17 Ray 5	I AM Healthy and Abundant on all levels of my being Now. I AM Living from my Spiritually Abundant Heart. "And... So It Is!"	I Invoke the Sacred Flame and Ray of Healing and Manifestation – to Heal my life and Create Abundance of Health, Wealth and Happiness.	Date:

Day 18	I AM in Perfect Spiritual Health and Wellness. My Mind, Body and Spirit are Perfection. "And... So It Is!"	I Invoke the Sacred Flame and Ray of Healing – to Spread the Green Emerald Fire throughout my Body, for Perfect Health and Wellness.	Date:
Day 19	I AM Totally Abundant and Prosperous Now. "And... So It Is!"	I Invoke the Sacred Flame and Ray of Healing and Manifestation – to Bring unto me Absolute and Total Abundance and Financial Prosperity, I Call upon the Sacred Flame of Resurrection – to Resurrect all the Abundance of Finance that is my birthright, as a child of The One, the All That Is.	Date:
Day 20	I AM Healed and Purified on all levels of my four Body Systems. I AM One with my Spirit in the Divine Perfection of All That Is. "And... So It Is!"	I Invoke the Sacred Flame and Ray of Healing – to Heal me on all levels of my being. I call upon the Sacred Ascension Flame of Purification – to Transform all within me to the Spiritual Purity of Divine Perfection.	Date:
Day 21 Ray 6	I AM the Resurrection of my Life. I AM Resurrected to the New Encodements of Divine Perfection. "And... So It Is!"	I Invoke the Sacred Flame and Ray of Resurrection – to Resurrect me to the New Encodements of Divine Perfection.	Date:
Day 22	I AM in Devotion to the Sacred Flame and Ray of Resurrection. "And... So It Is!"	I Invoke the Sacred Flame and Ray of Resurrection – to Revivify my Belief in being Devoted to the Functions of the Resurrection Flame and Ray. I Call upon the Sacred Flame of Transcendence – to Bring clarity and certainty to that devotion.	Date:

Day 23	I AM in Selfless Service of God, Humanity and Planet Earth. "And... So It Is!"	I Invoke the Sacred Flames and Ray of Resurrection and Divinity – to Assist me in being of Service to God and Humanity.	Date:
Day 24	I AM Born to the Spiritual worship of the Divine Heart of God. I AM my True Spiritual God-Self Now. "And So It Is!"	I Invoke the Sacred Flames and Rays of Resurrection and Transcendence – as I Resurrect my life and Transcend all in order that I AM the Divine Spiritual Heart of God.	Date:
Day 25 United	I AM Healed Completely by the Source energies of the United Twelve Sacred Flames of One Unity Consciousness. "And... So It Is!"	I Invoke the United Twelve Sacred Flames and Rays of One Unity Consciousness – to Merge with me and Bring Source energy to all areas of my Physical, Mental and Emotional Bodies.	Date:
Day 26	I AM the Embodiment of The One, the Supreme Creator God of All That Is. I AM my True God-Self Now. "And... So It Is!"	I Invoke the United Twelve Sacred Flames and Rays of Christed Light Consciousness – to Unite all parts within me to be of One Unity Consciousness.	Date:
Day 27	I AM in Gratitude and Love for the unending work of the Twelve Sacred Flames and Rays in keeping our Mother Planet Earth Alive. "And... So It Is!"	I Invoke the United Twelve Sacred Flames and Rays – to Encapsulate my Spirit, and my four Body Systems to Oneness with Mother Earth.	Date:
Day 28	I AM my God-Self State of the Holy Spirit of One United Consciousness Now. "And... So It Is!"	I Invoke the United Twelve Sacred Flames and Rays – to encapsulate and permeate every particle of my Spirit, Mind and Body; I AM One with the Holy Spirit of Oneness.	Date:

The Twelve Sacred Flames and
Rays Clearing – Part 2

28 – Day Clearing, Using the Affirmations and the Sacred Flames and Rays of Christed Light Consciousness for Flames and Rays 7 to 12, Plus the United Flames and Rays

Instructions: Before beginning your clearing process, make a photocopy of this original document. File your original and just use the copy. You can then redo the whole clearing process again at a future date, by simply doing another photocopy of the original.

When you finish the whole clearing process, destroy the photocopy to complete the cleansing. In order for the process to be most effective, do the full 28 days of the clearing consecutively without a break.

The Unconscious Mind clears progressively and frees you up at each stage. Say the affirmations below at least once a day, preferably three times a day.

The Sacred Flames for Healing will lessen the reactions that may occur, and bring the Wisdom and Understanding required for Complete Healing to your Conscious Awareness.

To help you combat any feelings of vagueness at work or elsewhere, use the affirmation below:

- Whatever happens as a result of this clearing, I release and let go of during my sleep period.

Day	Affirmations	Invocations	Date:
Day 1 Ray 7	I AM Justice and Fair, Merciful, Compassionate and Caring toward myself and others. "And... So It Is!"	I Invoke the Divine Principles of the Violet Flame from the Violet Planet of Omri Tas – to Bring Healing to me Now.	Date:
Day 2	I AM the Divine Violet Fires of Freedom and Forgiveness. "And... So It Is!"	I Invoke the Divine Justice and Divine Truth of the Violet Fires – to Be within me Now.	Date:
Day 3	I AM the Freedom that gives Opportunity and Growth. "And... So It Is!"	I Invoke the Sacred Violet Flame and Ray – to Transmute all energy within me – to the Light of Freedom, Opportunity and Growth.	Date:
Day 4	I AM the Temple of Grace; I AM Divine Love, Compassion and Gratitude. "And... So It Is!"	I Invoke Lady Portia, Chohan of the Great Violet Flame Temple – to Be with me Now.	Date:
Day 5 Ray 8	I AM the Self-Actualization of my Truth as a Master of Light and Love. "And... So It Is!"	I Invoke the Sacred Flames and Rays of Transcendence, Illumination and Purification – to be within me. I AM a Master of Light and Love Now.	Date:
Day 6	I Have Clarity of Thinking in All Situations; I AM Clear and I AM Certain of my Ascension to the 5th Dimension and Beyond. "And... So It Is!"	I Invoke the Healing Powers of the Sacred Flames and Rays of Transcendence, God's Will and Illumination – to Ensure that I AM Clear, Purified and Ready for my Ascension.	Date:
Day 7	I AM Living my Life in Truth, Balance and Harmony. "And... So It Is!"	I Invoke the Sacred Flames and Rays of Transcendence, God's Will and Illumination - to aid me in my Journey to Truth, Balance and Harmony.	Date:

Day 8	I AM Cleansed and Cleared of ALL my old false belief patterns and judgements. "And... So It Is!"	I Invoke the Sacred Flames and Rays of Transcendence, Purification and Illumination – as I Surrender to the Will of God.	Date:
Day 9 Ray 9	I AM my Original Blueprint of Divine Perfection of my Lightbody – Freedom and Forgiveness – to Be the Divine Light and Divine Love that I AM Now.	I Invoke the Sacred Flames and Rays of Highest Potentials, Cosmic Love and Purification – to Permeate and Surround my Entire beingness Now.	Date:
Day 10	I AM the Love and Joy, the essence of the Divine Mother, Lady Mother Mary. "And... So It Is!"	I Invoke the Sacred Flames and Rays of Highest Potentials, Cosmic Love and Transmutation – to Transform me to be essence of Lady Mother Mary.	Date:
Day 11	I AM Grateful for All the Talents and Abilities that Have been bestowed upon me in my Life. "And... So It Is!"	I Invoke the Sacred Flames and Rays of Highest Potentials – to Permeate and Saturate my Entire being Now.	Date:
Day 12	I AM the Rose, the Beautiful Flower in the Crown of Heaven. "And... So It Is!"	I Invoke the Sacred Flames and Rays of the Synthesis of Rays 1 to 7 – to Be within me now.	Date:
Day 13 Ray 10	I AM the Truth of my Divinity; I AM I AM the Spirit of my Divine God-Self. "And... So It Is!"	I Invoke the Sacred Flames and Rays of Divinity and Ascension – to Assist me in my Journey to Spirit, to be my True God-Self.	Date:
Day 14	I AM Completely Awakened to the Truth of my Divine Spirit, the Truth of Who I AM. "And... So It Is!"	I Invoke the Sacred Flames and Rays of Divinity, Purity and One Unity Consciousness – to Manifest the Truth of my Divine Spirit Now. .	Date:

Day 15	I AM my Lightbody Now; I AM Power, Love and Light, in Balance and Equilibrium. "And... So It Is!"	I Invoke the Sacred Pearlescent Flame and Ray of Divinity – to Permeate my Lightbody with Love and Peace.	Date:
Day 16	I Invoke the Sacred Flame of Divinity –to Encapsulate and Permeate, my entire four Body Systems, Now! "And... So It Is!"	I Invoke the Sacred Flames and Rays of Divinity, Purity and Christed Light Consciousness – to Reside within my Spirit Now!	Date:
Day 17 Ray 11	I AM Activated, Awakened and Aware of the Illumine Truth of my Life. "And... So It Is!"	I Invoke the Sacred Flames and Rays of Illumine Truth and Cosmic Love – to Encapsulate my Entire beingness Now!	Date:
Day 18	I AM in Wellness of Mind, Body and Spirit; I AM Reborn and Rejuvenated to Perfect Health. "And... So It Is!"	I Invoke the Sacred Flames and Rays of Illumine Truth, Resurrection and Illumination – to Bring Waves upon Waves of Source energy into my being Now!	Date:
Day 19	I AM that JOY in All things, and Know and Feel the Deepest Serenity within my Spirit. "And... So It Is!"	I Invoke the Sacred Flames and Rays of Illumine Truth, Cosmic Love and Resurrection – to Be in my Heart Now!	Date:
Day 20	I AM the Representation of the Illumine Truth in my Life; I Live in the Awakened Awareness of all that I AM. "And... So It Is!"	I Invoke the Sacred Flames and Rays of Illumine Truth into my Life. I Request the Wisdom and Understanding that I require for my Learning to come to me in Ease and Grace.	Date:

Day 21 Ray 12	I AM in Total Oneness and Complete Remembrance with the Source of All Life, the All That Is. I AM my Spiritual God-Self. "And... So It Is!"	I Invoke the Sacred Flame and Ray of One Unity Consciousness – to Encapsulate every Particle of my being to be in Total Oneness with Source, the All That Is.	Date:
Day 22	I AM Totally Surrendered to The One, the Holy Spirit of the Supreme God of All Creation. "And... So It Is!"	I Invoke the Sacred Flames and Rays of One Unity Consciousness and Divinity – to Allow the Divine God-Self that I AM to Be One with the Holy Spirit of God.	Date:
Day 23	I AM in Acceptance of All That Is, as What It Is – Divine Spirit Perfection. I See the Divine Spirit Perfection in All Things and in All Situations. "And... So It Is!"	I Invoke the Sacred Flame and Ray of Harmony – to Saturate and Permeate every Particle of my being – to Be in Acceptance, Harmony and Oneness with All Things in God's Creation.	Date:
Day 24	I AM the Sacred, Humble Loving Strength that comes from the Wisdom and Understanding of my Beloved Mighty I AM Presence. I AM One with my Beloved I AM. In Spirit We are One. "And... So It Is!"	I Invoke the Sacred Flames and Rays of One Unity Consciousness, Divinity, Illumination and Harmony – to Bring to me the Wisdom and Understanding of my Beloved Mighty I AM Presence.	Date:
Day 25 United	I AM Healed Completely by the United Twelve Sacred Flames of Healing and Harmony. "And... So It Is!"	I Invoke the United Sacred Flames and Rays – to Merge with me and Bring their Source energy to all areas of my Physical, Mental and Emotional Bodies.	Date:

Day 26 United	I AM the Embodiment of The One, the Supreme Creator God of All That Is. I AM in Harmony with All of Creation. I AM my Divine Spirit of my God-Self. "And... So It Is!"	I Invoke the Sacred Flames and Rays of Christed Light of God Consciousness – to Unite within me – to Be One United Holy Spirit of God Consciousness Now!	Date:
Day 27 Cosmic	I AM my Divine Holy God-Self; I have The Divine Holy Spirit within me Now. "And... So It Is!"	I Invoke the Sacred Flames and Rays of the Cosmic Christed Light of God Consciousness – the Source energy of All Life – to Be within me Now!	Date:
Day 28	I AM the Gateway to the Stars. I AM my True Divine Holy Spirit Now. The Holy Spirit of Planet Earth is Resurrect the New Encodements of Divine Perfection. "And... So It Is!"	I Invoke the Sacred Cosmic Rays of Light – to Encapsulate Planet Earth with Peace, Harmony and Oneness; Resurrecting the Holy Spirit of Planet Earth to the New Encodements of Divine Perfection of the Holy Spirit of God.	Date:
Cosmic	I AM the Cosmic Light of the Holy Spirit, that Shines upon Planet Earth; I Bring Spiritual Peace, Harmony and Unconditional Love to All Life.	I Invoke the Cosmic Light Rays of The One, the Ultimate, Supreme Creator God of All That Is – to Permeating Planet Earth with the Holy Spirit of Cosmic Love, Cosmic Light, Peace and Harmony.	Date

Inner Guidance: Healing and Purification Processes, and Charts

Purification Process

<u>8 Week Purification</u>   Commencement Date:

Readings: Parts 1 and 2 - Inner Guidance: Key Prayers for Cosmic Ascension

<u>Commitment to Purification</u>

Beloved One, the Supreme God of All Creation, my Beloved Mighty I AM Presence, Lord God essence of my being, I ………….......... Do solemnly Declare that I Commit to these Purification Processes with all of my Spirit, Heart, Mind and Body.

Select from the Listing of Purification Intentions those that your Heart desires for the 8 Weeks of Purification, or choose Purification Intentions other than those listed. Write in the Intention on the list below.

a) I Commit to The Purification of my entire being – Soul, Spirit, Heart, Mind and Body.
b) I Commit to The Peace, Balance, Harmony, Self-Love and Oneness necessary for bringing in my Lightbody.
c) I Commit to Purifying my thoughts and emotions to be Still and Calm within.
d) I Commit to Purifying my Physical Body, Etheric Body, all Subtle Bodies and Spirit - to be in Wholeness and Oneness with my Mighty I AM Presence.

e) I Commit to Being the 5ᵗʰ Dimensional Energy of Unconditional Love.

f) I Commit to Exercising in a Healthy way, one that will help me heal all levels of my physical beingness (walking, running, swimming, and dancing and movement exercises).

g) I Commit to A Diet that is Nutritious and full of all the vitamins and minerals that will sustain my being and aid me in becoming my Lightbody.

h) I Commit to Giving and Receiving the Source energy of the Christed Light Consciousness.

i) I Commit to Being of Service to Humanity and to Supporting my Spiritual family in every way that I can.

j) I Commit to Saying Prayers daily.

k) I Commit to Drinking Pure water and Eating Wholesome foods, which will enhance my being on all levels.

l) I Commit to Adhering to the Codes of Conduct for a Disciple of the Holy Spirit.

m) I Commit to Living my Life as a Master of Light and Love.

n) I Commit to Surrendering to the Divine Spirit that I AM; I Surrender to the All That Is.

o) I Commit to Being the Holy Spirit of my True God-Self. "And... So It Is!"

p) I Commit to

q) I Commit to

r) I Commit to

s) I Commit to

t) I Commit to

u) I Commit to

v) I Commit to

w) I Commit to

x) I Commit to

y)   I Commit to

z)   I Commit to

I AM All That Is, I AM Divine Perfection already, because I Have Fulfilled all my Commitments to The One, the All That Is and to my Mighty I AM Presence. "And... So It Is!"

Signed:_____

Part 1 4 – Week Purification Process – Rays 1 to 6

The Purification Process focuses on one or two different Sacred Flames and Rays per week.

Part 1: Read each of the four Prayers for each of the Sacred Flames and Rays, (three times).

Week 1 of the Purification Process – Rays 1 and 2

Week 2 of the Purification Process – Rays 3 and 4

Week 3 of the Purification Process – Ray 5

Week 4 of the Purification Process – Ray 6

Week 1: Monday, Tuesday, Wednesday and Thursday

The 1st Ray: The Sacred Flame and Ray of the Will of God, Discipline and Trust.

Read four Prayers for this Flame, three times daily; and write down the affirmations for each Flame, (three times a day).

Week 1: Friday, Saturday and Sunday

The 2nd Ray: The Sacred Flame and Ray of Illumination, Wisdom and Understanding.

Read four Prayers for this Flame, three times daily; and write down the affirmations for each Flame, (three times a day).

Week 2: Monday Tuesday Wednesday, and Thursday

The 3rd Ray: The Sacred Flame and Ray of Cosmic Love, Compassion and Creativity/

Read four Prayers for this Flame, three times daily; and write down the affirmations for each Flame, (three times a day).

Week 2: Friday, Saturday and Sunday

The 4th Ray: The Sacred Ascension Flame and Ray of Purification and Immortality.

Read four Prayers for this Flame, three times daily; and write down the affirmations for each Flame. (three times a day).

Week 3: Monday through to Sunday

The 5th Ray: The Sacred Flame and Ray of Healing and Manifestation.

Read four Prayers for this Flame, three times daily; and write down the affirmations for each Flame, (three times a day).

Week 4: Monday through to Sunday

The 6th Ray: The Sacred Flame and Ray of Resurrection, Devotion and Restoration.

Read four Prayers for this Flame, three times daily; and write down the affirmations for each Flame, (three times a day).

Part 2 5 – Week Purification Process – Rays 7 to 12

The Purification Process focuses on one or two different Sacred Flames and Rays for week.

Part 2 - Read each of the four Prayers for each of the Sacred Flames and Rays, (three times).

Week 1 of the Purification Process – Ray 7

Week 2 of the Purification Process – Ray 8

Week 3 of the Purification Process – Rays 9 and 10

Week 4 of the Purification Process – Rays 11 and 12

Week 5 of the Purification Process – United Rays 1 to 12

Week 5 of the Purification process covers Avatar of Synthesis: the Mahatma – Unification of the Twelve Flames and Rays of Christed Light of God Consciousness.

Week 1: Monday through to Sunday

The 7th Ray: Sacred Flame and Ray of Transmutation, Freedom and Forgiveness.

Read four Prayers for this Flame, three times daily; and write down the affirmations for each Flame, (three times a day).

Week 2: Monday through to Sunday

The 8th Ray: The Sacred Flame and Ray of Transcendence, Certainty and Clarity.

Read four Prayers for this Flame, three times daily; and write down the affirmations for each Flame, (three times a day).

Week 3: Monday, Tuesday, Wednesday and Thursday

The 9th Ray: The Sacred Flame and Ray of Highest Potentials, and the Synthesis 1 to 7

Read four Prayers for this Flame, three times daily; and write down the affirmations for each Flame, (three times a day).

Week 3: Friday, Saturday and Sunday
The 10th Ray: The Sacred Flame and Ray of Divinity, Peace and Opulence.

Read four Prayers for this Flame, three times daily; and write down the affirmations for each Flame, (three times a day).

Week 4: Monday, Tuesday, Wednesday and Thursday
The 11th Ray: The Sacred Flame and Ray of Illumine Truth, Joy and Serenity

Read four Prayers for this Flame, three times daily; and write down the affirmations for each Flame. (three times a day).

Week 4: Friday, Saturday and Sunday
The 12th Ray: The Sacred Flame and Ray of One Unity Consciousness and Transfiguration

Read four Prayers for this Flame, three times daily; and write down the affirmations for each Flame, (three times a day).

Week 5: Monday to Friday
The Avatar of Synthesis: the Mahatma Prayers: The United Sacred Flames of One Unity Consciousness.

Read four Prayers for this Flame, three times daily; and write down the affirmations for each Flame, (three times a day).

The Twelve Sacred Flames and Rays –
Chohans and Archangels Chart

Ray	Amplified	Colors	Archangels	Chohans	Flame Purpose
1	Monday	Blue	Michael and Lady Faith	Master El Morya	Will of God, Surrender, Focus, Trust and Discipline
2	Sunday	Yellow	Jophiel and Lady Christine	Lord Lanto and Master Kuthumi	Illumination, Mind of God, Wisdom, Understanding and Truth
3	Tuesday	Pink	Chamuel and Lady Charity	Master Paul the Venetian	Heart of God, Love, Compassion, Mercy and Artistic Creativity
4	Friday	White	Gabriel and Lady Hope	Lord Serapis Bey	Ascension, Purity, Hope, Discipline and Immortality
5	Wednesday	Green	Raphael and Lady Regina	Master Hilarion	Healing, Science and Manifestation
6	Thursday	Ruby/Gold (Orange)	Uriel and Lady Aurora	Lord Sananda	Resurrection, Devotion, Ministration Service, Restoration and Revivification.
7	Saturday	Violet	Zadkiel and Lady Amethyst	Lady Portia and Master St. Germain	Transmutation, Freedom, Unconditional Love, Transformation and Forgiveness

8	Wednesday	Aqua/Sea Green	Aquariel and Lady Clarity	Lady Nada	Transcendence, Calmness, Certainty, Clarity and Clearance
9	Tuesday	Magenta	Anthriel and Lady Harmony	Lady Mother Mary	Synthesis of Rays 1 to 7, Divine Qualities, Harmony and Highest Potentials
10	Friday	Pearlescent	Valoel and Lady Peace	Lady Vessa Andromeda	Divinity, Inner Peace, Opulence and Crystalline Lightbody
11	Thursday	Peach	Perpetiel and Lady Joy	Lady Quan Yin	Illumined Truth, Joy and Serenity
12	Sunday	Gold and Opalescence White	Omniel and Lady Opalescence	Lady Pallas Athena	Transfiguration, Opalescence, Self-Oneness and One Unity Consciousness
Cosmic	Daily	Crystal-Prism Clear, Platinum, Rainbow, Gold and Silver	Lord Metatron	Lord Zohar and the Cosmic Logos: Avatar of Synthesis: Mahatma	United, Integrated Holy God-Self. Harmony and Oneness with Christed Light Consciousness.

Twelve Sacred Flames and Ray Chart Developed by Amerissis Kumara

Twelve Rays	Chakra	Glands	Gems Crystals	Main Qualities	Colour And Toning	Arch-Angels	Chohans	Elohim
1 Will of God. Blue Ray and Flame Monday	Throat	Thy-roid	Lapis Lazuli, Blue Lace Agate, Blue Sapphire, Bornite, (Peacock stone). Calcite, Blue Sodalite.	Omnipotence Protection and Faith	Blue Sounds: MONG or HAM	Michael and Faith	Master El Morya	Hercules and Amazonia
2 Illumina-tion and Wisdom. Yellow Ray and Flame Sunday	Crown	Pineal	Tigers Eye Golden: Topaz, Amber, Citrine, Yellow: Peridot, Kunzite, Anatase, Carnelian and Sapphire	Illumination, Wisdom, Omniscience, Understanding, Perception, Precipitation, Comprehension Discrimination.	Yellow Sounds: AUM or OM	Jophiel and Christine	Master Kuthumi and Lord Lanto. World Teachers and Masters of Ancient Wisdom	Apollo and Lumina

	Heart / Base of the Spine	Thymus / Adrenals		Unconditional Love	Rose Pink / White	Chamuel and Charity	Paul the Venetian / Lord Serapis Bey	Heros and Amora / Purity And Astrea
3 Cosmic Love. Rose Pink Ray and Flame Tuesday	Heart	Thymus	Rose Quartz, Strawberry Quartz, Ruby, Pink: Kunzite, Fluorite, Agate, Coral, Tourmaline, Regency Rose.	Unconditional Love, Omni-presence, Compassion, True Brotherhood, Charity, Love in action.	Rose Pink Sounds: AH or YAM	Chamuel and Charity	Paul the Venetian	Heros and Amora
4 Ascension. White Ray and Flame Friday	Base of the Spine	Adrenals	Azurite, Snow Quartz, Pearl. Chal-cedony, White Coral, Kunzite colourless, White Agate, Sapphire.	Purity, Wholeness, Christed Light Consciousness.	White Sounds: Groan or I AM	Gabriel and Hope	Lord Serapis Bey	Purity And Astrea

	Chakra	Gland	Gemstones	Quality	Colour	Sounds	Archangel	Master	Elohim
5 Healing and Manifest-ation. Emerald Green Ray and Flame. Wednesday	Third Eye Brow	Pituitary	Emerald, Jade, Chrysoprase, Ruby Zozyte, Green Sapphire, and Kunzite, Spinel, Daphnite deep green, Moss Agate.	Healing at all levels, truth, constancy, creation through manifestation	Green	Sounds: EE or HAM-KSHAM	Raphael and Regina	Master Hilarion	Cyclopea And Virginia
6 Resurrect-ion. Ruby and Gold Ray and Flame Thursday	Solar Plexus	Pancreas	Citrine, Pyrite, Golden Calcite, Honey Calcite, Pyrite, Golden Beryl, Red Agate, Ruby, Garnet, Bloodstone.	Ministration of The Love of Christ and devotion to Humanity	Purple and Gold	Sounds: Loud HUM or RAM	Uriel and Aurora	Lord Sananda	Peace and Aloha

	Sacral	Gonads	Amethyst, Violet Fluorite, Kunzite Purple, Sugilite, Ametrine, Lavender Kunzite, Purple Rhodolite, and Sapphire	Freedom, Forgiveness, Trans-mutation and Diplomacy.	Violet	Sounds: OO or VAM	Zadkiel and Amethyst	Lady Portia and Master St. Germain	Arcturus and Victoria
7 Trans-mutation. Violet Ray and Flame Saturday									
8 Trans-cendence. Aqua Ray and Flame Wednesday	Causal Above Crown	Pituitary + All	Aqua-marine, Adventurine, Peridot, Green: Kunzite, Fluorite, Calcite, Apatite, Amazonite	Certainty, Clarity and Trans-cendence.	Aqua	Sound: OH	Aquariel and Clarity	Lady Nada	Over-lighed by Helios and Vesta of the Great Central Sun
9 Highest Potentials. Magenta Ray and Flame Tuesday	Etheric Heart Above the Heart	Heart + All	Red Garnet, Ruby, Raspberry Quartz, Red Jasper, Rhodonite, Rubellite, Almandine Red	Highest Potential, the Synthesis of 1-7	Magenta	Sound: HAH	Anthriel and Harmony	Lady Mother Mary	Over-lighted by Lord Goyana

10 Divinity. Pearlescent Ray and Flame Monday	Soul Star Above Causal	Pineal + All	Moon-stone, Clear Fluorite, Icelandic Spar, Dolomite, Pearl and Shimmery Shell, Dolomite, Serpentine	Divinity, Peace and Opulence	Gold	Sound: OR	Valoel and Peace	Lady Vessa Andromeda and Allah Gobi	Over-lighted by Lord Huertal
11 Illumine Truth. Peach Ray and Flame Thursday	Star Gate Above Soul Star	Thyroid + All	Peach Agate, Spessartine Garnet, Peach Spinel, Morganite Beryl, Peach Calcite, Hessonite, Cinnamon Garnet.	Illumined Truth, Joy and Serenity	Peach	Sound: AYE	Perpetiel and Joy	Lady Quan Yin	Over-lighted by Lord Semveta

12 Oneness and Trans-figuration Gold Ray and Flame Sunday	Universal Chakra Above the Star Gate	Pineal and Pituitary + All	Golden Calcite, Golden Beryl, Gold, Yellow Sapphire, Yellow Fluorite, and Peridot, Heliodor, Beryl, Gold Adventurine	Oneness and Unity Consciousness Transfiguration and Transformation	Opal/ Opal-escent Gold and White Sound Soft HUM	Omniel and Opal-escence	Lady Pallas Athena	Over-lighted by Lord Ardal
Cosmic Rays of Light and Love. Prismic All Rays and Flames Daily	All 352 Chakra's	All Etheric Glands and Light body	Diamond, Herkimer Diamond, Selenite, Clear Sapphire, Goshenite, Beryl, Transparent Crystal	Avatar of Synthesis Mahatma Energy One Unity Consciousness of the Twelve Flames and Rays	Clear and Trans-parent Sounds: 3 OM and 3 AUM	Lord Meta-tron	Maha Chohan St. Germain and the Great Divine Director Master Ragoczy	Elohim Council of Elders. Cosmic Logos: Mahatma Avatar of Synthesis

Chart:

As one works with the Twelve Sacred Flames and Rays that represent the Twelve Major Chakra System of our physical and metaphysical being, we clear and cleanse the blueprints that are contained within each of these chakras. We resurrect them, to the New Encodements of Divine Perfection from the Christed Light of God Consciousness of The One, the Ultimate Supreme God of All Creation, the All That Is. The Twelve Sacred Flames and Rays, along with the Cosmic Rays, heal the Human Cod and Resurrect the Twelve – Strand DNA to the New Encodement of Divine Perfection.

Much has been written about the Chakra System, with information coming from many different sources. There are many healing modalities that can be successfully used for Chakra Balancing and Alignment.

We on the Cosmic Ascension Pathway are dealing with the Chakra System differently by using the Twelve Sacred Flames and Rays and their corresponding Crystals and Gemstones. We have choices in applying the principles of the Twelve Sacred Flames and the Rays to each of the Chakras in the System, and also to the four Body Systems, Spiritual, Mental/Emotional, Physical, Etheric, all Subtle Bodies and Body Elemental.

We ask the Chohans, Ascended Masters, Lady Masters and the Archangels and Angels of the Twelve Sacred Flames and Rays, to help us in our Self-healing work.

This gives us an enormous boost in our healing of core issues, because core issues that we have in our being are imbedded into the chakra that cover that period of our Life.

We not only contain and retain energy within our physical and metaphysical organs; we also hold the energy within the Chakra System.

Our Ascension process is greatly enhanced by our using the Twelve Sacred Flames and Rays, and the Crystals and Gemstones relating to each of the Chakras.

<u>Toning</u>:

When Toning the Chakras, proceed with care. The OO sound is recommended for all. Tone softly into the higher chakras; more power can be added to the lower chakras in the way of toning. It is recommended that No overtoning should be used in applied healing to others.

Use pure sound only, as this will indicate to you when there is a blockage to the chakra. Chakra imbalance affects the tone sound that you are producing – possibly causing the sound to be wobbly, unclear or stuck. Continue toning the chakra until the sound is clear and pure; you may feel the need to change the pitch of the sound.

<u>Toning</u> (as per the chart) –

<u>Example of How to Use the Chart:</u>

On Monday, the Will of God, the Blue Ray – meditate for at least 15 minutes and hold a gemstone in each hand (the left hand is the receiver and the right hand is the transmitter); it is important to hold a gemstone in each hand.

Use the gemstones as shown on the chart.

During this meditation tone, the sound for the Blue Ray, MONG or HAM (softly) and focus on the Throat Chakra and the Thyroid Endocrine Gland.

Call in the Maha Chohan, the Chohan and the Ascended Masters, Lady Masters and the Archangel for the Sacred Flame and Ray concerned, to assist you in your Healing Journey.

<u>Intention: Set an intention based on the main qualities of the Chakra</u>

Meditations done on the day stated in the first column of the Chart for any of the Rays, will amplify the healing benefits of the Gemstones, Crystals, Toning Sounds and Intentions. The Governing Forces are strongly enhanced for the Rays on their special day.

The Twelve Sacred Flames and Rays –
Attributes and Related Gemstones

The Crystals and Gemstones mentioned in the Chart below are relevant to the attributes assigned for each of the Sacred Flames and Rays. When used in conjunction with a meditation on any of the Sacred Flames and Rays, worn as jewellery or placed within your environment, these crystals and gemstones assist you in attaining and sustaining the attributes assigned for each of the Sacred Flames and Rays.

Ray	Color	Ray Attributes	Crystals and Gemstones	Crystals and Gemstones
1	Blue	God's Will, Surrender, Power, Will-to-Good, Vitality and Discernment. Individuality, Purpose, Clear Vision, Protection, Direction and Faith. Omnipotence, Order and Focus. Activation of the Will of Mother/Father God.	Lapis Lazuli, Peacock Stones, Angelite – Blue, Turquoise – Blue, Calcite – Blue Iolite – Blue/Grey or Violet, Sodalite, Bornite – (Peacock Stone)	Sapphire – Blue, Agate - Blue Lace, Celestite, Fluorite – Clear, Herkimer Diamond, Sapphire – Indigo, Fluorite – Blue
2	Yellow	Illumination, Wisdom, and Discernment. Understanding, Precipitation, Patience, Endurance, Intuition, Clear Intelligence, Faithfulness, Perception and Discrimination. Activation of the Mind of God. Omniscience and Comprehension	Tigers Eye, Topaz – Yellow, Citrine, Amber, Peridot – Yellow or Green, Spinel – Yellow, Analcime – Yellow	Fluorite – Yellow, Sapphire – Yellow, Carnelian – Yellow, Kunzite – Yellow, Iolite – Yellow, Anatase – Yellow, Tourmaline – Yellow

3	Pink	Unconditional Love, Compassion, Omnipresence, True Brotherhood, Charity and Love in Action. Love of The Holy Spirit, Initiation of the Heart Chakra; Beauty, Devotion, Generosity and Living in the Now	Rose Quartz – Love, Pink Tourmaline – Stone of Unconditional Love, Kunzite – Pink, Strawberry Quartz Fluorite – Pink, Agate – Regency Rose	Ruby, Rubellite, Rhodochrosite, Rhodonite/ Rhodolite – Pink, Morganite – Divine Love. Coral – Pink, Kyanite – Aids Meditation
4	White	Purity, Wholeness, Clear Mindedness, Ascension, Honesty, Transparency and Protection. Christ Consciousness and becoming God through the Consciousness Of the Divine Mother. Truth, Mental Illumination, Focus and Philosophical Studies	Azurite, Chalcedony, Black Tourmaline, (Purification and Protection). Coral – White, Sapphire – White, Kunzite – Colorless, Clear Quartz (Male,) Frosted Quartz (Female)	Snow Quartz – Quartzite, Diamond, Lemurian Seed, Fluorite – Clear, Herkimer Diamond, Agate – White, Serpentine – White, Kundalini, Analcime – White
5	Green	Healing, Truth, Constancy, Creation through Manifestation, Abundance, Balance and Harmony. Common Sense, Independence, Keen Intellect, Detachment, Details, Magnetizing of Universal Energy, Intellectual, Science and Mathematics	Jade Nephrite, Chrysoprase – Green Daphnite – Deep Green, Malachite, Moss Agate, Kunzite – Green, Lepidolite, Spinel - Green	Emerald, Ruby Zozyte, Sapphire – Green, Tourmaline – Green Yttrian Fluorite – Green, Iolite – Green, Black Tourmaline, Kyanite – (Aids Meditation)

6	Ruby/Gold Orange	Love of Christ, Selfless Service to God and humanity. Devotion, Spiritual Worship through Love, Devotion and Reverence. Regeneration and Revivification. Idealism, Tenderness, Intuition, Loyalty, Resurrection and Restoration	Citrine, Calcite – Golden, Calcite – Honey, Ajoite – Angel White, Pyrite (Fool's Gold), Kunzite – Yellow, Beryl – Golden	Ruby, Red Agate, Garnet, Carnelian – Red, Strawberry Quartz, Bloodstone
7	Violet	Freedom, Forgiveness, Transmutation, Transformation, Diplomacy, Ritual and Ceremony. Strength, Courtesy, Self-Reliance, Science of True Alchemy and Unconditional Love. Connection to the Divine Spirit of All That Is	Amethyst (all), Sugilite – (Cleanses the Pathways). Ametrine, Kunzite – Lavender, Apatite – Purple, Rhodolite – Purple, Penninite - Violet	Fluorite – Violet/Purple, Kunzite – Purple, Iolite – Dark Violet, Yttrian Violet Fluorite, Agate - Purple Sage. Mica – Violet, Sapphire-Purple
8	Aqua	Certainty and Clarity; Listen to Heart; Calmness, Courage, Justice, Integrity, Unity, Stability, Balance and Harmony. Unconditional Love, Joy, Clearing and Cleansing. Understanding, Infinite Expansiveness, Transcendence, Crystalline Lightbody, Building and Wisdom	Aquamarine, Peridot – Green, Calcite – Green, Amazonite, Apatite – Apple Green, Zircon – Green, Herkimer Diamond	Chrysocolla, Nephrite Jade, Moss Agate, Adventurine, Fluorite – Green, Kunzite – Green, Plasma Agate - Green

9	Magenta	Synthesis of Rays 1-7, Attaining the Highest Potential, Truth, Joy, Splendor, Mercy, Higher Self, and Integration. Creativity, Compassion, Peace, Order, Divine Guidance, Unity, Justice, Creation of my Crystalline Lightbody. Embodying Christed Light Consciousness.	Ruby – Deep Red Garnet – Red, Jasper – Red Rhodochrosite, Rubellite, Kunzite – Lavender/ Pink, Spinel – Red, Raspberry Quartz 1-7 Syn.	Plasma Agate – Red Yttrian Fluorite – Red/ Brown, Rhodonite/ Rhodolite – Red, Coral – Red, Zircon – Red, Scapolite – Red or Pink Almandine – Deep Red
10	Opal - Pearlescent	Balance, Harmony, Justice, Love, Power, Infinite Wisdom and Self-Mastery. Detachment, Attainment, Responsibility, Peace, Direction, Opulence, Divinity and the Integration of one's I AM Presence	Moonstone – Male and Female Balance. Icelandic Spa, Milky Quartz, Orthoclase, Calcite – Milky White. Selenite – Gypsum, Kunzite – Grey, Serpentine – White	Fluorite – Clear, Dolomite, Serpentine, Opal/Pearl/ Shell – Shimmery. Agate – White. Beryllonite, Alabaster – White Gypsum
11	Peach	Illumined Truth, Joy and Serenity. Discernment, Regeneration, Healing, Rejuvenation, Regeneration and Rebirth. Strength, Kindness, Generosity, Abundance, Organization and Discernment	Agate – Peach Chrysoprase – Green, Spessartine Garnet, Spinel – Peach, Calcite – Peach, Fluorite – Colorless, Morganite Beryl, Carnelian (light).	Hessonite, Garnet – Cinnamon, Rhodochrosite, Padparadscha, (Sri Lanka). Sapphire – White, Coral – White, Calcite – Peach.

12	Gold	Oneness, Unity of Consciousness, Transfiguration, Wisdom, Understanding and Love. Devotion, Illuminating Intelligence and Power. Balance, Harmony, Peace, Inspiration, Magnetism, Creativity and Enlightenment	Citrine - Golden Celestite, Fire Agate, Pyrite, Chrysoberyle, Adventurine – Gold Carnelian (deep) Gold Nugget.	Beryl – Golden, Smokey Citrine Quartz, Fluorite – Yellow, Heliodor Beryl – Golden, Sapphire – Yellow, Tourmaline – Yellow Peridot, Kunzite – Pale Yellow.
All	Cosmic	Avatar of Synthesis Mahatma. Transparency, Immortality, Cosmic Rebirth, Integrated and the United Twelve Flames and Flames of God Consciousness, Oneness of Humanity, Cosmic Rejuvenation. Peace, Unconditional Love, Balance and Harmony to Earth.	Goshenite Beryl Tanzanite – Stone of Magic, (Personal Power and Actualization). Diamond, Apophyllite, Selenite, Sunstone (Balance), Prismatic Calcite, Spinel – Colorless, Crystal Quartz Male,	Sapphire – Clear, Herkimer Diamond Azeztulite, Coral – White, Phenacite, Topaz – Colorless, Kunzite – Clear/ Colorless, Fluorite – Colorless, Anglesite – Colorless. Crystal Quartz Female.

Afterword

Blessings to each and every person who reads and uses the healing processes in this book,

I trust that your journey throughout these prayers and processes will Support, Transform and Transport you in your Cosmic Ascension – through the many higher dimensions of this Universe, the Multiverses and Omniverse beyond.

As you become more in tune with your being and in Oneness with yourself, and your Mighty I AM Presence, you thereby become more into the Oneness, with Others, Humanity, the Elemental Kingdom and All the Kingdoms and Realms of this amazing Being that is Planet Earth, Our Beloved Mother, to whom we owe so much.

I ask that you take the time to Be in Gratitude and Bless our Beloved Mother Earth, for the Beauty and abundance that through her Great Love, Compassion and Wisdom, she gives to us freely. Go forth and stand up for her in every way that you possibly can. No effort is too small in preserving her Health and Splendor. In so doing, we give thanks and appreciation for all that we receive in this now moment of time.

As WE give, so WE receive. ALL is a Reflection of our Hearts. Let our Hearts be Free, with Boundless, Unconditional Love for ALL. And the Unconditional Love is returned, Reflected unto us as Free and Boundless, Whole, Complete and in Total Oneness with The One, the Ultimate, Supreme God of All Creation – the All That Is.

"And... So It Is!"

About the Author

Amerissis Kumara facilitates Spiritual Retreats in Australia and the United States of America; she is a Spiritual Healer, Teacher and Channel for the Elohim Council of Elders and the Ascended Masters.

Amerissis has a B.Msc; she is a Reiki Master Teacher Trainer, NLP Master Practitioner, Associate Accredited Certified Meta-Coach, Breathwork Practitioner and Transpersonal Counsellor, specializing in Spiritual Healing of Humanity and Planet Earth through the Sacred Flames and Rays of God Consciousness.

She has helped many people to elevate their consciousness and therefore achieve their Cosmic Ascension to the 5th Dimension and beyond in this lifetime.

Printed in the United States
By Bookmasters

THE
TROPHY
TREE

A Fictional Story of Illegal Immigration
along the US and Mexico Border

DAVE WILCOX

authorHOUSE®

AuthorHouse™
1663 Liberty Drive
Bloomington, IN 47403
www.authorhouse.com
Phone: 1 (800) 839-8640

Published by AuthorHouse   09/11/2019

ISBN: 978-1-5462-5433-1 (sc)
ISBN: 978-1-5462-5432-4 (e)

Library of Congress Control Number: 2018909199

Print information available on the last page.

SMART AND COMPLEX, THE TROPHY TREE IS AN INTELLIGENTLY WRITTEN STORY ABOUT ONE OF THE MOST PRESSING ISSUES FACING NORTH AMERICA TODAY. THE BOOK IS ALSO DEEPLY HUMAN, A MUST READ FOR EVERYONE.

— ARTIS HENDERSON, EDITOR

This book is proudly dedicated to my son, Kevin Wilcox for being who he is, and his twenty-year service in the United States Navy, and to the men and women of the U.S. Border Patrol whose service and dedication are rarely recognized.

ACKNOWLEDGMENT

Bob Wells's thoughtful suggestions and advice improved the content and strengthened the story. I remain grateful to him for introducing me to the writing of Cormac McCarthy.

Fellow writer Dick Rimrodt's experience and sage advice kept me on track and focused.

George and Sue Goley, and Steve Schwinn, who valiantly suffered through the first chaotic draft, and exposed my many errors.

Gil Martz for his technical and computer skills.

My wife Mary, whose support, encouragement, and patience added insight and enabled the completion of this project.

1

*L*ate for his appointment with Ignacio, whose advice he had no intention of accepting, Miguel Gutierrez increased speed, producing a dust cloud visible for miles. The old truck rattled as though complaining of the treatment.

As Miguel was a man of the desert, many plants were old friends. After a rainfall, cacti burst into a panorama of vibrant colors blending as far as the eye could see into a coalescing hue reminiscent of the Matisse landscape his wife, Maria, had shown him at the Vargas hacienda. That opulent evening and her aunt's letter from Tucson had changed everything.

Brown and gray road dust saturated roadside vegetation. Two mountain ranges soared to heights exceeding nine thousand feet. The pueblo squeezed into a valley between them beside a railroad track where an unpredictable train periodically stopped to pick up passengers for Hermosillo, the capital of Sonora State. Once a year, he and Maria took the train there to shop. Usually, they did not buy anything because they had no money.

Most Friday evenings, Miguel raced Maverick, a quarter horse he had miraculously saved from certain death when the mare died during birthing. Miguel remained in the barn until the foal survived on its own. In appreciation, Vargas gave Miguel a gold watch engraved with "Maverick," a reference to Miguel's independent reputation.

When it was clear Maverick would survive, the hacienda owner Ernesto Vargas, gave Maverick to Miguel who trained him to race. Together, they won most of the Friday races.

Miguel never intended to leave his family or Mexico. Born of the desert, a mestizo of Spanish and Indian blood and larger than most men, he expected deference. A third-generation vaquero, he worked on the thousands of acres owned by Ernesto Mendez Vargas, whose conquistador ancestors had acquired the land from the Spanish Crown in the fifteenth century. Vargas was also Mexico's secretary of the interior.

Dry, remorseless, and intimidating, the Sonora Desert had not changed in millions of years. Miguel loved its brooding temper of violent flash floods and unpredictable sandstorms. He identified with the creatures that lived in the unforgiving environment. Unlike humankind's rules, to Miguel, the Sonora Desert was always unforgiving, only survival mattered. There, human *values of right and wrong were meaningless. Either you understood and acted accordingly or you perished.*

Miguel viewed the cartel wars the same way. Having recently spent two years in the Mexican army, he had witnessed cartel violence. They wanted to acquire, expand, and protect their territory, so they acted accordingly. Extortion and smuggling drugs and people meant millions of dollars, and what the hell, everyone, including the government, got what they wanted, except, of course, the victims.

There would always be victims, his father, Jose, had taught him. Life was harsh. Humans were imperfect and vulnerable creatures. "I've never ceased to be amazed at the tragedy and violence we can impose upon each other," Jose would say while watching the sunset from his back porch.

Miguel's job was to make the most of life and protect his family. Was that not the way of the world? The cartels just wanted more. Each cartel wanted to control everything.

Such ambition was understandable, especially with the world's largest market for their products at their northern border. So far, such a life had not tempted Miguel.

Some locals had joined. Sure, they had approached him. In fact, the very man he was meeting today tried to recruit him. Vargas had convinced him to join the army instead of joining the newest cartel. Many believed that so long as you did not take sides, kept your mouth shut, and stayed out of their way, you survived. Just like the jackrabbits: as long as they avoided rattlesnakes, they survived. Besides, Las Flores was an isolated pueblo in the middle of the desert, too far from the beaten path to interest the cartels.

The narco style was too messy and too undisciplined for Miguel. He was more comfortable with military organization and efficiency, which suited his expectation of order, and, of course, military activities were usually legal.

From his military experience, he knew narcos were sloppy, vicious, undisciplined, unorganized, and illegal. He also recognized that sometimes a blurred distinction existed between the military and the cartels. In the end, only money truly mattered, especially American dollars. To Miguel what mattered most was family and survival.

Maria was the one determined to go to America. Miguel knew nothing of gringo rules, what lay beyond the border, their language, or their customs. Though skeptical about finding a better life, as she expected by simply crossing the border into Arizona and sharing a house with her aunt and uncle in Tucson, he had nevertheless reluctantly agreed to meet with Ignacio to learn how to go to America. Maria's concern about what sort of life their new son, Juanito, could expect growing up in the increasing violence of the cartel wars was a valid and important consideration. Miguel understood the danger of crossing, but she had dismissed his concerns as mere inconveniences. He had heard his father and the elders describe how the gringos had cheated the Mexicans out of half their land. "They are bullies, telling us what to do, how to live. They should clean up themselves," his father had said.

The men also said, "You can make good money there, money you can send back to your family." Moreover, the letter from Maria's aunt Rosa inviting them to come live with her and her husband reported there was plenty of work. Her aunt also suggested that Antonio, Maria's uncle, thought that with Miguel's help, they could have their own landscaping business.

A few miles outside the pueblo, Miguel passed a cross on a hill. In the afternoon heat, the scenery danced and weaved like ghosts of the ancient ones who occupied the desert in the beginning. Often, he thought of them.

At the junction, he turned onto the rutted street. Strewn about were junk cars and pickup trucks. Bottles, paper, and cardboard swirled in the small whirlwind he had caused. When he turned at the junction, he recalled the evening Maria's parents had died in an accident at that junction. A truck pulling a horse trailer crashed into their car after the Friday-evening horse races. Maria was with her cousin, aunt, and uncle at the cantina. Her father died at the scene. Her mother died a few days later. Maria had lived with her aunt and uncle at the cantina until she married Miguel.

As usual, Las Flores appeared deserted, except for a small pack of dogs meandering in the street. In the center of the pueblo, a dusty late-model SUV seemed out of place in front of the cantina. Miguel parked behind it. One of the dogs left the pack, sniffed at a wheel, and then lifted his leg. The liquid ran down it, making a moist trail through the road dust.

For almost a minute, Miguel remained motionless behind the wheel, staring at the SUV. The purpose of the meeting suddenly seemed overwhelming. His hand lingered on the door handle. There was still time to turn around and drive away. He did not know how he would explain to Maria why he did not attend the meeting. Sighing and then catching his breath, he slowly opened the door, swung his legs around, and set his boots unsteadily in the road. He slammed the door and watched the dust drop from the chassis before he turned and left the truck.

The cantina occupied a faded-green concrete-block building. An equally faded Corona sign haphazardly clung to the wall above a covered plank porch stretching across the front. Several tattered, unoccupied chairs and benches provided seats for those awaiting the bus or loitering away from the sun. The door was open, spilling narcocorrido music into the street.

Even before he entered, he smelled beer and mildew. Seconds passed before he adjusted to the dark interior. A ceiling fan rotated slowly. Maria's cousin and best friend, Inez, stood behind the bar turning the pages of a ragged gringo catalogue while her baby slept in a small carrier placed on the bar near her.

A large refrigerator with a glass door displayed Cokes, other soft drinks, and Mexican beer. A shelf nailed to the wall behind the bar held various bottles of liquor: mescal, tequila, Jose Cuervo Traditional, El Jimador, Bacardi, and Torres 10. A soiled curtain partially covered a closet door, revealing boxes containing additional bottles and cigarette cartons. Inez lived with her husband, Florio, and their baby in an attached structure accessed by a door next to the refrigerator and partially covered by a curtain.

Miguel clomped through the front door. The scratched and pitted floor planks creaked beneath his boots. Inez acknowledged him with a slight toss of her head. He removed his straw cowboy hat and nodded.

Except for a man occupying a table in the dark back corner, the cantina was empty. Miguel slowly approached and noticed a bottle of beer on the table next to a half-filled glass. A felt hat screened the man's eyes. While they were similarly dressed, Miguel noted the man's clothes. A pleated seam ran down his jeans, and his starched white shirt seemed out of place in the cantina. The boots were expensive ostrich and shiny. In contrast, Miguel's clothes were permanently dirt stained, and his cowhide boots were covered with manure. The man used a forefinger to lift the brim of his felt hat, displaying his face. Miguel recognized Ignacio.

Ignacio raised his bottle and yelled at Inez, "Bring Miguel one!"

She grabbed a glass from a tray on the bar, wiped it on her apron, took a bottle from the refrigerator, looked at her baby, and then crossed the room. She smiled at them, lifted the bottle and glass up to eye level, and poured the beer, leaving room for foam.

Ignacio clapped. Miguel joined in when she set both the glass and bottle on *the table. She smiled at them, spun around, swinging her hips with the rhythm of the music, and returned to the bar. She turned off the radio.*

"Hey, man, what's happening? It's been a long time, no? I am at your service." Without changing position, Ignacio extended his arm and dangled his hand toward Miguel.

Miguel noticed his grip was firm and his hand calloused. Miguel's recollection of Ignacio went back years. They attended the same small room at the church on the days when an itinerate priest taught there. He remembered Ignacio as a foolish boy who was always whining. The bigger boys bullied him. Now he seemed of some importance by displaying that little pile of pesos on the table for him to see, ordering Inez to get another beer, and wearing such expensive clothes, as if he were some jefe accustomed to giving orders. A confident aura and a semiautomatic pistol in his waistband made Miguel wary, like the way a lone man reacts in the desert when a hungry coyote trots toward him with the pack out of sight but not far behind.

They sized each other up. Miguel was taller. He did not want to tangle with Ignacio, unless, of course, he had to.

"Sit!" Ignacio said.

To Miguel, it was an order ... the way he ordered his dog, Rascal. His impulse was to leave, and he scowled at Ignacio. But he had promised Maria he'd hear what Ignacio had to say.

Ignacio kicked the chair toward him. Miguel spun it around and shoved it against the table. He sat straddling the back of the chair. Ignacio smirked. Miguel placed his hat on the table.

"So how is Maria?"

"Fine," Miguel replied. There is a nasty edge to him, he thought.

"And Juanito is fine also?" Ignacio wiped his hand on his jeans as though removing Miguel's dirt.

Miguel recalled that when they were school-age, Ignacio followed Maria wherever she went and promised her he would be an important man one day, able to give her the things she deserved. Miguel raised his glass to drink. He wanted to pour beer over Ignacio, stain his clothes, and wipe the smug smile from his face.

"Let's talk," said Ignacio and turned to Inez. "Leave us," he shouted.

She walked outside. Miguel watched her place the baby on the porch. She then stepped into the deserted street, lit a cigarette, and blew smoke into the stagnant air suspended like a little motionless cloud stuck there with nothing else to do. Miguel frowned and wondered why he made her leave.

"She listens and talks about what she hears. We need privacy," Ignacio noted.

Miguel shrugged.

Each man sipped his beer.

"Maria wants to live in America, right?" Ignacio asked.

Miguel nodded.

"There are several ways." He looked at Miguel as though expecting a reaction. There was none. He swiped at dust on his jeans. Ignacio held up four fingers. "You can go to an American consulate and apply for a visitor card, or visa. Or, if you have a passport, you can walk across at any border checkpoint." He paused, took a sip, and set the glass noisily on the table.

Except for the soft whir of the ceiling fan and the hum from the refrigerator, the cantina was silent.

Ignacio continued. "You can apply for a work permit if you can show you work for a gringo. Without such documents, you must sneak across the border and hope you are not caught or lost. Getting documents takes time and money. You pay the officials to get them; plus, the government charges. Peons like you ... well, they pay taxes to the police and border guards to let you pass, not to mention the cartels for allowing you to go through their territory. That is not even considering being robbed by other illegals. Once you cross into Arizona, there are bandits who will rob you or, worse, rustle your group." Ignacio paused, watching Miguel turn his hat. "Lots die in the Arizona desert," Ignacio continued as though death meant nothing. Lifting his hand, he examined his fingernails and took another swig of beer.

"You can do as Inez's parents. Pay me, and we will take you across, and you don't have to worry about the rest. We'll protect you." Ignacio let his chair settle on the floor, sat up straight, and closely watched Miguel. Finally, Ignacio stood and leaned on his arms, his hands pressing the table. "You called me. I guess you have papers and don't need my assistance. By the way, amigo, we control this plaza now, all the way to the border. I am the plaza leader and the only one who can help you."

"What do you mean by plaza?" Miguel asked.

"A plaza is the territory controlled by a cartel. We took this plaza from

the Morales Cartel. The plaza includes a trafficking corridor all the way to the Arizona border and the Nogales Port of Entry.

"You are illegal. We cannot take you through the port of entry. We cross the border using another area. From the border, you walk to a drop site and are driven to a stash house in Tucson."

"What does your assistance cost in this matter?" Miguel tried to sound sophisticated.

Again, Ignacio settled into his chair. "You plan to take Juanito? I advise against it . . . too dangerous. Babies are trouble, die, and are tossed away in the desert. Once you get settled in America, we can get him there."

"No, we discussed it," Miguel answered. "He stays here with my parents."

"Okay then. You pay me five thousand American each. Once you give it to me, I contact El Coyote and make the arrangement. You must get to the meeting place on your own. I can help you with all of that. You each pay El Coyote another thousand dollars before he takes you across."

Miguel's dislike for Ignacio grew by the second. "We don't have that much."

"Many expenses, we pay people at the border, the police, and maybe soldiers. If you can't pay it all now, you can arrange to work the debt off after you get to America. That's what most do." He pointed to Inez. "That's what her parents did. How much you got?"

Miguel had not saved much . . . maybe five hundred, plus some from his parents and a little more if he had more time. He could borrow from their families. Maria's aunt wrote in the letter she could send some. It was not enough. He did not want to try to cross without help. Perhaps if he went by himself, but with Maria, it was too dangerous.

Ignacio smiled. "You know me, and we are friends. I can help you."

Miguel squinted and looked at him.

The smile slid from Ignacio's otherwise expressionless face. "You have something I want," he noted. "We can make a deal."

"What?" Miguel could not imagine anything a man like Ignacio would want from him.

"Give me Maverick, and I'll take care of your expenses."

Miguel stared at Ignacio, who resurrected the arrogant smile.

Miguel sighed and looked away from Ignacio, realizing he had lost. Ignacio had somehow managed to find the one weakness he could not challenge . . . a *choice between Maria and Maverick. If they remained in Mexico, he could maybe protect Maria and Juanito and keep Maverick.*

Ignacio said, "You can't take Maverick with you, can you? What I am suggesting is a reasonable solution."

Miguel had not considered what he would do with Maverick. In fact, he had not thought seriously about the entire situation. He had mostly been humoring Maria until now. The beer rose up in his esophagus, and he gagged. The horse was as much a part of him as the desert.

Finally, Miguel realized the importance of a decision between leaving and remaining in Las Flores. As Maria had said, "The future for Juanito, if we stay in Las Flores, is a choice to either remain a peon working on the Vargas hacienda like you, Miguel, or join a cartel. Is that what you really want, Miguel?" He knew she was right. It was his job to make things better for the three of them.

He had loved her from the moment he first saw her kneeling in church. Her black hair flipped about her face when she turned her head as he passed, and she smiled at him.

Miguel's hand shook as he drank from the glass until it was empty. Ignacio walked behind the bar to the refrigerator and removed another bottle, returned to the table, and poured it into Miguel's glass.

"There are considerations. I have to think," Miguel said.

Miguel had been told he might be placed in charge of the hacienda's horses. He had dreamed of this opportunity. Maria told Miguel that Vargas would never do something like that for a peon like Miguel, and besides, Ignacio had assured her they could do much better in America.

Miguel needed to think. He had to ride Maverick into the desert, see the mountains and the clouds, feel the sun, and let the spirits whisper to him and clear his head. Such a decision could not be rushed.

Miguel looked at Ignacio and said, "I'll let you know."

Ignacio stood and started to walk toward the door but then turned and looked at Miguel. "We need men like you. If you join us, you and Maria can cross for free. With us, you will be paid more than you get from Vargas. He recommended you by name, Miguel, when he heard you might leave."

"I don't understand. How would he know? I have said nothing, nothing about leaving. Who said such a thing?" He grasped the edge of the table, his hands turning white from the strength of his grip. He paused, trying to distill

his thoughts and then shook his head and said, "Vargas is part of this Sonora Cartel … He recommended me? I don't understand."

Ignacio looked down at Miguel and held his eyes until Miguel looked away. "He knows your reputation in the army. He followed your activities there. He said you are a leader and said your commander was disappointed you did not consent to officer's training."

"I'd have to reenlist. I just wanted to be home with the family, not hunting drug lords." He shook his head. "The army," He stammered. "They do things. I did things there. Sometimes it's hard to tell the difference between …" He shook his head again, trying to stop the pounding and looked out through the doorway. Inez stood on the porch in the shadows.

"This is war, Miguel, a war between the Morales Cartel and the new one, the Sonora Cartel. I am the plaza leader for Sonora and control plaza territory. Men with your reputation, Miguel, cannot escape this fight. You must pick a side. Think of Maria, Juanito, and your parents."

"No! They cannot be part of this. They can't hurt anyone."

"They are the insurance. You must realize there will be no escape from a decision. This is all on you now. You know how to find me."

Ignacio left. Inez returned. She looked at Miguel's glass, nodded, walked to her station behind the bar, and brought a new bottle.

Miguel held the glass between his hands, absorbing the coolness. He wanted to forget Ignacio and not think about the past or try to anticipate the future. Yet he knew what Ignacio said was true. He had witnessed what the cartels did to hostages.

No longer was their life clear and simple as he had hoped when he had returned home. He could keep Maverick, continue to race him, and try to ignore Maria's concerns. It might even be smarter to remain with Juanito. With the cartels fighting, he could protect him and his parents.

But maybe crossing was simple after all. They did not have much to lose if they tried. If caught by the dreaded US Border Patrol, it was not a big deal. They would just send them back, Maria had said. Yet leaving his family was an immense sacrifice. If Miguel was correct about the danger to them if the cartel war reached Las Flores, that danger would be eliminated if they joined Maria's family in Tucson.

Later, after Miguel returned to the compound, he walked to the small pasture. He spotted Maverick grazing at the far side and whistled. Maverick lifted his head, looked at Miguel, and trotted to him. Miguel stepped through the gate. He placed feed in the rack, took the bucket, pumped in water, and hung it from a hook. He did the same for the older horse. He grasped Maverick's halter and walked Maverick to the corral where his father, Jose, sat on the top rail.

Jose climbed down from the rail and held the lead while Miguel brushed Maverick.

"Maria is determined to go north," Miguel said. "She hasn't talked about it before. She's unhappy here and thinks it's too dangerous for Juanito."

"Women must have their say. She talked to your mother."

"She did? She only got a letter from her aunt yesterday."

The withers trembled as he moved the brush down Maverick's flank. "No, not yesterday maybe a couple of weeks ago. Inez was there. They talked about it. I heard them. Inez said they were thinking about going too. I thought it was nothing. You know many people talk about it, and it usually means nothing. I didn't see any reason to mention it to you."

Miguel reached down and lifted a front leg. With a pick, he removed the caked dirt from the hoof. When he was done, they left the corral, leading Maverick to the trailer. Jose watched while Miguel walked Maverick. Together, they loaded Maverick inside. A saddle, blanket, and bridle were already in the truck. The race was between two horses. They had to run a quarter mile beside the railroad track.

When they arrived, men were waiting in the parking area. Jose and Miguel removed Maverick from the trailer. Jose slipped on the bridle and held the reins while Miguel mounted. Maverick tossed his head, blowing and prancing. Miguel turned him in small circles to calm him and then led him to the starting gate.

"Go with God," Jose said and pushed, shoving Maverick inside before turning to the men to write down their bets.

Miguel bent forward and patted Maverick on the neck. Lowering his head next to Maverick's ear, he said, "You can outrun any horse. Make us proud."

With a sound of whistles and ringing bells, the gates flew open. From a dead stop, Maverick was full speed by the second stride. Dust rose, and the horses' hooves pounded the ground like drums. Miguel leaned forward and encouraged the horse. He felt the power surge between his thighs. The wind blurred his eyes. The mane swept his face.

The men cheered when he passed the finish line first. Dust settled on them and drifted farther down the tracks. Miguel walked Maverick until he cooled. As they walked, he told Maverick how proud he was of him, patted his neck, and wiped him with a towel. Miguel smiled, and the men crowded around, congratulated him, and shook his hand.

"Glad you are back," a man shouted.

The others cheered, followed by another round of handshakes. He thanked them while Jose collected their winnings.

The following morning, Miguel rode Maverick bareback into the desert. Rascal ran with them for half a mile and then returned to the compound as they began to ascend a trail that led up the mountain to a lookout on a narrow ridge. He felt part of the animal, as though he were Chiron, a half-man, half-horse Centaur from Greek mythology. When he was young, the itinerant priest and teacher at their one-room school in the church in Las Flores told the story of a mythical creature with a horse's body and the torso, arms, and head of a man. Miguel still remembered. He had thought of himself as Chiron, someone who had sacrificed his life so Prometheus could live. His own valor, however, remained untested.

Last night's rain left the desert in a colorful bloom of millions of flowers stretching as far as he could see. The aroma fresh on the breeze cleansed the air.

Miguel swung his right leg over Maverick's haunches while holding the reins in his left hand, slid to the ground, and stood next to the horse. The compound appeared small and insignificant in the vastness of the desert.

The sun crested the mountain, pleasantly warming his back. Soon, he would have to return home to meet Jose and the work bus. For a few moments, the serenity was an engulfing blanket, sheltering him from acknowledging the decision while Maverick carried him to the ridge. He looked below, into the area the patron let them occupy. Never had it seemed so small.

He watched Jose walk to the outhouse. At this distance, he was a miniature figure, wearing his felt sombrero, a gift from the patron for completing a project long since forgotten. Small, however, was not an adjective used to describe his father. Jose taught him how to be a man by both words and example. They had built the compound together. Future improvements were now, of course, out of the question.

From Miguel's perspective upon the mountain, he attempted to see the compound from Maria's point of view. A speck on a vast, empty desert was *not the place for a woman. He knew she did not understand the desert. To Miguel, the Sonora Desert was a thriving and vibrant world of predictable behavior with rigid rules for survival. His mother managed and sometimes complained, but she never had an interest in America, for her life was about acceptance and family.*

Dreams belonged to Maria and Inez: beautiful dresses, parties, movie stars, big houses, and fancy cars. They listened to narcocorridoes, a popular music genre that glamorized the narco lifestyle in a garish, screaming sound passing for music. The boys fantasized about being bad-ass narcos with pockets of dollars, AK-47s, and girls clinging to each arm. Miguel shunned that fantasy, leaving it to Ignacio and the others.

Ignacio and Maria were correct, he reluctantly acknowledged. Times had changed. Juanito's future in Las Flores was dismal. He would either join a gang or remain a farmworker all his life. There was no choice. Maria's aunt and uncle had left last year. They were in Tucson. Without them, Miguel knew Maria felt isolated.

At least they had a destination. Never had he felt such dread and despair. He rose, looped the reins over Maverick's head, and swung onto the horse's back. As he edged Maverick forward, he knew this was their last ride.

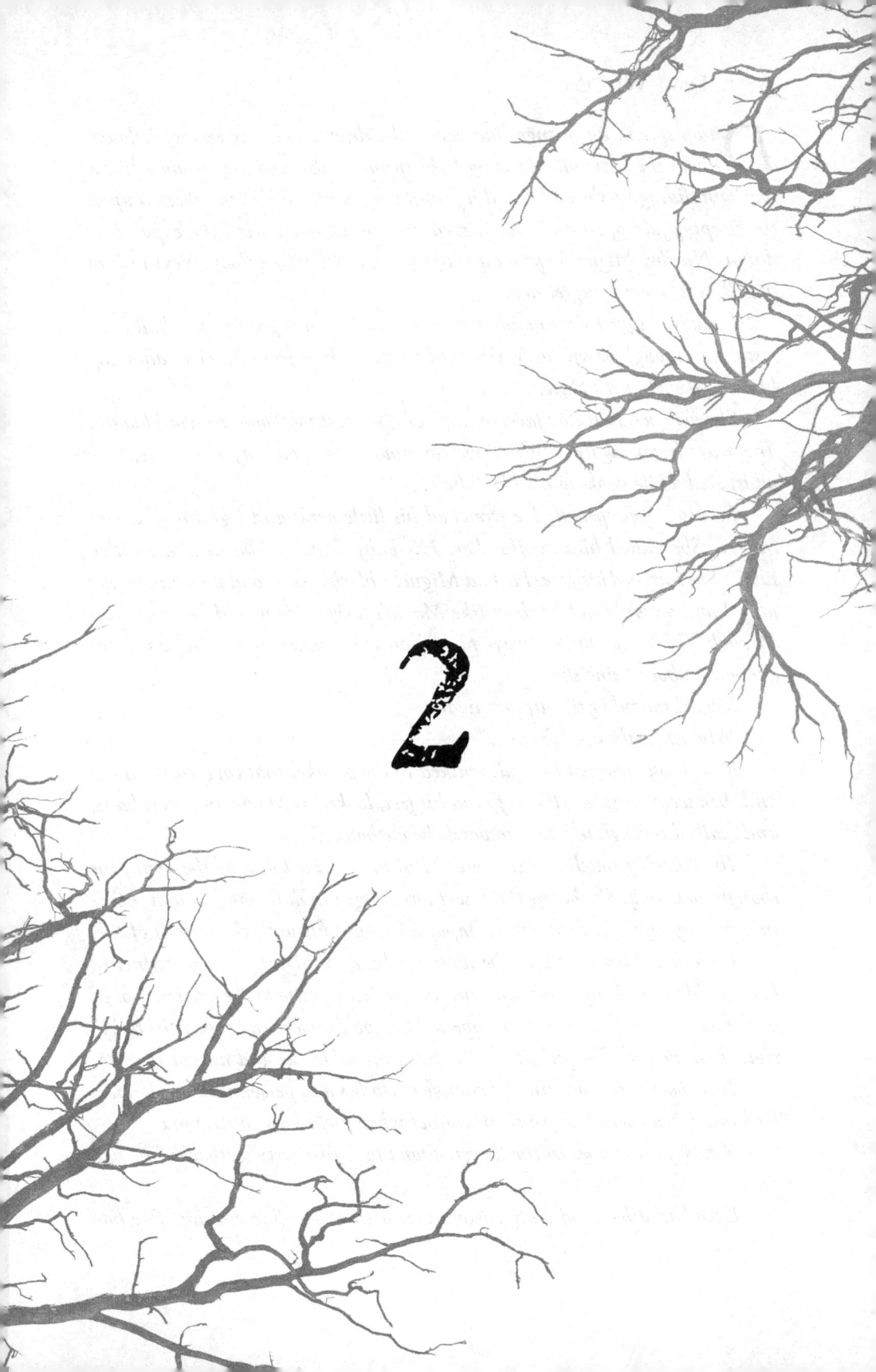

2

*D*awn spread an orange hue across the desert. The sun emerged slowly above the horizon. Morning light funneled through the window like a spotlight sliding up the wall until it found the crucifix and then reflected upon the sleeping face of Maria. She stirred and rolled away from the expanding dawn. Nearby, Miguel slept on a tattered mattress on the floor. Next to him was Rascal, their mongrel dog.

Usually, Miguel slept beside her on the bed. Last night Juanito had been restless, as though he knew. Maria had retrieved him from his crib, allowing him to take Miguel's place.

She watched Juanito's face, so innocent, so trusting. Soon, he would walk. The tears began again. "What we do now is for you, my little one," she whispered while stroking his black hair.

Juanito's eyes opened. He stretched his little arms and legs and watched Maria. She pulled him against her. His baby skin was warm and smelled sweet. She searched his face. He had Miguel's black eyes, broad nose and strong jaw. Juanito would not be short like Maria's father. He would be strong like Miguel. The bigger men always picked on the smaller ones. Life was hard enough without being short.

Miguel snored softly, almost awake.

"Miguel, wake up. It's time!"

Rascal rose, wagged his tail, walked to the blanket that covered the door, and then went outside. Miguel found his feet, looked at Maria and their baby, and walked through the door toward the outhouse.

The morning smelled of creosote. Must have rained during the night, she thought to herself. She heard the desert wren begin its daily song from its home in a nearby saguaro. Soon, the compound would fill with the sounds of life. Tears moistened her cheeks as she watched Juanito. Sighing, she straightened her shoulders. Shifting her attention, she carried Juanito to the dresser, looked at the worn letter from her aunt, opened the top drawer, and tossed the baby's clothes on the bed. She pulled a chair from the table, sat and nursed Juanito.

Their backpacks contained a change of clothes and personal items. Ignacio had instructed them to have clean clothes when picked up in Arizona.

"Leave your clothes in the desert. Don't look like dirty wetbacks," he had said.

Each had a bottle of water. More was available before crossing. She had *folded and placed their new athletic shoes, jeans, shirts, underwear, and jackets in their backpacks.*

Miguel carried the cradle and backpacks to his parents' casa. Maria placed Juanito in the cradle. Breakfast was frijoles, corn tortillas, and coffee. Miguel's mother, Yolanda, gave each a lunch bag.

"We'll send money when we get some," Miguel said.

Yolanda began to cry. Miguel and Maria walked hand in hand to the table. Smiling, Juanito looked first at Maria and then Miguel.

"We don't know when we will see you again," Maria said, lifting him. "I will not see you walk." She held him so that Miguel was able to enclose both of them in his arms. Together, they placed Juanito into the cradle and then slowly turned away with Miguel's arm around her waist, her head against his chest.

"We must go now," Miguel said, checking his watch. Jose gathered their backpacks, containing all their worldly possessions, and tossed them onto the truck. Miguel followed him as he had all of his life in almost everything.

They turned toward the corral. Maverick was in the far corner. He lifted his head and trotted toward them, stopping at the gate. Jose and Miguel both approached the horse and stood quietly while Miguel stroked his nose.

When he turned back to Jose, there were tears in both their eyes. Miguel stretched out his hand. That was not enough. They clasped each other in a long, lingering embrace, turned, and looked around the compound to all the things they had accomplished together. Their plans for additional improvements would never be realized. Miguel could not look back at Maverick. When he turned toward the truck, Rascal ran to him and stood on his hind legs, his front paws on Miguel's legs. Miguel squatted and pulled the dog against him.

Maria took her backpack to their casa where she shoved her modest collection of jewelry and a silver broach from her grandmother into a small pouch she hung from her neck. She remembered that Miguel had told her to leave her valuables with his parents. She shoved them into her backpack along with a picture of Juanito and her aunt's letter. She then held up her head and walked from their casa.

Two hundred American dollars were in a leather pouch hung around Miguel's neck. They had agreed to work off a balance of $10,000 after they arrived in Tucson. A sheet of paper from Ignacio with instructions, a hastily drawn map, and the telephone number, address, and phone number of Maria's aunt were in Miguel's pocket. They squeezed into the truck's cab. When they *approached the small pasture, Maverick was at the fence. Lifting his head, he trotted inside the fence until it ended. Miguel looked away. Silently, they continued toward Las Flores.*

Leaving Juanito was the hardest thing Maria had ever done. It seemed like the right solution until last night when reality had set in. Maybe it was a mistake to leave Juanito behind. Ignacio refused to estimate how long it might take to send for Juanito. Would Juanito even remember her by then? Really, she wondered. How hard could it be for the few days it will take us to cross the border? Men always exaggerate everything. Miguel's concern about her stamina to complete the journey was annoying. She was strong. Miguel was experienced. Ignacio said El Coyote was the best. She wondered what he would be like. Because Ignacio was in charge of the plaza and all the smugglers, she was confident he would not let anything happen to her. Yes, leaving was best. Regardless, now it was decided. The desert flashed past. Soon, she'd be gone for good. She saw the cross on the hill. "Be there soon," she sighed.

At the cantina, Inez gave Maria and Miguel each a gallon of water in a plastic jug. Maria and Inez then went to the corner to talk. She waited inside with Inez and her baby while Miguel rocked slowly in a porch chair reading the map and instructions from Ignacio. After an hour, an approaching dust cloud turned into the rickety bus that was to take them to a small village beyond Hermosillo where they would spend the night in an old church that took in travelers.

The bus dropped them at a small pueblo. They walked to the church that Ignacio had noted on the map. Miguel rang the bell next to the closed gate. Through the gate, Maria saw the church, a graveyard, and a small house. The wall seemed to surround the entire property.

"Just like a prison," Miguel said.

The corner of a one-story building was visible, along with several live oak trees and benches, all just as Ignacio had described.

"That must be the barracks," Miguel said.

An older gringo walked from the house toward the gate. "I am Father Michael," he said. "How can I help you?"

"We were told we could spend the night here. We'll leave here tomorrow," Miguel began.

"Yes, yes," Father Michael interrupted, looking at their backpacks. "I see." He opened the gate. When they entered, he stepped outside and looked both ways. He locked the gate. "Follow me please."

Father Michael led them to the house. Invited inside, they followed him to a small sitting room with a soiled sofa and two worn chairs. He motioned them to the sofa and then sat at one of the chairs beside a table on which were neatly stacked sheets of papers.

They set their backpacks on the floor between their feet. A small woman entered the room with water. They drank the water and leaned back into the sofa, sinking into the stuffed pillows that had long ago lost their stuffing and support. Maria sighed, rolled back her head, moved it from side to side, and rubbed her eyes. She felt dirty.

"You plan to go to America," Father Michael said.

They nodded.

"You were told of this place by the person who made the arrangements."

Again, they nodded.

"They tell of the church where we can take you in, supposed to be safe here. No one will harass you. That is not the same after you leave." He shook his head and looked sternly at Maria.

Maria tried to settle into a more comfortable position by leaning back, but the couch was worn, and she thought it better to slide to the front edge where she could at least get her feet to touch the floor.

"There are some things I must tell you," Father Michael said, looking at her.

She thought he sounded like someone who had given this same speech many times. On the wall behind Father Michael was a picture of the Virgin of Guadalupe. Maria thought she was watching them.

"I came here as a missionary when I was much younger. The church in America supports my work here, as does the Mexican government and the local mayor." The priest frowned, carefully scrutinizing Miguel. Finally, he focused on Maria, through eyes that Maria thought seemed to be inspecting her soul. "This is your first time to cross, yes?"

"Yes, Padre," she said, wondering how long this was going to take. She heard Miguel sigh.

"You can only stay here this night. I have room. A dining room is through there." He pointed to the door the woman had entered through.

Maria saw part of a table.

"Where do you live?" he asked.

"Las Flores," Maria replied.

"That's not so far. Many come from as far away as Guatemala and stay. Everyone thinks it will be better in America." Father Michael sighed and shook his head. *"It is not so nice."* He paused and continued to watch Maria.

She sighed, rolled back her head, moved it from side to side, and rubbed her eyes. She still felt dirty.

"You are married, are you not?" He did not wait for a response. *"And you have children."*

"Yes, a small baby. His name is —"

Father Michael raised his hand and shook his head. "Please, I don't want to know any names. Go back to Las Flores! Forget about America. It is a long and dangerous trip. Much can happen to you. The desert is treacherous. There are banditos. Many illegals get sick and die or are left behind."

Maria looked at Miguel, hoping he would say something to make the priest hurry, and then turned back to Father Michael and said, "Padre, we are strong and healthy and young. We are used to the desert. We have lived there all our lives."

Miguel glanced at her and then looked down.

"Do you have family in America?" Father Michael asked.

"Yes, my aunt and uncle live in Tucson."

"How do you get there?"

"El Coyote will take us to a stash house. Then we call my aunt. She will tell us what to do."

"I see." Father Michael said. Taking a deep breath, he looked away from her and toward the window before turning to Miguel. *"This is what everyone is told. Do you have work in Las Flores?"*

"I work on a hacienda. We live in a compound. My family has lived there for generations," Miguel replied.

"You are lucky ... more fortunate than most. Go back there."

Maria gasped, surprised at the priest's emphatic response. "We want a better life, Padre. We can never have anything here. Now, it is not even safe. Gangs take everything. They will take our son. My aunt, she says it is much better there even if you are illegal. I have her letter." She reached into her backpack, but he waved it away and glimpsed at Juanito's photo as it fell out of her backpack.

"Not necessary to see." Pausing, he sighed. "Perhaps you should dispose of that picture."

"Padre, that is my baby! I need a picture of my baby."

"If they see a baby picture, they may try to find the baby, steal it, or, worse, sell it."

She gasped and turned to Miguel. "Ignacio never spoke of such things, nor did my aunt. They know best. This can't be true." She was sure Ignacio would have told her if such things were true. She believed the priest was just trying to scare them.

"Give me the picture," Miguel said and held out his hand.

"Miguel, no!" His expression was intense.

"Tear it up!"

"That's best," agreed Father Michael.

Miguel yanked the picture from her hand and tore it apart. She struck him.

"Always the same, every time." Father Michael looked at Miguel, who kept his eyes on the floor. "I still say it is best you return to Las Flores, but I see you are determined, like all of them." He paused, shifting his penetrating gaze first to one and then the other.

Maria held his eyes. Miguel continued to study the floor.

Father Michael shrugged and rose as though he had done all he could do to dissuade them. "Tonight, you have dinner here. In the morning, you will take a lunch from the table, water bottles, and go catch the train."

He then took a paper from the table. "Here!" He handed it to Miguel. "The open border people have prepared this paper for you if you can read. It is in Spanish. Along the trails in Arizona, you may find places where they have placed blue water containers. A blue flag is sometimes visible from a distance. Having water is important, a gallon each."

Miguel started to speak, but again, Father Michael interrupted him. "Yes, I know a gallon is heavy. You can live out there without food for a while but not without water. This paper has numbers to call if you need help after you cross: the sheriff, border patrol, open-border groups, and churches that provide sanctuary. Also, it shows some landmarks and trails in case you are lost or left behind."

Father Michael walked to the sofa. "This is important." He pointed to the paper in his hand. "Here's the phone number of the Mexican Consulate. Inform the Mexican authorities if you are arrested or mistreated. Here is a list of your rights if caught." He looked at Maria and then at Miguel. "Questions?"

"What's an open-border group?" she asked.

"An organization that advocates no borders between Mexico and the United States, so people can cross freely without being stopped."

Maria took the paper from Miguel, looked at it, and gave it back to Miguel.

"Also, churches and other sanctuaries are listed along with phone numbers. You have rights. The US Border Patrol is too aggressive, too anxious to use force. We encourage migrants to press charges."

"What are rights … Rights for what?" Miguel asked.

"The people who catch you must treat you well. That's the law there. More questions?"

They shook their heads. Maria glanced at Miguel.

"Okay then. The rail yard is a half mile from here." Father Michael pointed north. "The train is called the Beast and may leave somewhere around six thirty in the morning. Best to get there early. The police watch. If they catch you, they will ask you for money or arrest you. In addition, others will try to get you to go across with them. Do you have arrangements to cross? If not, there are boys who can take you over, for a price of course. Oh, and some migrants on the train may try to rob you. You must be careful. You can't trust anyone."

Maria felt Father Michael's eyes dig into her while she looked down at the floor. She heard him say to Miguel. "It is not too late. Take the bus. Go back to Las Flores!"

Miguel looked at her.

"Padre, it is not your place to tell us what to do," Maria said, wondering why Ignacio had not explained all this.

Father Michael said, "The women, they …" He shook his head slowly and looked into her unflinching eyes. "The women," he repeated, turning back to Miguel, "are vulnerable, very vulnerable."

The older woman who had served them water when they arrived walked into the room. "Others are waiting," she said with her hands on her hips, tapping a foot on the floor.

Father Michael stood and made the sign of the cross over Maria and

Miguel. *"Be careful climbing on the train. Many are killed."* He slowly shook his head, looking at her. *"If I don't see you in the morning, go with God."*

On benches under the live oak trees in the courtyard, Maria had seen people of various ages with anonymous faces sitting quietly or sleeping.

Now, despite the presence of others, for the first time in her life, Maria felt utterly alone. The more she was learning, the more concerned she became. She was upset that Ignacio had not informed her of all the problems, if, indeed, the priest was correct. Yet convinced she would be able to manage, she remained anxious to get going, reunite with her aunt and uncle, and begin their life in a new world. In a way, though, this experience was an adventure. Also, she knew the sooner they settled in Tucson, the sooner they would get Juanito.

Miguel, however, dreaded what lay ahead. He felt lost in a vacuum of unreality, as though the world had become an illusion while he stood outside watching life unfolding around him. The priest's concern about the vulnerability of women languished in the back of his mind like a poisonous pond in the desert, luring the unsuspecting to drink.

Miguel and Maria found the elongated windowless box of a room that reminded him of a windowless military barrack. The stench of human sweat nearly overwhelmed him. Because the two rows of cots along opposite walls did not have two unoccupied adjacent beds, Miguel led Maria to a single bed in the back corner. She lay down while he sat on the floor between her bed and the thin bathroom wall. Maria quickly fell asleep.

On the floor, wedged into the corner with his knees practically in his face, Miguel knew he would be listening to the flushing toilet all night. Sleep seemed impossible. Darkness spread into the unlighted room, Miguel rose and walked outside into the fresh air. The moon was nearly full and illuminated the courtyard in a ghostly effervescence. Beneath a grasping banyan tree, a sudden glow and the smell of tobacco drew Miguel's attention to a young man sitting on the ground smoking a cigarette.

"Where you from?" Miguel asked.

"Guatemala. I left three weeks ago. I go by buses and trains and walking."

A drag on the cigarette eerily lit his face. He was young, maybe fourteen, Miguel guessed. *"Alone?"*

"No, with my brother. They were going to kill us."

"Who?"

"The gangs who take money from our father. He didn't have more to pay, so they said they would kill us. So, we go north for money like many others."

Miguel looked around for the brother. "Where's your brother?"

"Dead. He fell off the Beast. A wheel sliced his head off."

"The Beast? What's that?"

"The train everyone rides to get here from Guatemala. You sit on top of the boxcars. Goes all the way from Guatemala to Arizona. It stopped here yesterday."

Miguel remembered the priest's instructions about the train. "You're not going back now?"

"To what? They may be all dead by now. Have to make some money and try to go back and pay the gang. They may still kill my family."

"You are traveling with others?" Miguel questioned.

"No."

"What's your name?"

"Emilio, yours?"

"Miguel."

Emilio stood almost as tall as Miguel. "Taking the Beast tomorrow?"

"Yes. With my wife."

"I saw you when you passed. Maybe we can help each other."

"How far are you going?"

"To the United States. They say there is plenty of work. You can send money back to Guatemala."

"I don't know about the work," Miguel noted. "We have family there. We'll stay with them until we get a place. How old are you?"

Fifteen."

"What work you do?"

"Whatever needs doing. I work hard like my father and my brother. We had a store, gone now, I think. Maybe when we get there, you think we can work together? Did you work there where you are from?"

"Yes. I was to be in charge of the horses maybe, at a big hacienda."

"Why you leave there then?"

"We have baby and want a better life for him. Lots of trouble here."

"Where's baby?"

"Stays with his grandparents until we can get him." Suddenly, Miguel remembered Father Michael's caution. "Got to go back inside now." He *was uncomfortable with the conversation, remembering Father Michael's warning about what can happen if a cartel or gang gets hold of a baby. Maybe Emilio, because he seemed almost desperate for money, would willingly supply information to someone regarding Juanito.*

Miguel returned to the darkened dorm, encountering a variety of sounds: crying babies, snores, coughing, moans, and muffled voices. Maria remained asleep. Weary, he stretched his long body along the wall, used his backpack for a pillow, and succumbed to a fitful sleep.

3

*M*iguel held Maria's arm and looked down the track. They were behind a storage shed, waiting since five thirty until it was light enough to sneak aboard the train. Fifty yards away someone dashed from behind a building only to be stopped by a police officer. The officer's back was to Miguel.

"Let's go!" Miguel said, shoving Maria toward a railcar. Without stopping, Miguel grabbed her wrist with one hand, half dragging her the twenty yards to the boxcar. He grasped the ladder, swung onto the first rung, and then climbed to the second, yanking her onto the first rung just as the train whistle screeched into the expanding dawn.

Like a nest of disturbed fire ants, people swarmed from the shadows and rushed toward them. The wheels behind the engine screeched. Each coupling yanked the following car, sending a jolt through the length of the train, finally reaching the front coupling of their car.

A loud and sudden lurch almost threw Maria off the train into the frantic crowd shoving to get to the ladder. Miguel's weakening grip on her wrist held while she dangled in midair, a human pendulum swinging away from the car. Miguel clung to the ladder with his other hand. Others attempted to pull her from him, and his grip slowly weakened. Just then, he saw a figure shove through the frenzied crowd, jump to the ladder, grasp her around the waist, and lift her high enough to grasp the next rung. The man covered her body with his own and held both sides of the ladder pinning her there as the boxcar swayed. Miguel crawled onto the roof. He reached over the edge and pulled Maria up behind him. Miguel saw the man's head, and then a face appeared. Miguel recognized Emilio. With Emilio on the roof, they looked for a safe place with decent handholds.

"Thanks for your help," he said to Emilio. "I won't forget this."

The train increased speed. All possible handholds were taken. Two boys were close by. A searing glance from Miguel made them move.

A young man attempting to climb the ladder on the car behind them was not as lucky. Miguel watched him running beside the train, reaching to grasp the ladder rung. Men tugged at him. He slipped, lost his grip, fell, and then dragged along the tracks until he disappeared beneath the following car.

The Beast gathered speed. Their car swayed precariously, requiring them to concentrate on maintaining secure grips. Two men carefully crawled around them and grabbed handholds farther along the roof. A third clung to the *ladder, and another straddled the coupling. Those on the roof warned of bridges and overhanging trees.*

"How could we have done this with Juanito?" Maria asked. "Ignacio's advice to leave him was correct. I told you he knows best."

Late in the afternoon, the train pulled into a station. Before it stopped, people jumped off and ran toward the woods.

"Where are we?" Miguel asked a man.

"El Huerfano," came the response.

Huerfano was their second day's destination, according to Ignacio's map. They followed those heading north toward an opening in the trees and the location of a trail leading north. During the day as they followed the trail, Miguel periodically noticed Emilio following at a long distance.

"This is an ancient Indian trail," Miguel said to Maria, recalling Ignacio's explanation. "The trail takes us to Huerfano. There, we meet our group. Following this trail north beyond Huerfano leads to the border. Ignacio said locating the route into and through Arizona requires knowledge and experience to find the drop site."

While light remained, Miguel selected a grove of pecan trees in which to spend the night. The sound of nearby traffic indicated they were not far from a major highway. Coyotes howled in the distance. Small creatures scurried about them in the darkness. Maria questioned every noise. His arm turned numb from her grasp. Near midnight, the moon disappeared into a jumble of clouds, and a drenching rain soaked their clothes and backpacks. Sleep was impossible. By morning, they were shivering in wet clothes. When they heard others shuffling along the trail, they joined them.

Walking and a warming sun helped to dry their clothes. Nothing prevented the trail mud from finding every porous entry in their shoes.

Finally, they reached Altar. At a small grocery, they bought food and more water. A young man approached them as they left the store.

"Do you intend to cross the border?" he asked.

Miguel looked around and saw several illegals speaking with a muchacho. One tapped him on the shoulder and said, "I will take you to the border tonight. Only two thousand dollars per person. If you don't have that much, you can work it off once you get there. No problem. You then cross with a coyote."

Maria pointed to several people following another boy behind the store.

"We don't need your help," Miguel said.

Ignacio had explained there would be many boys trying to get business for coyotes. He had explained to Miguel that some people would be robbed and not taken across. Others would be taken to the border then left on their own to find their own way.

According to Ignacio, illegals who had not made previous arrangements were the most vulnerable to bandits. They were the people most likely to be caught and sent back to Mexico.

Following Ignacio's instructions, they found the trail next to the river shown on Ignacio's map.

"My feet hurt," Maria said after walking several miles on the rugged trail.

Miguel knew she was tired and wanted to rest. They saw the trail ascending a mountain ahead of them. They looked at each other and nodded. "We must be there on time," she said.

The trail narrowed. The vegetation changed as they climbed higher. Now Miguel recognized gray thorn, ocotillo, yucca, juniper, evergreen oak, and pinyon pine. They climbed carefully to keep from stepping on loose stones. The trail meandered into a cluster of trees where a freshwater spring and a light breeze cooled them. They continued until dusk and slept in a small cave with a soft moss floor. He had lost track of Emilio.

At dawn, they began negotiating the rocky trail. Dark clouds gathered behind the mountains to the east. Around noon, the storm broke. By the time they reached their second stop, the afternoon sun had partially dried their clothing. They located the store where they expected to meet El Coyote who was to take them across the border the following day. Others arrived asking for El Coyote. They decided to spend the night on the ground beside the small store with the others.

Behind the store, a windmill pumped water from a well to a small water tower over a shower stall. A rope tied to a showerhead attached to a hose leading from the bottom of the tank supplied water. A few boards stuck haphazardly to the forms supporting the tank, almost providing incidental privacy. Maria showered in her clothes in the cold water.

Near dusk, a swirling dark cloud approached like a small ominous intruder. The cloud became a dirt-stained pickup truck that stopped in front of the store where Miguel and Maria, along with thirteen others, were preparing to spend the night.

When the dust cloud trailing the truck caught up to where they stood, it blocked their view of the vehicle. Miguel heard a door open. After it closed, he noticed three men covered in dust sitting in the truck bed. They removed the bandanas covering their faces. They resembled muskrats with patches of road dust in places not covered by the bandana. One man rummaged under a tarp and removed an AK-47 and backpack. From the backpack, he removed a rag and wiped down the weapon. He vaulted over the side. He took an attack pack chest rig containing multiple magazines and put it on. Holding the AK, he stood next to the passenger door.

A broad-shouldered, big-bellied man emerged wearing blue jeans, hiking boots, a long-sleeved blue shirt, and a baseball cap that read NYC. A holster attached to his belt held a 9 mm Glock semiautomatic pistol. From the rear of the truck under the tarp, he removed two backpacks, gallon jugs of water, and a camouflage jacket.

As the man leaned into the truck, Miguel noticed a knife in a sheath tucked in the middle of his back sticking partially out of his jeans. He recognized it as a KA-BAR seven-inch fighting knife. The man with the AK-47 watched the group.

Maria clutched Miguel's arm. He felt her shiver. "That's the meanest looking man I've ever seen," she whispered.

After apprising the group, the man with the knife stopped in front of Miguel and Maria. He looked up at Miguel. Miguel noted the harsh facial line that looked like a dried-up river bed in the middle of summer. Maybe in his early forties, his expressionless face lacked any pretense of human kindness. His black eyes seemed hollow seemingly, stuck into narrow sockets like a death mask.

The man looked Maria up and down, smiled, and stepped back. He lifted his arm, making a small circle over her head. "Let's see the rest." She did not move. He said to Miguel, "Is she your wife?"

"Si," Miguel answered.

The man nodded. "Nice." He reached out to touch her face. She tried to pull away, and Miguel instinctively stepped in front of her. The man's eyes became slits. The two men stared at each other without either giving ground. The man sneered at Miguel, rested his hand on the Glock, turned, and walked toward the others who had surrounded them in a tight little circle to observe the confrontation.

"Get in a line facing me. Quickly!"

Except for Miguel and Maria, the group rushed to comply. Miguel waited until the line formed and then led Maria to the end where they joined.

"I am El Coyote; I am the boss of this plaza. I will lead you into Arizona to a drop site. There, you get transportation. The most important thing is you do as I tell you when I tell you. Many people, especially illegals, die here. No one cares. You keep up, or I leave you. Now make two lines, one for men and another for women."

He gestured toward the areas he expected them to stand. When they complied, El Coyote began carefully inspecting each one. The man with the AK-47 stood nearby. Finished with the men, El Coyote approached the three women and two teenage girls, ran his hands over their bodies, and slid his hands down their legs. He checked their backpacks and plastic bags.

He then took a small paper from his shirt pocket. "Who is Miguel?" El Coyote barked.

"Here!" Miguel replied.

"So, it is you. This must be Maria. You two stand over there. The rest of you must give me a thousand dollars except for Miguel and Maria here. If you don't have the money, you leave now. Or, we can work out an arrangement." He turned and smiled at Maria.

He collected the money from each, and after carefully dividing it in half, he stuffed it under his shirt. He walked to Maria. "So, you are Maria. You, I won't forget. Ignacio told me about you. He did not exaggerate." He pointed to Miguel and then looked at the bleary-eyed guard with the AK. "Does Miguel look tough to you, amigo?"

"No," the man said, smiling a nearly toothless grin.

"Me either."

They stood in the middle of the street in a valley between rocky hills. The group consisted of seven men, two teenage girls, three grown women, and three teenage boys. The girls seemed to be with parents. The boys traveled alone.

A dry creek bed of stones was adjacent to the road and extended north through a growth of oaks along the valley's edge leading toward a higher range of hills somewhere near the border. The sun was about ten degrees above the hills and settling fast.

"We leave and cross into Arizona tonight. This is the last time I will mention any location. Each of you buys food and a bottle of water at the store. We walk through the desert for two days and two nights. Keep up with me, or

I will leave you behind. When we get to the drop site, you will change clothes so you look like gringos. Leave your stuff there to make room in the cars. That means everything except the clean clothes you intend to wear. You can keep your backpacks if you want. If we do not get to the pickup area on time, they will leave without us. If they are intercepted or they don't come for us, we keep walking."

As El Coyote spoke, another dust cloud appeared. A black Expedition with opaque windows approached. El Coyote stopped speaking.

The guard with the AK-47 said something to the two men with him and pointed to the Expedition. They went to the rear of the Expedition and struggled to remove two large bundles wrapped in burlap with burlap back straps.

Miguel watched the man use the muzzle of his weapon to poke the men as they struggled to swing the bundles onto their backs. Miguel decided to call the man Pedro … a name he used for men he did not much like. Here was a scrawny little guy, brandishing a machine gun that made him appear larger than life. Miguel was not impressed.

El Coyote walked to the passenger's side window and spoke to someone inside. When he turned back to the group, the Expedition left.

El Coyote reached into a duffel bag slung over his shoulder and removed a cell phone. Shortly, two small trucks arrived.

"Get in!" El Coyote ordered.

Pedro lowered his weapon and began swinging the muzzle back and forth between them and the rear of the trucks as though directing traffic. They groaned and mumbled, struggling to squeeze into the truck beds. Pedro sat in the front seat of one. El Coyote sat in front in the lead truck.

As they started to move, a military jeep blocked the lead truck. Two men wearing military uniforms pointed handguns at the lead truck. El Coyote got out and walked to the jeep. Taking money from the stack he had in his shirt, he gave some to each man. The jeep drove away.

The trucks drove cautiously northeast for an hour along what was hardly more than a cattle trail. The hills were angular and rugged with thick cactus and thorny brush. They stopped, and except for the drivers, they all got out.

Miguel held Maria's hand. They fell in directly behind El Coyote. The others lined up behind them. Miguel wanted to be as close to El Coyote as possible, not only to keep an eye on him but because he considered it the safest position. The two mules carrying the bundles and Pedro kept about ten paces behind.

After walking another hour, a man waving a rifle stepped from behind a mesquite grove. Miguel saw other armed men watching in the shadows. Without saying a word, El Coyote gave him money. The man pointed at the youngest girl and at the other men with him.

El Coyote pointed to Pedro who had managed to slip around them and now had the drop on the small group. El Coyote gave the man more money. They continued. Close to the border in dense cover they stopped.

"Absolutely no talking," El Coyote said. "No lights. Nothing. No one move until I say!"

After the sun settled below the mountains, El Coyote removed a handheld radio from a bag. He turned it on and listened. Though the sound was low, Miguel heard the radio.

"They are going to the diversion site," a voice said.

El Coyote led them another one hundred yards. Miguel saw the outline of a barrier of crossed railroad tracks that looked like X's strung in a row and separated by a single bar that, from their position, seemed to stretch endlessly east and west through the trees and foliage.

He had wondered what sort of barrier marked the border. This strange fence apparently had no other purpose than to keep out vehicles.

Car lights appeared on a nearby hill on the other side of the border, and an engine started. Headlights pierced the sky and seemed to be dancing with the clouds before swinging down in their direction.

"Get down! Flat on your face. Don't move. Do it now!"

The outline of a US Border Patrol Ford Bronco descended toward them. The front lights swept the trees above their heads. Before reaching the fence, the lights swung east, bouncing along a dirt road that ran next to the barrier on the Arizona side. The red taillights disappeared, and engine noise faded. They did not dare to move.

El Coyote rose and holstered the Glock. "Let's go! Now!" He ran toward the barrier and crawled through.

The others followed in line, squeezed through, and then lined up behind Maria and Miguel who remained as close as possible to El Coyote. Pedro and the Mules brought up the rear.

Miguel saw a barbed wire fence across the dirt road. Even though it was now dark, there was enough moonlight to make out some details.

El Coyote led them across a cattle guard, over a gravel driveway, and onto ranch property, walking through the front yard with a darkened house less than fifty feet away. A covered porch wrapped around the front and sides.

To Miguel, choosing this location to cross an international border was irrational. They stood in the midst of occupied property. Logic dictated the crossing ought to be an empty, unpopulated area. He expected gunfire from the house any minute.

Maybe the property is deserted or the family is hiding, he thought to himself.

A broken-down tractor was beside the driveway, and a horse was in the corral next to the barn. It snorted and shied away. The presence of a horse indicated people lived there. From what Miguel could make out, the horse was about the size of Maverick with similar coloration. The barn's windows were smashed. At the end of the barn beside the driveway was a horse trailer with a broken axel. He heard cattle in the distance.

They approached a barbed wire fence. El Coyote stopped at a repaired section. With hands on his hips, he shook his head and kicked at a post, trying to push it over. He then removed his backpack and pulled out wire cutters, cut the wire, and knocked over the post.

After breaking through another fence, they scrambled into a wash that meandered northeast. Branches and brush left from a recent storm when the wash carried water from the mountains combined with the darkness made walking difficult.

The girls began to talk to each other. El Coyote stopped, halting the line. He slowly walked toward the girls. They continued to talk. The mother of one of the girls stepped toward El Coyote and opened her mouth. Before the woman said anything, El Coyote shoved her to the ground and then stood over her. He pulled the KA-BAR from behind his back. Slowly, he resumed walking toward the girls holding the ugly knife in his hand.

They clung to each other. Grabbing the arm of the nearest, he slung her to the ground and stood over her. As he looked down at her, she began to cry. He stepped away from her, walked to the older girl, grasped the back of her neck with his left hand, pulled her face close to his, and placed the point of the KA-BAR against her throat.

"Keep talking, and I will kill both of you," he said. El Coyote turned to their mothers. "If you don't follow my rules, I will leave you out here by yourselves. No one cares."

Soon, the clouds dissipated into a star-filled sky.

They stumbled along in the wash all night, trying to negotiate the slippery, loose rocks. Many tributaries and junctions joined the wash. El Coyote knew which to follow. Maria tripped and tore a hole in her jeans. They continued. She appeared short of breath and limped.

The trail steepened, and they began to climb. An older woman lagged farther behind. Miguel stopped and turned.

Maria grabbed his arm. "Miguel, this is not our business. An old woman should never make this journey. She will hold us back. We can't let her."

Miguel looked behind, saw her still struggling, and said, "I know I can help her and still keep up."

"No. No, Miguel. I need you more than her. I am your wife. She's just an old lady."

Pedro, the last man in line, walked past the woman without a glance. Soon, everyone lost sight of her.

During the night, they had no sense of direction or location and numbly followed the person in front of them. The darkness prevented visibility to see what might be beneath their feet. Heat lightning flashed across the sky. They placed a hand on the back of a person walking in front of them so they would not stumble or lose the trail. With the thick brush in some cases extending across the trail, it would have been easy to lose the trail, which would mean becoming hopelessly lost.

By morning, they were well into the mountains following washes and steep trails leading north. Encountering a thick grove of mesquite trees, they climbed out of the wash, stopping in an area covering a half acre filled with garbage and human feces. They found places to sit or sleep as thousands had done before them. The mules dropped their loads, while Pedro reconnoitered. After an hour, Pedro returned and spoke with El Coyote.

"Let's go," El Coyote growled.

They got in line and followed a trail leading deeper into the desert. The sun was intense, and several began to drink heavily from their plastic water bottles. Ahead loomed another rugged mountain range of crumbling cliffs, jagged rocks, and deserted mineshafts from a time when miners used pickaxes and shovels to search for silver and gold. Now they were accessible only by four-wheel-drive all-terrain vehicles or horses. Cattle grazed the lower areas.

The distant deep and rhythmic thump of an approaching helicopter forced them off the trail to hide among the cactus. Miguel hesitated, concerned about rattlesnakes. El Coyote pointed his pistol at him and several others. Pedro shoved them to the ground.

Miguel realized nothing prevented El Coyote from killing them. He already had their money, and the desert creatures would quickly strip their remains into a pile of unidentifiable bones. In a small mesquite grove, Miguel pulled Maria to the ground and lay on top of her. Others lay in prickly pear and creosote bushes. Some sprawled in tough, lanky la cholla and ocotillo. Barrel cactus formed a miniature city surrounding them. Many were stuck with painful needles, which later would fester if not removed.

The helicopter remained high and changed neither direction nor altitude, so it did not seem to be searching for them.

Near midnight, Miguel and Maria, who were following closely behind El Coyote, saw him reach for a handheld radio he had clipped to his belt. El Coyote listened for thirty seconds without responding and clipped the radio back to his belt. Then he pulled the semiautomatic from its holster and stopped. When they squeezed up behind him, he said, "Off the trail, now! Get down. Don't move. Don't breathe. Bandits looking for us. They find us, they take you with them and seek ransom from your families. Spread out. Lie down again in the brush."

Miguel saw Pedro and the two mules fall back fifty paces. They retreated down the trail about another twenty-five yards. Pedro made them separate before shoving them into the brush. Miguel heard Pedro rack the AK-47 as he followed them into the brush. The noise was loud and unmistakable. The bandits would have heard it if close enough.

Once time had passed without an incident, they set out on the trail again. Some removed their backpacks, half carrying and half dragging them along the trail. Miguel watched a man who had remained near the back of the group begin moving toward the front. Upon reaching Maria, he slowed and stayed closely behind her. When they rounded a bend in the trail, Miguel nodded to Maria and let her round the bend first. The man moved closer to her, grabbed her backpack causing her to fall, and tripped over her. Miguel yanked him to *his feet and slugged him in the face, knocking him to the ground. The line of illegals stopped. When he tried to role away, Miguel slung him into an ocotillo.*

El Coyote turned when he heard the ruckus. He glanced at Miguel but did nothing. The others stepped around him with barely a look. He thrashed, struggling in the tangled, thorny branches to free himself.

After a painful night stumbling along the meandering trail, El Coyote gathered them together again. "This is the last day we walk. This afternoon if all goes well, we will arrive at the pickup area. There we get our transportation. For a while, we will be close to roads and populated areas where we are exposed to more people and the border patrol. We must be very careful. Do as we say if you want to survive."

They walked for almost an hour before El Coyote stopped the line. He walked into the brush and emerged carrying a stand that seemed out of place and smashed the camera that was attached to it. The US Border Patrol used the camera to record activity along the trail.

Occasionally, especially at higher levels, they saw roads and heard traffic in the distance. When they descended into the valley, they passed close to homes and ranches. The vegetation became thick again as they entered an area of cactus and mesquite trees.

Tired and lacking water and food, El Coyote herded them into a small clearing surrounded by mesquite trees, prickly pear, and dense vegetation. Except for the sun's location, Miguel had no notion of their location, just that they were in southern Arizona. The very air grew more stifling the farther they walked. Maria coughed.

The growing stench reminded Miguel of a garbage dump. The trail gave way and opened into a clearing. Decaying litter surrounded them: blankets, backpacks, shoes, underwear, plastic bottles, toiletries, toilet paper, comic books, and burlap. Fearful of tripping and falling, they cautiously avoided decaying food, feces, hats, jackets, paper, pencils, discarded cell phones, and trash entangled in tree roots.

Maria grabbed his arm. "Miguel, look over there." She pointed to a pile of diapers, baby bottles, baby clothes, toys, and blankets. A ragged teddy bear was visible beneath a couple of discarded shoes. "Can you imagine people bringing babies all this way?"

"This stuff must cover an acre," he replied. "No one would believe what we've seen or been through these past few days. They'd have to see for

themselves." He waived his arm over the rancid accumulation. "These sorry dregs of humanity are a collage of the desperation to find a better life. I wonder," he said almost in a whisper, "if they've found what they thought they were seeking here. God help us all."

"Miguel, do you think we've made a mistake?" Maria questioned.

Before Miguel could reply, El Coyote ordered, "Sit!" He spoke as if they were trained dogs.

The area was somewhat open, giving them some room to spread out, but the odor remained overwhelming. They dropped their backpacks and sat, except for Pedro who remained standing. Miguel watched him swing the weapon from the attack rack chest rig and grasp it in a ready position as if he thought they might have enough strength to escape or attack. The few with water remaining drank. No food remained.

El Coyote circled and watched them, as though this was the first time he had seen them. "Change clothes."

No one moved.

"Now! You want to look like you belong here, not like the wetbacks you are."

As they changed, El Coyote and Pedro walked about them smiling, finally stopping by the girls, while they shed their clothes and changed into fresh ones, modesty no longer an issue.

"It seems like a ritual of some sort, a celebration maybe for reaching the end of the line," Maria said to Miguel. "You know, like symbolic, take off your clothes, and emerge as a new person."

"It's sick," Miguel said. "My God, look there, Maria." Miguel pointed toward a large mesquite tree near the center of the clearing.

She looked at the tree, and then gasped. Panties hung from many of the branches. "What is that?"

In their clean clothes, the group began to move closer to El Coyote.

"Don't do that," El Coyote said, backing away and placed his hand on his pistol. "I'll call transportation. We have a few things to do first." He nodded to Pedro. Pedro smiled and moved closer to El Coyote.

"Get your backpacks. Drop them on the ground here beside me. Then get into your lines. Women here by me. Men over there!" He pointed toward the opposite side of the clearing.

El Coyote placed his backpack with Pedro's on the ground near the others.

He chose the nearest, opened the top, and then turned it over. A shirt, a pair of shorts, a notebook, pencil, a cell phone, and a pocketknife fell out. After kicking the clothes toward the pile, he picked up the cell phone and tossed it into the pile. He opened the notebook and skimmed the pages before tossing it to Pedro who put it in his own backpack. A pocketknife went into his own pocket. The next one contained money, which El Coyote removed, folded, and placed it in a pouch that hung around his neck. He followed the same procedure with each backpack until all were inspected.

The contents either became part of the trash, or if they contained useful information, such as telephone numbers, names, and addresses, they went into Pedro's backpack.

Miguel was accustomed to demoralizing treatment from those more privileged than he and his family. However, this was beyond that kind of indignity. Angry, he wanted to stop him. For El Coyote to take such advantage of virtually helpless and unsuspecting people who trusted him and relied upon him to lead them to a new and better life, this was unconscionable and inhumanly callous. Besides, all were Latino, supposedly in this together. Gringos were supposed to be the enemy. Worse, he knew the group could do nothing to defend themselves against an AK-47. Half-starved and without the strength to defend against El Coyote, an escape seemed impossible without help. Calling the authorities afterward was also out of the question. All were illegal.

Miguel remembered what the priest had said; "Call the sheriff or US Border Patrol if you get into trouble."

The paper the priest had given them had phone numbers and information about lawyers and open-border people and the Mexican consulate; people who were supposed to help them. In the middle of the desert in a foreign country without knowledge of the language, now confronted by two armed men, their means of communication, information sheets, and money now possessed by the smugglers; such advice was now meaningless. Was this treatment a tax for their delivery and further an indication of what to expect in America?

All of this was his fault, Miguel acknowledged. He realized he should have known better. From the very start with the meeting with Ignacio at the cantina, everything had seemed too easy, too simple. He had heard and ignored the horror stories of what happened to illegals, how they were taken advantage of and preyed upon like defenseless rabbits in the desert. He now believed Ignacio only pretended to help them. It was all a pretense for something else he had yet to discover. He had ignored the lessons taught by the Sonora Desert. There, the only thing that counts is survival. He thought of the ancient ones, hoping they were present in this American part of the Sonora Desert. He wondered what his father would think of all this.

Miguel noticed El Coyote and Pedro standing aside talking and looking at them. "Get back in your lines. Men over there, women by me. I need one more search. The first was just for weapons. This will be the final one."

They quickly formed up again as instructed. El Coyote stood so close in front of Miguel that the man's sour breath made him gag. While Pedro pointed the AK at Miguel's head, El Coyote lifted Miguel's arms. He noticed the gold watch Sr. Vargas had given Miguel for saving Maverick. El Coyote removed it, placed the watch on his own wrist, pulled back his sleeve, and waved it in front of Miguel.

After El Coyote searched the men, Pedro forced them to stand in a line, holding them at bay. Pedro watched El Coyote like an entranced voyeur. El Coyote approached Maria. He made her stand in front of the men. He meticulously searched her. She trembled as tears dripped down her cheeks. He stopped and looked at Miguel and then turned to Pedro. Both smirked at Miguel.

When El Coyote touched her again, it was a red cape before a bull. Rationality deserted. him. He rushed El Coyote, ignoring Pedro and his weapon. El Coyote was the real danger. Pedro jammed the rifle into Miguel's chest, knocking him off balance. He stumbled and fell back into the line. El Coyote laughed.

The second search was more thorough. El Coyote discovered a few pieces of jewelry Maria had tried to conceal after she had changed clothes. Miguel was surprised. He thought they were going to leave such trinkets with his parents. With a smirk and another glance at Miguel, El Coyote felt under her shirt and jeans, lingering until her cheeks were awash in tears, and then he smugly nodded to Miguel and removed a small bag, opened it, and turned it upside down until a broach and a necklace she'd inherited from her grandmother dropped into his hand.

Before they had left Las Flores, they had agreed that her jewelry would remain in Las Flores with his parents. They were to retrieve it when they returned for Juanito. He wondered why she had changed her mind and why she had not told him. Now they were completely without the means they had hoped to use for a new start. After returning the jewelry to the bag, El Coyote put the bag into his backpack.

Once El Coyote searched the rest of the group, he placed their items, including their money, into his own bag.

When El Coyote finished with the women, Pedro made them stand together by Maria apart from the men. He joined El Coyote, holding the AK at the ready. El Coyote nodded to Pedro and walked toward the women. Pedro lowered the weapon and walked toward Miguel.

"Come with me," El Coyote said and grabbed Maria's arm. She resisted. He snarled, turned, and began to pull her toward a small break in the brush.

"No," she cried. "Miguel, Miguel!"

Like before, Pedro jabbed the muzzle toward Miguel's chest. Being considerably larger than Pedro, Miguel understood his own advantage and was ready. Miguel anticipated Pedro's move, knocked the muzzle away, and slung Pedro to the ground. The weapon slid toward the trash pile. Miguel started toward El Coyote, who seeing Miguel advance and Pedro on the ground, drew his pistol and pulled Maria against his bountiful belly. He placed the barrel to her head. "You come any closer, she dies!"

With the pistol at her head, El Coyote shoved her faster. She turned and looked helplessly at Miguel. El Coyote yanked her hard, throwing her to the ground and began dragging her.

Miguel, now enraged and convinced he had nothing to lose, started after them. Without releasing Maria, El Coyote turned and saw Miguel coming for him, aimed his pistol, and fired. Blood appeared at Miguel's head. He fell to his knees, tried to rise, and staggered, almost reaching El Coyote who raised his pistol to fire another round.

Miguel fell and lay motionless. Maria screamed and struggled, but El Coyote drug her into a mesquite grove. Her moans and cries for help along with El Coyote's grunts tortured the night. No one moved.

Apparently, the incident was just a minor disturbance, like the old woman who could not keep up or the man Miguel had thrown into the ocotillo. Miguel's motionless body was just another piece of garbage to toss on the pile, merely a discordant chord that soured the sound of a favorite melody. Pedro retrieved his AK-47, wiped it clean, and then pointed it at the illegals.

Finally, El Coyote emerged, tugging a whimpering Maria from the brush. He held her panties. As they passed the large mesquite tree known as the trophy tree, he tossed them over a branch near dozens of others, and then led her to Miguel, his blood leaching into the desert.

She checked his pulse and looked at the others. They ignored her. She sat next to Miguel and began rocking, she did not look at him again or speak. Her tears soon dried, and all expression left her face.

Pedro gave the AK-47 to El Coyote. He selected the youngest girl, drug her into the brush, brutally raped her, tossed her panties on the trophy tree, and then gave El Coyote a thumbs-up.

While they waited for the vehicles to take them to a stash house, the only sound was the girl's mother quietly crying. Apparently, she annoyed El Coyote. He scowled and walked to where she sat, cowering at his approach. She stopped crying and held her daughter, slowly rocking back and forth while tears rolled down her cheeks.

The sun slowly descended behind a distant mountain as the forlorn howl of a coyote faded into stillness so intense that all sense and meaning seemed to evaporate with the sound.

Three vans arrived. An armed young man stepped from each and stood near the rear doors. El Coyote checked Miguel's pulse, forced the other men to drag him to the first van where they struggled to lift him, and managed to slide him facedown across the floor. His feet remained outside the doors. A man crawled over him and pulled while several others pushed until his feet were inside. The rest, except the mules and Pedro, tumbled into the rear, attempting to avoid the blood seeping from Miguel's head. El Coyote made them lie down on top of Miguel.

El Coyote shoved Maria into the second van. The other women attempted to scramble away from her within the confines of the van, as though she had an infectious disease. The two mules and Pedro remained at the drop site. El Coyote entered the front seat of the women's van with the driver.

The men's van bounced along the dirt road and then turned onto a highway and increased speed. They swayed. The stench of unwashed bodies in the confined space was noxious. The tires slapped loudly on the road as the strained springs and shocks magnified every bump. Those in the back bounded about like clothes in a washing machine in a chorus of groans and grunts until the van turned into an area of nice homes, slowed, and pulled into a driveway at a house with a large garage. The van with the women and El Coyote disappeared into the night.

Two muchachos with pistols quickly herded the men inside. Another warned them to silence. Four others carried Miguel into an empty bedroom with a dirty carpet and no furniture. After they dropped him on the floor, one muchacho yanked his arms behind his back and secured them with plastic ties as another cuffed his ankles. Blinds and a blanket covered a window.

The other men sprawled on the floor, also restrained with plastic ties. They moved away from Miguel. One started to speak, but a muchacho hit him with a buckle attached to a black leather belt. Blood ran down the man's cheeks and dripped on the rug. After that, no one spoke.

A woman entered the room carrying bandages, several towels, and a bowl of water. She cleaned the wound stretching alongside Miguel's head, covered it with a bandage and tape, and then turned to the other man who had been struck with the belt buckle and treated.

Near dawn, Miguel regained consciousness. His head throbbed. He wanted to feel the source of the pain. He tried to reach for his head, but he was unable to move. His wrists and ankles hurt. He heard rain splashing against the window. He heard cars and muffled children's voices. His face was sticky from dried blood. A bus stopped outside, its air brakes reminding him of the bus that stopped to pick them up at the compound in Las Flores.

The room smelled rank, causing him to throw up. His vomit covered his shirt and the floor and stuck to his face. Sensing motion nearby, he turned his head slowly. Others were on the floor, also shackled. He recognized them from the group. He remembered Maria's scream and El Coyote dragging her.

"Maria!" he yelled. Nothing. He tried again. "Maria!"

"Quiet. She's not here," a voice said. "The women are not here. Just us and muchachos with guns. They want us to be quiet, or they will beat us."

Miguel tried to move, to roll over to see the man but the pain was too intense.

"We thought you dead. So much blood. No movement. We couldn't see if you were breathing."

"This is hell then," Miguel noted.

"Yes, hell, but I am afraid we are alive," another man said.

Out of the corner of his eye, he saw a muchacho standing by the window holding an AK-47.

He thought he must have slept because the next thing he knew, people were moving in and out of the room. Shortly, a muchacho about the same age as the ones guarding them entered and helped him up, cut the ties at his ankles, and escorted him into the living room.

Miguel saw a ragged couch, several chairs, and a desk. An adjacent room contained only a dining table. Standing in the center of the room was a man dressed in khaki slacks, a blue button-down shirt, and cowboy boots.

He studied Miguel. Removing a knife, he flipped it open with one hand, walked behind Miguel, and cut the handcuffs. He then folded the blade into the handle.

"I am Manuel, the boss here." He turned to the muchacho. "Wait outside the door."

Manuel was shorter than Miguel. His smile not only seemed out of place but was also somewhat askew, as though his face were twisted. "What is your name?" he asked.

"Miguel. Where is Maria?"

"Who is Maria?"

"My wife," Miguel explained.

"I don't know. I don't care. There are no women here." He walked to the desk, sat, and looked at a sheet of paper. "Oh, yes. Miguel and Maria Gutierrez."

Manuel rummaged through a pile of backpacks on the floor behind the desk. Reaching into one, he removed the letter. He said, "Here is a letter to Maria in Las Flores from a Tucson address." He opened the envelope and removed the letter. "Let's see ... yes, Rosa and Antonio Rodriguez. Well, what do you know, right here in Tucson, easy to find them, with names, address, and a phone number, do they have the money to pay off your debt? Are they legal?"

The room was spinning. Miguel had never had such a headache, never felt so weak. Through the uncovered window in this room, Miguel observed the house next door. Bougainvillea entwined a trellis in a mixture of red and yellow flowers that seemed out of place in the starkly drab reality of his situation. The exterior of the house was stucco, matching the color of earth. The roof was red tiles. At most, the house was only twenty feet away. If he got there, maybe they would help.

Manuel followed Miguel's interest in the house. "No one's there," he said, gesturing toward the window. "They just come during the winter." He walked to the window and closed the curtain. "We will be gone by then. I need three thousand dollars from each of you before I let you go. If you can't get it, each of you can work off your share. You stay here, Miguel, until what you both owe is fully paid. Maria stays with the women."

"Get the money from that sick bastard, El Coyote," Miguel snarled. A ringing in his ears joined the pounding in his head. He shook his head, trying to clear it. He wanted to throw up. "He took everything we have. He raped Maria."

Manuel shrugged. "That's just a tax for crossing the border."

"I will kill him," Miguel growled with a guttural sound and an intensity he had never before experienced. His hands closed tightly, his nails dug into them, drawing blood, and his eyes narrowed. He felt faint and walked to the edge of the desk, placed his hands on the front edge, and leaned forward on them, attempting to understand and calm down.

"That is your business. You are to pay me another three thousand dollars each before I let you go."

"Your man took our money. Get it from him!" Miguel repeated, stepping toward the desk.

Manuel took the knife from his pocket and snapped it open. "Muchacho," he said toward the door.

A boy with an AK-47 stepped into the doorway. Manuel nodded toward Miguel and then sat at a desk opposite him, placing his hands behind his head and leaning back in the swivel chair.

"No one said I needed that much money," Miguel said, trying to fight dizziness.

"No? But you are here now, are you not? You are in no position to tell me what to do, amigo. Remember, we have Maria." He shrugged again. "We also now know where her aunt and uncle live, not far from here. We know you are from Las Flores where your parents are. If you do not have the money, you will both do what I need so you can work it off. That's the way it is, Miguel. Nothing matters now, only what I tell you." Manuel nodded to the muchacho standing in the open door holding an AK-47.

"I'll be right here," the boy said and moved out of sight.

Manuel continued, "You will go with another to pick up some bundles and take them to a place where they will be unloaded. You will then return here where you will remain until you work off the rest."

"What of Maria? What does she have to do?" Miguel asked, afraid of the answer.

"Whatever we need her to do to get our money."

"Where is she?" Despite the pain in his head and dizziness, he struggled to constrain himself from crawling over the desk and wringing the man's neck. *I will kill him*, he thought.

As though reading his mind, Manuel said, "Don't do something stupid, Miguel. We have her. Believe me, we will kill her. Believe me, no one but you, cares about her, death might be a blessing for her."

For this? Miguel, asked himself. *This is what we crossed to America for? This is worse than Mexico.* His anger included not only himself but also Maria who had naively insisted that all their problems would end once they crossed the border. His anger extended especially to Ignacio who lied to both of them. He felt helpless, trapped with no other choice, if only for Maria's and Juanito's sake, to do as they asked until he could figure out something.

Manuel looked carefully at Miguel. He reached into his pocket and brought out a paper. "I know you are Miguel Gutierrez from Las Flores. Your family lives there. I know you were in the Mexican Army. I am told you are the kind of man we are looking for to help expand our business. I also know you have refused to join us. You refused even though you know it is dangerous to do so. Is that true?"

"Yes. I refused. Who told you this?

"Ignacio. You seem smart, Miguel, able to take care of yourself. You know what I'm saying?"

"No."

"Miguel, join us."

Miguel glared at him. "I don't want this kind of work. You treat people like cattle. You rape women. You speak of killing as though it were nothing. What kinds of men do this?"

"The kinds who see things as they are. Those like you who are as large and as tough as the desert. Other men don't mess with you, right? There is money for men like us. This cartel is much better than being a slave at a hacienda or a landscaper or picking tomatoes or cabbage on some gringo farm and living in a plywood box or jammed in a house in a barrio where gangs rule. That is your future. You can do nothing. No papers. You live in the dark. Everyone takes advantage as we do of you now. You will end up selling on the street *the very dope we supply and having to fight the gangs that want to take your business, and you will go to prison or die in the streets of America before you reach thirty. A big, smart man like you we can use. You join us, we will forget the additional money, and there will be much more. You can make Maria and Juanito happy."*

"How do you know what Maria wants ... about Juanito?"

"Ignacio." He extended his hand to Miguel. "I am the boss here. Look, here is money." Manuel pulled a bundle of dollars from his shirt. "This I can give you if you join us now." He tossed the wrapped bundle of dollars on the desk.

Miguel stepped back as though the money was poison. "I want to see her."

"She is not here. The coyote took her and the other women somewhere else. The men will stay here because they do not have the money for payment." He put his hand on the money. "This is for someone recommended like you, not for those muchachos who stand guard over you and make only a few hundred dollars to kill someone. This is to start being part of an expanding organization that will run things ... something that is important, something with power."

He pushed the money toward Miguel. "Something important that Maria will be proud of and for Juanito to have a good life, go to a good school. Maybe important in Mexico or maybe even in America. Now you say yes?"

"Where is she?" Miguel repeated.

"They took her to another stash house until the money is paid or until you join us. You can't see her. She will be whored out until she can pay us off."

Miguel continued to look toward the window. Ignacio had told him the same story. "Join and you won't pay."

This was not a bad dream. The room, this man was all too real. The pressure he felt was beyond any he had experienced. The first decision had been either Maverick or Maria. He had given up Maverick, of course, because it was what she wanted and there was nothing more important than her and Juanito and his parents. Maybe it was worth a chance, especially if there was a narco war, which would certainly engulf Las Flores as it had so many Mexican pueblos. There was no room there for two cartels. The description of what life would be like for them in Tucson was very different from what Maria's aunt had written. Yet Maria's aunt said life was better there. Maybe, once they had paid off their debt, it would be better as she wrote. He doubted it. Even if they paid the money, why would these people just turn them loose as long as they could continue to produce money for the cartel or, worse, simply kill them to get them out of the way?

Even if her aunt was willing to pay a ransom, he doubted they would pay for him. If anything, they would only pay for Maria. They had never liked him. They had wanted her to marry Ignacio.

Whether he joined the cartel was not a decision he could make without Maria. What could he tell his family? His father would never approve. Yet Miguel knew Maria would want him to do whatever necessary to end this nightmare.

If he worked off the money, he would be reunited with Maria and not have to make a commitment to the cartel. He knew he would be a criminal, assuming he even survived because he knew what they would want him to do. What was the choice? Once he had worked it off, was it really over? Would she be safe, and they would be on their way? Really? What he might be required to do was one thing. What they expected Maria to do was unthinkable. Father Michael's warning rang in his mind like a fire alarm. The flames may have already engulfed her. There was no choice now.

"I won't join you," he said. "I don't understand this. I will do as you say so we can finish this thing and live here."

Manuel shouted to the door for the muchacho to take Miguel away.

When Miguel was outside the room, the boy jabbed him with his AK-47 to make him move faster and tried to shove him into the room with the other men. Miguel stopped, forcing the muchacho to push harder. The boy was smaller and not as strong as Miguel. The boy cursed. The men in the room watched. "Move!" the boy shouted.

An older boy appeared, and when he saw what was happening, he said, "I will hurt Maria."

Miguel turned and glared at him. The boy had a semiautomatic, so Miguel moved into the room. They put him in plastic handcuffs again and then left.

The men had no food until noon when they ate soggy tortillas and beans washed down with water. They used the tortillas to scoop up the beans.

*L*ife *for US Border Patrol Agent Nate Gonzales always seemed intense. Usually, he liked it that way. Near midnight he was on duty in a Bronco parked on a hill just off Ruby Road. He was preparing to meet with the line leader of a border watch group. The line leader had just called him to report illegals they had spotted from their stakeout along the road to Elephant Head.*

Gonzales's secure phone hummed and vibrated in his pocket. He recognized the voice of Maj. Gen. Manny Marcus who was Nate's commanding officer during the Afghan war. "Call me back!" the message said.

Nate punched in the number Marcus left. "Me," Nate said.

"Need to meet. I am stuck here. Day after tomorrow," Marcus told him.

"Yes, sir. What time? Where?"

"Noon. I'll get a table in the back. Civilian clothes, Nate. Georgetown. Crazy Hog Cafe. I've made a reservation for you at Davis Monthan Air Force Base for a direct cargo flight to DC. I'll clear all this. They won't know."

"Yes, sir." He hung up. The last time he had spoken with Marcus was shortly after he had returned to the States after completing a tour in Afghanistan just before he had joined the border patrol. They had met at the same restaurant in Georgetown. Blustery old coot, he recalled, and a great boss who loved good intel. He looked forward to seeing him. Stuff always happened when General Marcus was involved.

Nate started the engine, turned on the Bronco's lights, and pulled out of the brush onto Ruby Road. He turned on his flashing blue emergency light, which weirdly gave a bluish tinge to the plants by its rotation on the top of the cab. He turned east toward the interstate, then south and turned onto a road that lead to Elephant Head. At the north-south railroad crossing, he stopped beside two jeeps. A man and a woman with holstered pistols stood by the jeeps. The back door of one was open. An ice chest inside was filled with water bottles. A third man, Nate recognized as the group's line leader, was bent over a young Mexican sitting in the middle of the railroad tracks drinking from a bottle of water.

"I called you because we spotted a man and woman walking toward us along the tracks," the line leader said to Nate. He gestured toward the railroad tracks crossing the road from the south. "We have five two-person cars stationed just off the road in the brush about thirty yards apart, spaced in sight of each other."

The line leader pointed to a man and woman standing beside a Jeep.

"Those two were hunkered down in folding chairs in the brush watching the railroad tracks coming from the south. Two illegals approached their position walking along the tracks. They called me. I called you. The female illegal is wearing a red jacket. The male also wore a jacket and a baseball cap. I don't think they saw us." He pointed north. "They crossed this road walking north beside these tracks until the bend up there." He pointed up the tracks.

A distant siren seemed to be getting louder.

"A little later, this guy stumbled toward us. He said he saw us. He collapsed where you see him now. He asked for water. I called the emergency squad. That is probably their siren we hear in the distance."

Nate radioed to report the situation and then walked to the boy sitting on the tracks. Kneeling beside him, he said in Spanish, "I am Nate Gonzales, border patrol. How do you feel?"

"Not good. We walked a long way. I am thirsty, very thirsty." He started to slump forward. Nate held him. "They left me behind. I couldn't keep up."

The siren was close. Soon, an ambulance approached and pulled to a stop. A man and a woman carrying small knapsacks went to the boy.

"I'm going up the tracks and check it out. See if I can tell anything," Nate said. He turned on his flashlight and walked north along the railroad, following footprints in the gravel. The tracks turned toward the east. Rounding the curve, he saw a red jacket caught in the brush. The flashlight displayed broken twigs where they had left the right-of-way. Returning to his car, he radioed the information to the dispatcher, who would send a notice to be on the lookout for the man and woman.

The male medic said, "He'll be okay. We'll take care of him."

They placed him on a stretcher, and with the help of Nate and the line leader, lifted him into the ambulance.

When Nate returned to headquarters, he approached his station chief to report the trip to Washington. Miguel was surprised his station chief already knew.

Two days later, Nate caught a military cargo flight from Davis Monthan Air Force Base on a scheduled military cargo flight to Washington arranged by General Marcus. Along with several others, he sat on a bench in a harness attached to the fuselage and wondered what General Marcus had in store for him. The general also had arranged for transportation to the restaurant. He *leaned back against the fuselage and closed his eyes, listening to the engine noise and the vibration until he slept.*

Nate's parents came to the United States illegally. Nate was born in the United States, making him a US citizen as well as a citizen of Mexico. His father started a landscaping business in Tucson and became a talented and respected landscape designer. Both parents were naturalized citizens. His grandparents and other relations remained in Mexico, except for an uncle who had a green card and worked with Nate's father. Growing up he spent holidays and other family occasions in Mexico.

Nate was equally at home in both cultures. He assimilated easily into American culture growing up with gringos and Mexicans while at the same time clinging to his Mexican roots. Occasionally, he had mixed feelings as he attempted to balance both cultures.

At Arizona State, he joined La Raza to support Mexican causes as a way to identify with his Latino roots. He was pressured to join Aztlan's Reconquista Movement to reclaim US land once belonging to Mexico prior to the Mexican-American War. The Treaty of Guadalupe Hidalgo, signed February 2, 1848, ceded 55 percent of Mexico to the United States. The Rio Grande River became Mexico's northern border. When Nate refused to join, his tires were slashed, and he was labeled a traitor.

Nate assumed that after graduation from Arizona State, where he excelled in athletics and academics, he would join his father and uncle in their landscaping business. Shortly after graduation, however, 9/11 changed his life. He joined the US Army, anxious to do his part. After his discharge, a Mexican American convinced him Mexicans were treated well in the border patrol. He decided to join.

Some called him a traitor for joining the US Army and especially the US Border Patrol because they arrested and jailed Latinos.

A childhood friend said, "I hate gringos. My mother was arrested then deported." She had sought sanctuary in a church. After she was deported, Nate's friend became a ward of the state. He lived in various foster homes, got into trouble, was sent to prison, and joined a Mexican prison gang for protection. Now he was the boss of a stash house in Tucson.

Nate sympathized with people who risked everything to improve their lives by entering America. It is what his parents did. He probably knew many illegals. He did not report them. How do you know? They will not say. How can you ask someone whether he is illegal without having cause?

His own perspective on life and the priest at a local church enabled him to deal with his conflicting pressures. The small church was originally a one-room mission on land donated by the gringo who owned the pecan grove on which the church stood. Initially, the parishioners were almost all Mexicans who worked the groves. Not only did they build the church but also, and almost as important, the men who worked in the fields learned valuable construction skills that enabled them to earn a decent living in an area that was steadily growing with new construction.

The church was the center of family activities. Gringos were also attracted to the church. The reputation of the priest spread among the community. The congregation became a mixture of Latino and Caucasian families. Fiestas preserved the culture and attracted an increasing number of gringos. They worshiped together in bilingual services, celebrated, and participated in religious holidays and traditional processions. Every Sunday they enjoyed mariachi music at Sunday Mass.

When the plane landed, Nate saw a man holding a sign with his name who delivered him to the Crazy Hog Cafe in Georgetown. He entered the dimly lit anteroom. The man behind a stand stepped in front of him, asked his name, and stepped aside, saying, "The general is in the back corner on the left."

Nate paused in the doorway, straightened his posture, and then stepped into a large and surprisingly quiet main dining room. This was a more solemn atmosphere than he remembered.

The room was crowded. The tables were discretely separated. All were occupied. Nate was glad he had worn a suit, for all the men wore suits and ties. Women wore dresses and high heels. Leather purses, briefcases, and various devices adorned the tables or sat on the floor within reach. The atmosphere of the large room seemed to emit a low-level, barely audible sound effectively disguising conversation. The waitstaff stood off to the side out of earshot, ready to respond to a request. Solemnity seemed to underscore what were doubtless important business and political discussions occurring at every table.

Nate saw General Marcus in a small booth in the farthest corner. It was the first time he had seen him out of uniform. The lighting was constrained, and what had seemed to be a black suit was, at closer inspection, actually blue.

Marcus appeared the same, perhaps balding. What hair remained was still the standard crew cut. When he stood, he was the same height as Nate, maybe more of a pouch, which he tried to suck in. Incredibly, Marcus wrapped his arms around Nate in a big hug ... something he would never have done in their army days. It was as though they had never parted.

As soon as they sat, Marcus started to talk about the Afghan war.

"Remember the border stuff, the intel ops, sneaking around trying to get info?" Marcus asked. "As I remember, you got to be pretty good at that."

Nate had not thought of those operations in a long time. It started to spark his memory. "Yes, sir." He knew Marcus had not whimsically brought this up.

"Do you remember periodically working with a unit commanded by a Brigadier named Reginald Delany who led special ops on the Afghan/Pakistan border?"

"I never met him. His reputation was legendary."

"Delany is now attached to a secret operation under the Department of Homeland Security. No one knows where he is. It has to do with government corruption, intelligence, and law enforcement, particularly on our southern border. Heard anything about that, Nate?"

"No sir, not a word. Not likely to either, at least not at my pay grade."

"Maybe we can fix that." Marcus noted.

The server interrupted. "You boys look deep in thought. Care to order, General? Your regular?"

"Yes. You want a steak, Nate? On me."

She looked at Nate. "You won't be sorry," she said. "Martini, boys?"

They nodded, and she left them alone.

"I just want to be sure we are on the same page here before I get to the bottom line," Marcus said when she left them. "Some history first."

That is a bit ominous, Nate thought. He recalled that General Marcus always placed operations in a historical context so everyone knew as much as possible about a mission.

Marcus looked at the nearby tables and then back at Nate. He cleared his throat. "As the cartel violence in Mexico spread, corruption, a staple of Mexican culture, also increased."

Nate nodded.

"With the Colombians' drug trafficking role diminished, Mexican cartels took over. Generations of peon families have grown cannabis in the mountains. Families living along the border for generations smuggled contraband both

ways across the border, generally unimpeded. The growers eventually expanded to control the smuggling routes and developed trafficking organizations to move marijuana, Colombian cocaine, and Mexican methamphetamine. As they increased their wealth, they displaced the small independent smuggler guides."

Their server brought two martinis. They tipped their glasses. Marcus sipped his and placed the glass on the table. Nate sipped and held onto the glass.

"Centuries of Indian and animal trails leading north became lucrative trafficking lanes driven by the insatiable American demand for drugs and cheap labor." He looked at Nate. "You are too young to remember this, but this smuggling stuff was learned during the prohibition era when liquor was the commodity of the time. The Mexicans were busy then in the same way as now. The merchandise now is different and more valuable, that's all.

"Mexican farmer families, many supported by local state governments and local police, became cartels. Competition for the favored routes to Brownsville, El Paso, San Antonio, Laredo, Douglas, Nogales, Yuma, and San Diego turned violent. Jamaican street gangs were once the primary vendors in America who received their product from Colombia. They were replaced by black and Latino members of convict prison gangs who obtained their product from Mexican cartels, first by affiliation with existing prison gangs and, more recently, direct operations and corruption on both sides of the border. My group is tasked to flush out corruption and gather cartel intelligence."

"I thought that was the DEA's job."

"Mostly they do the drugs and trafficking part. I am talking about US government corruption."

Nate started to see a little light in the discussion. His pulse increased. Marcus had mentioned Reggie Delaney. He did not think that was simply idle conversation. There had to be more to it than merely investigating corruption. He did not ask Marcus. He knew things were not always what they seemed. You keep your mouth shut until asked. He recalled that Delaney had a reputation as a skilled operations leader. It was unlikely he would be satisfied with merely sneaking around looking for bad people. Killing them, maybe, but someone had to identify them first.

There were some tough hombres in that group, he recalled. He had met them, but their faces were always covered. They had tried to train Afghans and coordinate their missions. He remembered one of them saying it was like trying to herd cats.

"The US Border Patrol," Marcus continued, changing the subject, "is an amazing organization. Whether its merger with US Customs proves a good decision remains to be seen. I have my doubts. When you realize what these people do, mostly individually, undermanned, in terrible environments, under gunned, and underfunded, it draws your respect and admiration."

"How well I know," Nate responded, glad to know someone he respected understood. He remembered a night during training when he chased illegals through the desert all alone. In the pitch darkness, it had been an adrenaline rush trying to trace their footsteps and follow their trail. It was not until afterward that he realized the extent of the danger. That had been more than a year ago. Now, it was standard procedure to be alone out there.

He also thought of Brian Terry, a border patrol agent killed with a weapon allegedly supplied to a cartel by the ATF. Nate had walked that area alone many times.

"Not only do you have to worry about the bad guys," Marcus continued, "but our own citizens attempt to interfere in your pursuit of illegals. They also try to gather evidence of misconduct and criminal harassment by BP agents."

Nate nodded in agreement.

Their steaks arrived. While they ate quietly, Nate tried to piece together where this discussion was going. He knew Marcus had something important in mind. Nate admitted to himself that whatever it was, he was interested.

Nate noticed tables occupied by people enjoying quiet, if not animated, conversations. *Here I am, the son of wetbacks, in the heart of the world's most powerful capital city, discussing important stuff affecting my country, perhaps among others doing the same thing.* He felt the importance of being part of the elite and wondered what the other conversations might involve. Looking at his steak, he waited to discover what any of this had to do with him.

"Even the politics are against you," Marcus continued as he sliced off another piece of meat. He looked at Nate as he sipped his martini. "No one has a clue about what you do or the problems, unless they live in the border region. The border patrol is an organization that receives lip service support, while assets are diverted elsewhere to more politically beneficial agencies or to political districts and states with greater political return for the buck. Frankly, in my opinion, combining it with customs and immigration confuses the mission, dilutes resources, and increases bureaucratic jealousy. Anyway, with a low pay structure, there is at least, theoretically, strong motivation for corruption.

"The cartels have more money than they know what to do with and a lust for violence and power. However, there is remarkably little corruption in the BP. Agents respect the job, and until recently, morale remained high.

"We believe the rush to put on more agents because of political pressure has introduced some bad apples who are overlooked. Less polygraph testing, rushed background checks, and time constrains prevent detailed vetting of applicants. Some political appointments are also suspect. These are the dangerous ones because their tentacles can potentially extend throughout our federal bureaucracy. The cash available by cartels to invest in the United States is incredible. They want access and influence, to eliminate problems and competition, and to clean their dirty money."

"Intelligence makes the world go around," Nate suggested, using a phrase he had learned from Marcus, now understanding where the general was leading. "At least it was true in the war."

Marcus nodded. "And I kid you not, this is war." He paused, looked around, and lowered his voice. "Also, we are concerned Mexico will become a narco state, either by the emergent dominance of one cartel or a confederation of several cartels."

Marcus put down his fork, leaned back in his chair, and intensely looked around the room before he turned back to Nate. "There are those who advocate violence to encourage this development. We look the other way at the inevitable violence. After a cartel or other entity emerges, without informing the Mexican government, we make our peace with the cartel. We want to control immigration and human and drug trafficking and provide economic development. This plan includes US support for a Mexican insurrection." Marcus sighed heavily and leaned back. "This plan presupposes if we can't find such an organization then we create one."

Nate was numb. He could not immediately respond. This disclosure of inside information was overwhelming. He looked at Marcus who was closely watching him. Though Marcus had not warned him, Nate knew that this was eyes-only intel, which was unquestionably classified. He did not know whether he still had a clearance and, if so, at what level.

"This is very interesting sir, but what does it have to do with me?"

"I need somebody inside the BP in the Tucson Sector I can trust. You will remain in Tucson. I think the Homeland Security Sector official named

Adrian Wolforce is corrupt. A member of the Office of the Director of National Intelligence appointed him to the position."

"Arrest him!"

"Can't got nothing on him," Marcus said with frustration. "I am almost positive he is connected with a cartel but cannot prove it. That's where you come in." He paused.

Both sipped their martinis. Their server started toward them. Apparently, she saw liquid remaining in their glasses and turned around.

"Why me? What would I have to do?" Nate questioned.

"I know you, and know you can be trusted. You know the territory. You have the training, stamina, ability, language, and respect to work undercover on your own within the normal operating practices of the Tucson Sector, as well as finding the moles … and you are not married."

"How do I find these people?"

"Blackmail or money. For instance, you arrest a mule. For agreeing to provide you intel, you suspend the charges against him, pay him, or promise a favor. Doesn't really matter whether you keep the promise. Once he is hooked, he can't get away. He knows you can out him. He's dead meat once it's known he's a snitch."

"Sort of like what you are doing to me, right? What do I tell the Tucson Sector Chief? Technically, he's my boss."

"Nothing."

"I have a relationship with the Pima County Sheriff. Known him since college. Also, a contact in the state police."

"Great. No reason not to stick with it. You all can help each other. Just don't blow your cover. I may have a contact for you as well."

"I've heard of this Wolforce," Nate said.

"I know."

"Assuming he is what you say and he discovers what I am doing, I am dead meat, right? If he is connected to a cartel as you think, he'll stay clean. I will be killed, or my parents in Tucson or family in Mexico. I have aunts, uncles, nieces, and nephews in Mexico. Can you get them here? Protect them?"

"I don't know. Well, they can cross, but I don't know if I can get documents without breaking your cover."

"Sir," Gonzales said, pushing. "We have a very porous border."

"Go on."

"Well, sir, it is only a matter of time before Isis or the Taliban or Hezbollah figure out how to cross it, or some other group or terrorist recognizes our vulnerability or, and this is my worst fear, hooks up with a cartel."

"Yes," Marcus said. "Unfortunately, this issue is treated as a political matter, rather than a security issue."

On the return flight to Tucson, in spite of the risks, Nate had made the decision to go undercover for Marcus. The border patrol was not just a job. It was a cause. He hated the corruption. It was destroying Mexico, he believed. Yes, the border had always been lawless and never been tamed, and now a violent, morally destructive cancer was spreading northward, infesting and corrupting as it advanced. Nate was not surprised that it might reach into the halls of the US government.

5

*A*t gunpoint, a muchacho led Miguel to a van parked in the driveway. The driver, an older Hispanic with hair turning white at the temples, glanced at him and then started the engine and began driving.

The house where they held him resembled all the others in the area, with trimmed lawns and sidewalks and streets intersecting one after another in an almost identical pattern. Though of varying colors, each home was more or less the same, just like the casas he remembered in Hermosillo. They were very close together. He was surprised to see Mexican flags. At a corner was a grocery store. The sign was in Spanish. They turned onto a much broader street having four traffic lanes. They waited at a red light. They passed a school, and in the distance, he saw several tall buildings. A large white church dominated the skyline.

"What ciudad is this?" Miguel asked the driver.

"Tucson."

He recognized the name and wondered if Maria's aunt and uncle lived in one of the houses they had passed. She could be anywhere. He looked at the driver. He knew he could take him, make him stop the car so he could get out. Perhaps he would find someone in the neighborhood in one of those houses with a Mexican flag willing to help him. Where would he start? No, he had to play along until he had more information. He knew they had her. Manuel said they would kill her if he did not go with this man and do what he said. If they threatened to kill her, then she must be alive, or such a threat meant nothing. Maybe Manuel was bluffing. Maybe she was already dead. Until now, Miguel had not allowed himself to think of that possibility.

They crossed a wide, dry riverbed and then turned west on Highway 10 into the sun, which was slowly setting behind the mountain ahead. The sky changed to orange, pink, and purple the same way the western sky did in Las Flores. As the shadow crept down the mountain, lights sprinkled the mountainsides and glittered like shards of glass placed there to decorate and form neat patterns.

They turned south onto a major highway. He observed landmarks and noticed a road sign that displayed a 19.

"If we stay on this road, we will be in Nogales in about an hour and a half, but we don't get that far," the driver said. He looked in the rearview mirror and slowed. A green and white Bronco passed them.

"That's the US Border Patrol. We do not want them to stop us. This is my fourth trip to do this. I am very careful. No problem."

"How long you been here?" Miguel asked.

"Four months."

"You do this to pay them back?"

"No," the man noted. "Now they pay me."

"Where are you from?"

"Guatemala."

"Alone?

"Yes. I see you have a ring. You are married and your wife? She is here?"

"Yes, I was brought to that house. They took her somewhere else," Miguel explained. "Do you know where?"

"They have many places. I don't know. They make the women do other things." He glanced at Miguel who stared straight ahead.

"What things?" Miguel finally asked.

"Well, they cook and clean the houses and do things to bring in money."

"Like what?" he asked again.

"Steal from stores, things like clothes and beer and whatever can be sold. The pretty ones are prostitutes or assigned to service the men at the houses or the warehouses or on the streets in Tucson and Phoenix. I heard some are returned to Mexico for the cartels."

Miguel clinched his fists and sat up stiffly, his head nearly touching the roof. How long do they keep us?"

"Depends. Don't know," the driver said. "Maybe, until there is no more money that they can get from you or your family. Or maybe if you are to work for a company, until the company pays or a broker buys you. I don't know how they decide things."

"What's a broker?"

"A person who pays the cartel for the illegals and then makes the illegal work for him or rents him out to someone else. Better to work for the cartel. That way you get the money. The cartel pays well, but you can't leave."

"You decided to work for them?" Miguel questioned.

"Yes."

"Why?"

"For the money. Now I can't leave. But it's okay. Better than Guatemala," the driver admitted. They drove into a rest stop. "We'll wait here until we are *called and then we go to the drop site where we get the bundles." He took a cell phone from his pocket.*

Each used the restroom. They waited for fifteen minutes. Vehicles pulled into the parking lot. Many had Mexican license plates. He saw one from the state of Sonora with two kids in the back. He watched them until they drove away toward the border. He wondered whether Ignacio was taking care of Maverick and if Juanito was all right. Would he ever see them again?

"Are you not afraid you will get arrested?" Miguel asked the driver.

"We are careful. Someone is always watching. We have scouts up there," he pointed toward the mountain. They have high-power telescopes and night-vision equipment. Spotters warn us of problems like the border patrol or sheriff or a border watch group."

"What's a border watch group?"

"Small groups of people who watch for illegals who cross the border. They call the border patrol when they spot illegals." Just then, the phone rang. The man listened and then said, "Time to go." The moon was merely a visible sliver between clouds. "They have night-vision goggles," the driver continued.

Miguel frowned at him. The driver looked back at him and smiled as though proud to explain things. "It lets them see at night. They have GPS too, for directions. Some even have listening devices. A man on top of the mountain watches the trail and looks for the border patrol or others who may be around and have radios and cell phones. Almost everything gets across and picked up like a game of hide-and-seek. There's not enough to catch us."

He turned off the pavement and drove slowly with the lights out along a dirt trail leading south.

"We are looking for a green ribbon tied to a tree next to this trail. There's a flashlight in there." He pointed to the glove compartment. "Get it."

When Miguel had the flashlight, the man slowed the van to a crawl.

"I think I see it." Miguel said.

"That's it." He stopped the car. "Get out and walk that way." The driver pointed toward a small break in the brush. Go about twenty-five yards. I will turn the car around and come help you. The bundles are fifty to seventy pounds. The mules will be gone. The bundles are in the brush beside the wash or in the wash."

Miguel slowly approached the area. He entered through the break in the brush and carefully followed a path to the edge of the wash. Turning to follow along beside the wash, his foot caught an exposed root. He fell into the wash and landed on something. He gasped, realizing he had fallen on a body. He rose to his knees to run. The body did not move. He slowly crawled up the side and pulled himself over the top.

Miguel followed the wash, searching for more bodies and bundles. By now, he'd gone twenty-five yards.

"Everything okay?" The driver had caught up to him.

"Two bodies. No bundles so far."

The driver pulled a pistol, pointed it at Miguel, turned around, and ran into the brush, leaving Miguel stranded in the wash. He heard a car door slam. The engine started. Miguel heard tires spinning in the dirt and the chassis pounding the ground as the car bounced through the brush. Suddenly, all was quiet. Miguel held his breath, not daring to move. The night tightened about him. Now alone, he trembled, an indication of impending fear that might immobilize him. He had to control the negative effects of such fear. Perhaps there were others still out there. Maybe they were not far away. Nothing made sense.

Why would the man panic like that? Panic was the only way Miguel could describe the reaction. Maybe it was fear or knowledge that something dreadful had happened. It was obvious to Miguel. The bodies were mules. They were killed by a rip crew for the drugs they carried, probably an ambush. Were they still there? Maybe that is what frightened the man. Maybe he thought Miguel was part of it. Maybe the driver was part of it or was double-crossed or thought he would be blamed. For now, whatever reason caused the man to panic no longer mattered. Now what mattered was survival and finding Maria.

The darkness seemed vast. Miguel crouched into the exposed roots of a mesquite and remained obscured by the creosote bushes surrounding it. As long as he remained quiet, it was almost impossible to see him.

He relied on sound. The Guatemalan had mentioned night-vision goggles, and if killers had those, they would find him. Obviously, it took several to hijack this group, the gunmen and enough people to carry the bundles. He dared not move, carefully listening until he heard the sounds of desert creatures. Their presence told him he was the only live human present.

The night passed slowly, but to him, it was a comfort. The desert was as familiar as the compound at home. The bodies were starting to smell, and the buzzards were circling. He knew insects had found them.

Approaching daylight crept over the ridge to his east. He emerged from the wash and found a dirt road. He saw tire tracks in the dust and followed them north until he reached an intersecting trail. He checked for footprints. He did not want to follow the rip crew, and because there were no prints, he decided the trail was safe. Not long after first light, he crossed a paved road and followed the trail north. Near noon, he approached another paved road. Seeing no tracks, he believed it to also be safe and started across.

"Alto! Don't move!"

Miguel turned. A border patrol agent stepped from the brush holding a semiautomatic pistol pointed at the ground. He pointed to the side of the road and repeated the order in Spanish.

Miguel hesitated and looked around him. The brush was thick and close.

"Sit down!" The voice was now threatening, and the pistol pointed at him. "Hands on your head. I will shoot."

Miguel moved to where he pointed and sat. The agent removed a handheld from his belt and spoke into it. A green-and-white truck pulled onto the pavement a half mile down the road, drove to them, and stopped. Another agent got out and made Miguel stand and place his hands against the side of the truck.

The first agent held the gun on him while the other searched him. "Agua?"

"Si, gracias." Miguel drained the bottle.

They swung open the rear door. The agent offered him another plastic bottle from an ice chest, and when he finished drinking all the water, he handcuffed him. Miguel climbed in and sat on a bench along the side.

They drove for a half hour and then parked by a restaurant with large steer horns extending across the roof. They made him walk to a black-and-white bus with bars over the opaque windows. He climbed inside. Three men and two women sat separately. They looked at him. No one spoke. A man with a pistol in a belt holster stood outside next to the door, talking to a second man and to the two BP agents. An hour later, another BP truck arrived, and five more people entered the bus.

They must have been in a wet wash because their clothes and skin were muddy. The BP agents were equally dirty. Another hour passed before the bus left, heading north along Highway 19, past a church and a hill covered with saguaro trees. Finally, they turned into a parking lot and passed through a gate into an area enclosed by a chain-link fence topped with razor wire. They were rushed into a large building and shoved into a holding cell.

Miguel saw a bench along the wall, and looking at the men who already occupied it, he decided to sit there anyway. He thought they looked smaller than him. The smallest one got up and let him have his place on the bench. No one spoke, and soon a guard opened the door, gestured for Miguel to follow, and led him through a hallway to another closed door. The guard knocked, opened the door, and stepped aside to let Miguel enter.

They completed paperwork and then took his picture, fingerprints, and DNA. They removed his shoes and took pictures of his feet, measured his feet, measured the shoes, photographed, and returned the shoes. The same guard led him back to the holding cell, and an hour later, he returned and led Miguel to an interview room. At a table sat the border patrol agent who had arrested him.

Nate Gonzales stood eye to eye with Miguel staring into his eyes. With deep-brown eyes and black hair interspersed with a few graying streaks, he looked like Rhett Butler.

"I am Nate Gonzales," he said in Spanish. "Sit down!"

Miguel nodded and sat. "I am with the border patrol. You are being held for murder." He turned and then stiffly sat in a chair directly across the table from Miguel. "You have a right to have an attorney present. We can get you one if you want. This interview is being recorded." He pointed to a video camera. "You don't have to say anything. If you do, we can use whatever you say against you."

Without hesitation Miguel replied, "No. I have killed no one!"

Nate held up his hand. "Before you say anything more, let me tell you what I have. Say nothing until you get a lawyer. We can assign one. You understand?"

Miguel nodded, recalling the instructions from Father Michael at the church.

"Okay, it's like this, Miguel. Last night I dragged the trail that crossed the road. I took a rake and removed footprints. This morning, I returned and found footprints on the west side of the road and another set of the same footprints on the other side. I know that trail. We drove to where it crosses another road. No footprints were there. I dragged that site the night before

also, so I knew someone was between the two roads. We waited. Do you follow me so far?"

"Si, you waited to see who comes." He shrugged his shoulders. "It was me. Okay, but I killed no one."

"I returned and backtracked. Mules walk to the highway after dumping their loads to catch a ride to the border. I wanted to find the drop site. What I found instead were bodies, lots of footprints, and shell casings. Many prints and marks went west. Only yours went north and east. In addition, one set of tire tracks of a vehicle that turned around, came back to the site, and stopped. Footprints in and out of the wash match your shoes. Your shoes and shirt are bloody."

Nate opened a folder and showed him pictures of his footprints, his shoes, and the tire tracks, as well as the bodies and the murder site. "Your feet are larger than most."

Miguel glanced down at his shirt and shoes and saw the blood. He was exhausted with little sleep and almost no food since leaving Las Flores. His head throbbed. Until now, he had managed to maintain control of himself. There had been no time to think, just react to the moment by instinct and necessity. He slumped back into the chair.

"Tell me what happened, Miguel. I know you were there. Your footprints are everywhere … near the bodies, in the wash, on the trail. I have not found a weapon. None on you and no ballistic residue, though they are still looking for shell casings or other evidence. Obviously, you could not have hijacked and killed those mules alone. Come on, Miguel. Let's have it."

Miguel sighed heavily. This situation seemed hopeless, just another wound to fester and add to the others. No one knew where he was. Feeling lost with nowhere to turn, he believed his only recourse, the only hope to survive and find Maria, depended upon this border patrol agent. Maybe if he were not so tired, he could be rational.

He explained everything that had happened: the letter sent by Maria's aunt, the meeting with Ignacio, the offers to join a new cartel from Ignacio, El Coyote, the trophy tree, the stash house, the trip to the drop site, and Manuel. He did not intend to say everything, but he lost control once he started. Because Nate was Mexican, Miguel hoped he might be sympathetic and, perhaps foolishly, thought that explaining might help him find Maria.

"All we want is a better life in America for ourselves and Juanito. My job is to protect her. I don't know where she is." He lowered his head. "I don't know what she has to endure. I must find her."

Nate let him talk. He had heard Miguel's story many times by others. Instinctively, he believed him because he wanted to. The discussion with General Marcus still rang in his ears, and so did the name Manuel. He wanted to check out Miguel if he could. He left Miguel seated at the table.

When he returned, Miguel was sleeping, his head resting on his arms folded on the table.

"Miguel," he said, waking him. "Maybe we can help each other. I am going to put you in a cell where you will be isolated. No one will see your face. It's very important that you do not talk to anyone about any of this, not about Maria, Juanito, or your family in Las Flores, not even the officers or workers here and especially not to other detainees. I will get back to you as soon as I can. You must trust me."

Once Miguel was taken to his cell, Nate removed the videotape from the video machine. Near midnight, Nate released Miguel from the isolation cell. They went to another interview room.

Miguel remembered what the priest said about his rights. "I want to call the Mexican Consulate," he said.

"That is your right. They tell you to do that. However, you should know some things first. You are in a bad way right now. Talking to the consulate will only make it worse. You have no papers. They will want you to file a charge against the border patrol. They claim we treat illegals badly. They write reports they can use to try to get charges filed against us and use the incidents to get publicity and money from organizations who want open borders. They cannot help you find Maria. They can't protect your family."

Miguel did not care about filing charges. He had no interest in open borders. His only interests were in finding EL Coyote so he could locate Maria and get back to Las Flores. So far, no one had asked for money; yet, intuitively, he knew Nate did not believe he had killed anyone. Perhaps because the man was also Mexican rather than a gringo, he just might be able to trust him. However, the man wanted something.

"As I mentioned, maybe we can help each other," Nate repeated.

Miguel was afraid to ask, but there was nothing to lose. No one knew where he was anyway, and Nate seemed his only hope. "How do you help me?"

"Find Maria. Drop the charges, and don't arrest you for illegally crossing the border."

"What do I do for you?" Miguel thought he knew the answer. Obviously, money. He knew his father did not have enough to help him.

"Could you recognize the stash house? The place they took you?"

Miguel was surprised and did not know how to respond or what Nate expected him to say. He folded his hands on the table. "What good would it do? She is not there. If you go there, they will know it is me who informed, and they will kill her or hurt my family."

"What do you expect to do if I release you?"

"Find El Coyote. Make him tell me where he took her, but they'll make me do what they want until I pay off the debt. I planned to do that and find Maria. Now I'm caught. They will think I ran away or took the drugs. I have to get back so they don't think I ran."

"Are you really that naïve, Miguel? Once they realize you can make money for them, they will use you both for more money. Once they dry out your family, both of you will have to work for them."

Neither one looked directly at the other. Miguel tried to make sense of everything Nate had said, wondering what it all meant.

"Listen to me," Nate said, breaking the silence. "I will help you find the stash house. I will drop you off so you can walk there as though you were walking for two days and nights. We will watch the house. After you are back for a while, we will let the sheriff know it is a stash house. He will raid it. You will be arrested. You will be brought back here. I will send you to Las Flores."

"That does not help me find Maria."

"Just wait a minute. If you stay here, they will think you are protected. We send everyone back or detain them. If I let you go now, you cannot find Maria. If you find El Coyote, he will kill you or have someone else kill you, or he will kill Maria himself if he knows where she is, unless, of course, you did not tell me the truth before. I believe what you said that you don't know anyone here.

"Maria's aunt and uncle live in Tucson. They are illegal," Nate said. "I checked. You are illegal. You have no money, right?"

Miguel nodded.

"They took it all, didn't they?"

"Yes, they took it," Miguel said.

"And you can't even speak English. It is hopeless. You won't find her without my help."

Miguel remembered the many homes he saw two nights ago in an area that looked like it was all Mexican. *"The Mexican community, they will help me find her."*

"Many there are illegal. Believe me, they cannot help. They are more afraid of the cartels than they are afraid of us. Most have relatives still in Mexico, like me, like you."

Miguel knew what Nate said was true. *"There is no solution,"* Miguel said, his voice barely audible.

"There is a solution. It is not an easy one. This is your choice. Here's the way it is right now. We can prosecute you for murder, we can let you walk away on your own, or you can work with us. If we let you walk away on your own, you can stay in the States, try to find a place to hide, and try to find Maria after you get out of jail. Or you can work with me now, and we do this together."

"I don't understand." Miguel replied.

"You said they asked you to join the Sonora Cartel, right?" Nate asked.

"Yes," Miguel agreed.

"I also want you to join the Sonora Cartel. We don't know much about this organization. You will provide us information about them. Also, I want you to identify people who have arrangements with the border patrol. There are rumors and some evidence of corruption within US Border Patrol and Immigration and Customs Enforcement. That is who I want. In the meantime, I will try to get a lead on Maria, and I will keep in contact with you. We have resources that can help you. However, you must go back and join there." He paused and looked Miguel in the eyes. *"I must warn you that if El Coyote or someone or anyone learns we are looking for Maria, they will kill both of you."*

"How do you contact me?" Miguel asked.

"I will find you. Do you have a picture of her?"

"It was taken away from me at the stash house."

The two men remained quiet for a moment.

"If it is so easy for us to talk, won't these people know I talked to you? Won't they know I'm a snitch? The people here even, won't they know? You said no one here can be trusted."

Again, Miguel knew he was trapped into another decision that offered no real choices: leaving Las Flores to protect Juanito and Maria, giving Maverick to Ignacio as payment for crossing the border. This was the warning he had felt and ignored from the ancient ones as he had passed the cross on the hill on his way to meet with Ignacio.

"What about my arrest for murder?" All this mess is the trouble he had tried to explain to Maria … why he didn't want to do this or to leave Mexico. If he had persisted, perhaps all this might not have happened. None of that mattered now. What has happened is history.

"There's still that," Nate said, referring to Miguel's question. "I'd have to report you to the feds, and you'd likely be transported to the Pima County Jail until we confirm your story, if we can, or try you for murder. Even without witnesses, the circumstantial evidence is overwhelming. You will stay locked up for a long time, and even if you are cleared, you will be deported to Mexico. Maria, Juanito, your parents, what happens to them?" He paused. "On the other hand, with no witnesses and no evidence except for what I know, there is no reason for anyone to think you are involved."

"You have the video from the last time we talked."

"I do indeed. No one has seen it. If you do not do this, I will turn you over to Immigration and Customs Enforcement. They will arrest Maria's family."

Now it was all clear. Nate wanted to use him to spy on the cartel. Again, he was confronted with making a choice between alternatives forced upon him by someone with power over him. If he did not agree to help this man, he would be in jail for a long time. If he agreed, he would be sinking into a way of life he detested. Again, there was no choice. In jail, he could not find Maria. In jail, he could not defend against the cartel's suspicion that he had something to do with the hijacked drugs and the murders. That meant his family in Las Flores was also in danger.

The only winners were El Coyote and Nate. He was sure El Coyote had her if she was alive. If he worked for the cartel, he was certain he would run across El Coyote and find Maria. Either he went to prison, or he joined the cartel and played Nate's game.

"I will do what you want," Miguel finally agreed.

Most of the early hours before dawn, Nate and Miguel looked for the stash house. Nate found it quickly based upon Miguel's recollection of features from the drive to the drop site. Two miles away, Nate stopped the car. Miguel left it and walked toward the stash house.

As dawn inched into Tucson, Miguel drew close and noticed a muchacho *watching at the corner. They recognized each other. The boy called on his cell phone and then put the barrel of his gun against Miguel's side. They walked to the house.*

Manuel took him into the living room and shut the door. "Where is the driver?" Miguel asked as Manuel searched him.

"He didn't return," said Manuel. "At first, we thought you ran away, but we weren't sure, and then we learned that the mules had been killed and the drugs stolen. The driver thought you set it up. What happened?"

"When we got there, I got out. I found dead men but no bundles. I told the driver. He took off, leaving me there. I started walking out to find the big highway. I found a bathroom area. I asked a Mexican in an old pickup truck to take me. He dropped me near where the 19 road and 10 road come together. I walked from there. It was a long walk to here. I didn't think I'd find it. I thought you might think I ran. I was afraid of what you might do to Maria or my family if I didn't get back."

Manual looked at Miguel as though he was not buying the story. He said, "You are resourceful." He shrugged as though it did not matter. "Okay. After we heard from the crew who killed the mules, we knew you didn't do it. They wanted money to give the stuff back to us. I thought you ran. We will find them. It is not good they do this on this side of the border. Just makes the gringos more determined to stop us." Then he laughed. "They can't stop us. Money rules, especially for gringos.

"It is a new rip crew. They wanted us to know. We will find them. It doesn't change anything. We need you to steal some cars. The cars or trucks we use for pickups and deliveries we steal. Okay? I'll let you know."

"What about that Guatemalan driver?"

"We'll find him. You want him?"

"Maybe. If I do this will you let me and Maria go?"

"It is not for me to say. Stealing a truck is not enough to pay your debt. I don't know where Maria is."

Two nights later, a loud crash and the sound of people yelling and running awakened Miguel along with the others still handcuffed on the floor. In darkness, sheriff's deputies made all of them stand outside the stash house,

searched them, and placed them into several vans. At the Tucson detention center, Miguel followed and was taken with the others to a holding cell. After an hour, a deputy removed Miguel from the cell and walked him outside to a parking lot where a car waited. A deputy removed Miguel's handcuffs, opened the passenger's door, and placed Miguel in the front seat. Miguel was surprised to find Nate Gonzales sitting in the driver's seat.

"I am taking you to the Nogales Port of Entry. You are returning to Mexico. At the Port of Entry, there will be a few questions. Just give them this." Nate gave him a sheet of paper.

When they reached the Port of Entry, Nate drove behind the building into a restricted area and parked. Neither moved. A bus arrived and stopped. "Those are illegals being sent back to Mexico," Nate said quietly.

Miguel watched the illegals step from the bus. He remembered what Nate wanted him to do. He said, "The only thing I am interested in is finding my wife. How do I know you will keep your word?"

"You don't. However, if she is still alive, you can never find her on your own. We are in this together, Miguel. I need you to trust me."

They sat quietly. Finally, Nate broke the silence. "Promise," he said. "If she is alive, I will find her. I need you to join the Sonora Cartel. Together, we can help each other. We will meet again soon."

They stood. Nate extended his hand to Miguel. Miguel looked into his eyes, and they shook hands. For some reason he could not explain, Miguel felt a bond with this border patrol agent.

Nate handed Miguel a packet of money. He watched as Miguel walked across the border and entered a bus with the other illegals. Nate removed his phone. The bus passed through the gate and turned south. He dialed a number.

"It's me," he said. "Done."

6

*J*ose entered the cantina. Inez pointed to a table in the corner. Miguel slept. His head rested on his arms. On the table were a half-empty bottle and an empty plate. Inez and Jose helped Miguel get in the truck.

A long breath escaped Miguel's lungs. He felt relieved to be home and anxious to see his mother and Juanito. By the time they reached the compound, he had somewhat recovered and tried to store the events of the recent past into an isolated notch in his mind. He went to his empty casa, fell onto the bed, and slept. He awoke the following morning. Rascal lay on the floor beside the bed.

At his parent's house, he reunited with Juanito who was on the floor in the cradle he had built. His mother, Yolanda, sat next to the cradle. Miguel rushed to Juanito and lifted him into his arms. He carried Juanito to Jose's chair and sat. He pulled the baby tightly to him, unable to speak as the lump in his throat grew. His hands shook. Finally, he succeeded in controlling his hands. Juanito grasped Miguel's finger, cooed, and smiled.

Miguel had held Juanito many times. This time was different. He knew this is where he and Maria belonged: helping their son, teaching him to ride, Jose explaining the world and individual responsibility, and most importantly where Miguel could best protect all of them. Nothing was more important than family. That was central and most important. Everything else could wait until tomorrow.

It was not that he had not paid attention to Juanito before. But his experience with the real world had changed his perspective, perhaps also changed his soul and hardened him.

He looked toward the corral, now vacant without Maverick. Without thinking, he whistled, hoping he would see his horse trot to the fence. He felt a duty to make things right again. Nothing made sense except the baby in his arms. Only the things you touch make sense. He looked away from Juanito's expectant face and wondered how this had happened. He wanted life to be the way it was when they were all together.

He looked toward the kitchen where dinner warmed, expecting to see and feel Maria's presence. Home was incomplete without her.

At dinner, he told his parents of their crossing, their separation, and how the border patrol had arrested him because he was undocumented and sent him home. He did not mention the cartel or Nate Gonzales or the rape or the dead mules lying in the wash or the trophy tree. The only indication of something more serious was the bitterness reflected in his voice.

"I must go back and find her," he said. "The longer it takes, the harder it will be."

"What if you are caught again? You know no one. You are illegal. You do not have a job. How can you find her?" Yolanda was crying.

"She wants to find her family in Tucson. I don't have their address or phone number. If I had that, I could find her because that is where Maria is going. We will get together there. I can't just leave her."

Jose looked skeptical. "How do you get back there?"

"I do the same as before, through Ignacio, to get to El Coyote. Then he will tell me where to find her."

"But you have no money. How can you pay?"

"I have some money … enough." He did not want to look at his father.

Jose looked at Yolanda and then said to Miguel, "You haven't been gone long. There is more trouble already. People we don't know in Las Flores the other day asking for Ignacio. The men at the cantina, they say they are narco. In addition, they say Ignacio is cartel. Do you know this?" He held Miguel's eyes until Miguel looked away.

Miguel looked at Jose. He saw Jose knew. "That is the only way to get there and to find her." He wanted to tell Jose about Nate and being undercover. He knew Jose would be proud of him.

"I see." Jose stood and walked to the cabinet and removed a bottle and two glasses. "Ignacio did not get Maverick to win any races."

Jose remained standing at the table. The bottle was unlabeled. He poured some into each glass. "Vargas gave me this bottle a couple of years ago. He claims this mescal was from Oaxaca and stored in barrels for over four years. I have not tasted … waiting for a special occasion. So, you being home, that is a special occasion, no?"

"This we take outside and sit and watch the sunset," Miguel said.

They went out back onto a porch and sat on a sofa with the stuffing falling out. Yolanda followed with Juanito. She set him down where he unsteadily stood next to Miguel, grasping Miguel's leg. They faced the mountain. There was no need to talk.

They used to sit there when he was as young as Juanito, silently accepting their lives as they were. Now they wanted more. Miguel looked at Juanito and wished to turn it back. Rascal trotted from around the corner of the house and lay at Miguel's feet.

"Sometimes you don't appreciate what you have until you don't have it anymore," said Miguel, looking at the distant mountain.

The mountain seemed closer than he remembered. He saw where the tree line stopped. He always thought it was interesting how the foliage changed as the elevation increased. First, there were many trees, then they got smaller, and finally they ended just below the top. A creek began there, meandering down to the desert floor. The water usually flowed all year. It originated from melting snow and seeped from inside the mountain. The mountain seemed close, but it was almost twenty miles away.

"What of the gringos?" his father was saying.

"Saw a lot in Tucson where everyone looks like baby rabbits scurrying everywhere. Big pueblo. Mostly though, I saw many Mexicans where I was. One boy from Guatemala." He shook his head slowly.

"I was in Mexico City once," said Jose. "It is big. The place was suffocating with so much smoke, dirt, crowds, garbage, and stench. You can't see the sun. The mountains were nearly hidden in the haze. Such a place says Mexico is important, I guess, but look here at these mountains and look at all this open area. We have nothing, true, except we have this and many tomorrows." He stretched his arms toward the expanding sunset.

Miguel looked at him. He was his father's son. He looked at his own son, Juanito. He remembered his grandfather. He saw life at that moment in its fundamental essence, perhaps now lost forever. "Mexico has changed, even here," he said sadly.

"This is true, Miguel. Human nature has not changed. There was a time of nobility my grandfather used to speak of, even though he was very poor and lived a hard life. This dope, these narcos, they lack nobility. Even now in Las Flores, people are afraid. They are afraid of men like Ignacio. The country is washed in blood. It is not like before when we fought for independence. Now we fight each other to grow poppies and make chemicals for what they call meth, and we kill to control routes to America. Now, Miguel, we make drug addicts of our own people. It is one thing to have corruption. We have always had corruption. This now is what hell must be like."

They sipped in silence, the liquid as slick as silk.

"It is because of the gringos," Jose continued. "They want the drugs. We want their money, because we cannot make enough here. Our government encourages immigration, illegal or not, so they will send their money back here."

Maybe there was much more to say. Instead, they watched the desert turn colors as the shadows extended and the light softened. The mescal was almost gone.

"Maybe when you do find her, you will come back here. Your mother worries about the danger and what you will get into and fears we won't see you again." Jose rose unsteadily. His hand shook.

Miguel stood and took the bottle. He poured mescal into his father's glass and the rest into his own. Some of it spilled. In unison, they raised their glasses, put the glasses to their lips, looked at each other, and then spit the liquid on the ground. Steadying each other, they entered the house where Yolanda was feeding Juanito.

Miguel wanted to remember this time so he could tell Juanito about his grandfather.

7

*E*xcept for Ignacio, Inez, and her small daughter, the cantina was empty. Miguel joined them at the same rear corner table.

"So, we meet again, amigo." Ignacio offered his hand, and Miguel took it. "Things did not go so well, I hear."

"You didn't warn me about El Coyote. He stole our money and raped Maria. He took us to a stash house, he separated us, and she is gone. I don't know where she is. They are making me work for them until I am able to pay them. They threatened my family and Maria if I don't do what they say. They want even more money. The border patrol arrested me and sent me back here. No, it did not go so well. Why did you not explain everything to us?" He wanted to pull Ignacio out of his chair and do him bodily harm … something that would take him but little effort to accomplish. However, he needed Ignacio to find Maria.

Ignacio sat up straighter in his chair and looked at Inez and then back at Miguel. "I tried to explain some of those things to her. She didn't tell you?" He looked back at Inez. "Inez was here too."

Inez nodded.

"When?" Miguel asked Inez.

"When she got the letter from my mother," Inez replied. "We talked with Maria about immigrating. I told her about my parents' crossing."

Miguel turned and walked toward the door, trying to control himself. Nothing made sense. He tried to remember when Maria might have gone to the cantina. She would have taken the bus, or maybe she drove the truck. He wondered why she had never mentioned the conversation. When he reached the door, he turned and walked back toward the table. Inez and Ignacio watched him. Ignacio said something to her. She nodded and returned to the bar with her baby.

"Ignacio, I need you to get me across the border again with El Coyote. Can you stop them from harming my family?"

If Ignacio was concerned, he did not show it. "It didn't go so well with Maverick. When I race him, he does not come in first. What do I need to do?"

"What do you know about horses?" Miguel questioned.

"I can ride," Ignacio noted.

"Not enough. That is only the beginning. You and the horse have to be like one person, especially with Maverick. I raised him from a foal. We talked. He knows how I think. It will take time, maybe never."

Inez brought the beer.

"Horses don't talk," Ignacio said.

"You don't know how to listen."

Slowly, the sun crept through the open door and the windows and made patterns on the scarred floor. Miguel, standing over Ignacio, watched it advance along the floor toward them. He did not understand why he had to go through all this and struggled to get control of himself.

Again, he said, "I need you to get me across the border with El Coyote. Can you stop them from hurting my family?"

Ignacio poured the beer into both glasses. "I am sorry about Maria. It is what sometimes happens. It is a matter of competition between the coyotes, a macho thing. This one is the most feared, an experienced knife fighter. The human smugglers view these people as sheep, as merely smuggled products like any commodity. A pretty woman like Maria and young girls are vulnerable and fair game, like the leader of a wolf pack taking a bitch just because he can. That's why they have trophy trees to confirm their dominance so others will acknowledge." He sipped and then raised his hand dismissively and shrugged. "The women should expect it as part of the price. Not only do the coyotes rape them, the other men, the illegals, they do also."

Ignacio took a couple of sips and then wiped the back of his hand across his mouth.

"What do they do with the women at the stash house?" Miguel asked.

"Gringos buy them, sell them into the sex industry, or hold them as hostages to get more money from their families."

"You are a big man with this cartel, Ignacio. You are a plaza leader. You must control or know about these things and have influence."

"This is some of the perks, another way the coyotes get paid. You walk out of civilization when you enter the illegal immigrant world. Humanity disappears. The coyote is the most powerful person, the giver and taker of life. They follow him along like sheep, possibly to a slaughter. Out there, the coyote is the only law. There is no right or wrong. Humans become merely inventory. People are nothing, not even victims, just a commodity. The power is overwhelming. They can do as they want with the illegals. Who's to stop them?" Ignacio shrugged. "El Coyote is a businessman, Miguel. He has his own crew. He only takes important packages across the border like the marijuana smuggled by your group. He makes sure it is delivered to a stash house or as

instructed. He also trades in people, selling the women or kids to others. We get dollars for that also. El Coyote has done this for a long time. In addition, he tries to find out the names of relatives and where they live. Most illegals have relatives in Mexico or South America. They use the information for ransom."

"He doesn't work for you? You are the plaza leader."

"He is an independent contractor," Ignacio explained. "I pay him to take the illegals and contraband across and deliver it to where he is told. He can do it himself, or he can hire others in turn. He'll work for whoever pays him the most."

"What if he doesn't do what you want?"

"Simple. We don't hire him, or if he won't cooperate, what do you think? We kill him. Who cares about a dead coyote?"

Miguel shook his head, stood and walked toward the door, turned around, walked back to the table, and made the same tour two more times before stopping over Ignacio. "What of Maria? Where is she? How could you let this happen?"

"This is just what it is, Miguel. I don't know where she is. She is not with us at the hacienda. El Coyote is the only one who knows." He paused, closely watching Miguel. "This is the reason you must join us. It's the only way you will learn what's happened to her. The offer is still open. We are having a little war now. We can protect your family if you are with us. We need men like you to help us expand and get more control."

"Why me?"

"You are considered a tough man and smart ... a leader."

"Who says this?" Miguel asked.

"Those who know you at the hacienda: Vargas, the priest in Las Flores, and the men at the cantina. They all say so. If you don't join us, you must join the ones who are trying to take control from us here. They want you as well or to get rid of you. For people like you, there is no neutrality unless you have power. You have no power, Miguel. You must think of it like an invasion. This is our home. We defend what is ours. They want to keep control. You are either with us or against us, and, amigo, you will not have to pay back the cartel. The cartel is our power, Miguel."

Miguel wondered if these words were just bluster, another trick, an attempt by a small self-important man to prove his courage or to impress him with his knowledge of the cartels.

Agent Gonzales's instructions had now settled in Miguel's mind. He had gone over and over the alternatives. They were clear: remain in Mexico, return to the United States alone, or join the cartel. If he remained in Mexico, he could continue his life the way it was before crossing, perhaps be in charge of the horses. That alternative posed a life without Maria. Every time he let his thoughts loose, he relived the scene at the trophy tree of El Coyote dragging her toward the opening into the brush, of her screams, then nothing until he was forced to stand by a muchacho at the stash house.

Without himself and Nate's resources, how could she find her way to live with her aunt in Tucson? She would have to work off the money herself. The cartel would hound him and his family, just as they did with Emilio's father in Guatemala, leaving the family impoverished. He remembered how Emilio had saved Maria on the Beast. He wondered how Inez's parents had made the trip without such help.

He had to find her. He wanted to be with her and Juanito. No other purpose mattered, except killing El Coyote.

"If you don't join us," Ignacio said, interrupting Miguel's thoughts, "We cannot protect you or your family. If you don't join us, you are our enemy. We may kill you, especially now that you know so much about our business. Your choice is either them or us. Also, do not forget, we have Maria. Only you and I care whether she lives. If she dies, it's of little consequence."

"What do you mean, just you and I care? You have known her as long as me. We all came from here. It is not like she is some stranger." Miguel looked at Inez. They attended the same school. He edged forward, rested his elbows on the table, and held his head, rubbing his fingers along his temples.

Ignacio shrugged and calmly sipped his beer, his boots on the chair in front of him, the same smug way he had sat when Miguel first met with him. "We have a little war now."

Miguel stared at Ignacio. "What are you talking about? There is no war here. I've heard nothing. We are in the middle of nowhere."

"It hasn't officially hit Las Flores yet. Vargas has hired armed guards for the hacienda. We provide the security. This is about power and politics and money, mostly money. Why should people like us not get our share? Is there somewhere else you can go to get as good a job?"

Miguel replied, "Because, if we fight, we will die? Because, what you do is illegal?"

"People have crossed and smuggled things from both sides since there was a border, first the Indians, now us. The gringos say they want to stop us now, but it belonged to us. We just may get it all back anyway if our immigrants continue to cross and grow more Mexicans. Our government cannot stop us from going there even if they wanted. Besides, the government needs the money. It goes to the big shots, not to us. There is no job here. You'll go to the cities and live crammed into a suffocating barrio. You want to live like that? You have seen it there?"

"No. I had a good job, the horses, the family, the desert, the races. What's so bad about that?"

"Ask Maria."

"Ask Maria?" Miguel sat quietly for a moment and then gave Ignacio a hard look. "You discussed crossing with Maria?"

"And with Inez. Maria wants more for the both of you."

"What makes Maria and Juanito your business?"

Ignacio appeared to sink into the chair. "Well, we sometimes talked. And, uh, well, you know with Inez?"

"Where's Florio when you are having these discussions with his wife about his business?"

"Well, uh, working at the hacienda, like now."

"And when you were discussing these important matters with Maria, what she wanted for herself and Juanito, that was where exactly?"

"Well, we … you know, while you were in the army." Ignacio suddenly straightened up in his chair. "Listen, Miguel, you need me if you are to find El Coyote and Maria."

They sat quietly. Shadows blanketed the sun's pattern on the floor. Two men entered. Miguel recognized them from the pueblo. They worked on the hacienda. He nodded to them. They went to the bar, and Inez served them.

"I will join," Miguel finally agreed.

"You know you can't leave … not ever."

"Yes."

"There are a couple of things you must know now if you didn't know already. This is the Sonora Cartel. We are led by El Anglo. Don't know his real name. He is building and consolidating his control over Sonora and wants to control all the way to the southern border of Arizona and beyond. This is a rich plaza for taking people, drugs, and other things across the Arizona border.

El Anglo says most of the violence will stop if there is only one cartel in Mexico. Both the government and the people will benefit. Such a vision is beyond me. We are a transnational business, he says, like a holding company, and a small army. He has important contacts in the Mexican government and some say in El Norte and elsewhere.

"We operate up there through street gangs as well as our own people. He makes it sound like some kind of Mexican cause, like maybe a new Reconquista, but the only cause I care about is me." He sipped his beer.

"That is enough for you to know. You cannot talk about this. You must also be aware that the Morales Cartel will try to prevent our further expansion. They do that by hijacking our deliveries and attacking us. We must always be alert. They will try to get you. You must be careful of what you say to others. They torture for information. I am in charge of this plaza. Meet me back here in seven days, and I will have a job for you. This assignment will be to confirm your abilities and your loyalty before I can send you to find El Coyote."

Miguel returned to the fields to help his father and the others clear an irrigation ditch that had clogged with sand. Several young men armed with rifles patrolled near the compound, and others were nearby when he worked. On the second day, he was asked to be a guard.

Later, he also informed his father he was leaving for a few days.

"Where are you going?" Jose asked.

"It is best you don't ask."

"Have you met again with Ignacio?"

"Yes! I must find Maria. I do what I must for her and Juanito."

8

*M*iguel found Ignacio in a car behind the cantina, just as Ignacio had instructed. Ignacio left the car and spread a map on the hood. "Your destination is a truck terminal north of the Nogales Port of Entry, right here." He tapped his finger on a mark several miles into Arizona. "An hour before you arrive at the Nogales POE, call this number to learn which gate to enter and the time to be there. You know how to use a cell phone?"

"No."

Ignacio showed Miguel the cell phone. "All you have to do is hit this number. It will contact the person on the other end who will be expecting your call. This button here will let you answer if he calls you. This one lets you end the call. Another car will follow you once you cross the border. It is one of ours. He will tell you where to park at the terminal.

"Here is your identification card and your visa. Counterfeiting documents is just another one of our businesses," Ignacio explained. "My job is to ensure this plaza is secure. I identify and pay people to allow our traffic: the governor's representative who pays the police, the army, the agent at the Mexican border, and the one at the US side. The most danger is from the other groups who want this plaza. This is part of our little war. The last time they tried it, we killed all of them. Your only responsibility is to drive the car. Better the border patrol or sheriff catch you than get captured by another cartel or bandits. A rip crew will torture you before they kill you. That is why I only tell you what is necessary.

"We have followed this routine many times without incident. This is an important delivery. I did not want to use one of the groups we pay who hire the expendable couriers. If caught on the American side, it means jail. The odds are against it. We lose only about 10 percent of our merchandise," he said as though it was not important.

"Be very careful at the US gate. Don't do anything that creates suspicion. Watch your behavior and appearance. Do not appear nervous, and do not be too bold. Remember, you are going to Tucson to shop at the mall and are returning later. If you are not in the correct line when you get there, they may arrest or search you, though if you do not seem like a smuggler, they may let you pass anyway. With our guy, it's just safer."

He made Miguel walk away from him and then called him back. "It's good you are wearing nice clothes so you don't look like a wetback. Only answer what they ask. Be polite. Say yes sir and no sir or ma'am. Don't pay attention to the dog. It will sniff around your car for drugs. We disguise the smell. If you *act nervous, they will notice. Someone will call you and tell you which gate to drive through on the American side. You will also receive a call telling you what car to follow once you are through. We do not provide this information in advance because we don't want anyone to know. They will speak Spanish. Any questions?"*

"No, I don't think so." Miguel was not sure he would remember anything because the instructions came so fast. He felt confused, yet strangely calm. At least now he felt he was on Maria's trail instead of just floundering.

"Okay," Ignacio said. "You will also bring merchandise back to Mexico. We will meet you at the border on the Mexican side. They will give you the next instructions and, if necessary, make the payments."

Miguel surmised he was carrying drugs. He had no idea where in the vehicle they stashed them. He wanted to ignore the danger. He watched every vehicle and remained alert for any activity in which someone paid attention to him.

A block before the Nogales POE he encountered long lines of cars, trucks, buses, and motorcycles. He could not see the entrance. Vehicles pinned him between them. He called the number as he joined the slowly moving vehicles.

"Lane two," the voice said and hung up.

He slowly maneuvered into what he hoped was the second lane. Ignacio's instructions were specific: go where the voice said. The voice said the second lane when he entered the US side and the second lane only. A half a block ahead was a corner where the lines turned toward the port of entry. He hoped he would see entrance 2 then, and if he was in the wrong lane, he could maneuver to the correct one. Even so, such a movement might give him away. It took about a half hour before he turned the corner. He seemed to be in the correct lane.

Slowly, he moved forward to the Mexican border with the others. He passed through the Mexican side without having to stop.

Entering the United States, a customs officer directed a car in the right lane to pull over. An agent escorted the driver inside a building. The US agent in lane 2 was older. Miguel regarded him carefully while the customs agent examined each car ahead and asked the drivers questions.

Miguel was next. He took a deep breath, knowing this was the most critical point. The agent's name tag read "Walker."

"Good day, sir," Walker said, looking at Miguel through brown rimmed glasses. "Identification please, sir."

Miguel removed the identification card, Mexican driver's license, and green card. He handed them through the window to Walker.

Customs Agent Walker nodded to Miguel. "You are a Mexican citizen?"

"Yes, sir," Miguel replied.

Walker was about five nine or ten with a memorable plastic face. Although he thought it hard to tell the ages of gringos, Miguel guessed he was in his fifties.

Walker slowly studied the documents, looked at Miguel and then at the card and back at Miguel. He returned the cards to Miguel. Walker stuck his head inside the car and looked into the back seat. Walker nodded to Miguel and said, "Have a nice day, sir." He stepped back and waved Miguel through.

As soon as Miguel had cleared the area and saw the POE in the rearview mirror, he released his breath and placed the cell phone on the dash. He drove about five miles. He began to worry because he had not received a call. He wondered what to do if he did not receive a call. Another two miles passed. The phone rang.

"I am going to pass you. Follow me."

Miguel followed the car into a large truck terminal and stopped in front of door 10. A car pulled alongside. The gringo driver walked over to him.

"Let me check things out," he said in Spanish. He disappeared for a minute, returned, and said, "Get out. Give me your keys."

The gringo drove the car inside a large garage. As he returned to Miguel, the garage door closed behind him. "Okay, let's go eat," he announced before driving Miguel to a nearby truck stop for lunch.

The gringo looked at his watch when they finished. "We must get your car. You will take Interstate 19 back to Nogales. I will follow you to the border. I'll call and let the others know you are crossing. They take care of everything. Once you are across, there is a large parking lot next to the Mexican customs building. They will be waiting for you. You park, and they will find you. They will stay with you all the way to Hermosillo and show you where you will leave the car. They will take you to the bus stop for the bus to Las Flores."

Before midnight, they arrived at a small warehouse in the outskirts of Hermosillo. Miguel pulled inside where two men were unloading weapons and ammunition from a trailer.

Following the instructions of the man who seemed in charge, he left the car at the warehouse. Everything had gone as planned. On the bus to Las

Flores, he finally relaxed. In Las Flores, he spent the remainder of the night in the cantina.

Having spent a restless night on a mattress on the floor, he awoke to the noise of the family arising. Florio caught the truck that took workers from the pueblo to the hacienda.

When Ignacio arrived, it was early afternoon. He walked to Miguel, who was standing at a table. His back was to the bar. "The trip must have gone well. I haven't heard any bad news."

"Yes," replied Miguel. "Everything went as you said."

Ignacio reached inside his shirt, removed an envelope, and gave it to Miguel. "That was an important delivery. Were you worried?"

"Not much," he said. He looked at the bills in the envelope. It was close to $5,000. Miguel closed the envelope and stuffed it into his shirt. He had never seen so much money in one place. "The instructions were clear." He reached into his pocket, pulled out the cell phone, and gave it to Ignacio. "It's just a job," Miguel said, as though danger was merely an expectation in a job description. "What have you found out?" he asked Ignacio.

"Nothing about Maria. They know you completed this task without incident. They wanted you to meet with people at the hacienda near Hermosillo if this job was successful. I would say the job was very successful, especially for a first try. This was an unusual trip with lots of contraband going each way. People who shop on either side of the border do most of these crossings. The hacienda is the headquarters for the Sonora Cartel, at least until we get larger and more organized. Now we are recruiting." He gave Miguel directions on a folded sheet of paper. "When you get there, they'll have your name on a list at the gate."

Outside, a car stopped. Doors slammed. Whoever was out there took their time entering. The hazy shadow of two men with assault weapons outlined in the blinding sunlit doorway caused an adrenalin rush. Miguel and Ignacio looked toward the entrance. Both tensed and focused on two men.

The first, the larger, held an M16 at his waist as he checked out the room. A muchacho holding an AK-47 remained at the door watching outside. The older one moved quickly toward Miguel and Ignacio. He glanced at Miguel who had shoved back his chair, preparing to rise.

The man turned his back to Miguel and turned to Ignacio who reached for the semiautomatic pistol in the holster on his belt. Inez screamed, picked up her baby, and started to step back from the bar. Ignacio's back was to the bar. He was between the bar and the shooter. As he stood, he started to raise the pistol.

"This is what happens to traitors," the man shouted, firing a short burst just as Miguel shoved the rifle and grabbed the man around the neck, knocking the rifle and the man to the floor. Miguel kicked it away. He stepped over the man lying on his back, reached down, grabbed the weapon, fell to the floor, and rolled onto his stomach.

Surprised, the boy standing just outside the door turned around and tried to shoot off balance as he rushed into the room. The rounds mostly peppered the ceiling. The boy moved to fire again. Miguel fired a short burst from his weapon and then rolled over, seeing the boy fall on a table and then to the floor.

Realizing Inez was wounded, Miguel growled like an enraged animal, turned, and shot the first man as he tried to rise. He turned back to the boy with the AK-47 who was lying on the floor bleeding. Miguel had made sure he was dead. Most of the boy's face was missing. The older man groaned and tried to move. Miguel turned and emptied the magazine into him. Miguel knelt by Ignacio to check his pulse. There was none.

Hearing a noise at the bar, Miguel stood and turned toward Inez. Wide-eyed and still holding her baby, Inez stared at him. She slumped out of site behind the bar. Miguel went to Inez and walked behind the bar. A round had passed through Inez's neck, and probably also through the baby's head, which only partially remained. Other rounds had punctured the bar and the wall behind it, shattering bottles. Liquor flowed to the floor like a waterfall.

Miguel searched the bodies of Ignacio and the two shooters and took their money, along with Ignacio's car keys and cell phone. He gathered all the weapons.

The cantina was deathly quiet except the overhead fan, which provided a surreal rhythmic sound. He saw and smelled the blood draining from the five bodies. Miguel slipped on the bloody floor before looking back at the bar where Inez's feet extended beyond the corner. He hesitated, as though he expected her to get up.

He then walked out the door and searched the killers' car. A bag containing magazines and ammunition was on the floor. He took it before slipping into the driver's seat of Ignacio's SUV and drove to the hacienda.

Miguel arrived after dark. It had taken him almost the entire drive to calm down. *The events felt like a slow-motion scene. He thought it ironic that his participation was unthinkingly reactionary, without a moment's reflection of what he ought to do. He'd never seen an M16, let alone fired one. It had a trigger, and that's all he needed. Even more baffling was that he felt no remorse, no prick of conscience for killing two people. He felt nothing at all . . . except for Inez, his niece, and Ignacio.*

Miguel found his father in the shed cleaning tools. Jose turned and saw Miguel's blank face.

Without emotion Miguel said, "I killed two men in the cantina. They killed Ignacio. They killed Inez. They killed Angel."

"Oh my God," Jose said. "Are you all right?"

"Yes. Somehow, I am okay. It is a mess there."

"Who did this?"

Miguel explained everything that happened. He did not tell his father about the smuggling, the border, what he had done, or where he had been.

"Los narco!" Jose said, shaking his head. "They say there is a fight for Sonora, that there is a new capo building an organization. They say he is more vicious than Los Zetas or the Sinaloa's and has more power."

Jose found a stool and sat, while Miguel paced slowly.

Finally, Jose said, "What is your part in this?"

"I can't say. I must leave here. After killing those gangsters, they will find me, or they will hurt you if they know I am here and find out you are my family."

"Who saw you?"

"No one. No one alive is still there." He thought for a moment. "I spent the night with Inez and Florio. Florio knows I was there. He was gone, probably at the hacienda when this happened."

"He didn't see what happened?" Jose asked.

"No," Miguel assured him.

"So how would anyone know you killed them?"

"They wouldn't, I guess."

"Did you leave anything there?"

"Nothing. I took their money, their guns, Ignacio's keys, and his car. That's it." Miguel walked outside to the car. The sky was clear except for clouds that

looked like they were caught in the mountain peaks. He took the AK-47 and its magazines plus the extra rounds from the SUV and returned to the shed.

"Here, take these for protection!" he told his father. He then took the money from his shirt and gave Jose several thousand dollars. "To help with Juanito. The quicker I leave, the safer you all will be. I don't know when I will see you again."

Jose sat on the stool looking at the rifle and the money and then looked expectantly at Miguel who turned away. Miguel walked to the SUV, opened the door, stopped, turned, and looked at the compound and his now deserted casa. He was still proud of having built it.

He wondered about their future. Could they ever be together again? Could they ever return here? He turned and faced north toward Arizona. What would happen to Yolanda, Jose, and Juanito? He had brought this trouble upon them all. He must find EL Coyote and through him, with Nate's help, Maria, and then he must end all this. He got into Ignacio's SUV. As he sat behind the wheel, he wondered how the killers knew Ignacio would be at the cantina. They must have followed Ignacio from somewhere. Who sent them?

Miguel got out of the car and looked around the compound. He wondered whether others had followed him. Everything had irrevocably changed. He got back in the SUV. The M16 lay on the seat next to the map Ignacio had drawn to the hacienda near Hermosillo. He knew they would come for him. He did not want to think about whether they would come for his family. Maybe Vargas would protect them. Maybe the Sonora Cartel would protect all of them.

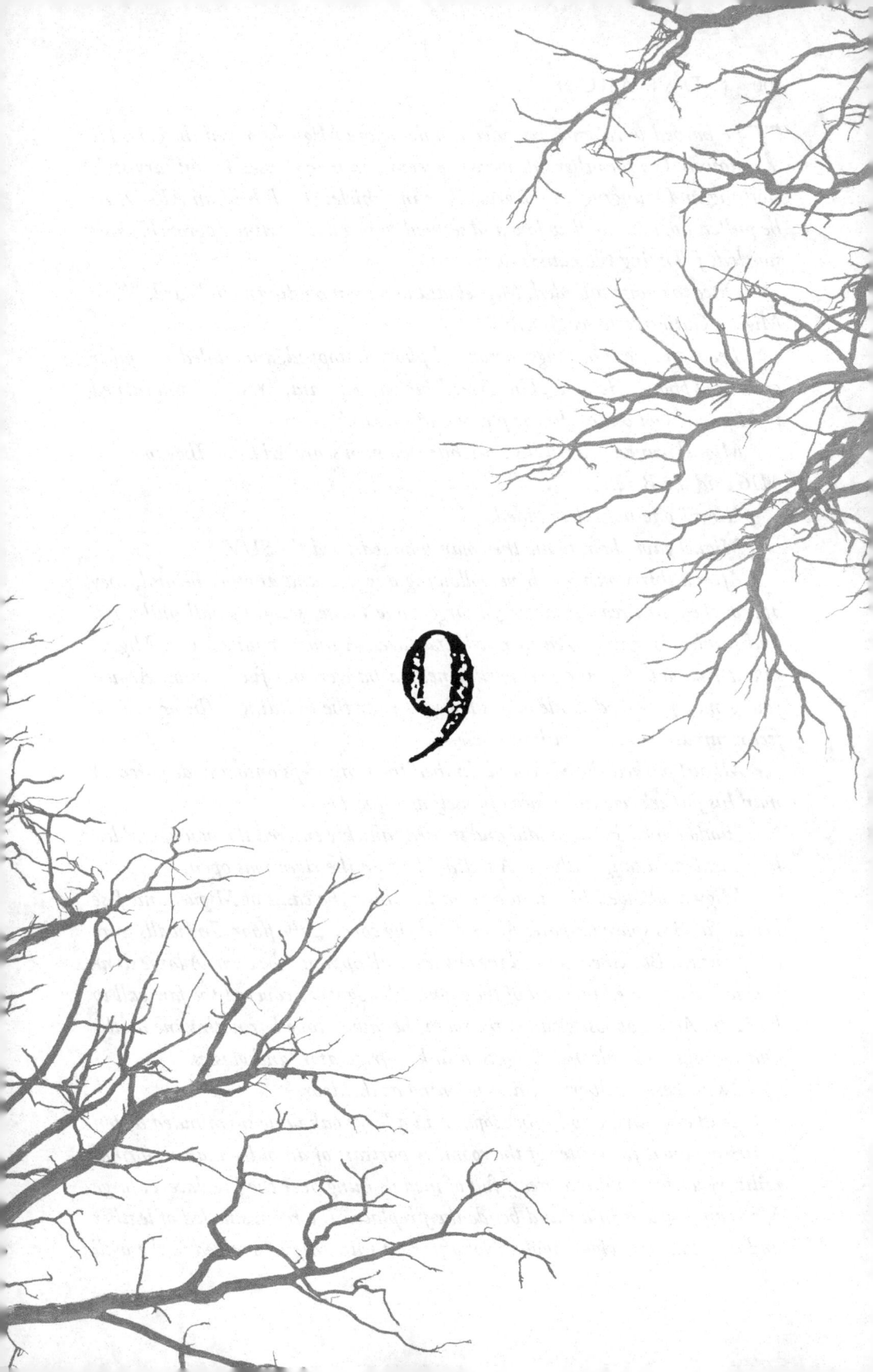

9

*T*he barbed wire fence extended a mile before Miguel noticed the gate. He slowed. On the other side were five jeeps and men dressed in military-style clothing and lounging on the ground or in vehicles. Each held an AK-47. As he pulled up, a plane flew low and seemed to be on a landing approach. Dust swirled, following the plane's wake.

Once the noise subsided, Miguel said to a man holding a clipboard, "I am Miguel Gutierrez to see Alvera."

The man traced his finger down a clipboard, stopped, and dialed a number on his cell phone. He said, "Gutierrez." He paused, said, "Yes, sir," and turned to Miguel. "Get out of the car please and spread."

Miguel leaned against his car while two men searched him. They took the M16 and the Beretta.

"Keys!" one man demanded.

Miguel gave them to another man who searched the SUV.

After a thirty-minute drive, following one jeep and another behind, they approached an area containing a large stone house, several small buildings, and stables. Horses grazed in nearby pastures. A quarter mile away, Miguel saw a runway. A plane was parked near a hanger and fuel pumps. Armed young men patrolled while others lounged near the buildings. The organized feel reminded him of a military base.

Miguel parked the SUV and climbed the front steps onto a wide porch. A man his father's age introduced himself as Filberto.

"Follow me," Filberto said and turned, quickly entered the house, and led him inside to a long hallway. A sliding door on the right was open.

Miguel followed him into a room in which the casas of Miguel and Jose would fit with space to spare. An oriental rug covered the floor. The walls were oak paneled. Bookshelves lined the outside wall opposite the door. A large stone fireplace dominated one end of the room. Photographs covered the far wall to his right. At the opposite end of the room, he saw a stone bar with wine bottles and various other alcohol delights, a sink, refrigerator, and glasses.

"Wait here," Filberto said, remaining at the door.

Leather chairs, two leather sofas, and a large oak table surrounded by ten chairs occupied the center of the room. A portrait of an older man in formal military uniform with a breast full of medals hung over the fireplace. A large Mexican flag was in a stand beside the fireplace. The room smelled of leather and oak and stale cigar smoke. Not offered a seat, Miguel walked to the wall *containing the pictures. The photos were mostly old black-and-whites depicting soldiers and fighters, some in large sombreros, others in various uniforms with World War I Mauser rifles and bandoliers draped across their shoulders.*

Other photos depicted various scenes, probably the ranch and perhaps the family, some riding or leading horses. A framed map that might have been of the hacienda, and a variety of individual portraits of both women and men and children were likely family members. One of the pictures was familiar. He tried to recall a familiar man with a large sombrero and mustache holding a rifle.

"That man is Poncho Villa," said a voice behind Miguel. "It was taken shortly after he returned from raiding Douglas, Arizona. The man standing next to him is my grandfather."

Jose often spoke of Villa while they watched the sunset on the small back porch. He liked to repeat stories and legends of the revolution. Jose regarded Villa a hero.

The voice behind Miguel said, "My grandfather rode and fought with Villa when they were young Mexican bandoleros in the Sierra Madre Occidental in Durango and Chihuahua."

Without turning around, Miguel replied, "My father tells that Villa after he'd killed an army officer and served time was called Francisco Poncho Villa after his own grandfather Francisco Villa."

"That's right, Miguel. If you want to understand present-day Mexico, you must know the history of the revolution. Men like Poncho Villa planted the seeds of today's Mexico. It was a time that has yet to end. That table there is sometimes where they'd plan their strategy," the voice continued.

Miguel turned. The man was pointing to the large table dominating the center of the room. "Villa liked to hide here. See that picture with the old car?"

Miguel nodded.

"In 1923 he was assassinated while driving through the town of Hidalgo de Parral. If you look carefully, you will see some of the bullet holes in the car."

Miguel leaned forward to scrutinize the picture. He turned to see a man in his late forties, tall, wearing a white shirt, tan slacks, and immaculate handmade hand-tooled classic boots. He had jet-black hair graying around the temples, saddle brown complexion, a perfectly trimmed mustachio, and black penetrating eyes; he was an aristocratic composite who screamed of conquistador heritage.

"You are Miguel Gutierrez," he said, advancing toward Miguel with his hand extended. "I am Arturo Alvera. Welcome to my hacienda."

Miguel felt awkward. He knew Alvera was an important man in Mexico. The military was under his department. Miguel's boots were filthy, his clothes tattered, his hair long and unkempt, and his hands dirty. He should have entered through the kitchen and never been in the presence of such a man.

Miguel looked toward the door, thinking of escape. He did not know what to say and hesitantly shook Alvera's hand.

As though attempting to put him at ease, Alvera said, "My friend Ernesto Vargas said good things about you. Please sit." He pointed to one of the leather chairs. While Alvera was doubtless genteel and sophisticated, there was no mistaking he was in control, an exhibition of confidence and subtle power.

Alvera looked toward the door as a man entered the room. He was younger than Alvera and taller, with an unmistakable military bearing despite his ponytail. Not Mexican, he seemed about the same height as Miguel. He was clean-shaven with brown hair and blue eyes and an intense gaze, through which he carefully scrutinized Miguel. He sat across from Miguel.

"This is El Anglo, Miguel."

Filberto appeared in the doorway. "He has arrived," Filberto said and stepped aside to let Ernesto Vargas enter. Vargas was the hacendado of the hacienda at Las Flores where Miguel and Jose worked. He nodded to both Alvera and El Anglo and then turned to Miguel.

"It is good to see you again, Miguel." He took a seat in a leather chair. "Maverick is now at the horse barn here, where you will be staying. I am sure Alvera will take very good care of both of you."

Filberto entered and sat on a sofa.

"What happened with Ignacio?" El Anglo asked when everyone seemed settled.

Miguel told them the story in precise detail. He finished by saying, "They only seemed interested in Ignacio. Inez and her baby were merely collateral damage. We were simply in the way. I do not know who they were or how they knew he was there."

El Anglo watched him closely as he spoke and looked to Alvera who nodded. "We think they were a hit squad, hired by a cartel we are challenging. Doesn't sound like they were professionals. Sloppy work. Someone must have informed about his whereabouts. Probably hastily arranged."

"I am concerned about my family," Miguel said without letting El Anglo continue. He turned to Vargas. "I must find El Coyote. He has Maria. He raped Maria and took her." Miguel knew Vargas knew his family and Maria well. "Ignacio thought you could help."

El Anglo glanced at the men and nodded. "Ignacio said you had joined us. We will protect them. We will get you to El Coyote. However, we expect you to undertake an important mission Ignacio was assigned. Your participation in this is the price for our helping you. You understand? We demand your loyalty."

"Yes, I do. However, I do not understand why I am doing this. I mean, there must be many others with more experience. I know nothing about this … about drugs or smuggling or death squads or stash houses or cartels." He lifted his arms and let them drop in his lap.

"There is more to this than what you mention, much more," Alvera repeated. "Most of the young men who join cartels are peons who do it for money or to be part of a gang or because of the excitement or because there is nothing more they can do. They listen to the narcocorridoes and are inspired. They hear about the lifestyle. They see the money that impresses girls. These people are not leaders. They are the soldiers. According to Vargas, you are a leader."

"You are part of this Sonora Cartel?" Miguel asked. He looked at Vargas, who did not answer.

Alvera responded. "I said before, there is more to this than what you mentioned. This is about Mexico. You remember this man Villa whose picture you just saw?"

Miguel nodded his head.

"This man was more than a smuggler and bandit, was he not? He was a man for Mexico, a man for the people. He fought the army, fought for land redistribution, built his own army. He was also a bandito who did what he had to do to get money to support his troops and operations."

Alvera gestured toward the flag. "This drug war we must stop. It is destroying Mexico. Some say for it to end there must be only one cartel, that one should be Sinaloa, and that this man Juaquin 'Chapo' Guzman should be the leader. The Americans have him. There are many scores to settle. There are scores here to settle first. We oppose Chapo. We can only save Mexico from becoming a narco state in one way. We must destroy the others: Los Zetas, the Gulf Cartel, La Familia, and the rest.

"We must do this ourselves. The gringos betrayed us before. They betrayed Villa, and they will take our sovereignty. Their insatiable demand for drugs and workers has sucked the life out of Mexico. Instead of helping us build a stable country so both of us prosper like Canada, they try to exploit us. We cannot trust them. They are our enemy. We must use their weaknesses to defeat the enemies of Mexico. We must make other alliances. We must blend all these divisive groups into one organization. One day this continent will be one." He looked at El Anglo. All four men, including Filberto, nodded.

"For this movement to build and be successful," Alvera continued, "we need leaders like you, Miguel. This is not an easy task. The responsibility is ours. We must lead Mexico in the way Mexicans understand. It will be a long battle. We will do what we have to do. This is all I will say to you on this subject for now ... except to say that you have a reputation with this man" he pointed to Vargas, "who has spoken to your military leader and his own manager, and both are very positive about you."

These men were not like others Miguel had known. The few leaders he had seen in the army did not compare to Alvera or Vargas. The words moved Miguel, especially the talk of a New Mexico. These were important ideas. His father had also spoken of Mexico in this way, but not so eloquently as Alvera.

An older woman brought them coffee. She left and then returned with a pastry tray and napkins.

El Anglo said, "You will stay here for a few days. There are rooms attached to the stable with showers. Tomorrow we will take you to Hermosillo for clothes and the things you will need to cross the border just as you did before. You are to escort two men, to join with El Coyote, and cross into Arizona. These men will be taken to Manuel at a stash house in Tucson."

"El Coyote raped Maria. He tried to kill me," Miguel snarled and turned to Vargas.

El Anglo, now all business, said, "If he knows what happened to her, this will give you a chance to find out where she is." His Spanish was American. "Nothing must happen to these two men. There will be others watching on both sides of the border to prevent a hijacking. They belong to gangs that operate on both sides. We hire them to do this. They are not part of this movement. Don't trust them. They do this for the money and to stay alive, not for patriotism. With Ignacio's death, we assigned this important plaza to Eduardo Mendez. You will work with him and El Coyote."

Miguel shook his head. "I don't understand. These people are not Sonora Cartel? Is it not better they should all be under one command?"

El Anglo smiled and looked at the others. "No, we hire them to do things we don't want blamed on us. They cannot do anything else. We can't train them. We don't have to defend them. If they mess up, we get rid of them one way or another."

Alvera leaned forward in his seat, his face stern. "At all costs, including the migrants and your own life, you will protect these two men. You and El Coyote will have radios, cell phones, and GPS. El Coyote will have a night-vision scope. At the drop site, you, Eduardo, and El Coyote will take separate vehicles to different locations. El Coyote, Eduardo, and the illegals will go to a stash house. You and the two assassins will go to a different stash house, and then they will be transferred to another location. Before you leave the drop site, you will have the opportunity to confront El Coyote."

Vargas looked into Miguel's eyes. Miguel continued the eye contact with him and nodded his head.

"Miguel, El Coyote cannot be trusted to remain quiet about the two men you are protecting. He will talk to anyone who pays him for information. He will only understand they are important. These two assassins don't speak Spanish or English." Vargas turned to El Anglo and nodded.

El Anglo said, "We believe El Coyote informs the Morales Cartel when he takes a group across. Morales was the cartel that controlled the Nogales Plaza before we took it from them, our first major operation. Ignacio belonged to that cartel before we took the plaza. He joined us.

"Many times, there are last-minute changes and additions. We use this plaza and El Coyote to transport contraband, including people. There may be last-minute changes for various reasons. That is why we usually meet him at the last minute to reinforce our directions and to make sure we receive our payment before he crosses the border. He is as well paid as he is vicious. Eduardo will tell El Coyote he is training you to be a smuggler at our request."

"What if he recognizes me from before?"

"Well, he thinks you are being trained, and he knows this is a way to pay off the debt due from your previous crossing, so it's not so unusual. However, your history with him creates a highly volatile situation. He is unpredictable. The bottom line here is that you must protect these two men. You do what you have to do to make sure they get to the stash house. Only then is your assignment *over. If there is a physical confrontation, your biggest threat from El Coyote is the knife. He is deadly with it. Take your Beretta. Also take your M16."*

The room remained quiet to let the instructions sink in. Miguel caught his breath and said, "When I crossed before with El Coyote, there was a man who backed him up. I think he was there for the mules. He had an AK-47. Will there be another such man beside El Coyote this time?"

"No mules this time," El Anglo said. "El Coyote has his own crew. He will know you represent us. El Coyote realizes the repercussions if he turns on you."

Alvera crossed his legs, displaying hand-tooled boots inlaid with silver that glowed and reflected the sunlight splaying through a nearby window.

El Anglo continued, "You and the two men will stay at the stash house until contacted. Once they leave, your mission is over. You will receive ten thousand dollars for each man. Then there may be time to look for Maria."

Vargas nodded to the others. They stood. Vargas grasped Miguel's hand, placed his other hand on Miguel's shoulder, and said, "I am very sorry about Maria. We want to help you find her. I respect Jose and the work of both of you at the hacienda. Our work here is very important for Mexico. You are to take your instructions while here from that man." He pointed to Filberto. He then turned and walked toward the door.

"Follow me," Filberto said.

Miguel walked with Filberto toward the stable and the adjacent buildings. Along the way, they encountered armed young men patrolling the area. "These men are members of our security team. Some have wives. Most are not married. However, they have families." He looked at Miguel who interpreted the words as a warning. "If you are interested, there are young women in that building." He pointed to a smaller barrack. "We take care of them, and they take care of the men, if you know what I mean.

"When not on duty, practice with the weapons we have here. We have a range. You can practice with any of the weapons, and you can get instruction. The instructors are ex-soldiers. When not on duty, some of the men like to use peyote. You can also if you wish. Here, we maintain discipline, just like an army. The mess hall is over there." He pointed to a single-story building.

They entered a building attached to the stable and an enclosed arena. Miguel looked toward the stable hoping to see Maverick.

"Here is where you will stay until the men you are to protect arrive. That may be at any time. Tomorrow we will take you to town for new clothes and

whatever else you need. We will pay. We do not want our people hanging out in town, no cantinas or anywhere that will draw attention to you. It is in such places that you are easily attacked."

Miguel thought of the cantina in Las Flores and of Ignacio, Inez, and Angel.

"In the meantime, before your mission, we want you to learn about the weapons and be able to use them."

"Can't you be attacked here?" Miguel asked.

"It would take a well-organized effort. The army is supposed to protect us, and we are capable of defending ourselves. Here is your room."

Miguel entered a small room with a cot and a chair. His M16, magazines, and Beretta lay on the cot. He smelled horses, hay, and straw. He was anxious to check out the stalls and locate Maverick.

"The latrine and shower are at the end of the hall. The mess schedule is posted on the bulletin board next to the latrine. One final thing that is very important: Do not talk to anyone here about what happened at the cantina in Las Flores or that you were there or that you live in Las Flores. We assume there are informers here. That includes the army. You can trust no one. The best way to protect your family is by not disclosing your identity or your home. From now on, you will be known as El Caballo. Using your real name puts your family in grave danger."

Miguel ate dinner in the mess hall. No one spoke to him. They looked and nodded but left him alone. They were a mixture. Some were workers and caretakers. Others were guards or otherwise affiliated directly with the cartel. Men entered and left in a continuous flow like bees to a hive.

After dinner, he walked into the stable. For a minute, he looked down the center aisle. He whistled. Maverick stuck his head over a stall. Miguel walked to the stall, excited and anxious to see him and feel a connection to Las Flores.

Later that night, tired, Miguel lay on his cot and tried to piece together the events of the last weeks. Nothing seemed real. Even his killings and Maria's rape, events he'd never thought he'd experience, were events seemingly outside of himself and foreign. He recognized he was on a surreal journey that ended with Maria. Though he was among many, he felt alone.

In the darkness, smelling the hay, listening to the horses in their stalls, and wondering where Maria was, he tried to understand how and why their lives had become so desperate. Where was she? What was she doing? What might they be doing to her? He was not sure how much she could physically take.

Now he wondered whether he possessed the confidence, ability, and stamina required to find her.

10

*A*t dawn, Filberto awakened Miguel. "You need to eat and head to the range. The instructors want you to work with a rifle."

One of the instructors, who had been a member of the Mexican Special Forces Airmobile Group and had trained in the United States, introduced Miguel to a slightly modified, scoped 30-06 Remington 700 rifle. He practiced shooting with silhouette targets at distances between three hundred and five hundred meters.

Afterward, Miguel saddled Maverick and followed a trail leading up the mountain. The solitude spread as the trail ventured higher until they reached the tree line where the trail ended at a ledge with an expansive view of the hacienda. Of course, the scene reminded him of the view of the compound in Las Flores; only here, the view was more overwhelming. He saw the highway he had driven to the hacienda, the airfield, the hacienda, the barracks, cattle in one pasture and another pasture with several horses grazing near the stable, the shooting range, and a maintenance building with various vehicles neatly parked in orderly rows. Men appeared like ants in the maintenance area. Others patrolled in jeeps and walked the premises. Not far from the stable, he saw a racetrack.

Miguel rode back down the trail to the racetrack. He put Maverick through his paces, ending with a run around the track. They then returned to the stable. Miguel groomed and fed Maverick before returning to his room, relishing in an almost overwhelming feeling of normalcy.

Shortly after midnight, he heard a plane arrive. In the morning, two security guards and Filberto took Miguel to a clothing store in Hermosillo to buy new clothes. After lunch, Filberto brought him to the hacienda. Waiting in the large room were Arturo Alvera, El Anglo, and two men.

At their first meeting, Miguel thought El Anglo worked for Alvera, perhaps a bodyguard, but this time it was different. El Anglo was in command. His presence dominated the room. Alvera was obviously differential to him … not by what he said, but mostly by his body language. Everyone looked to El Anglo. El Anglo looked at Miguel.

El Anglo's Spanish was Castilian, as though he learned it formally at school rather than the streets.

"These men are not Mexican," El Anglo said, looking at Miguel. They were shorter than Miguel and El Anglo and dark skinned. "They speak neither Spanish nor English."

"It's your job to see they arrive safely," El Anglo continued. "Tomorrow you will travel with me. We will deliver them to El Coyote. We want this to look like a normal illegal crossing. Your job is to protect these two men and make sure they arrive safely. We will have a diversion so that it is easier to cross without detection. Take your M16, the Beretta, extra mags, and your backpack. I will provide you a GPS and a cell phone. There is more danger once you are across than here because of the unpredictable gangs and the border watch groups in Arizona.

"Our man Eduardo Mendez is the new Nogales Plaza leader. His people are already covering us here and on the route to the border. If there is a problem, they will call you. It will be up to you to decide what to do. You must avoid the US Border Patrol and the border watch groups. If you do get in trouble with the border patrol, you must kill these men." He gestured to them without taking his eyes off Miguel. "They cannot be captured. They know this. They have no ID. I don't know their names, and neither do you."

He paused, watching Miguel closely. "El Coyote has no idea of this mission. To him, they are illegals like anyone else. I will give him money to pay for them and some for himself. I will also tell him you work for me." He nodded to Filberto who left the room with the two men and shortly returned.

"You understand the importance of this mission, right?" El Anglo said to Miguel.

"Yes, sir."

"Questions?"

"No."

El Anglo looked at Filberto, Alvera, and Vargas. "And you?"

They shook their heads.

"Okay. I guess we are set."

Alvera and Vargas stood. They all walked to the door.

"Good luck," they said to Miguel and El Anglo, standing side by side.

Dawn's gray hue began to spread along the mountain ridge cresting ahead of the following sun. Three black SUVs waited in front of the main house. The two assassins, Miguel, and El Anglo walked across the veranda. A man Miguel's age stepped from the passenger's side of the first one and opened the front door of the first car for El Anglo. Miguel was beside him.

El Anglo said, "This is the man who takes Ignacio's place, Eduardo Mendez." To Eduardo he said, "This is El Caballo. He is with me."

Miguel was surprised that El Anglo called him El Caballo. Eduardo sat in the back seat of the first car. El Anglo sat in front. The assassins entered the second SUV. Miguel sat in front. Several men Miguel recognized from the hacienda appeared holding AK-47s and entered a third car.

They arrived in Altar at dusk without incident. Soon, they stopped in the village where he and Maria first met El Coyote. A group of six people stood before El Coyote, who was speaking to them. Miguel felt his pulse increase at the sight of EL Coyote. When the cars stopped, El Coyote interrupted his instructions and walked to the middle car. El Anglo rolled down the window just far enough for El Coyote could see his eyes. Miguel left his car to join them.

"You know who I am," El Anglo said.

"Si," replied El Coyote.

El Anglo jabbed his thumb toward Miguel and Eduardo. "These are my men. Eduardo is the new Nogales Plaza leader." El Anglo pointed at Miguel. "He is El Caballo. I want you to show him how to be a coyote."

El Coyote carefully examined Miguel. "You are familiar."

"You hear what I said?" El Anglo asked. "He will not interfere."

"Si, I understand," El Coyote agreed.

"You got my instructions that you are to show him this work?"

"Yes."

Eduardo turned to El Coyote. "Where's the money?"

El Coyote glared at him and reached into his shirt, pulled out bills, and handed them to Eduardo, who counted and then said, "You are short a hundred dollars. The thousand extra dollars these people pay is not enough for you? You take ours?"

El Coyote grinned sheepishly, exposing yellow teeth, reached again into his shirt, and handed Eduardo another hundred. "Sorry, I miscounted."

Miguel slung the M16 across his chest, turned, joined the two assassins, and walked with them to the illegals. The illegals looked at the weapon and then at Miguel. He wore new hiking boots, a backpack, new clothes, and a baseball cap pulled low, leaving only his eyes visible. El Coyote looked intently at Miguel without expression. The SUVs left.

Miguel watched the illegals milling about near the front of the store where he and Maria had waited. This time, the scene was different. Except for the two men for whom he was responsible, the other illegals seemed like a group of chickens milling about a chicken coup instead of individuals with unique identities.

Miguel watched before following El Coyote and helping Eduardo push the illegals toward a truck. It reminded him of herding sheep. He counted ten, including two women. Miguel shoved them to get them to climb onto the truck bed, just as he recalled Pedro doing. The largest illegal grabbed the smallest woman, slung her over his shoulder, and tossed her into the truck like a bag of dirty laundry. El Coyote stood to the side watching. She tried to get to her feet.

The rest struggled with each other to get on the truck. The truck was too small for the number of people. They shoved and knocked the woman to the floor where she lay on her stomach. She tried to crawl along the bed toward the front. Someone grabbed her ankles, pulled her back, and then crawled over her. The process reminded Miguel of the scene at the railroad siding where they boarded the Beast. The girl needed help. Miguel started to climb on the truck. El Coyote and Eduardo restrained him.

"No!" El Coyote shouted. "Let them be and work it out for themselves. It is not our responsibility to look after them. We lead the way, that is all. They are animals now. Better that way. Helps them survive the desert."

The two assassins had remained aloof. Miguel directed them into the bay of the second truck. Eduardo and El Coyote sat in the front seat of the truck transporting the illegals. Miguel crowded onto the bed of the second truck with the assassins for the ride to the border.

They waited in a grove of trees and brush until long after dark. El Coyote received instructions on his handheld radio. Near midnight, they crossed. El Coyote was first, crawling under the railroad ties. Eduardo stayed close to El Coyote. Miguel waited until the others crawled across and brought up the rear with his two men. They formed a line and began to walk. Miguel paid no attention to the ranch house or the barn. If the horse made a sound, he did not hear it. The illegals slid and fell over each other, trying to keep up with El Coyote.

By the second day, Miguel herded them like sheep, prodding with the M16, urging them forward to keep them moving and together. He had learned that lingering increased the odds of discovery. Their faces became anonymous masks, seemingly uncaring about each other. As their food and water depleted, they grew disorderly and annoying.

By the second night, Miguel wanted rid of them. Two women kept up an annoying chatter until El Coyote finally told them to shut up or he would leave them alone in the desert. In contrast, the two assassins took the pace in stride and stayed together as though strolling in a park on a pleasant Mexican family Sunday afternoon outing.

Eduardo joined El Coyote at the front of the line. They stopped for a short rest. Eduardo talked with El Coyote and walked back to Miguel standing with the two assassins at the end of the line.

"El Coyote said when we get to the drop site, he wants the younger girl. I am the plaza boss, and I thought I should get her. He insisted, so unless you want seconds, take the older one. They don't have the power to stop us, you know. Most accept it as part of our payment, like a tax to take them across the border. These people, they become animals out here. Who cares? No one knows anyway. Who can they tell?" He shook his head. He pointed to the younger of the two women who were standing together watching them. "Let's just take them over there," said Eduardo. He pointed toward some brush. "We take all these risks for these people. They come to us. They will do anything to go to America."

El Caballo said nothing.

"What's your problem? You don't like girls?"

"You are my problem." He was reliving the scene with Maria at the trophy tree.

El Coyote joined them, looked at the two women, and said to Eduardo, "Not now. We must get going."

They walked through the night, stopping for short periods to rest. By late the following day, they approached the area of the trophy tree. Miguel recognized the stench before he saw the tree. More panties hung from the branches.

Eduardo and Miguel formed the men into a line. Eduardo then separated the two women from the rest and guarded them. Miguel kept the two assassins away from everyone.

El Coyote advanced toward Miguel. "Who are these men? Why are you guarding them? El Anglo forgot to tell me who they are. This is my business."

"Perhaps he does not trust you," Miguel replied in a voice barely audible; yet nevertheless, it held the chilling deep-throated snarl of a wolf just before it attacks.

El Coyote stiffened as though attempting to match Miguel's height. "El Anglo and I are partners. He must have forgotten to inform me. Who are they?"

Miguel shifted the M16 so that he held it in his right hand near the trigger, the muzzle pointing at El Coyote's belly. "This is no concern of yours. You just do as you're told."

"You don't order me, amigo, not out here. You do as I say."

Miguel decided that if El Coyote reached for his knife, he would kill him. However, what he most wanted to know now was Maria's location. Killing him could wait.

"You guard these people while we check the rest for valuables, and then we will take care of these women," El Coyote said. "I must know who these men are."

Eduardo guarded the men, except the two who stayed with El Caballo. El Coyote took their money and whatever he thought was valuable, including their family information, following the same routine as before. One man refused to disclose family information. El Coyote spun the man around, drew his knife, and placed the blade to the man's neck. The man removed a paper from his shirt and handed it to El Coyote. As before, he searched the women, taking anything he wanted.

"Change your clothes," El Coyote ordered. He grabbed the youngest girl, causing her to fall to the ground. While holding the girl's arm in one hand, he punched his phone with the other hand to summon transportation.

"Let her go!" Miguel growled.

"Fuck you!" El Coyote said, yanking her to her feet and dragging her toward the brush.

"This is none of our business," Eduardo said. "Your responsibility is these two men. We do our job. You do yours. You want this girl? Take her when I am done with her. There is no morality here. If we don't use them, then these illegals will. They may still do so when we are finished with them. That's the way it is out here, El Caballo."

Miguel remembered that he had ignored an old woman, leaving her to die. He had also left a man tangled in a cactus for attempting to steal their water. He had felt nothing for those on the train, with the young Guatemalan, Emilio, trying to stay alive to keep his family alive. He had felt no remorse in killing again at the cantina with both Inez and her baby lying in a puddle of blood, except at the time an overwhelming rage for the slaughter of Inez and Angel.

El Coyote and Eduardo walked out of the brush, each carrying panties, and tossed them on the tree. One woman followed meekly behind them. Like before with the others, Miguel did nothing. He turned his back, wondering at the depravity of life. How easily he had succumbed when no longer restrained by social mores.

El Coyote approached Miguel. "I know you. Where do I know you?"

"You raped my wife right here. You shot me. Her name is Maria. Now do you remember? After we separated in Tucson, she disappeared. I am told you took her."

"Ah, yes, now I remember." A scowl crossed El Coyote's face. "So, you are not dead. I thought I killed you. I told Maria you are dead. Nevertheless, here you are, El Caballo, one of us," he said, shaking his head. "You should understand these things. You have not learned yet about real life. Maria told me you are a fool." He paused. "You want this girl? Take her now." He pointed to the girl walking unsteadily from the brush. "Forget about Maria. I sold her."

Miguel smashed El Coyote in the face, knocking him to the ground.

Eduardo shoved his AK-47 into Miguel's ribs. "I will kill you for sure, El Caballo. We make this delivery. That's all that matters out here."

El Coyote struggled to his feet. "Yes, I admit I raped her. So, what? It is my bonus." He quickly glanced at Eduardo, and their eyes met.

Eduardo raised the AK-47 and pointed it at Miguel, his finger on the trigger.

El Coyote nodded, stepped back, and turned toward Miguel. "Most of these girls are happy to be with me. I am an important man. Another raped Maria at the stash house after we got there. She is a nice piece. They took her to another house where she had sex again. They sold her to a gringo. That's all I know." He shrugged. He pointed to the M16 lying near Miguel. "Since you are one of us, you must now understand that these people are merchandise. These are the things El Anglo wants you to learn."

El Coyote motioned in the direction of the illegals as though indicating a small herd of cattle headed to the slaughterhouse. "They are nothing to me except money. I risk my life every time I bring this junk across the border. It's only right that I get a few benefits." He tried to smile only to cough up blood. "I forgive you of your insolence now that you realize who I am."

Miguel stepped toward El Coyote. "Tell me who you sold Maria to."

"Why do you care? She is no longer the girl she was before she met me. If you really want to know about her, you should ask the man who ran this plaza first, Ignacio. He can tell you a few things. He knew her well. Better than you, I bet. She is used goods. By now, many others have used her."

The expression on Miguel's face was grotesque. His hands clenched into hammers as he moved toward El Coyote.

El Coyote stepped back and covered his face with his hands. "I don't know, I don't know," he whimpered. "Someone said a Mexican picked her up in a yellow Humvee. My share was five thousand dollars. That is a decent price. Most bring a lot less. I can't get that much for that girl, and she is younger."
He gestured toward the girl he had just raped. "Maria went to an important gringo. That's all I know."

"What do you mean, important?" Miguel asked.

"Gringo businessman, big shot. Forget her. Such girls like her, ambitious, pretty, undocumented, they live with important gringos, do cleaning, watch children, have sex, and live better than you can ever provide. She is better off where she is than with you. That is the way it is with gringos. They say they do not want us to dirty up their country, yet they anxiously buy my merchandise: the boys, the girls, and the dope. My last trip back from good-old USA, I brought back a young girl I bought in Nogales from some guy who took her while she walked to school in Tucson. I've done business with him before. Here's his number." He pulled out his cell phone. "Grow up, Miguel."

Laughing, he wiped away the blood oozing from the side of his mouth and then spit. "Gringos can't get enough of this merchandise I provide. Now that you belong to El Anglo, extortion, kidnapping, and selling girls, boys, and drugs to gringos is what you will do. You will make them work for almost nothing. They will stay in crowded shacks afraid they'll be arrested by ICE and deported. They will wonder whether both Mexicans and gringos will take advantage of them." He gestured toward the huddled group. "They have nothing more to lose. Maria, however, is with a wealthy American. Forget about her. She is happier now than she could have ever been with you. She does not want you. She thinks you are dead."

Just then, two vans arrived. El Coyote instructed all of them, except the assassins, to get in the vans. An SUV picked up the two assassins and El Caballo and drove to a stash house in Tucson. It was not the same as the previous stash house. Manuel, the boss at the first, greeted Miguel as El Caballo.

Dried blood covered the front of Miguel's shirt. "Get cleaned up," Manuel directed. "We will burn that shirt. I will take you to dinner. We make a stop afterward where we will stay in town all night."

"What of the two men I brought here?"

"They are already on their way."

11

*M*anuel drove carefully, keeping one eye on the rearview mirror and changing directions frequently. After a half hour, he pulled into a neighborhood shopping center and parked behind a restaurant. Waiting five minutes, they entered the rear door, walked through a narrow hallway, and opened a door into a crowded dining room. A woman nodded to Manuel. She led them to a corner table and removed a reserved sign. They sat. A waiter promptly brought menus, water, chips, and salsa and then nodded to Manuel before leaving.

"What was that all about?" Miguel asked. He wore new khaki trousers, a light blue polo shirt, and brown boots, resembling a businessman attending a casual business dinner. He felt uncomfortable and out of place. Manual had insisted upon the clothes so they blended into the local atmosphere. The customers appeared to be families and business people. All were Caucasian.

"I wanted to be sure we weren't followed. We are meeting another. But let's order first."

Miguel looked around. Many black-and-white photos of vaqueros adorned the walls: branding, herding, lassoing steers, and lounging around fires. Colorful sombreros, lariats, serapes, horseshoes, bridles, bits, and branding irons were in glass cases. Several old rifles and pistols were in a case near the door. Miguel's neck ached from stretching to see everything.

Finally turning to Manuel, he said, "No Mexicans. We stand out."

"In the kitchen are Mexicans, and the waiters are Mexican. We can easily tell if any Mexicans come in. They serve only Tex-Mex here, so mostly gringos come here."

"I don't understand. We are the only ones speaking Spanish."

"Most Mexicans prefer traditional and don't come here. The owner is Greek, and the cook is Italian. Besides, this place is expensive for Mexican food; many snowbirds come here during the season. Considering the usual places in the Mexican community, this is upscale and caters to gringos. People here are accustomed to hearing Spanish. It's no big deal. We are unlikely to encounter the folks in our crowd here." Manuel chuckled.

"What's a snowbird? I don't think I've ever seen one."

"They are not birds," Manuel laughed. "That's what we call people who live here in the winter. They fly here on airplanes. Then fly back north in spring, usually after Easter." Manual looked at his watch. "Soon, you'll understand why we are here."

"*They fly? How do —*" *Miguel shook his head.*

Manuel started to laugh and then stopped. "Never mind."

Nothing made sense to Miguel; a Greek owner and an Italian cook and Mexican waiters and Tex-Mex food, whatever that was.

"*The gringos, they pay money, apparently lots of money, for this?" Miguel squinted and looked at Manuel. He remembered his father once telling him after a few sips of peyote, "Gringos are crazy."*

He looked around the room. People had to be staring at them. No! It was he doing the staring. People occupied all the tables. They stood in line at the entrance. This was crazy. He did not know what to think. Finally, he said, "I have to try this stuff."

"*Okay, what do you want to drink?" Manuel asked.*

"*Do they drink beer?"*

He then nodded to the waiter. "How about you try a combination plate?" In Spanish, he read aloud what was included.

"*Okay, I guess," Miguel said and shrugged.*

The waiter looked down at them, grasping his pad.

"*Two combinations," said Manuel. "And two beers."*

A motion at the back door caused them to look. Miguel saw a familiar man who advanced toward them, dressed in casual clothes. Miguel could not place him but then realized he was the border patrol agent who had caught him, Agent Nathaniel Gonzales.

Looking at Nate, the waiter asked, "And you, sir?"

"*Beer." He grabbed a chair that faced the entrance. Miguel's back was to the front door. "I won't stay long," Nate, told them. "How are you both, Miguel, Manuel?"*

"*Bien," Manuel said.*

Miguel's mouth hung open like a half-closed garage door.

Shocked and realizing Nate knew Manuel, Miguel looked back and forth from Nate to Manuel several times. "What is this?"

Nate nodded his head toward Manuel. "He is undercover like you." Now Miguel realized why Manuel was not at the stash house the night of the raid. Nate must have warned him.

"*What do you think of the Cucaracha?" Manuel asked.*

Miguel squirmed in his chair. He looked down at his boots and along the strip forming a chair rail the length of the wall at table height.

"There are cockroaches here?" he asked, glancing about him.

"No, no, the name of this restaurant," said Manuel, chuckling again, "La Cucaracha."

"The gringos name a restaurant for a cockroach? This, I don't understand either. Do they serve cockroach here?" Miguel looked about at plates on several nearby tables.

"The song, Miguel, do you not remember the song about the cockroach, 'La Cucaracha'?"

Miguel sat back and looked across at them as they attempted to stifle laughter. Finally, he recalled the song. "Yes, I think so, but —"

"Well, the gringos don't know Spanish, see, but they know cucaracha was the name of a popular Mexican song, so they named the restaurant La Cucaracha so everyone will know this is a Mexican restaurant. Okay, now you understand?"

"These gringos, they are loco, no?" Miguel noted.

"Okay," said Nate. "Let's move on to a different subject."

Manuel was holding his stomach, trying to withhold his laughter without falling from his chair. People at the next table looked concerned.

"Just tell me anything I should know. I won't stay. How did you know to go to the terminal?"

"From the man on the phone. He told me how to find it. He said to stop at garage 10. A car followed me to the terminal once I left the POE. The driver, a gringo, took me to lunch."

Manuel looked at Nate. "Did we get that traffic?"

"Don't know. Nate was writing in a small notebook as they talked.

"Exchanges were made while we ate lunch. We didn't use names," Miguel told him. "When I passed back through Nogales, no one checked my papers on either side. I followed another car to a large barn near Hermosillo. It was late. I drove into the barn. In the light, I could see men were loading weapons into a van."

"Where did you stay when you got back to Mexico?"

"A large hacienda south of Hermosillo. The owner, Arturo Alvera, is a big deal in the Sonora Cartel."

"We did not know that he was involved. He has an important position in the Mexican government, I believe."

Miguel continued. "The part I saw is a compact military base: firing range with ex-military instructors, an armory, a small group of security, dining hall, landing strip, large machine shop, fuel, not to mention a large stable, a bordello, and various vehicles. My gut says the cartel's operations boss is a gringo called El Anglo. The others, Vargas, the owner of the hacienda where I worked, and Alvera, deferred to El Anglo in operational questions."

"Would you say they are the board of directors?" Nate pressed.

"I don't know what that means. I think they are the commanders; Alvera seems to be the capo. They seem most interested in something bigger than just the cartel stuff of drugs and the rest. That's where they get the money to do the other stuff. They referred to Poncho Villa and how he was a bandit to get money to fight for the revolution. They want to get control of all the plazas and cartels."

"What do you think of this, El Anglo?"

"Not Mexican. I would guess he's American just from his name, maybe early forties. Don't make sense to me. For some reason, I felt a connection with him."

"Did you learn anything more of Maria?"

"Some. El Coyote told her I was dead. Said he sold her for five thousand dollars to a man driving a yellow Humvee. Said he's supposed to be a gringo big shot."

The concern he saw in Gonzales's eyes seemed both real and distressing at the same time. He choked, and his voice trembled. "He claimed she was raped repeatedly." He looked away, feeling the tears gathering into his eyes. They remained quiet, sipping their beers.

Nate covered Miguel's hand with his own. "I guess I don't have to tell you how important what you are doing is for us. However, it is also extremely dangerous for you and Maria. You must be careful. The life you are in now has no rules except violence: no loyalties, no friendships, no values except survival, no future, no recognition, no moral justification, no redemption. You are in hell, Miguel, because of your skills and vulnerability. You unfortunately seem fated to fulfill a role in this godforsaken tragedy that is the antipathy of humanity."

The waiter brought their food. The beans were like slush, the rice brown and tangy. Watching Manuel, Miguel spread butter on the tortilla, took some hot sauce, and spread it across the enchiladas. After a few minutes, Miguel mixed the beans and rice together and then dripped some hot sauce on the mixture. "Umm ... not bad."

As Manuel and Miguel ate, Nate resumed. "Miguel, you must understand that Maria is in a bad place. Sex slavery is alive and well in an underground network that is as well organized as drug trafficking, often conducted by the same cartels or their associates. Young women like Maria are particularly vulnerable when they are indebted to the cartel as you and she are. They will have isolated her, drugged her, and raped her before deciding how to use her. She may be held for ransom. She can be sent to the streets to whore and steal, returned to Mexico to service a cartel, kept at a safe house to service gang members, or sold to a broker who will pimp her to the porn industry or pimp her to a man for any purpose he may want. On the other hand, if the man is wealthy, he may have bought her to be his personal sex slave. This doesn't even include providing her to subcontractors who supply businesses with laborers to clean offices and hotels. Have you ever seen a snuff video, Miguel?"

"No."

"Do you know what it is?"

"No."

"They take a video of killing someone. Sometimes they take a young girl and rape her on the video, kill her, and then sell copies. Gringos buy them as do people all over the world."

Nate's words astounded him. He gasped. Miguel thought of the girls he saw at the hacienda in Hermosillo. He recalled Filberto's remark that he could have any one of them he wanted, like a piece of candy from whom you tear off the wrapper, enjoyed, and then tossed away.

Father Michael's words urging them to return to Las Flores rang in his ears again. In his mind, he saw Maria the way he remembered her at the church when they were young, her dark eyes and black hair that flowed down her back with a flower somehow entwined. She would look at him over her shoulder when he passed or as she kneeled with her cousin, Inez, aunt, and uncle in church. The dusty alameda on Sunday evenings where everyone pretended for an hour or so that they were Castilian and aristocratic, on a paseo in which the senoritas strolled and the caballeros watched and absorbed.

"You let these things happen in your country?"

"It's not what we want, but it is the result of human trafficking into a dark world that exists in the shadows of every country. We pretend it does not happen here."

They ate silently. Afterward, Miguel could not recall the taste ... only Nate's introduction to a side of life that had no explanation and no comprehensible resemblance to the world of simple survival he knew in the desert.

Nate broke the silence. "Manuel told me of the first plaza boss." He looked down at his notes. "Ah, yes, Ignacio." He looked up at Miguel. "He was killed, yes? Manuel says he was the Nogales Plaza boss for the Morales Cartel and remained the boss after Sonora took over. You were there when he was killed?"

Miguel said nothing, wondering where Nate's information originated. "You killed the shooters, true?"

Miguel again said nothing.

"Who killed them?

"My wife's cousin was killed, her baby also."

Nate looked down at his notes. "She and her baby and three bodies were found by Florio. Her husband?"

"I don't know. Who found them?" He paused. "What? Say that again."

"I said Florio found five bodies ... a baby, Inez, the two shooters and Ignacio."

Manuel said. "Okay, let's forget about the shooters for now." Nate flipped the page of his notebook. "Why did you cross into Arizona again?"

"I was told to take two assassins across the border with El Coyote. It was a test for —"

"A test? What do you mean?"

"For me to learn about smuggling people, about being a coyote. It was really to see if I am good enough to join them. We used El Coyote."

"Who else?" Nate asked.

"Eduardo Mendez, who took Ignacio's place."

"Okay." Nate wrote in his notebook. "Who are these two assassins?"

"I don't know. I was to guard them with my life. If the police or the border patrol discovered them, I was to kill them. They do not speak English or Spanish and are dark skinned."

Nate turned to Manuel. "These two must be the same two that were picked up at the stash house."

"Yes. I am sure.

Nate closed his notebook. "This yellow Humvee is a good clue to find Maria. It's rumored Humvees are popular with narco big shots, particularly in this area. It is almost a joke, like some kind of status symbol. Don't know for sure if the rumor is true. A big house on a hill might suggest narco lifestyle.

If the important gringo who has a yellow Humvee is also the man who has Maria, then this is a man we can find."

Nate remained quiet for a minute before reopening his notebook. "Do you recall the name of the man at the Port of Entry?"

Miguel wrote the letters he remembered. "I think that's what the badge said, forties, five eight, balding, older gringo than the others. Brown rimmed glasses."

Nate turned to Manuel. "Heard of him?"

"No."

"Okay! That's where we start."

Nate gave Miguel a report on El Coyote. "This is a copy of El Coyote's background, so you know who you are dealing with." Miguel read the report as Nate and Manuel watched him.

Background on El Coyote:

Born in El Salvador. At twelve, he migrated through Guatemala with his parents into Mexico where Los Zetas attacked their bus in an attempt to rob them. They raped his mother and then killed his parents. He made his way to the US border by himself and crossed from Tijuana to San Diego. A local gang hired him at thirteen as a lookout for their street dealers. Two years later, his reputation with a knife earned him the position of an enforcer, and he joined the gang after an initiation in which he killed two members of a rival gang in a turf battle. He subsequently raped and killed a young woman and severely mutilated her husband. He escaped capture and retribution from the other gang by fleeing to Mexico, becoming a mule, and trafficking drugs in Yuma where he was captured by the border patrol, convicted, and sent to prison There he encountered MS-13 and joined them in prison.

Following his early release from prison in California, he returned to Mexico, remaining with MS-13 and hired by Sinaloa in the drug wars, earning a reputation for violence *and as an assassin working alone. When the Morales Cartel won the Tucson corridor, he was smuggling migrants, mules, and drugs in southern Arizona and leading attacks upon independent coyotes encroaching on the Tucson corridor. When the Sonora Cartel won the corridor away from Morales, El Coyote became an independent contractor smuggling important contraband for Sonora. Believed to sell information on Sonora to Morales and vice versa.*

"Would you have done it?" Nate asked, staring into Miguel's eyes.
"What?"
"Killed the foreigners in cold blood?"
"Yes."

12

"*O*ne of the responsibilities of a plaza leader," Manuel said when they returned to the car, "is to deliver information and money to the hacienda or to wherever instructed. We are on our way now to meet with a courier for a pickup at the Marriott. It is my first time. Ignacio explained the process a couple of times in case he could not do it. Quique, the finance guy, contacted me. He will meet us there. The money is in dollars totaling one million in large bills, which Quique will launder through various outlets once we get it to the hacienda.

"The dope is smuggled across the border in bricks to a distribution center or stash house where dealers pay for the delivery. From there, bricks are sold to various destinations to traffickers who break down the bricks and sell the small baggies to the street venders and gangs."

Miguel recalled the delivery he made across the border to the large truck terminal north of Nogales.

"The payment for the delivery to the distribution center or stash house is made in cash. When the total reaches a million dollars, it is delivered to a courier who arranges for a pickup to take it across the border. That is who we are meeting." Manuel dropped Miguel at the entrance and drove to the parking garage.

Miguel went to the check-in desk. When he gave his name, the desk clerk smiled and said, "Senior Alvera made arrangements for three rooms. One is here already." The clerk pointed to Quique sitting in a chair in the lobby.

"Another is parking the car and will be here in a minute," Miguel said. He had not stayed in a hotel before and thought he had better wait for Manuel until he felt comfortable with the procedures. At least they spoke Spanish.

The attention he received surprised Miguel. The desk clerk ignored others standing in the check-in. Another stopped what she was doing and smiled at Miguel when she heard Alvera's name.

Manuel arrived and received the same treatment. Each carried a small backpack. Nevertheless, the bellman insisted on showing them to their suites. All three followed the man into an elevator that ran up the outside of the building, providing a breathtaking view of the city. They stopped at the top floor. He took the key card from Miguel and led him to a door. Manuel gave him a twenty-dollar bill.

Miguel was speechless, again believing both Jose's and Miguel's casas would fit within the suite's living room.

Twenty minutes later, they walked through the lobby with Manuel guiding Miguel to prevent him from running into objects he might damage as he tried to see everything at once.

"Here's what's to happen," Manuel explained. "We are meeting a man who is giving us one million in cash."

Miguel stopped short.

"It's only money," Quique said, a smile lighting his face.

For a moment, Miguel wished for the desert where life was familiar and certainly simpler and taught a deeper truth than this building of designed opulence. The Sonora Desert did not care about any of this. The desert equalized life in a natural order, and complacency meant death. There, money, men, and women meant nothing.

Miguel wondered what Maria would think of the hotel. This environment he knew was the sort of place she would enjoy. He also recalled Father Michael's advice: "Return to Las Flores." He recalled the homilies of their priest in the little church in Las Flores who frequently spoke of good and evil. Such distinctions seemed simple and clear then, as he had tried to understand the ideas while sitting in a pew as a kid. He wanted to ask both to explain what was happening to him and Maria now. How would they justify laundering money from drugs and human trafficking? Where does any of that fit into the scheme of the life they now experienced. Nothing seemed simple or clear. Right and wrong had blurred into decisions limited to surviving, finding Maria, and protecting his family.

Like the three musketeers with the largest, Miguel, in the middle. They stopped upon entering the lounge to let their eyes adjust from the glaring lobby lights into the subdued lounge lighting. Manuel pulled back his jacket just enough for Miguel to see the Glock.

"Can't be too careful," Manuel said. "Just because it's a ritzy joint don't mean nothing.

A mahogany bar and swivel stools extended the length of one wall where two men and a woman dressed in tuxedo-style outfits tended to customers. The wait staff used a small space to fill drink orders, certainly a contrast to the cantina in Las Flores. A dance floor occupied the center of the room with various colored lights in both the ceiling and beneath the floor.

An empty bandstand and DJ station was in the corner near the far end of the bar. Instrument cases were on the floor beside each chair.

They stopped and stood near the bar, letting their eyes adjust to the lighting.

"Back there in the corner," Manuel said, nodding his head to a man sitting alone. "See him?"

They nodded. The man looked in their direction and stood. Miguel was wary, not only because of the money or because of the uncomfortable surroundings but because the lounge was crowded. The corner was a trap. He had no weapon.

They cautiously walked toward the corner.

The courier's head rotated like an oscillating fan. Miguel thought he must also be wary of an attack.

The courier was maybe five eight or nine, tops. The darkness obscured facial features. Miguel had learned to anticipate trouble by watching body language. As they neared the table, the man tensed. He appeared to be in his fifties with graying hair and glasses. His head was in constant motion, one moment turned toward their approach, the next observing the whole room like a lighthouse sweeping the ocean to warn approaching ships. He did not seem threatening.

The man's suit was threadbare, his shirt was wrinkled, and he appeared uncomfortable as he pulled at his collar. Sweat beads on his upper lip reflected light. Miguel thought him familiar.

Manuel extended his hand and said, "A beautiful night, sir."

"Still hot, though," the courier replied. He looked at Miguel. He extended his hand to Miguel and hesitated as he looked up at Miguel. He looked at Miguel's hand and grasped it, his grip flimsy like a floppy hat, and avoided further eye contact. When he released his grip, Miguel expected him to wipe his hand as Ignacio had at the cantina.

Miguel felt vulnerable. He wanted his back to the corner in order to view everything in the room, but the courier occupied that space.

"Where is Ignacio? What are you three doing here? First, a Mexican on the phone says Ignacio is not coming. Then you three arrive." The courier looked them up and down, a smirk at the corner of his mouth. To Miguel, this behavior was typical and consistent with what he was learning about most gringos, who would look at him as if he smelled of chili pepper.

"Speak Spanish!" Manuel said.

At first, he ignored Miguel. Then the expression on the courier's face, the peering eyes, the scrawny build, and the glasses seemed familiar ... and there was the clue, the glasses, the voice. Now he recognized him, the American ICE agent with the nametag of Walker, who had let him pass through gate 2 at the Nogales Port of Entry.

"I'll be damned," Miguel said aloud, shaking his head. He nodded to Manuel who frowned.

Walker slid behind the table where he could see the room. Miguel squeezed in beside Walker, forcing Walker into the corner. Quique took a side chair. Manuel sat across from Walker and Miguel. A server arrived and took their order.

Walker's eyes continued to roam the room as though he were expecting trouble. "Your package is waiting," Walker said. He removed a ticket and a key from his jacket pocket and held them out to Miguel. "Here is a hotel parking ticket, fourth floor, a tan Toyota. Just give it to the attendant and pay when you leave."

Miguel did not take it and nodded to Manuel. Manuel put the ticket and key in his pocket.

"No problem passing through Sasabe. We will have a spotter on the mountain. A car will cross ahead of you. Both cars have handheld radios and will warn you of problems. Use channel 2." He gave a card and key to Miguel. "Be ready to pay once you cross into Mexico. They might say something like, 'We may have to keep you here for a while and check things out. If you don't offer and the Mexican Border Agents find the stash, they may keep it all. Just pay what they ask."

The server brought their beers with a plate of chips and salsa. She nodded to Quique. They watched her walk away.

Miguel turned to Walker and impulsively said, "If that money is not in the trunk when we go to check it out, you are a dead man!" The man had gotten to him and made his stomach churn.

Walker looked away and smirked at Manuel. "Not in the trunk. Concealed within the car. The car is made special just for this purpose."

"You've heard of El Caballo, no?" asked Manuel.

"No one has heard of him. Just another wetback narco," Walker replied.

"You will know of him soon enough," Manuel assured him.

Walker turned to Miguel. "All the money is there."

"For the time being, you can give your information about the plazas to El Caballo," Manuel said.

"Where is Ignacio?" Walker asked.

"Let's just say he had an accident," El Caballo said.

"You run the plaza now?"

"El Caballo causes accidents," Manuel said. "You should remember that." He nodded to Quique who gave Walker an envelope containing dollars.

"No unusual border operations scheduled for the next month," Walker reported. "The patrols will follow the current schedule for the next month also. Border watch groups continue to operate, but their locations and times are unpredictable. They have grown and are more aggressive since Fast and Furious and now carry long arms."

Miguel had no idea what Walker was talking about. Walker seemed more contrite now that he had received the envelope.

"I know a man who can hook you up with a supplier for Spain. Ignacio had asked for such information. It's too dangerous for me to contact him directly, but I can let you know." He paused and looked at Manuel. "My daughter is sick and needs a heart transplant."

They stood. "Let's go!" Manuel placed a hundred-dollar bill on top of the check.

To Miguel, Walker was a pathetic little man beaten down by life and, like himself, caught up in something beyond his control. He hoped Walker did not personify his own future.

"I hope your daughter will be okay. We will keep her in mind," Manuel said.

Upon their arrival at the hacienda without further incident, Filberto met them.

Quique took the suitcase containing cash.

Filberto said to Miguel, "You are staying here now, Miguel. Follow me." He climbed the stairs to the second floor with Miguel following like a puppy.

At the rear were two rooms. They entered one. "Eduardo is next door. This room may be temporary."

The room contained a small living area, a bedroom, a bathroom, dresser, closet, chair, and small refrigerator. In the closet was his M16 in a metal gun case with a new scope attached and a bulletproof vest. To Miguel, the room seemed almost as large as their casa in the compound.

"*The previous occupant of this room is dead. El Anglo asked for you. Good luck.*"

"*Wait! Wait. What is this? What does it mean?*"

"*It is for El Anglo to say.*"

When Filberto left, Miguel went next door. Eduardo invited Miguel to join him in the mess hall for dinner.

"*I guess you heard,*" *Eduardo said as they settled into their seats after passing through the chow line.*

"*What?*"

"*They made me leader of the Nogales Plaza.*"

"*Congratulations,*" *Miguel said. He had already heard it from El Anglo and Filberto. Apparently, Eduardo had forgotten their previous introduction. Miguel, on the other hand, had not forgotten the barrel of Eduardo's rifle jammed against his ribs.*

Miguel spread butter over a corn tortilla, rolled it up, and stuffed most of it in his mouth before tackling the refried beans.

"*Looks like gringo food,*" *said Eduardo.*

"*Tex-Mex,*" *Miguel explained, feeling a bit more sophisticated since his visit to Tucson. "Good stuff. What exactly does a plaza leader do?*"

"*Well, I am looking for a new guide and someone to organize the hawks. You interested?*"

Miguel nodded toward the hacienda. "I'm waiting for them to tell me what to do."

"*I'll tell you what to do,*" *Eduardo harshly replied. "I didn't see you at the stash house. Didn't see Manuel there either." He paused to shovel food into his mouth. "I was there to check things out.*"

"*We went to dinner.*"

Eduardo loudly belched and quickly tried to wash the food down his gullet, causing him to choke. He pouted like a child. "Manuel didn't invite me. He knew I was coming. Doesn't that seem strange to you since I am now his boss?"

Miguel shrugged.

Eduardo folded his napkin into a neat square, tossed it on the table, and then slid his chair closer.

"*Okay. Listen." Eduardo looked around the room. "What do you think of Manuel. He is supposed to work for me, right. You were there, right?*"

Miguel was suspicious. What he recalled from taking the two foreigners across was that Eduardo was a pawn of El Coyote. He believed there was a relationship. "From what I know, Manuel keeps a tight rein on everyone there. I guess he does his job."

"What else do you know?"

"About what?"

"What did you talk about at dinner?" Eduardo asked.

"Not much really. Just about El Coyote and gringos and Tex-Mex. Manuel just wants to help me find my wife." As soon as he mentioned her, Miguel wished he had not said anything.

"Did he say anything about me?"

"Like what?"

"I don't know," Eduardo said impatiently. "Just wondering. Just anything about the people in charge around here. I need to know what's going on so I can do my job." He smothered butter on a tortilla, rolled it up, and shoved it in his mouth. He patted Miguel's knee. "You know Manuel, right? They say you were a friend of Ignacio. And so was your wife, Maria, I hear," he said as though sharing a locker room secret.

"What about her?" Miguel glared at Eduardo over the top of his glass.

"She'd know stuff, right? I mean, maybe if you have found out something from Maria that she had heard from Ignacio, you can tell me, right?"

"No!"

"No? You forget I am your boss now, El Caballo. You do as I tell you. Don't forget."

"I don't know anything. I don't want to know, but what they tell me to do, I do and then forget."

A sustained uncomfortable silence created a wall between them.

"And leave my wife out of this," Miguel added.

Eduardo slid his chair closer to Miguel. He bent forward until he was inches from Miguel's face. Miguel saw the saliva at the corner of Eduardo's mouth. He knew he could sling Eduardo across the table. Taking a deep breath, he kept control.

"You are just a new soldier here, El Caballo, not the jefe you think you are. What is your real name? Everyone knows you are a kiss-up to Vargas." Eduardo backed away. Changing his tone, he said, "You have respect. It means something. Look, I expect to be as important as Ignacio was, maybe even more important. I can help you if we are friends. Know what I mean?"

"No. I'm tired." Miguel stood.

"Okay. Think about it, Miguel. Tomorrow morning there is a shooting contest. I'm going."

"Me too."

"Okay, well you shouldn't waste your time. I am an expert shooter. Lots will watch. How about a little side wager, huh?"

"Got to go," Miguel said and shoved back his chair, standing noisily. For a moment, he stood over Eduardo with clenched fists, the reference to Maria angrily ringing in his ears. Others looked in their direction. He turned away, heading into the darkening sky.

Nearby, horses grazed in a small pasture. A muchacho with a pitchfork tossed bundles of hay from a wagon to several horses.

Troubled by the conversation, Miguel decided to walk. He instinctively approached the fence to watch the scene. He glanced at the boy. Looking at the horses, he gasped and whistled. Maverick lifted his head, snorted, and trotted to Miguel at the fence. The boy followed Maverick.

"Ola, El Caballo."

Miguel looked closely at the boy and remembered. He'd saved Maria from falling from the Beast.

"What are you doing here, Emilio?"

"I was stopped by this cartel. I had no money. That hombre, Filberto, he paid, so I was working to pay him back. Now they pay me. I can send money home."

"This is the same with me. What do you do here?"

"I take care of the horses. They are teaching me to shoot with a rifle. I do it very well."

"This horse here used to be mine. His name is Maverick. He is special."

"Yes, they told me the name. He is a very fine horse. I will take very good care of him for you, El Caballo."

"How do you know to call me that?" Miguel questioned.

"Filberto. I saw you when I was with him. I said the name Miguel. He said only to call you El Caballo."

The following morning, a large crowd gathered to watch the shooting

contest. Eduardo, Miguel, and Emilio, among others, participated. Emilio won and accepted the trophy. The others cleaned their weapons. Eduardo stalked off, walking the road back to his quarters.

After he cleaned his weapon, Miguel also began walking back. Filberto approached him in a jeep. "Get in. I'll take you."

They caught up with Eduardo trudging along the dirt road. When they passed, a dust cloud engulfed Eduardo.

"El Anglo has an assignment for you," Filberto told Miguel. "A meeting is scheduled this evening in the library at eight o'clock. You and Eduardo are to remain outside the room. Bring your 16, loaded, and at least two large mags. Should not be trouble. However, be ready for anything. Both of you wear a balaclava so they won't recognize you and wear your vests. You will protect these people. They may stay after the meeting for drinks. You are in charge of the inside detail. Several others will be inside but not near the room. You are responsible for all of them too. Understand?"

Filberto paused. Miguel opened his mouth and looked at him.

"This is your responsibility, El Caballo. No one gets near the room except me. Some of these people may have bodyguards. We will keep them outside. The guests, as well as our people, and of course our guest's security cannot recognize your faces or know your real names. Our people will protect the outside."

"But if they have their own security, why—"

"We can't trust them. They are supposedly on our side. The man who did this job before you got killed taking such things for granted."

"Why did you leave me out there," Eduardo snarled. He was covered with dust except for the area around his nose where he had obviously tied a bandana. His eyes bored into Miguel, his arms were motionless and stiff, and his fists clenched. Miguel fought to keep from laughing.

Stepping to within inches of Miguel, Eduardo looked up at him and started to point a finger as though he intended to poke him in the chest. Miguel stiffened. His eyes mere slits. Eduardo stepped back.

"Ask Filberto!" Miguel snapped.

"What's the assignment?"

After Miguel explained, Eduardo again glared at him, but said nothing.

Miguel returned to his room. A knock at the door announced Filberto. "I am here to take your picture. Go stand by that wall."

Yet another puzzle.

"Passport," Filberto explained.

13

*M*iguel pointed to the place he wanted Eduardo to stand. *"Stay here to cover anyone approaching from the interior of the house."* Miguel stood inside next to the library door. Shortly after assuming their positions, the house shook with the roar of a landing aircraft. Soon, three men led by Filberto entered the front door. Filberto smiled at Miguel while Miguel held the library door open for three stern-faced men and Filberto.

Miguel recognized Arturo Alvera and Ernesto Vargas, the patron at Las Flores. The third man he recognized from pictures, the governor of the Sonora State.

They settled around the table. Alvera sat at the head. After some chatter, they quieted and looked at Alvera.

"We need to select an assistant for El Anglo," Alvera began. *"I don't mean an orderly. More like an aide de camp, someone who can carry out his orders and El Anglo can rely on. El Anglo has suggested we consider El Caballo. Remember that Ernesto Vargas recommended Miguel."* He nodded to Vargas. *"He also recommended Ignacio, and that proved a good choice. Ignacio had said Miguel is smart, a hard worker, and has potential to become a good leader.*

"We've had a chance now to observe El Caballo. He handled without incident a smuggling assignment. He acquitted himself well in the attack upon Ignacio in Las Flores. He did well in the important delivery of two foreigners across the border. He and Quique made a successful cash delivery from Tucson."

A knock at the door interrupted Vargas. Filberto went to the door opened it. He took the tray of coffee and set it on the table. After they had taken their coffees, Vargas turned to Filberto. *"I'd like your thoughts, Filberto, and maybe some background or anything else you want to say about Miguel. You have had the most contact with him."*

"The only reason he joined us," Filberto began, *"is because he wants us to protect his family in Las Flores and help him find his wife. I think he is smart. He seems interested in our business. I think he will work with us until he finds her. He has the temperament for more responsibility. However, I guess I am concerned about his loyalty. Once he finds her, I think he will leave. He is self-reliant and takes directions well, even from me, so I think he would work well with El Anglo."* He paused and looked at each of them. *"Still, he is an unknown quantity. We know of his physical skills and his bravery, and we know from contact with his army commander that he wanted Miguel to stay in the army, attend officer training, and remain in the army after finishing*

the academy. We know he is resourceful. He does not associate with the others here, does not mess with the girls, and does not indulge in the drugs or the liquor. I know his stay here has been short, and perhaps there has not been time to thoroughly evaluate him."

Filberto looked at the men surrounding him at the table. All were important, wealthy Mexican patriots. Filberto was not of their social class. He had worked for the family, as had his father before him. Nevertheless, he believed himself a patriot also. He thought Miguel was a good choice for their cause, yet that was mostly a feeling rather than certainty of fact. Men needed testing before being given responsibility, he believed. Miguel had handled assignments well. They were moving ahead. Still, Filberto wanted more time to evaluate.

Filberto was more to Alvera than an assistant or house manager. He was an alter ego, a voice of wisdom and experience. Alvera sought him for advice and evaluation of all his important decisions. Filberto had performed the same function for Alvera's father, and when he died, Filberto became a father to Alvera. When Filberto was present, he seemed almost invisible, listening and observing. Anyone who dealt with Alvera understood his importance.

Three years prior in Mexico City, Alvera's wife, son, and daughter Katia, who was their chief financial officer at the time, waited for Alvera to meet them at a restaurant before attending a concert. The meeting was with the president and his cabinet. A presidential aid interrupted the meeting and whispered to the president. The president's face went pale as tears formed in his eyes.

"Arturo, your family was killed along with others in an attack at the Capital Restaurant," the aid said. "Your family's security was apparently compromised. They are dead. If there is anything the government can do, we will do it. We will hunt them down. We will find out who ordered it."

During the period Alvera worked through the tragedy, Filberto managed the estate following Alvera's instructions and assisted Quique, the accountant and CFO, who had replaced Alvera's daughter.

Filberto continued, "Miguel is not like the people here, though; that is clear. You don't know what's going on inside his head, and that is worrisome. He keeps his mouth shut, and he is trustworthy, something that is almost unique here. Until now, we know his only interest is in finding his wife. I don't see any broader motivation like money or dedication to any other cause or special loyalty to us. Nor do I see a criminal personality nor, for that matter, any trend to some moral creed. He simply does what he must do to stay alive. He is trapped here. Furthermore, I understand why Vargas and El Anglo believe in his leadership potential. I just do not know what he is really thinking, and that bothers me. I am not sure I trust him. I nevertheless believe, despite my concerns, that he will have a leadership role in achieving our purpose."

"What about Quique?" Alvera asked. "He's been our financial guy since my daughter Katia died."

Filberto opened a file. "He graduated from Arizona State in accounting and finance. He is a CPA, not married, knows the money and accounting stuff. He's done some innovative things in money laundering. However, he is not a warrior, not like Miguel, not like El Anglo."

"Any idea how Miguel might react to our real agenda?" asked the governor.

"We've hinted at it," Filberto continued. "He hasn't responded one way or another, although I think he is curious."

Alvera said, "I think what El Anglo likes are some of the things that disturb you Filberto, you know, not having a relationship with the others, not making judgments about what he is asked to do, and a sense he can be trusted. Miguel has a military background and operational experience, which, of course, appeals to El Anglo. I think with a little more experience Miguel will make an excellent executive officer. He also believes Miguel displays the disposition and the courage for a combat leader." He looked at Filberto. "Any further thoughts?"

Filberto shook his head.

"His family has been part of our business for several generations," Vargas added. "His grandfather was with Poncho Villa, as was mine. That is how the Gutierrez family came to live in the compound. My family set aside the land for them. They built their casas, the barn, and the corral. Miguel is a very good and loyal worker." He explained the background with the horse, Maverick. "We expected to give him more responsibility. The men respect him."

"Additional thoughts or misgivings?" Alvera asked, looking around the table.

They all shook their heads.

"Are we agreed then on the next phase?"

The men nodded in agreement.

"Let's pull Miguel in a little further and see what happens," Alvera suggested. "If we are wrong about him, we know how to fix it."

They nodded once again.

"Let's get El Anglo in here and let him know." Alvera walked to the door and opened it. He motioned for Miguel to enter. The others stood around the table. "Tell El Anglo to join us. He's on the porch. Then you stay over there just to keep an eye on things." He pointed toward the corner. "Leave Eduardo outside near the door where he can see anyone approaching from either direction."

When Miguel returned with El Anglo, Miguel walked to the far end of the room and stood near the corner as Alvera had instructed. The men gathered around the large table in the middle of the room. El Anglo and Alvera joined the others standing around the table. After delivering their brandy, Filberto returned to the bar and began a second batch.

Alvera turned and raised his glass toward the Mexican flag. "Viva Mexico!"

The others lifted their drinks. An earsplitting explosion outside lit up the night. The windows rattled, and the room shook. The men looked at each other and started to turn in the direction of the door when the window opposite the bar shattered. The building shuddered from another explosion, knocking them to the floor. Gasoline fumes filled the room.

As suddenly as the attack began, an unnerving silence followed. The explosion had left them deaf except for a hum in their ears. Floating scraps of paper, dust, and small chunks of stone settled on them and around them while they lay on the floor. Trancelike, the men started to move, coughing, and sneezing, checking themselves for injuries.

Miguel, farthest from the blast, rose first. He quickly checked the others for injuries and helped them to their feet. Alvera, closest to the bar, was barely breathing, disoriented, and bleeding. Miguel tried to help Alvera, but he was unable to stand. Miguel left Vargas on the floor. He did not see Filberto. El Anglo managed to get to his knees. Blood dribbled from a scalp wound.

Miguel walked through the rubble that had been the stone bar. Because of the dust, he at first did not see Filberto and then gasped. He saw body parts and noticed the scalp of Filberto stripped away, exposing his brain. His torn remains wallowed in a puddle of blood. He must have caught part of the primary impact from a shoulder-launched multipurpose assault weapon that struck the bar wall.

Eduardo cautiously entered the room. He helped Alvera, who crawled along the floor and appeared disoriented. Miguel went outside to report to the security captain. Fire still engulfed the hanger, gas tanks, and an aircraft. They all blew at once, sending shrapnel in every direction.

Several men in balaclavas lay on the ground, profusely bleeding and probably dead. The captain jumped into a jeep with two others and, while talking on a radio, chased after a jeep that was attempting to escape. Another brought four men wearing balaclavas to the house who had been captured by the security detail. The dead attackers lying on the ground also wore balaclavas. The security men removed the balaclavas from the dead men.

Eduardo managed to get Alvera outside. Alvera could barely stand. Incoherent, he stumbled and then collapsed and fell. Eduardo stood over him, his own clothes covered with blood, all of it belonging to others. Both Eduardo and the captain watched Alvera.

Miguel approached them.

Eduardo turned to the captain and ordered, "Tie them up," pointing to the captured attackers in the jeep. "You know where to take them and what to do." He paused, looked at Miguel, and smiled. "Take this man also. He is El Caballo, one of them." He tried to shove Miguel toward the security chief. "Find out what he knows and who did this."

The captain apparently assumed that with Alvera down and unresponsive, Eduardo was in charge.

"Gag him and get him in handcuffs. This man is very dangerous." Three men finally took Miguel to the ground, handcuffed him, and shackled his ankles. One started to blindfold him.

"No!" Eduardo said. "Hold him up. Lean him against the side here."

Miguel continued to struggle.

"We can't hold him much longer," the captain said.

Eduardo hit Miguel first in the stomach and then in the face with a blow so hard, broke Eduardo's hand and knocked Miguel unconscious, his chin sinking to his chest as his legs buckled.

Eduardo walked to where he lay, poked him with his foot, stepped back, and spit in his face. "Get him in the jeep. Take him with the others. You know what to do."

14

*M*iguel smelled urine and sweat. Unable to see clearly, he heard muffled voices, which were followed by a blurred vision of others across the room. He felt restrained when he tried to move. His vision cleared. A muchacho grasped his shoulder, pulling him into a sitting position. The man shoved his back against a wall. His legs stretched out in front of him.

He tried to untangle his thoughts. He remembered the explosion and Filberto in pieces and Eduardo hitting him. He did not know how long he had been there. He knew it was dark when the attack began. It remained dark. Three lanterns provided light.

Miguel felt no pain. He tried unsuccessfully to move. Everything seemed intact. He was nauseous and light-headed and thought he had been sedated. He knew he would not know if he had injuries until the drugs wore off.

Finally, his vision cleared, and his face began to hurt. A masked man holding a chain saw stood before a man seated on the floor propped against the opposite wall. In addition, a third masked man was on his knees, grasping the arm of another captive and holding it on a large tree stump. A third masked man placed a hunting knife across the man's wrist and appeared about to cut off his hand. Instead, he sliced into a finger. The man screamed and tried to pull away, his blood-soaked face distorted.

"I don't know," he yelled. His other arm hung loose and twisted. His severed finger fell to the floor.

The torturer picked up the finger and dropped it in a sack.

The fourth masked man stood next to Miguel, recording the scene on a video camera. He stopped recording and turned to Miguel. "You informed that the meeting was taking place."

"No!" Miguel replied, trying to clear his head.

The man kicked Miguel in the stomach, knocking the wind out of him, and then resumed recording.

The boy holding the chain saw yanked the cord. The machine roared into operation. He placed it against the neck of the man sitting directly across from Miguel. The whirling chain sent chunks of skin and tissue and bone throughout the room like sewage from a ruptured sewer line. In seconds, the victim's severed head tumbled into his lap. The headless body leaned slowly sideways against a third captive, drenching him in blood. The man by Miguel continued to film as the head rolled toward him. After the head stopped, he filmed a close-up of the face whose eyes seemed to stare at Miguel.

The cinematographer stepped close to the next captive and nodded to the muchacho with the knife. The muchacho nodded, turned to his victim, and placed the knife to the man's neck with his right hand while holding his hair. The muchacho who previously used the chain saw held the man as both looked at the cinematographer who knelt before them.

"It was Eduardo, Eduardo!" the captive yelled. "Eduardo told them." The captive tried to scream but only managed a gurgle before the knife sawed back and forth across his neck. Suddenly, blood spouted like a fountain. His head fell and rolled along the blood-slick floor like a jagged soccer ball.

"We'll get a lot for this," the cinematographer said, putting the camera in his backpack. He made a call on his cell phone. Turning to Miguel, he said, "You are a lucky man, El Caballo."

Ignoring Miguel, they gathered the lamps, picked up their gear, and quickly left, leaving the chain saw behind. Miguel heard them drive into the night.

Shortly after, a commotion began outside. Men with flashlights and weapons entered. The captain found Miguel bound on the floor. He cut the plastic cuffs and helped him stand.

Miguel stumbled, trying to walk. Two security guards helped him outside. Miguel saw Eduardo tied and sitting in the truck's bed.

Several men pulled Eduardo from the truck and made him kneel in front of the truck in the headlights. The captain pulled an automatic. Turning to Eduardo he said, "Who ordered this attack?"

"I don't know," Eduardo answered.

"Take him inside."

Two security men drug him by the arms through the door.

"No, no!" Eduardo squealed.

Miguel heard the chain saw start and then stop. They dragged Eduardo back outside bathed in blood from the floor. They pulled him to his knees before the captain, again in the headlights.

"Spiro Morales," Eduardo yelled.

"Who told him of the meeting?"

Eduardo's eyes widened. He looked at Miguel and the others standing around him in a circle. "I don't know," he pleaded, his voice wavering.

The captain turned to another man. "We know where his family is?"

"Yes."

"No, no. I called Spiro. I called and told Spiro last night. Don't hurt them."

"Here, El Caballo." The captain tugged the automatic from his holster and offered it to Miguel. "This man accused you of being an informant. Do you want the pleasure?"

It was more than Miguel could stomach. "No, thanks. I thought him my friend."

The captain calmly walked behind Eduardo, placed the barrel to Eduardo's head, and pulled the trigger. Eduardo fell forward onto his face. They rolled him over. Most of his face was missing. The captain then shot him through the heart. "That's for Vargas."

They picked up the body and dropped it into an acid-laced well, along with the chain saw and the other mutilated corpses.

When they arrived at the hacienda, Miguel staggered to a grove of trees and threw up. He sat on the ground, shaking. It was almost dawn before he finally returned to his room.

For Miguel, having been a loner all his life, his closest and perhaps only friends were his father, Jose; his wife, Maria; and his horse, Maverick. The solidarity of the desert and the presence of the ancient ones had been more than enough to maintain equilibrium in the way he accepted the world. He now found his singularity inadequate to confront and deal with the events he witnessed at the kill house.

Until now, he had experienced relative comfort and confidence coping with the circumstances encountered in his life. Even in the army he had witnessed atrocities after the fact, experienced physical danger, faced the threat of death, and dealt with occasionally nearly debilitating fear. However, he had never witnessed a killing that included intentional brutality by mutilation or the pathologic pleasure these young men apparently experienced in administering pain. That anyone participates in such barbarism, such depravity, revealed the darkest and deepest fundamental nature of humans. That is what scared him most. Was that in him also? Is this what I have become?

Miguel felt a tug to the bottom of that pit. He'd left people to die in the desert, he'd killed men without remorse, accepted El Coyote's and Eduardo's view of illegals as cattle, as merely a commodity upon which the cartel hoped to achieve a financial return.

He recalled the words of Nate at La Cucaracha, "You unfortunately *seem fated to fulfill a role in this godforsaken tragedy that is the antipathy of humanity."*

Miguel had never felt so alone or impotent. He could not seek advice from his father. This was not the back porch with the view of the desert while savoring an unlabeled bottle of mescal, talking about life. This was not the corral with his father sitting on a crossbar as Miguel worked a horse while they discussed plans for the compound or tactics for the Friday night horse races. Maria was not in the bedroom bathing Juanito or discussing their next bus trip to Hermosillo or planning to meet with Inez or debating whether she ought to take Juanito with her or leave him with Miguel's mother. Now he was his own counselor. Worse, he thought that no longer mattered. There was no one he could turn to for advice.

He mentally escaped to Jose, Juanito, and Maria. Always, they were in his mind, the foundation of everything meaningful. They remained the only anchors securing him to a better place and time. They were what continued to drive his determination to remain alive until he negotiated the maze that he hoped led him to Maria. Not only were they his reason for living, but they were his only sense of righteousness, his only claim to sanity, and his singular remaining acquaintance to morality that was all he had left to negotiate a sea of faceless death and overwhelming violence.

He prayed his connection to them remained intact, despite the oppressive and powerful forces that he felt were dragging him in another direction he could not yet comprehend: money, luxury, respect, prestige, leadership, and events and circumstances he could not yet fathom, the very things Maria had hoped they would find in America.

Recalling again that day at the cantina when he killed the two shooters, which now seemed so long ago, and his subsequent and continuing lack of remorse, he wondered if that event was when he had changed or whether he had changed at all. Maybe it was then that his true self emerged. Perhaps the rational for his placidity with those events was as simple as the Sonora Desert, where life and death were merely functions in the continuing cycle of reality. You survived until you could no longer live, but the relentless desert endured, seeking revenge for those who tried to change it. He saw the kill house now as just one of the scenes that, as Nate said, he was fated to fulfill in this tragedy.

15

*M*iguel was surprised to find a squad of military staked out on a hill overlooking the grave sight of Filberto. Observing an officer who seemed in charge, Miguel approached him with his M16 slung across his chest.

"Sir, I am El Caballo, in charge of a security unit with Arturo Alvera. I did not know the army was also providing security."

They shook hands.

"The secretary of the interior ordered us to also provide security. With both of us here, this burial is secure, no?" The officer smiled.

"Yes, indeed, secure. I just need to know how you are deployed so we don't needlessly cause either of us a problem."

"We are deployed on this hill and can easily observe the mourners. Also, we've taken positions along the road leading to the grave site." The officer motioned to the hill and pointed toward the road.

"Okay, we'll fill in the gaps," Miguel noted.

When the hearse and the long procession of vehicles arrived, Miguel watched with Emilio, who had earned a reputation as an expert rifleman by outscoring everyone at the range. Miguel selected him to be part of his security team. Together, they posted their team members and began an inspection of the positions of the military to identify their locations.

Once the priest, family, and mourners settled at the grave site, Alvera, Vargas, and the governor sat beside the casket while dignitaries stood behind them. El Anglo remained at the hacienda recovering from his wounds.

Miguel decided to inspect the area again. Slowly he climbed the hill, recalling the first time he met Filberto almost a year ago. In a way, he had thought of him much like his father. As he moved higher through the brush, he saw Vargas and the governor clearly visible, seated beside the coffin. The priest solemnly moved to his position at the head of the casket. Bodyguards stood behind them, and mourners were behind the bodyguards. Several possible clear fire lanes from the hill appeared well within the accurate range of an assault rifle. Uneasy because he did not see, as he had expected, military on the hill, Miguel removed the M16 from the sling. He began to ascend.

A flash of sunlight reflected nearby, then another. Not recalling anyone in that position previously, he ducked behind a tree. A man in camouflage lay in a small alcove of trees just below the crest of the hill, his silhouette obscured against the sky. He aimed a scoped long gun with a suppressor down the hill.

Miguel yelled, "Hey!" and stood just as the man fired.

Below, a tall security man standing behind the governor fell. Miguel fired a burst from the hip, killing the shooter. Everyone fell to the ground, while the chatter of the M16 echoed among the hills and faded into a deathly silence.

Miguel spoke to Emilio through their handheld radios. "Let's be careful. There may other shooters. Let's expand our search."

They carefully searched the area. Believing everything secure, the service proceeded without further incident.

Hours later, Filiberto's funeral mass and burial remained fresh in Miguel's mind. Told to report to the library, he found El Anglo and Alvera waiting for him among the rubble. Dust covered everything. The torn Mexican flag covered the spot where Filberto had died. The picture wall seemed intact, perhaps a statement that the history the wall displayed would never be forgotten. The repairs thus far only consisted of equipment and tarps dumped in the corner where Miguel was standing when the attack began.

"We're sorry about the confusion," said Alvera. He paced, found a seat on the dusty sofa, and then stood and began pacing again.

Miguel knew he was referring to the treatment he had received from Eduardo after the attack on the hacienda.

Alvera turned to El Anglo. "We've got to get on this right away. If we leave this alone, it will encourage others."

"Of course," El Angelo agreed.

"I have to get to Mexico City." He turned to Miguel. "Good work today, Miguel. You saved lives. I am very sorry," he repeated. "If I'd realized what was happening, I'd have stopped it sooner."

The apology was the second or third time he had apologized to Miguel for Eduardo's accusation and his treatment after the attack. Alvera turned and left the room.

Nervously, Miguel remained with El Anglo. He instinctively looked for Filberto. Filberto would have stayed there so Miguel would not feel threatened. Having just attended the grandest funeral he had ever witnessed for a man he respected, he wondered how he might react to his father's death. They must have been close to the same age. It was unimaginable. The evening they shared Oaxaca mescal flooded his memory. His thoughts turned to Juanito, hoping someday to share the same kind of experience with him. Were they safe in Las Flores? Where was Maria? What had Nate found out?

El Anglo motioned to two dusty chairs and said, "Let's talk."

Miguel sat.

El Anglo stood over him. "You want something to drink first?"

"Cerveza!"

El Anglo left the room and closed the door, leaving Miguel alone. Miguel squirmed uncomfortably. To be served by so important a man was unnatural.

"Here," El Anglo said, returning and standing over Miguel. He gave Miguel a bottle and pulled a chair closer. After a few swallows, he leaned toward Miguel, continuing the silence while closely watching Miguel. Finally, he said, "I need to get a few things straight before we move on."

Miguel felt the pulse rate in his neck increase. His palms were sweaty. He crossed his legs and then uncrossed them and felt sweat gathering at his forehead. He wanted to wipe his forehead before it dripped down his face, but he did not dare move.

"Someone had to notify Morales of the meeting. When did Filberto tell you about it?"

This is an interrogation, Miguel thought, realizing he had as much opportunity to notify someone about the meeting as anyone.

"While I rode with him from the range after the shooting match. Filberto said you wanted me in charge of inside security for the meeting and to tell Eduardo."

El Anglo searched Miguel's face. Miguel tried to hold his gaze but could not. He sighed heavily again and placed his hands on his knees.

"Yes. Filberto reported he had explained the assignment to you on the way back from the range. When did you inform Eduardo?"

"As soon as he got back to his room."

"All right, that's probably when he called Spiro Morales right after you left. They told me Eduardo slugged you and ordered them to take you to the kill house. We found a cell phone on Eduardo's body. A call occurred during that period. He confessed before we killed him. I'm sure Spiro ordered today's attack also, with assistance from police and the army. If not for you, who knows how much damage there would have been. Today's funeral arrangements for Filberto were common knowledge, which means there was plenty of time to plan.

"Ignacio's murder was hastily executed, a revenge attack and a warning to

others for Ignacio switching sides. Of course, there could be other explanations as well, maybe an inside power struggle, for instance, or a revenge killing."

El Anglo stood, looked at Miguel, turned, and walked to the missing window. He stood there sipping his beer before turning and walking back to Miguel. "Here's to Filberto. May he rest in peace." They touched bottles. "By the way, you're moving to a new room next to mine upstairs here."

Miguel knew the last person to occupy that room had died in a shoot-out. Why would El Anglo do that? His place was the barn or the barracks.

"You have an assignment. Before I explain it, I want you to think about something. I believe that Ignacio's loyalty remained with the Morales Cartel. I think he and Eduardo and El Coyote were working together for the Morales Cartel or maybe someone else within the cartel. I have not shared this suspicion with anyone else here. This is only my theory. I have no proof. I am mentioning this to you so that you are on guard. You cannot trust anyone. I also know that you, Maria, and Ignacio were friends from Las Flores. Eduardo's role in this recent attack on us certainly raises questions. Did you know Eduardo from before, maybe in Las Flores?"

Miguel remembered that El Coyote and Eduardo seemed close during the crossing. "No, not until you introduced us."

"Okay, here is the assignment."

Miguel knew he would not like it.

"Kill the leaders of the Morales Grupo Cartel. There are three brothers, Spiro, Javier and Roberto. Spiro is the most notorious. He graduated from a university in America. We took the Tucson Plaza from them. We had to kill the father to get it." He sipped his beer, continuing to watch Miguel.

Miguel frowned. He had previously assumed that Ignacio was followed to the cantina that morning in Las Flores. He now recalled that the night before, he, Inez, and her husband, Florio, were all together. They had not talked about Ignacio and Miguel meeting the next day at the cantina. When Florio left to catch the bus the following morning, Miguel remembered Florio asking him to tell Ignacio hello for him. Florio must have known Ignacio would be there.

El Anglo changed position so he directly faced Miguel. "They still control a plaza between Sasabe and the California border. We want it. We want people to know we are the ones who killed them and that you, El Caballo, are Sonora. I have a contact that can get us in touch with a couple of hit men. They were once members of Los Zetas and, like you, trained for a short period

*in the States. They are freelance now. For this, it's fifty thousand for each kill
and double for you, plus expenses. Stick with them, and you will learn."*

Miguel gasped and coughed in spite of his intent to maintain control. He
was accumulating quite a few bodies, and telling Zetas what to do seemed
unlikely to prolong one's life.

He had heard of them, Los Zetas, of course. Everyone had heard of them.
They were once part of a unit with the Gulf Cartel and proclaimed themselves
the most ruthless of all. They broke away from the Gulf Cartel in 2010 and
created their own cartel.

Sweat dribbled down Miguel's face and annoyingly down his nose, where
it then dripped on his shirt. So far, he had attempted to rationalize his killings,
but this was different. This was what his father would call pure evil.

Killing people in the cantina he justified as self-defense. Killing the shooter
earlier today was certainly justifiable. What El Anglo wanted was assassination,
rationalized by an ambition to steal their plaza and earn respect and fear and,
ultimately, power. This killing was murder. No way could Miguel wrap that
up into a rationalization. His chest tightened. He wondered how he could
explain all this to his father and Maria. Would she think he had become a
monster?

Before Miguel fully grasped the idea of killing in cold blood, El Anglo
presented another task. "You are now leader for the Nogales Plaza. You get this
Morales business done, and the Sasabe Plaza will also be yours until you select
the next leader. Manuel will work with you and whoever else you choose." He
paused. "Any questions?"

Miguel stood and walked to where the bar used to be. He looked down at
the rubble where he had found Filiberto's remains after the attack. Bloodstains
and chunks of flesh and bone mingled within the rubble. He turned and
walked over to the wall of pictures.

This is my death sentence, he thought. Ignacio is dead. Eduardo is dead.
Both were plaza leaders. This was not the reason he was here. He was here to
find Maria and pull his own family together so they could have their own wall
of pictures and memories.

"What has been done to locate my wife?" he asked El Anglo. "That's my
cause, not to become a narco."

El Anglo stood and walked to Miguel and put his arm around his shoulder.
"Filberto was trying to identify the yellow Humvee to find a connection to her

down here. He thought she must still be in the States, not here. He thought *El Coyote* probably sold her to a gringo or to a pimp. If she is still alive, you must understand a sloppy investigation of any kind is dangerous for her. I do not want to scare you, but if whoever is holding her has the slightest inkling that anyone is looking for her, the easiest thing is to kill her and dispose of her body. No body, no problem."

The ranch manager had mentioned to Miguel before Maria and Miguel left Las Flores that he might be in charge of the horses and the stables. The idea had excited Miguel. What El Anglo now proposed, the assassination of Morales and responsibility for another plaza, was a significant advancement. The fact that one was legal and the other criminal, one was peaceful while the other violent were significant distinctions.

Similarly, in both situations, he was a prisoner. In Las Flores, he would never get beyond the compound, and as Maria had said, he would always be a peon. At least he would have self-respect for honest labor. Even if Maria was unhappy, he knew he would be satisfied with the mountains, the desert, the horses, and his family. These were what mattered.

"This means lots of money, Miguel," El Anglo said, as though money was all that really mattered.

Miguel knew he had no choice, and it was not, he reasoned, about money. It was either do as they wanted or death and an uncertain life for Maria. On the other hand, maybe he was part of doing something good for Mexico. If you did something evil like killing the Morales Grupo Cartel and the others causing the sickness that was destroying Mexican society, was that not a good thing? Was that evil? The army killed to protect the country. His father honored Poncho Villa, who'd become a criminal to get money to fight the government. Perhaps with the additional money, Maria's desires could be accomplished after all.

16

*T*he handlebar mustache nearly overwhelmed the man's face. Miguel paid no attention to him when he entered the cantina wearing a white shirt and white pants, sandals, and a large straw sombrero. Except for the precisely trimmed mustache that contradicted his otherwise peon appearance, he looked like an Indian from the state of Chiapas. The man approached the bar and said something to the bartender, who then nodded in Miguel's direction. When the man removed the sombrero, his ponytail fell to shoulder length.

Just like El Anglo's, Miguel thought.

He looked at Miguel and slowly approached the table where Miguel sat facing the door. Miguel observed him cautiously approach. Miguel dropped his hand to the Glock, just in case. Still holding his sombrero, the man placed it on the table, leaving both hands in plain sight and then placed his hands on the table as well, a gesture Miguel understood as a sign he intended no harm.

"You are El Caballo? I am Isdel."

The respectful tone surprised Miguel, who towered over him, and extended his hand. Isdel's grip was like a vise. His eyes peered into Miguel's eyes as though exploring the depth of Miguel's soul.

Isdel seemed familiar. Perhaps the length of his hair and his ponytail reminded Miguel of El Anglo. While he appeared as ordinary as dirt, also just like El Anglo, there was intensity in his eyes and in the slant of his body as though poised to strike quickly, again just like El Anglo. Knowing he was Zeta, Miguel remained cautious.

Isdel said, "Let's talk." He moved to the same side of the table with Miguel, the wall behind their backs. Both sat quietly observing the room.

"The barman," said Miguel, nodding toward the man watching them.

"He's with me," said Isdel. "He is my brother, Joaquin. Isdel nodded to him.

Joaquin approached them and said to Isdel while looking closely at Miguel, "Tequila?"

Isdel held up two fingers.

Miguel already had a beer.

When Joaquin headed toward the bar, Isdel said, "He's the contact with El Anglo. We work together. What do you want with us, El Caballo?"

Miguel had not decided how to describe what he wanted. He said, "To kill Roberto, Javier, and Spiro Morales."

He had expected a reaction. However, Isdel remained calm and waited *for the barman to deliver his order: two shot glasses of tequila, a lime wedge, and a salt shaker.*

Isdel pulled a knife from the sheath on his belt and set it on the table. As though he were laying out the instruments for open-heart surgery, he carefully set the shot glasses next to the salt shaker. He picked up the knife and the lime and sliced two small wedges. He wiped off the knife, stuck it back in the sheath, and placed the lime wedges by the shot glasses, leaving the lime by itself on the table.

"You don't mess around much do you," Isdel said, placing the empty shot glass on the table.

Miguel was not sure what Isdel's response meant. "Is it doable?"

Isdel swallowed and coughed. "Perhaps with a small army. A bunch of hawks to patrol twenty-four/seven."

"How about with just two of us?"

"You loco, El Caballo?" He smiled and shook his head. He made no movement to end the conversation. He lifted the remaining shot glass in his fingers, held the glass at eye level, and slowly rotated it in his fingers while peering through it as though the liquid contained the answer to all life's great mysteries.

"Do you think fifty thousand dollars per Morales brother might make it more feasible?"

"And expenses," Miguel added.

He licked his hand, sprinkled salt, licked again, slammed down the tequila, and bit the lime. He lifted his arm. Joaquin looked over. Isdel put up three fingers. "I knew I was going to like you, El Caballo."

A few days later Miguel received a call from Isdel who used a code agreed upon at the previous meeting. They met again at the same cantina.

"I staked out the Morales compound on the outskirts of Hermosillo," Isdel explained. "I know one of the men on their security team. He said they are flying to Phoenix to shop and spend a few days with family. It takes a while to organize such a trip. They will take a private flight from their airfield to Phoenix. I have checked out the route to the airfield. There is one place where I think will be the best location for an ambush.

"My informant says there will be only two cars. One car is for Roberto, Javier, and Spiro. A second car is for their security. There have not been

problems on that route because they don't believe anyone would be so stupid to try something on their own turf. I don't think they will suspect anything. My car is outside. We can go look at the ambush site, which is suited for two or three shooters."

"This informant," Miguel began, "what the hell keeps this snitch from running to Roberto? My experience says a snitch is a snitch no matter who is paying."

Isdel frowned at Miguel and calmly said, "We have his wife and, oh yes, also his kid. He knows I will kill him. The same goes for you and me. We have to trust each other to do this. There are never any guarantees. Only dead men don't tell lies."

The location Isdel had selected was a blind curve where the dirt road passed between two cliffs forming a small gorge and then turned sharply, exited the gorge, and entered dense brush. Isdel walked to the area where the cars would exit the gorge.

"They have to slow down to negotiate this tight turn. The first car will be security. We let it pass. Joaquin my brother will be in the brush down the road there." He pointed.

"The Morales brothers will be in the second car. We take it out when it slows to make the turn. There is adequate cover for us right here. See, the car's lights will display the opposite side at the turn of the road, and that's when we fire from this side. By that time, the lead car will be where Joaquin is waiting. He will take them out. To get to us, they would need to turn around or stop to let the security get out and run back here."

Skeptical of a plan that seemed on the surface too simple, Miguel asked, "Where is their security? They need more. Surely, they know, as we do, that this location is vulnerable. At Alvera's property, there is no way anyone gets this close without being discovered." Then he remembered the attack on the hacienda where security did nothing to stop the assault that killed Filberto.

They walked to the second site. Isdel pointed to a secure place they could camouflage the car.

"If we used more men," said Miguel, "we can ambush both cars at the same time. We will have only one chance. We miss, and they will be on us. I think we should at least have another man with your brother to take out their security car, just to be sure."

Isdel shook his head. "If we hire some hawks, they will have warned

Roberto. We cannot trust anyone, El Caballo, not anyone. We work alone for that reason."

After viewing a couple of alternative sites, they returned to the first one. Miguel stood at the edge of the road and slowly turned in a circle, examining the terrain. "This is perfect for a rocket-propelled grenade, if we can get one."

"Just takes money. Two would be better. One for each car."

"I want to add one more man to the team." He looked at Isdel. For the money he was paying Isdel, he did not think there would be an objection.

"It's your show, El Caballo."

"I want you to meet him first. He got here on his own from Guatemala. His brother is dead. He is young. We are training him to be a sniper. In addition, I want you to return to the hacienda with me. Your brother can go back to the cantina until we are ready to move."

During the drive back to the hacienda, Miguel explained to Isdel what he knew of Emilio's background. Miguel left Isdel at the stable in the room Miguel first stayed and then left to find Emilio in the barracks. He instructed him to meet with Isdel. He went to the main house to report to El Anglo.

"Amazing how much information you can get for a few dollars," Isdel said to Miguel and Emilio as they loaded up two bulletproof BMW SUVs with four RPGs. Since they had arrived back at the hacienda, Emilio had not been out of Isdel's sight. They checked the rest of their equipment, gathering what they also needed for Joaquin.

While still light, they drove to Hermosillo and stayed with Joaquin in an adobe hut behind the cantina.

Before dark the next evening, they drove to the site and deployed their equipment, which consisted of placing one RPG at the first location and the second farther down the road. Isdel and Miguel remained at the first. Emilio and Joaquin walked to the second. A black tarp covered the SUVs parked fifty yards away in the brush.

Two security vehicles passed their location about a half hour apart.

"Checking the route," Isdel said.

Almost to the minute of the time Isdel predicted, two distant vehicles projected long stems of light into the dark sky as they bounced over the unpaved road, their engines howling, drowning out other night sounds. Miguel estimated they were a hundred yards apart. Reaching the blind curve, the cars closed the gap and slowed to negotiate the sharp turn and the narrow passage through the gorge.

Far behind, another set of headlights appeared unexpectedly, probably another security vehicle. This unexpected event eliminated any opportunity for a recovery from a mistake. Miguel wondered what had happened to the first security car that passed them before. Now, he was glad he had acquired the two extra RPGs.

The first car rounded the rock-obstructed corner, started to pick up speed, and emerged just as the second car closed the gap.

The second car had just rounded the turn when Miguel fired an RPG, ripping the car into twisted metal. The first car had reached the second ambush location and started to turn back when Emilio and Joaquin fired, disabling it.

Immediately, small arms erupted but quickly ended. Isdel and Miguel quickly ran to the mangled and burning second car containing the Morales brothers. Just to be sure, Isdel shot everyone inside. The fire burned out quickly.

Miguel and Isdel moved to another location, anticipating the arrival of the third car whose lights they had previously observed. Isdel loaded and fired the RPG, and Miguel cleaned up with his M16, taking out the third car.

Emilio and Isdel removed the tarp from the hidden SUVs and drove to the first site. They rolled the bodies of Roberto and Javier inside the tarp. Spiro was not with them.

The following morning, two bodies hung from a bridge in Hermosillo along with a sign that simply proclaimed: "Sonora."

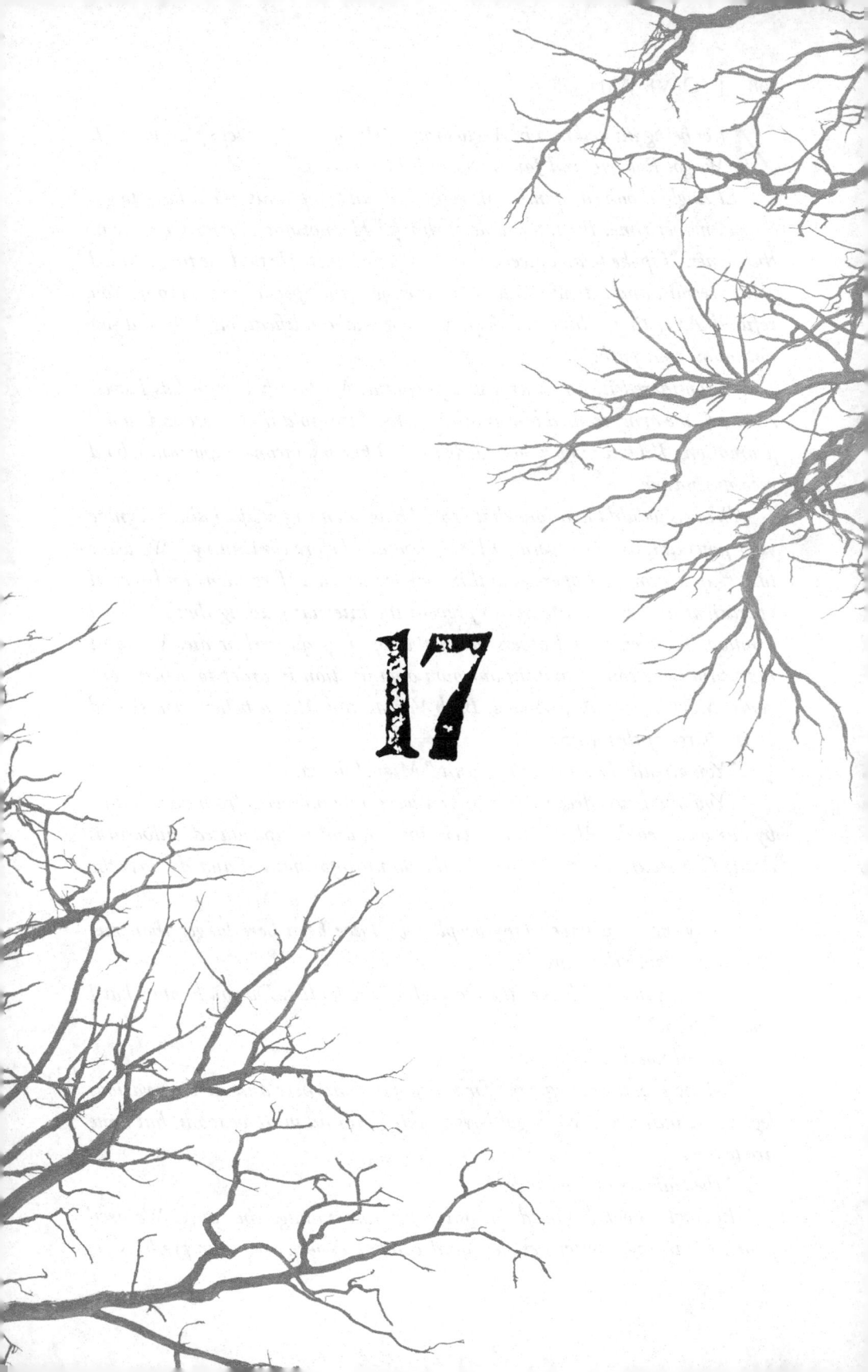

17

*A*fter being invited into El Anglo's room, Miguel said, "Isdel's plan worked. We got Roberto and Javier. Spiro is in America."

El Anglo shook his hand. "All right, we can't stop now. We'll have to get Spiro another time. First, a couple of things." He motioned toward a chair in the corner. "I spoke to an officer in your old army unit. He told me they wanted you to reenlist and attend the academy then join the Special Forces group. You refused. According to him, you display exceptional qualifications. Why did you not follow that path?"

"I considered it, but Maria was pregnant. My family was in Las Flores. At times, the army seemed like another cartel. I was told that to get additional promotions, I'd have to pay somebody unless I knew someone important who'd recommend me."

"Vargas would have done that. You'd have been set for life. I also recognize your potential, as has Alvera." El Anglo paused before continuing. "We want to set up a group to operate within Sonora as an enforcement and special operations unit in an attempt to prevent the internal feuding that's infected Sinaloa, Los Zetas, and others when the top dogs quarrel or die. We must maintain tight control within our own organization in order to achieve our goals. Much is at stake, Miguel. Both Vargas and Alvera believe you should be in charge of this unit."

"You already have a security unit," Miguel noted.

"You saw how effective that is. You were only moments from being killed by our own people. Alvera and I were injured and incapacitated. Filberto is dead. Our security captain thought the damn informant, Eduardo, was the boss."

"Why me? You have many people who have been here longer than me. They are all over the place."

"Yes, as you say, all over the place. They are bodies. Do you know what I mean by that?"

Miguel nodded.

"Many people are required for the jobs around here and Alvera's various legitimate businesses. We've got boys walking around with weapons, but none are leaders."

"The trainers at the range?"

El Anglo shook his head. "Mostly, they just manage the range. We need combat training. Better yet, we need combat experience. Our predecessors *here and yours are dead. That includes a couple members of Alvera's family killed by Morales and others. That's why you and I are here ... to build this organization."*

"I am not here because I care about all this. I am here to find Maria and return to Las Flores."

El Anglo stood and turned his back on Miguel who sat in the other chair watching him. He walked to the window, clasped his hands behind his back, and looked outside while rocking on his heels but saw nothing. After almost two and a half years, he finally had someone with the potential for helping the mission assigned by General Marcus: to develop a clandestine organization to take on the Mexican Cartels. They had started with a hairbrained scheme to follow the destinations of guns they let walk across the border. Because of weak political leadership and execution, they had lost all control of the mission. The only thing they had learned was that the guns turned up in some of the worst murders on both sides of the Rio Grande. El Anglo believed Miguel could be an important pawn in his mission's deadly game. He did not want to give him up. He empathized with Miguel's situation. He had lost his own family from a crazed intruder in his home while he was serving in Afghanistan.

El Anglo turned back to Miguel and returned to his seat. "You care about your own life, you care about her life, you care about Juanito, you care about your father, Jose, and your mother, Yolanda. No? What you now know about this organization and what you have already done is more than enough to put you in prison. We cannot just let you walk away. Do you not think that Spiro Morales will hesitate to kill them to get at you or get revenge or that we will not do the same? Did not Ignacio tell you that once you joined, you would not be able to leave alive? Think about it, Miguel. We are the only ones who can protect them and protect you. You leave, that stops. You are on your own. How do you expect to find Maria? Does anything else matter?"

From where he sat, Miguel saw the mountains and the desert. A dark cloud gathered over the mountain, and rain began to fall lightly and silently. He watched it approach. He felt he had no more control over his life now than he had control over the approaching rain.

Between the edge of the descending storm cloud and the clear sky, he experienced a vision of the ancient ones he sometimes saw in the desert when he felt troubled. What he saw in them now was vengeance. They had warned him often enough. He had not listened. As the moment slowly faded, he recalled some of what Border Patrol Agent Gonzales had warned in the Cucaracha Restaurant in Tucson. "The life you are now leading has no rules except violence: no loyalty, no friendship, no value except survival, no future, no recognition, no moral justification."

What Nate had further described about what might happen to Maria remained an added reminder of the horrible, unending nightmare. Staying focused on finding her had to remain his sole mission. According to El Coyote, Maria thought him dead. It was also possible she was dead. Where else could he turn to find her than to trust Nate, the resources of the Sonora Cartel, and, most importantly, El Anglo, who seemed to empathize with his situation. He had no choice unless he just wanted to throw up his hands, run away, and hide. He was now deep in the Sonora Cartel. He had to find out what had happened to her, no matter what she had been forced to do. He had to get her back. He knew it would be hard. They were different people now. He had not done his job. He had not protected her. Once they were reunited, they could work out the rest of their lives. He remained convinced the only pathway to finding her was through the cartel, El Anglo, and Nate. He could not simply go to the streets in America and locate her on his own.

Still overwhelmed from the ambush and El Anglo's thinly veiled threats, Miguel sank back into his chair. He stared straight into the center of the storm outside. He knew that while the storm would soon pass, his internal turmoil would not abate until they were all together again.

El Anglo remained quiet, watching Miguel. He rose, walked to a small refrigerator, and removed two bottles of beer. He gave one to Miguel and returned to his seat.

The rain pounded the roof. Together, they watched water roll down the stable roof and puddle in the corral. Miguel thought of Maverick. Maybe when the ground dried, he could ride. He had noticed a trail that appeared to ascend the side of the mountain. Maybe he could follow that to the end, as he did when he lived in the compound and rode Maverick to the ledge on the mountain. When seen from high above, the world appeared refreshingly beautiful. The distance made vision clearer.

El Anglo stood and walked to the window again, blocking Miguel's view. He turned and said, "There's another view of this situation you should consider, an opportunity to be a leader and a patriot and a hero in an important movement for Mexico, a historical change, a chance to be in the vanguard, perhaps a new Poncho Villa, a peasant like you." His stare was intense.

El Anglo walked to Miguel and looked down at him. "Poncho Villa killed to change Mexico. History tells of many revolutionaries, who, were they not deemed heroes, would instead be labeled killers and traitors. When one overthrows an existing order, is that treason, or is such violence heroic? Our humanity requires we understand the distinction."

Instead of answering, Miguel said, "I want Isdel in this squad and also his brother Joaquin, who is a good source of information about Morales. Also, I want the muchacho who won the shooting contest, Emilio. He is an excellent sniper."

El Anglo smiled. "You got him. I want Isdel to provide personal security for you. El Caballo is identified with Sonora Cartel and the assassination of Morales. Many may hunt you just to brag about killing you and gain favor with Spiro or others.

"Now, as I said before, if you get this job with Morales done, you will be the leader of the Tucson Plaza. This job was well done, so you have that responsibility, starting today. You have the support of Manuel, who is looking for another stash house."

"Why not Manuel?"

"He is not a good field leader. He is excellent at managing the houses, getting and transferring the money, and controlling the operations there. He will know shortly of your position."

"He will not object to my doing this?"

"It is not his choice that matters here, Miguel. If you are able to select someone else to take on the plazas, then we will listen to your choice."

"Where do I find such people?"

"Making the right decision for plaza leader is very difficult. Usually someone in the family takes it in order to retain control. Also, soon you will take a trip with me to South America. I'll explain more when the time comes."

They stood at the same time. El Anglo said again, "Miguel, good job."

Miguel walked through the rain to the stable carrying an apple. Entering, he whistled. He heard a snort halfway down the aisle. Maverick thrust his head over the top of a stall door. Miguel stepped inside and checked the condition of *the stall and the horse. Both were clean. He gave Maverick the apple. Maverick nuzzled him. Miguel hugged his neck, left, and walked to Isdel's room.*

"This is where I stayed when I first came here," he said when Isdel invited him in. I also found my horse here."

Isdel smiled. "I've heard the story from a couple of others. You are to be called El Caballo, yes?"

Miguel nodded. "We make a good team, I think. Would you agree?"

"Yes."

Miguel explained the plan to create the internal security squad and for Isdel to be Miguel's personal security. "I am driving to Las Flores tomorrow for a couple of days. We can talk about a security plan on the way."

After returning to his room, Miguel lay in bed thinking about El Anglo's advice regarding his appointment to Tucson Plaza boss. He would have to rely on Manuel for managing the stash house: money laundering, coordinating drop sites, storage, distribution, and enforcement. Reality was that he would have to learn from Manuel. Miguel could not contribute from his own experience. From what he had personally noticed while lying on the floor at the stash house, he thought there needed to be better control of the selection and control of the hawks, especially since he had now learned that loyalty at that level was virtually nonexistent. El Anglo said that the best way to ensure loyalty was to appoint family members. He had only one family member left, Florio, Inez's husband.

Miguel called Florio. No answer. He left a message. However, he was still unable to dismiss the possibility that Florio was the snitch who gave up Ignacio.

18

*A*t home, Miguel found a few changes as the result of the money he had sent to his father. Improvements were underway. A new truck was in the driveway, and new fencing surrounded the corral, enabling the horse to graze without hobbles.

Two armed men stood nearby. One he recognized from prior work details at the hacienda. Obviously, Vargas had provided security as agreed. Isdel got out and waited until Miguel stepped from the SUV and then walked toward the two guards.

Rascal ran from behind the shed, jumped, and almost tripped Miguel.

Jose looked Miguel up and down and then saw Isdel. His face remained a blank page, convincing Miguel that his father knew the source of the money. As they walked toward the house, his mother ran from the casa, smothering Miguel with an engulfing hug while Juanito stood in the doorway grasping the door for support.

"We have guards," she said, shaking her head and pointing her thumb toward the guards standing near the corral. "Jose has much respect at the hacienda."

Jose sent Miguel a knowing look. "Apparently, Miguel has one too. What is his name?"

"Isdel. He'll stay with the guards."

Miguel rushed to Juanito and lifted him into his arms. Juanito's arms tightened around Miguel's neck.

"Papa, papa," Juanito squealed.

Entering the casa, Yolanda said over her shoulder, "What do you know of Maria?"

"Nothing. I'm concerned." He hesitated about providing the details, not knowing how to explain to his mother about the rape and her disappearance, deciding instead to wait until he was alone with his father.

"Why do you need a guard?" Jose questioned.

"He's a friend."

"I see. Anyway, we are glad to have you back, and of course, your friend is welcome." Jose smiled innocently, as he lowered himself into a new chair. "You like how we spend your money?"

"You look good in that chair," Miguel said, relieved, understanding his father was not going to ask him about the cartel.

Yolanda walked to a new table and phone. She gave Miguel a note. "You had a call from Florio. Said he can meet you tomorrow morning at the cantina before the bus."

Miguel lay back on the old worn sofa and felt the springs jabbing against his back as he remembered and sighed, the familiarity warming him like an old blanket. Tears came to his eyes. "Home," he whispered to himself.

Isdel and Miguel drove to the cantina in Las Flores in Ignacio's SUV, spewing dust into a growing cloud behind them. While Isdel went inside to check the interior, Miguel remained outside in a chair on the porch, reveling in the quiet and peace that had eluded him. Isdel returned to the porch and asked Miguel to look at the young man sweeping the floor inside. Miguel did not know him.

"He probably also tends bar," Miguel suggested and noticed Florio seated at the same table Ignacio and Miguel had occupied the day of the massacre.

The subdued interior light failed to hide the bloodstains that discolored the bar and the floor. Bullet holes remained in the bar, the wall behind it, and the opposite wall, where someone had stuck a plastic flower in a bullet hole, perhaps to create a memorial to the tragedy. A new mirror hung on the wall behind the bar. A large picture of Inez and her baby and a crucifix hung together over the middle of the mirror.

What Miguel saw in the mirror startled him. His appearance resembled Ignacio's that bloody day: the jeans, the starched blue shirt, the fancy boots, the swagger as he walked. In fact, even his movements mimicked the arrogance he had despised in Ignacio. Even the semiautomatic pistol tucked in his belt was identical, just as the one Ignacio carried that day. Miguel removed his felt cowboy hat and set it on the table. He moved the chair around so that when he sat in it, he would have a view of the door. He wiped his hands on his jeans. Everything was the same as the day he met Ignacio at the very same table. The only real difference was that no dead bodies lay on the floor.

He hesitated, reliving the scene: the baby's blood spilled onto the bar, Inez's face a mask of blood, and the skin, tissue, and brains splattered on the wall. Unconsciously, he wiped his hand on his shirt and pants as though trying to remove the memory, like being awake and reliving a bad dream. He tried to tuck the memory away into the same mental folder that contained the others he had subsequently killed and were now merely items to file away in an unsuccessful attempt to remain forgotten.

He walked to the spot where Ignacio had fallen. When he turned around, Florio was watching him. This was the first time he had seen Florio Rodriquez since the slaughter of Florio's wife and baby.

"It was horrible," Miguel began after shaking hands and then paused, realizing that Florio might resent him for surviving … a question he had pondered also. "Florio, I am very sorry about what happened." He sat in the same chair where Ignacio had sat.

"What do you want, Miguel? I have to get out of here."

"It was the Morales Cartel that did it. We got two big bosses."

"Yeah, I heard." Florio glared at him. "You are a big man now, right, Miguel? Or should I say, El Caballo."

"You still working at the hacienda?"

"Yeah, I am in the fields most of the time. Run a tractor or I am here. What's it to you?"

"Are you interested in more money?"

"Doing what?" Florio questioned.

"You'd be responsible for the Tucson Plaza. I am the plaza leader now," Miguel explained.

"I'd work for you?"

"Yes." He shook his head and sighed. "How do you pay me?"

"You get paid out of the money we get from the plaza for your part. You select and pay the muchachos. I am the plaza leader now. They are not members of Sonora Cartel."

"What do they do?"

"What you tell them. Mostly they are lookouts for the coyotes. They also stop illegals. If they are not with a Sonora coyote, they must pay a tax. They don't know anything else, just what you tell them. They are not to know anything else. They are not loyal to Sonora. We only hire them as needed. You understand?"

"Who picks the coyotes?"

"Me, but you recommend new ones since you'd be in contact with them. I will call you when we need you. If you do okay, you can officially join us."

"What does that do for me?" Florio asked.

"Money. More than you make here. Protection," Miguel told him. "However, once you join, you can't leave."

Miguel was beginning to think he should not have said anything to Florio. He seemed to be pressing for some kind of confrontation.

The bus arrived. Several men who waited on the porch now stood and walked toward the bus.

Florio stood. "I'll let you know." He walked through the door without turning back.

19

*J*ose brought out the mescal. They went through the ritual, and Jose poured and placed their glasses on a small table. Miguel lifted Juanito onto his lap. Rascal rounded the corner to lie between them. The sun drifted lower. They remained quiet, listening to the sounds of evening: a car in the distance, a desert wren singing in a nearby tree announcing dusk, small creatures scratching, and nearby mesquite trees scraping together in the breeze. Even the evening released a soothing perfume to replace the remaining remnants of the day's shimmering heat.

"Any idea about Maria?" Jose asked, breaking the spell.

"We haven't located her. After we crossed the border, El Coyote raped her at a place called the trophy tree. I tried to stop him. He shot at me." Miguel lifted his hand as if he were holding a pistol and pointed it at Jose. "The bullet scraped my head." He touched the scar. "I don't remember anything more until I was at a stash house. They told me she was taken by a man in a yellow Humvee."

Miguel wanted to tell Jose about Nate Gonzales and working with the US Border Patrol. He knew Jose would be proud of him if he knew.

"People are looking for her." He looked Jose in the eyes. "There is no way I can find her by myself. I am illegal there. I do not speak English. I don't know anyone there who can help me. This cartel, though, has connections and people who are trying to help me. By now, she could be anywhere. She could even be dead. The man who took her, El Coyote, said he told her I was dead. When we got to Tucson, they said we needed to pay more money. El Coyote took all of ours.

"If I agreed to join them, they would forgive the debt, protect you here, and help me find Maria."

"You agreed to join them," Jose said.

"Yes."

"That's why the money, the guards, and Isdel to protect you. Do you have any idea where she is?"

"No. It must be awful for her. You know what they do?"

"I've heard things, rumors. I am very sorry."

"I have done things …"

Jose held up his hand. "Don't say. I don't want to know. You do what you have to do to stay alive and to find her. Now you can't walk away."

"Yes."

One of the guards approached them and looked at Miguel. "El Caballo, there is a man here who says he must speak to you. Isdel is checking him out."

"Okay, gracias."

"They call you El Caballo?" Jose asked.

"Yes. No one knows my real name, so others can't find my family." Miguel stood and looked down at Jose for a moment. This was where he wanted to be and again wondered how everything had gone so wrong. He took a deep breath and then followed the guard around to the front of the casa. Isdel, holding a pistol, stood in front of Florio as Miguel approached.

"I took this from him," Isdel said.

Miguel took the pistol. "What do you want, Florio?"

"I accept the job, El Caballo."

When they returned to the Alvera hacienda, Miguel noticed more men and guards. He started up the stairs to his room.

One of the men on the security detail stopped him. "You are to attend a meeting in the main dining room at eight o'clock. Vargas is here."

When Miguel entered the library, Vargas and Alvera stood near the bar, while El Anglo led Miguel to the opposite side of the room. They stood next to a map of Mexico that included the southern United States.

After hearing about Miguel's trip home, El Anglo said, "I want you to be responsible for Sasabe as well as Nogales." He placed his index finger on the location. "Sasabe is already established. With the death of Roberto and Javier Morales and Spiro presently in the States, we might be able to take control of that plaza. We will have to rely on the people already there, plus whatever you are able to put together with the team you are building. If we can accomplish this, we will be able to control the southern border of Arizona between Sasabe and Nogales."

Miguel noticed there were small circles on the map at Nogales, Sasabe, and Douglas.

El Anglo looked at Miguel and nodded. "Yes. Douglas is part of the plan also. We have reason to believe the Sasabe Plaza leader will turn just as Ignacio did in Nogales. It will take some time. Sasabe is not as busy as the Nogales Corridor.

"*The responsibilities include human and drug smuggling, warehouse storage facilities, stash houses, disciplining traffickers, payments to officials and snitches, as well as defending the territory and disciplining subordinates, trafficking guns and money, and dealing with various organizations across the border just like the Nogales Plaza. This will take time to organize. Manuel will assist.*

"*If we can turn the current plaza leader, getting control will be easier. That is what happened when we took the Nogales Plaza. A lot depends upon the depth of their loyalty to Spiro Morales. You have a reputation now and will doubtless receive credit for things you have not done. That's one reason to make sure they know about El Caballo. These people tend to venerate leaders. Still, that does not guarantee loyalty. If we can keep them, we will be able to expand our organization with experienced people.*"

Miguel was stunned and unable to speak. He turned and looked across the room where Vargas and Alvera stood next to the new bar, watching them quietly talking. El Anglo nodded. Alvera poured wine into four glasses and met the others at the table.

"*I don't know if I am able to handle this responsibility,*" *Miguel said.*

El Anglo said, "*If we did not think you could handle this responsibility, we would not give it to you.*"

Contrary to his feelings about narcos and his commitment to Nate Gonzales, when Alvera lifted his glass, Miguel felt he was part of something important.

20

*T*he road from Rio Rico ended at a stately stone house situated near the top of the hill. Adrian Wolforce turned the rental Mercedes into the driveway, stopping in front of an open garage door. Inside, the garage was a Mercedes-Benz SL550, a Cadillac Escalade, and a yellow Humvee. A middle-aged Latino holding a can of car polish stood next to the Mercedes. Wolforce shut off the engine and stared at the man in the garage. The man looked at him and then walked to the car, opened the driver's door, and held it open until Wolforce left the car. At least, Wolforce thought, he didn't stick out his hand for a tip.

As the Homeland Security informant had said, Morrison obviously did quite well. This house was only one of several the owner, Malcolm Morrison, allegedly owned scattered about the world. Morrison was chairperson of the International Contracting Corporation (ICC).

The front porch spread the length of the house. Wolforce climbed four steps and sucked in his breath. The view pulled him to the edge of the porch overlooking a hillside sloping toward the Santa Cruz River. From this distance, the river was a silver thread winding northward from Mexico through Rio Rico, Tubac, and Tucson.

Similar homes on other hilltops isolated the area from the ordinary world that squeezed into the town below. The nearest house could not have heard a shot fired from this location.

Elephant Head, an unusual rock formation resembling its namesake located near the foot of the Santa Rita Mountains, provided an artistic backdrop. A light breeze found Wolforce's face. The dry air was dramatically different from the sweltering humidity of Washington, DC. Situated at the farthest north end of the development, the house seemed the most isolated. Brush and rocks covered the mountainside ascending several thousand more feet. The sparkling river meandered through the narrow valley below, sharing the valley with a railroad track.

Adrian Wolforce was the self-styled important deputy to Ratcliff, an assistant to the secretary of the director of national security. Ratcliff rarely made a decision without Wolforce's advice.

The doorbell's chimes rang somewhere within the bowels of the house. Waiting, Wolforce looked at the large homes sprawling on the distant hilltops. Rumors purported the bigger homes belonged to Mexican cartel capos. Such rumors existed wherever expensive cars and homes were near the border. The properties contrasted to the homes of the residents of Rio Rico residing far below.

Before the chimes stopped ringing, a beautiful young Mexican woman opened the door and smiled at him. In accented English, she said, "You are Senior Wolforce?"

"Yes, I am," he replied.

"Please follow me, sir."

It is a pleasure, he thought, observing her walk ahead of him down a short hallway. The decor was southwestern. To his immediate left, a large painting that resembled the view from the porch hung on the wall. On the right, a mirror hung over a low cabinet. He slowed to observe his reflection. Staring back at him was a fortyish, nondescript, six-foot man with graying hair, glasses, and a trimmed beard wearing a wrinkled but lightweight dark blue suit and a red tie. He slowed to straighten his tie and then turned and increased his pace to catch up with the woman.

A few paces farther, an open door to the right displayed an office with bookcases and computer equipment. A closet was to the left along with another door, which was likely a bathroom. Beyond were steps leading upstairs. The hall emptied into a large family room with a tiled floor covered with thick oriental rugs. Along the rear wall, floor-to-ceiling windows and sliders opened onto a large patio and pool. The view from there was even more expansive and spectacular than the one from the veranda. Near the swimming pool were a fountain and a putting green, the only green grass in sight. Off to the side was a covered bar, complete with running hot and cold water, barbecue, bar stools, tables, and chairs beneath an enveloping awning.

Everything else was desert-tanned earth covered with stones, carefully designed landscaping of various desert plants, and neatly trimmed hedges. Beyond the pool and bar was cleared, level land, covering close to five acres gradually sloping downward out of sight to reappear as a hill more than three hundred yards away. Wolforce thought it an ideal location for landing a helicopter.

Morrison was an important man to cultivate. The report Wolforce had received on Morrison was sketchy and did not reflect whether he was actually involved in suspicious activities. What he had seen thus far painted a picture of wealth and added to his suspicion that Morrison was connected.

Wolforce, however, never put much stock in hunches. Two months ago, a source inside placed Morrison with Ernesto Vargas and the governor of Sonora

State at a swanky restaurant in Hermosillo, and though that did not necessarily prove a direct connection to cartel business, it gave Wolforce an opening.

Money was the real purpose of this meeting. However, the unexpected presence of this beautiful young woman in Morrison's home added another dimension to the accumulating evidence that Morrison was at least familiar with human trafficking. He knew if he was lucky, he might have fallen upon a dealer in humans. The suspicion was enough to give him an advantage and perhaps solve another pressing problem.

The young woman led Wolforce to the entranceway of an expansive family room. Malcolm Morrison, white-haired, handsome, debonair, and self-impressed, stood looking out the open sliders toward the pool. The woman approached him and said something. He grasped the girl's hand, turned, and led her back to Wolforce.

"Ah, Adrian, a pleasure to see you again. Maria, my dear, fix us a couple of drinks, won't you?"

She looked at him expectantly.

Morrison looked at Wolforce. "She makes an excellent martini, Adrian. May we interest you in one?" He looked at Wolforce, who nodded. "Okay," Morrison said, nodding to Maria. "That will do it. Thank you."

She smiled, turned, and walked to the bar.

Morrison gestured toward leather chairs carefully positioned to provide a view of the patio, pool, and the vast mountain scape beyond. Wolforce sat. Morrison sat in a leather recliner facing him. A nearby couch littered with various folders and papers completed the small seating area. Three other similar areas were also part of the room, along with a large wall television, several bookcases, a liquor cabinet, and various works of art. They watched Maria walk to the bar and mix their martinis in a crystal carafe.

"Very nice," Wolforce said to Morrison, referring to Maria.

She brought their drinks.

"Thank you," Morrison said to her. "That's all for now, Maria." He nodded toward the pool.

She smiled and left the room through a sliding glass door in the windowed wall that opened onto the patio and the pool. She removed her clothes, revealing a bikini, and then snuggled into a lounge chair.

"Some of these Mexican girls are lovely and grateful, if you know what I

mean." Morrison winked. "She's been with me for a while now." He looked at Wolforce. "Makes a nice martini too, no?"

Wolforce noticed two Mexican gardeners trimming brush and raking near the pool. Another, not standing far away, looked like a security guard with a concealed weapon. Maria did not pay any attention to them.

"I've taught her to drive. You should see her in the Mercedes ... stops traffic."

Wolforce smiled and nodded. He wondered what Morrison's wife thought of Maria. "How's Gretchen? The last time I saw her was in Tucson at that restaurant in Old Town."

Morrison frowned as though he did not recall.

"You had walked over from the DeGrazia Museum."

"Oh, sure. She's fine!" Morrison noted. "Been in Italy with friends. She's headed up to Florence for a couple of months. She's an art aficionado, you know."

"I figured that, with her interest in DeGrazia and all. Is she who selected these paintings?" He swung his arm in the direction of the far wall. Small ceiling spotlights highlighted the paintings. "Has good taste." He was quickly growing tired of this chatter. He wanted to press on.

"Yep, it's all her collection. A few of them she painted. She's not a bad artist herself."

Wolforce stood, glanced at the pool, and walked to the paintings. He turned and said, "Yes, very well done, indeed." His glass was already empty. Morrison had barely touched his.

Wolforce jiggled his glass. Morrison looked away and then nodded toward the bar. Wolforce walked to the bar and helped himself from the carafe.

"Did anyone talk to you about the foundation?" Wolforce asked as he walked back toward his chair, looking out toward the pool.

"Not since that time in Old Town. I thought that's why you are here," Morrison said.

"Yes. That's why I am here."

Morrison looked over at the sofa with all the papers. He sighed and shifted in his seat. "What is it you want, Wolforce? You asked for this meeting."

"Yes, of course, the foundation. I wanted to share some more information with you since Gretchen expressed her interest at the restaurant. She seemed very enthusiastic. I admit, I'd hoped Gretchen would be here."

"Rest assured, I am capable of explaining it all to her. She is interested in supporting the new gallery."

"Our members are a close group. Each has contributed one hundred thousand dollars for start-up funding. Gretchen, as I noted, would be a perfect member for our board. It is appropriate today to have women on foundation boards. Since she is already a donor to the gallery and she is so well known in the local art world, she'll go on the board, perhaps as chair." He paused.

Both men looked toward the pool while sipping their martinis.

After a few moments of silence, Wolforce said, "There are ancillary benefits that might interest you."

"Oh? Like what?" Morrison questioned.

"Well, nowadays, as you probably know, connections and access are valuable assets, particularly in international projects and business. The relationships that develop between board members and foundation contributors not only provide support for the beneficiaries of the grants provided by the foundation to the gallery, but the relationships developed between foundation members occasionally present opportunities between contributors and foundation members unrelated to foundation business."

Morrison stood up and walked to the bar. After pouring a drink for himself, he walked back, sat down, and placed the martini on a small table by his seat. "What are you saying, Wolforce?"

Wolforce could not repress his smile. He was almost certain Morrison had taken the bait. He just needed Morrison to swallow it. "My job with Homeland Security is to gather intelligence regarding the activities along our border. This includes developing information regarding the cartels. I collect this information and give it to my boss. He evaluates the intel, and we meet with a group of people involved with border security. We summarize the meetings, and the information is used in policy considerations at Homeland Security. We meet frequently with the US Border Patrol and other agencies that have responsibility for protection along the border. Over the years, I have developed contacts with people on both sides of the border. Many of these contacts I now consider my clients." He paused, watching a frown cross Morrison's face.

"For instance, I know you met with the governor of Sonora State at an upscale restaurant in Hermosillo. I know that meeting was to discuss a certain construction project under consideration to be funded in part by the State Department through a grant from the US government."

Morrison sat up and leaned forward. His frown deepened.

Wolforce continued. "Let's say, for instance, one of the board members of the foundation is a contractor licensed to do business in Mexico. Both of you might be able to benefit by participating in this project. Both of you could donate a few dollars to the foundation. My role in this matter is to facilitate such trade and information.

"The policy is that the general contractors for such projects sponsored by the government must not be involved in criminal activities. So, part of my responsibility is to submit whether contractors are involved in criminal activities. Now I am not saying that you are involved in any such activity." He looked away from Morrison and looked again toward the pool. "I am just exploring with you the idea of how relationships developed through the foundation can be beneficial while at the same time contributing to an important charitable cause. I have contacts with people and organizations on both sides of the border. Does this explanation help answer your question?"

Wolforce stopped to let the thought percolate. He looked around the room. Besides a baby grand piano and the bar, he now noticed two display cabinets with Mata Ortiz pottery worth thousands.

Morrison asked, "How familiar are you with the cartels?"

The directness of the question startled Wolforce. "Well, I know of them from our intelligence reports. It's my job to know who they are. I might know a few people with contacts."

"All right," Morrison said. "Tell you what, Wolforce. I cannot make any commitment right now without discussing it with Gretchen. In addition, I'd want to meet with the others in this … uh, foundation. I need to know more about these people. I am sure you understand."

"Yes, I understand. They need the chance to evaluate you also. How about I call you when we can schedule a meeting?"

"Perfect. You'll let us know then?"

"Yes," Wolforce said.

Morrison stood and turned toward the doorway.

Wolforce stood as well, but instead of following Morrison toward the door, he went to the sliding doors.

Morrison followed him.

Maria had not moved from the edge of the pool. "Where did she come from?" Wolforce asked.

"I don't ask. The less one knows, the better." Morrison paused, watching him.

"Eh, what does it take to get one?"

"What? Are you serious? One like her?"

Morrison nodded his head.

"A lot, I'd guess. You serious?"

"Maybe."

"I might be able to talk to someone who knows about this stuff." Then Morrison stepped back, shaking his head. "I don't know about anything like that."

Wolforce turned and looked him in the eye. "Of course not! Morrison, we both know better."

There was something repulsive about it. Nevertheless, Wolforce asked, "Another like her? That girl out there, she is documented, right? I mean, if I mentioned something to ICE, just in passing since part of my job is to report illegals. You know, start investigations, suspected human trafficking, and stuff like that. Phew, why even the hint of something like that. And the guy in the garage, of course he's documented, right?"

"Yes, he is."

"Okay, well. So, girls like Maria for instance, what's the going rate?" Wolforce asked.

"Very expensive," Morrison told him.

"Suppose I knew someone important who was looking for one for whatever purposes: nanny, housekeeper, care for an elderly family member, something like that. Or say, just for argument, a broker, a person who supplies workers, whether men or women, farmworkers or whatever. Okay? Can you also arrange people for that sort of thing?"

"No, I can't arrange anything. Like you, Wolforce, because of my business I know a few people who know people. I might be able to get a name. You'd have to do the rest."

Morrison partially turned. "You will be contacting us for a meeting then?"

"Yes," Wolforce assured him.

"Want to say goodbye to Maria?" Morrison asked.

"Sure."

Morrison went to the sliding door, opened it, and motioned for Maria to approach. She wrapped a robe about her. He led her to Wolforce, who then followed her to the front door.

When she returned to the room, Morrison was outside sitting with the security guard.

Maria collected the glasses, took them to the sink, and washed them. She turned and looked out toward the pool and the mountains in the background. This house was exactly the kind of place she had dreamed about when she had thought of coming to America with Miguel and Juanito. Only she thought it would be hers. The thought she would end up a housekeeper and a concubine had never entered her head.

Ignacio was the first to plant the idea into her head. He had promised her that they would live well in America, sharing their lives with Florio and Inez. Maria knew Ignacio was important in the cartel. He promised her he would take care of her and Juanito. He said he'd fix it with Miguel and Florio. She did not care to know about any of that or what he had meant by "fix it." Ignacio said she did not need to worry about anything.

At the trophy tree, however, everything changed. El Coyote killed Miguel. She was raped and then raped again at a stash house and then sold to Morrison. She had counted on Ignacio for everything and still could not understand why he did not warn her of all this. Where was he? He said he would help them when they got here, help her to get to her aunt and uncle and to get Juanito. There was no one, no one to help her now.

Morrison took good care of her. Just a little while longer, and she could mention Juanito to him. She wanted her baby, and maybe she could persuade him to get him for her. If Juanito grew up here, it would be far better than Las Flores.

Sleeping with Morrison was not as passionate as with Miguel, but he certainly knew how to please her. Gretchen did not seem to care. He did not want to share her with other men as she thought he might, and she did not care if he had other girls. They did not stay at the house. Others cooked and tended the house. She was the mistress and treated special. Under the circumstances, what could be better until something else came along? Still better than Las Flores.

21

*T*he *Gulfstream departed Mexico City Benito Juárez International Airport just after midnight carrying three passengers: El Anglo, El Caballo, and Quique, the Sonora Cartel's chief financial officer. El Anglo waited until the plane achieved altitude before explaining the mission.*

"Just the essentials," El Anglo began. "We call this explaining on a need-to-know basis. As you have now experienced, it is not a good idea to know too many details. Don't forget that. Everyone will talk when captured if tortured or drugged or when their family is threatened."

Miguel nodded, recalling the kill house.

"We have two destinations. The first is Asuncion, Paraguay. The second is Caracas, Venezuela. You are here for two reasons, Miguel. One is to learn. The other is to be our bodyguard." He pointed to Quique, who was holding a suitcase. "You already know each other."

"Yes," Miguel noted.

Continuing, El Anglo pointed to the suitcase. "In there, is cash … lots of cash. We are meeting with the general of the Paraguay Army. They have impeached their president. There is a new one and a new secretary of the interior. The guy who's really in charge is the general who rules through the military. He needs money to retain control. We want to establish an operation there. Paraguay is an important drug trafficking center."

A young soldier in the Mexican Army brought them coffee.

El Anglo sipped his coffee, looked out the window, and then turned again to Miguel and Quique. "We want to acquire product here so we can control distribution from dealers in Paraguay to the streets of America and beyond. Paraguay is the largest grower of weed after Mexico. We can use such a distribution channel for other commodities as well."

"Now we deal with various Mexican suppliers," Quique explained. "We want to eliminate the constant competition and expense for product by creating our own supply chain. We will need the help of this man, or whoever succeeds him, to do that. We want to pay the general enough money so he will not go into business for himself.

"We want a presence in Ciudad del Este to coordinate the acquisition of product and facilitate transportation to distributors in the US. Since few of these people know anyone but their immediate connection, they don't know, or don't care, about the cartel in Mexico. They only care about the product. They just know the person who is selling the product to them and the dealer they

sell it to. Once we get set up, we will have a valuable plaza for transporting intelligence, narcotics, and people to the United States."

Miguel looked at El Anglo. "I guess I don't understand. How do we ensure all these independent people will maintain the chain and not steal our product or not do what is expected or not go into the business themselves?"

El Anglo replied, "We hire enforcers to take care of troublemakers. We may let a trusted dealer buy product and pay for it later after he sells it. If he doesn't pay, there are consequences."

Miguel recalled the background sheet he received from Nate at La Cucaracha restaurant. El Coyote's description included "enforcer."

Quique said, "Everything we do in the cartel, Miguel, is about money. Trafficking illegal drugs is the most profitable business in the world. We live next to the largest drug market, the United States. Americans spend about sixty billion dollars a year on illegal drugs. Drugs are a commodity with an incredible profit margin. For instance, we can buy processed cocaine in Columbia for fifteen hundred a kilo and sell it retail on the streets in the US for sixty-six thousand dollars a kilo. Our biggest problem is what to do with the profits."

Shortly before dawn, the plane descended to an altitude that enabled Miguel to see the jungle beneath them. He felt the landing gear lock into place as soon as the plane leveled out. It banked to align with the runway at Asunción International Airport in the suburb of Luque.

"Now pay attention," El Anglo began, looking at Miguel. "When we leave the airport, we will be joined by soldiers in several cars. They will be our escort, as well as our guards. We cannot trust them. You will remain with us all the time. We will do our business and leave. There is a bulletproof vest for you. Put it under your shirt. You have your automatic, extra mags, and a Glock. There is no reason to expect trouble. You can't carry the 16 inside, but you can the Glock. It's when you don't expect an attack that it happens, and then you are not prepared. I doubt the general is foolish enough to harm us. It is unlikely anyone will try without his orders. Few know we are here. Nevertheless, awareness is preparedness."

They gathered their equipment.

"Okay, that's enough for now," said El Anglo. "We'll talk more when we complete this visit."

After landing, the plane turned off the runway into a private VIP area.

An armored Mercedes limo pulled up to the side of the plane followed by two vehicles. Men in uniform gathered beside the car waiting for the stairs. When El Anglo saw the car through the plane's window, he laughed and said, "Probably stolen from Brazil and brought here through Ciudad del Este," referring to the notorious smuggling and lawless Tri-Border Area.

A soldier inspected their passports with a roster. The drive from the airport into the capital, Asunción, took thirty minutes. Access to the military headquarters took almost an hour. To Miguel's further annoyance, they waited in hard chairs in an anteroom with two soldiers holding AK-47s. A young woman at a desk talking on the phone was apparently trying to buy a car. When she finished her conversation, she nodded to the guards. They escorted them into the general's office.

General Juarez rose when they entered. He was short and balding without even a casual resemblance to a military man in Miguel's view. The accumulation of medals and various braids tugged at his jacket. His trousers were haphazardly tucked into black jump boots. If anything, he looked like a dressed-up toad, pudgy, out of shape and bald.

After introductions, he settled into his oversized chair. A large window behind him provided a view overlooking the shantytown through which the polluted Paraguay River flowed on its journey. A guard stood nearby wearing camo and jump boots. Juarez waved him outside. He motioned them to chairs, and the conversation proceeded.

"Sir, as we previously discussed, we want to buy our merchandise directly from growers and processors here. We intend to select transporters to deliver product to Mexico," El Anglo began. "That means we want a secure facility near or in Ciudad del Este. We need access for our planes at your secure airport there. We want to establish a South American headquarters, a legitimate business, because we also need to launder money.

"Your laws are, shall we say, convenient. We will send cash here to deposit in a bank or banks you designate. We will invest in a business that you think is appropriate and hire a local manager."

"You need security for these operations!" Juarez interrupted.

"Yes, that's true," El Anglo agreed. "We'll use our people."

"No, I will supply them," Juarez responded. "You are locating in a dangerous area. We will protect you. We must keep out foreigners."

"As you wish. From time to time I will need a safe house —"

The generalissimo interrupted again, as though in a hurry to complete the discussion. "I understand. We are used to such requests." His hand waved in midair.

"General, as an indication of our good faith, we brought an option payment of one million dollars in cash plus a blank draft for an additional amount to be credited to your personal account here when we agree on a sum." Juarez leaned back in his chair, folded his hands across his ample belly, and let a barely concealed smile creep across his face.

"What seems reasonable?" Quique asked.

Without hesitation, Juarez said, "A million seems appropriate for the risk I am taking, does it not? And, of course," he added, "a percentage of what the merchandise costs you. Others must be paid."

What first amazed Miguel was the amount of money. He was now accustomed to paying bribes, a hundred dollars to a policeman or local part-time mayor, to let him transfer contraband through their territory. It was business ... but two million dollars? Then it struck him. The only difference was the importance of the payee to the success of the enterprise. The cost increased with the importance of the person. His father might describe it as corruption. Miguel was not so sure. He might argue that it was essential to maintain the political stability of Paraguay, a poor landlocked country.

"You drive a hard bargain, general." Quique said.

"I know you can afford it, sir. Without such consideration, the army could take things into their own hands."

"You have a new president. Will he share in your good fortune?" Quique asked.

"That remains to be seen. We shall see. We can pay him or shoot him." He laughed.

The others just stared and tried to chuckle.

After glancing at El Anglo again, Quique walked to the desk and placed the suitcase before the general as though presenting a jeweled crown to a monarch. He opened the suitcase, displaying stacks of cash. The general leaned forward. He removed one neatly wrapped stack of bills. After fanning the stack, he sighed. He shut the suitcase, leaving the stack on his desk near his hand. He looked at Quique and held out his hand. "Where is the key?"

Quique removed an envelope from his briefcase, opened it, and, after glancing again at El Anglo, withdrew the draft, filled out the amount for one million, and signed it. He placed the key on top of the draft and then slid the key and draft toward the general.

El Anglo appeared relaxed and accustomed to such discussions.

Nervous, the sweat dribbled down Miguel's back. "I know that after this meeting we will not directly contact each other. For our part, our primary contact for money is Quique. He is our chief financial officer. Your designee will be working with El Caballo or his assistant here for operational matters."

The silence was deafening. El Anglo paused.

El Anglo leaned forward in his chair and stared into the general's eyes. "We take our anonymity very seriously." *The edge in his voice was plainly evident.* "We expect secrecy. Both our successes depend upon trust. Our tentacles can reach virtually anywhere. No one else needs to know about this transaction."

"As can mine," *responded the general.* "I am aware of your reputation, El Anglo." *He leaned back in the chair. Slowly, he looked at each of them. The draft remained on his desk. Reaching into a jacket pocket, he removed a small notebook, turned a few pages, and tore out a page. A pen and pencil desk set sat on the desk. Removing a pen, he wrote some numbers. He returned the draft to Quique with the note.* "This is where you will wire the money from Mexico." *He nodded to the note.* "That's the bank in Mexico where I have an account. I need a fax or email when you make the transfers."

Quique picked up the note, entered the information into an iPhone, and shoved the note in his backpack.

"Now, is there anything else we need to do right away?" *General Juarez asked.*

They looked at each other and shook their heads.

"I believe our business here is finished for now," *El Anglo noted.*

Within two hours, the Gulfstream approached the Caracas Airport. Before they landed, El Anglo explained. "We will meet a Lebanese diplomat named Habib Gemayel and a Hezbollah operative. I do not know the agent. I have known Habib for some time. Hezbollah agents and a training facility are located here.

"Our business with these people includes two things. We want to control product and be the only supplier to Hezbollah in Venezuela, which has become *perhaps the largest world trafficker. In addition, we have agreed to smuggle their people or affiliates across the US border. Now they are dependent upon several sources to supply product, which is cumbersome.*

"The money from trafficking they use to support their operations in Lebanon and provide financial support to Iran, al-Qaeda in North Africa, and ISIS. With the sanctions, Iran lost its access to cash. The sanctions are now removed, so they will have cash for weapons and an expanding drug market that needs product.

"I can only guess what they do with the agents we shall smuggle across the US border. They will pay us well for that service. Otherwise, they have to get them into Mexico themselves where they must first travel through Guatemala and cartel territory, significantly increasing their costs, their exposure to hijackers, and their risks of interception and arrest. They are paying us to assume that risk.

"After this meeting, our formal contact with them will be through Ciudad del Este, except as may be necessary for confirmation or notification of shipments or delivery schedules."

Miguel asked, "Were the men I took across the border part of this?"

"Yes. That was a test for us. Gemayel needed to show his people he can smuggle folks over the US border. You proved it. I want Gemayel to meet you because further arrangements will be through you. You control the plaza now. You know how the system works for drugs and people traffic. We can't disclose this to anyone ... just the four of us."

"Just the four of us?" Miguel questioned.

"Me, Alvera, Quique, and now you."

"What will they do there?"

El Anglo shrugged.

"Who sells them the drugs now for Africa?" Miguel asked.

"Venezuela from Colombia or the Taliban in Afghanistan. They have their own source in Venezuela."

"Should we try to get that business also?"

"Not now," Quique replied. "It involves difficult politics and transnational groups. With the uncertainty in Venezuela's sinking economy, it's not a good time. However, Nicolas Maduro is rumored to want a larger piece of the drug trade, and that means a possible opening for us when the time is right."

They were hustled into another Mercedes with a military escort and driven to a private VIP room in the terminal where Gemayel was waiting with another man. The military contingent remained outside. The room was barren except for five chairs and a small table.

Miguel had expected Gemayel to be wearing robes. Instead, he wore a European-style suit, splashy red tie, heavily starched white shirt, and a neatly trimmed beard.

"I can order refreshments if you wish," Gemayel said with a British accent.

"No thanks," El Anglo replied. "We can't stay long."

"How is the general?" Gemayel asked. "Things go all right?"

"Yes, we should be ready to go by next month, in keeping with your timetable." He turned to Miguel and looked back at Gemayel. "I want you to meet El Caballo, the young man I mentioned. He will handle things personally, as you requested. How'd things go with you?"

"They are pleased. No suspicions, no problems. We expect to be ready for two more soon." He turned to Miguel. "You will do the same way next time?"

Since they were speaking in English, Miguel looked helplessly at El Anglo.

"Spanish!" El Anglo said.

Gemayel repeated in Spanish.

"If that is what I am told," Miguel said, looking at El Anglo.

"This mission is very important," Gemayel said. "If discovered, it will go very bad for everyone."

El Anglo said, "El Caballo knows what he's doing. It will happen unless it goes wrong on your side," threatened El Anglo. "Who is this man?" He pointed to the man standing in the corner.

"He is from Iran's Revolutionary Guard. He doesn't speak Spanish. They are very interested in this mission. There will be two men again, each at five hundred thousand dollars."

El Anglo looked at Gemayel. He slowly shook his head. "Not enough. We agreed on one million for each man. We take all the risk. All you have to do is get them to a safe house in Paraguay. We do the rest."

Gemayel walked slowly to the man in the corner. After a short discussion, the Iranian shook his head, turned, scowled at the Mexicans, and said something to Gemayel.

"He says no. Americans are too greedy."

"We are Mexicans," El Anglo said quietly with clenched fists. He turned to Quique and Miguel and in Spanish said, "Let's go!"

Walking toward the door, El Anglo stopped and turned back to Gemayel. Ignoring the Iranian, he said, "We went through this before. We agreed on one million each, and that's what we expect, or you can shove it."

The Iranian crossed his arms over his chest. He watched the Mexicans. When they turned to leave, he pushed Gemayel aside and said in English, "Seven hundred thousand dollars. If you don't like what we say, we get someone else."

"Fine." El Anglo said without turning around. They walked through the door.

"All right, all right," The Iranian shouted.

They returned to the room. Miguel shut the door. El Anglo turned to Gemayel and said in English, "Since I can't trust this whore, I want you to pay me two million in cash before we leave this room, or the deal is off."

The Iranian glared at them and started to walk toward them. El Anglo nodded. Miguel pulled the Glock.

El Anglo pointed to the Iranian. "If I ever see this man again, he will be a dead man."

The Iranian stopped and reached toward his pocket.

Miguel racked the Glock and leveled it at the Iranian's face. The Iranian's hands dropped to his sides. "The key," he said.

Gemayel took the key, went to the corner, picked up a briefcase, took it to a small table, and removed bundles of cash.

"Count it," El Anglo said to Quique.

To Miguel he said in Spanish, "Watch him! If the bastard moves, kill him."

Miguel was pointing the weapon at the floor, gripping it with both hands. He raised the Glock and made a show of thumbing the safety. The Iranian froze and stared at El Anglo.

They remained in their positions as Quique counted the cash. "Two million."

"Let's get out of here," El Anglo said. He headed toward the door.

Gemayel followed them. "I didn't know he'd changed the price," he whined. "Your escort to the plane is safe."

El Anglo nodded to Miguel, who reset the safety. The M16 was on the seat when they entered the car. Miguel holstered the Glock. When the car started, he laid the M16 across his knees. He handed the Glock to El Anglo. Quique pulled a Beretta 45 from his briefcase and placed it on his knee. The escort to the plane was without incident, as promised, and soon they were flying to Mexico.

22

"*L*et's meet," Miguel said in broken English when Walker answered the phone. "I have information for you, and you have some for me, I hear."

"Where?"

"You know where the Green Valley Walmart is, right?"

"Yes."

"Denny's. Be there! Tomorrow morning at eight o'clock."

Green Valley was a retirement community located midway between Tucson and Nogales. To the west were open-pit copper mines that from a distance looked like gray mesas. To the east, Mount Wrightson with its bare dome was the highest peak of the Santa Rita Mountains. The dome glowed in the early morning sun. Interstate 19 paralleled the old two-lane road called Old 19, or the Nogales Highway. It passed through a large pecan grove in Green Valley on its way southward to Nogales.

Miguel arrived early. Gringos and Mexicans stopped there for breakfast or coffee on their way to work. The restaurant was busy: loud voices, kitchen activity, hustling wait staff, tables and chairs scraping the floor, banging dishes and silverware, and an intermingling of two languages. He found an empty booth where he was able to see the door and the room. He opened a menu.

Hearing the door open, he expectantly looked up and was surprised to see Nate Gonzales in civilian clothes. Miguel knew Nate's presence was no coincidence. Nate looked at him and then walked in Miguel's direction. As he walked by Miguel, he passed him a small folded note. He sat at a table where he watched Miguel.

Walker entered, hesitated, saw Miguel, and walked toward his booth. Walker's appearance was different, though recognizable. He wore brown baggy shorts, a faded University of Arizona T-shirt, and sandals. A thinning head of salt-and-pepper hair was stuffed under a faded baseball cap pulled low over his eyes. The gray eyes and glasses were unmistakable. Miguel remembered how they darted about inside the Marriot's lounge. Walker seemed a man so common in appearance no one would notice his presence. Walker slid into the seat across from Miguel.

Miguel was not comfortable with his English, and after a formal greeting in English, he returned to Spanish. "I may have an important delivery to send through. What I want from you is to know when the best time to bring it across is. I need several dates and, of course, which gate to go through. It will be a truck, don't know what kind."

"What's it carrying?"

"They don't tell me. It's my job to get it across. It's yours to get it through. He paused for a moment and caught Nate's eye. He wondered how and why he was there.

"It's five thousand dollars to you for a few minutes of your time," Miguel continued. He showed Walker a thick envelope tucked inside his shirt. "Think you can handle that?"

Miguel had worked out a strategy to smuggle the two Hezbollah agents across the border. Because Walker's personal situation involved his daughter's expensive health problems, El Anglo thought him vulnerable to anyone who approached him offering money.

"If it's a truckload of drugs, the dogs will find it," Walker whined.

"It's not drugs."

Their breakfasts arrived. Both had ordered huevos rancheros.

"Do you have access to information beyond Nogales regarding work schedules and assignments and information of crossings by DEA, ATF, and other agencies?"

Walker picked up his fork and cut out a small slice. As he slowly brought the food to his mouth, he gazed at Miguel. "Yes. As a supervisor, I can access such information that gives current stuff at all the southern ports of entry, for a price of course. Oh, by the way, El Caballo," he said sarcastically. "What is your real name? All these nicknames you people use." He chuckled and shook his head. "Are you really the one who killed Morales? Doesn't seem likely. People want to know such a famous one. Why do they call you El Caballo?"

"I had a horse ..." Miguel stopped, realizing he had said too much.

Walker chuckled, smirked, and nodded like a bobble-head doll. "Now, young man, there has to be a reason for such an interesting name. How one as young as you can kill experienced men like Roberto and Javier Morales and their security people is worth telling."

"To you, I am El Caballo. You understand? That's all you need to know." The scowl that crossed Miguel's face caused Walker to sit back. He looked down at his food.

"Questions?"

"No, I understand. Oh, I just remembered something"

"What?" Miguel asked.

"You remember at the Marriott, I mentioned someone with a Spanish connection?"

Miguel nodded.

"I think I can set up a meeting with him. I know the name of his contact in Nogales."

"Who?"

"Won't say unless you are interested. Know what I mean?"

"Dinero."

"Of course. I don't say nothing until it's in my hand." He thrust a closed fist toward Miguel. "You narcos are dying all over the place. I get the money first to make sure. You know, case you get killed or something."

"I'll let you know when," Miguel said, "and if we are still interested in the Spanish connection." He removed the envelope from his shirt to give to Walker.

When Walker reached across the table and grasped the envelope, Miguel retained his hold so it appeared to be a small tug-of-war between them. Miguel stared unflinchingly into Walker's eyes and snarled, "I am paying you ahead of time. You mess this up in any way, I repeat in any way, I will kill you myself. Count on it, gringo."

23

*N*ate's note to Miguel read: *"Meet me at the first picnic area in Madera Canyon. I'll be waiting."*

Nate selected the meeting location because it provided a twenty-mile unobstructed view of the valley. As he made his way up the mountain, no one was following. The picnic area was deserted.

Miguel turned into the lot, parked next to the only car, and went to the table. Leaning against the front edge, he watched a creek with water so clear its freshness and gurgling passage produced an appealing smell. A noise behind him made him turn. Nate approached.

Spontaneously, they shook hands as though they were old friends. "Well, look at you," Nate said, stepping back, looking Miguel up and down. "You are different, no longer a peon working in the muck or cleaning up other people's messes."

Miguel wore pressed jeans with a crease down each leg, a blue button-down shirt, hand-tooled boots, and a Stetson.

"A caballero, definitely not the look of a narco soldier," Nate added.

Smiling, Miguel turned in a slow circle. "I owe it all to you, Nate. Even got a passport. Gets me across the border easy. What have you been doing?"

"Trying to keep up with you, El Caballo. I hear you have moved up in the world. Even have your own security, right? Manuel keeps me posted."

"How did you find me? Know I'd be at Denny's?"

"After your report at La Cucaracha, I requested telephonic interception and computer hacking to access Walker's home computer and devices. Also, we are monitoring his work phone. We intercepted your call to meet with Walker. What was this meeting with Walker all about?"

"I need to get a couple of guys across the border. I let him know so he would not stop them and clear the way through. Also, if he could provide information on special border operations he might hear about."

"What guys?" Nate questioned.

"Hezbollah, two. I told Walker."

Nate's mouth dropped open. "Really, Miguel?"

No, they are a couple of my guys, hopefully a diversion tactic to keep Walker busy while I actually take two special operators across.

Miguel explained the trips to Paraguay and Venezuela and opening the store in Ciudad del Este to organize buying and trafficking through Mexico to the United States.

"Where are they going when they get here? The turmoil in the Middle East and our concern about continuing infiltration into the US by terrorists are significant threats. This is just a further strain on border security along with everything else. Why are they coming here?"

"Don't know. They will not actually cross at Nogales. Walker is a diversion. I want Walker to think they are crossing there while I walk them across just like I did the first two, get them to Tucson, and stash them with Manuel. I plan to send someone through Nogales anyway to trick Walker just in case he tries to sell the info to someone else. He is probably working for another cartel besides us. I would guess it's Morales. Walker can also get me in touch with a man in Nogales who is a big shot. Claims the man can traffic cocaine to Spain. I told him I'd check with my boss."

"Who is your boss?"

"El Anglo, as well as you." He smiled at Nate.

Miguel reported the money-laundering meeting with Walker and Quique at the Marriott, the meeting, being accused of bombing the hacienda, and his treatment at the kill house afterward.

Nate quietly studied Miguel. "Good God, man, you've been through hell. What happens to Walker if he's also working for another cartel?"

"We can still use him, you know, if not, well ..."

"So, what's your job?"

"I'm with El Anglo and oversee the Tucson Plaza and the operation in Paraguay." He shrugged his shoulders.

Nate asked for the names of the people Miguel had met and then stopped recording. "Strange," he noted, "awfully fast for so much responsibility. Why do you think?"

Miguel looked at the ground and quietly said, "Maybe it's based upon how many people you kill. Or maybe because my predecessors are dead." He looked at Nate. "Life is short here."

Both men turned and looked through live oak trees to the serenely sterile stream that flowed down the mountain toward the Santa Cruz River. They not only saw the ribbon of road meandering through the valley far below but also the pecan groves, Green Valley, the copper mines, and beyond to another mountain range looming in the hazy distance.

"Madera Canyon is a world-class birding location," Nate said.

The two men sat atop a concrete picnic table with their legs dangling over the table's edge. Birds began to return, gathering in the trees, and resumed their harmonious colloquy.

"This is usually deserted and peaceful in the early morning. I find an unusual moment of solitude in this world that seems so consumed with intrigue." Nate pointed toward the mountains. "During dark nights, banditos and mules infiltrate the trails across the mountain and through these canyons." He looked at Miguel and sadly shook his head.

"There's something you need to know, Miguel. Walker was promoted. He is in charge of customs for the Tucson sector. He has access to lots of information. I have been checking him out since you told me about him. Seems he is connected to a big shot named Wolforce through a Mexican go-between that the sheriff has also been watching. This guy Wolforce has enough juice to get his recommendation for Walker's promotion all the way up through the bureaucracy. Wolforce is with Homeland Security. He reports to a man named Ratcliff who is an assistant to the director of Homeland Security. With Wolforce, both participate in periodic meetings with folks gathering intel here. That is all I know. Have you heard of him? He is suspected of working with a cartel."

"No. Now it is your turn. What have you learned about Maria?"

"Have not found her yet. We are still checking for yellow Humvees. My fear is that she is no longer in the area. We're identifying all owners of yellow Humvees. Manuel said one of the muchachos had seen such a car but didn't notice the driver or occupants. If it's parked somewhere in a garage, it may take us a while. We got registration records and are checking one by one. We feel strongly the car is still in the area. There are not too many of them still around. Do not know about the owner. Could be anywhere. The car should give us an identity. I am trying to get a permanent tail on Walker. We are watching a stash house where Manuel thinks they hold women; maybe a yellow Humvee turns up there. We have the word out on the street for yellow Humvees."

"You still think Walker is a source to find her?"

"Yeah, at least to find the car. These things unfold like a weak chain. One thing leads to another. He probably doesn't know anything about her, but he may inadvertently know someone who does or sees one crossing the border. We are trying to find out everyone he knows. I am working this mostly alone, unofficially, though I have a contact with the state police and a

longtime relationship with the sheriff." He paused and changed the subject. "You mentioned El Anglo. Know who he is yet?"

"No, but he gets lots of respect. As I mentioned, he wants to set up arrangements to do our own transportation from Colombia to Mexico and Venezuela. Also, he wants to smuggle people from Venezuela."

"Like the two Hezbollah guys?"

"Yeah. Also, to set up an office in Ciudad del Este to launder money, do business with Colombia traffickers, and trade with Venezuela."

"Who's setting all this up?"

"Me, for organization and operations. Quique, our financial guy."

"And Arturo Alvera, what does he do?"

"He's like el president, the patron. Runs and owns everything, the ranch, various businesses, mines, and lots of political stuff. I don't understand much of it. He and Vargas are close."

"El Anglo?"

"He runs all the cartel operations. I'd say he's head of the cartel part. He showed me an organizational chart like the ones the army uses. He said it was the plan to organize what they are working on."

"Any other big shots?

"Ernesto Vargas. He has something to do with the federal government of Mexico. Plus, the other guys at the hacienda there the night of the attack, are big shots somewhere."

"Anything else?" Nate asked.

"Well, they continue to bring young guys into the organization. Talk of building larger barracks. Don't know if this means anything, but Alvera and El Anglo speak of Sonora Cartel becoming the dominate cartel as though they want to start a new revolution to save Mexico. I've heard it several times. They indicated the purpose of all the drug stuff and human trafficking is to get financing to create and support the organization's operations."

Nate looked at Miguel without expression, recalling the dinner discussion about strategy with General Marcus in Georgetown when Marcus told him: "We are concerned Mexico will become a narco state, either by the emergent dominance of one cartel or a confederation of several cartels. There are those who advocate violence to encourage this development, while we look the other way at the inevitable violence this approach creates. After an emergent cartel or other entity is determined, according to this strategy and without informing the Mexican government, we then make our peace with the cartel and work out an arrangement, among other things, to control immigration and human and drug trafficking and to provide economic development. This plan includes US support for a Mexican insurrection." Marcus had sighed heavily and leaned back against the seat. "If we can't find such an organization, we create one."

"Okay," Nate replied. "We need a way to keep in touch. I have a phone you can use to communicate with me." He reached toward his pocket.

Miguel held up his hand. "No way. Someone is always watching. I am subject to search at anytime, anywhere."

"I understand. But without one, you are in the wind." He pulled a cell phone from his pocket. "This looks like an ordinary phone, but it is actually a satellite phone. Even if someone takes it from you, they'll believe it's a regular phone. You treat this like a regular phone. Trust me. Every time you use it, we will be listening." He extended the phone to Miguel.

"All right," Miguel said.

Nate resumed his perch on the table and watched Miguel walk to the SUV. Miguel slowly descended Whitehouse Canyon Road toward the Nogales Highway.

Nate called General Marcus. Before ending his report, Nate said to General Marcus, "One thing bothers me. I expected tension between us. There was none. There should have been. I am wondering where he stands. Surprisingly, Miguel did not hesitate to pass along information. If Sonora Cartel finds out, they will kill him.

"He seemed comfortable, in a way proud of his work in the cartel, almost like he's found a home or career. What is it? Is he trustworthy? Is his loyalty to the Sonora Cartel, to himself, to finding Maria, to us, or to something else? Can we trust him?"

There was a pause at the other end of the line. "Only time will tell. Good work, Nate." General Marcus hung up.

Nate wondered whether Miguel was one of those rare individuals who confront life as they find it, without expectations or preconceived notions and lacking a sense of loyalty. For sure, he was courageous, able to work alone in a hostile environment with no way to make contact if he was in trouble. Honorable? Unknown. A killer for sure. A murderer? Would not most in his *situation kill? What was his alternative? Whatever he was, Nate liked him and felt a connection with him.*

He watched Miguel driving down the mountain, disappearing and then reemerging until the car reached the Nogales road, turned south, and disappeared into the distance.

24

*A*drian Wolforce and his boss Mallard Ratcliff, assistant to the secretary of national security, waited for the others to leave the conference room. Wolforce's face was flushed.

"Who is this General Marcus?" Wolforce asked.

Stammering, looking at the door as the others left, Ratcliff said, "Well, I am not sure exactly. Marcus's name came up at an important meeting the other day, you know, one of the important meetings I have with POTUS seeking my opinion about the border here and other important things. Eh, well you know, it's classified."

Ratcliff looked down at his shoes and rubbed the top of his right foot against the back of his trouser legs. Ratcliff seemed satisfied with his shine.

"I think Marcus is some kind of operative from DOD.

"Well, something is going on. You better find out what it is."

Ratcliff looked at Wolforce. A stern expression spilled across his face as though he were speaking to a recalcitrant teenager. He looked about the empty room, walked to the door, looked both ways down the hall, shut the door, and turned the lock.

"Nothing for you to worry about, Adrian. Before the meeting, you mentioned something about girls, you know, like housekeepers and caretakers. I, uh, want to give my wife some help. Her birthday is coming up soon. You know, with the housework and the kids and stuff, it would be nice to provide her with, well, you know, some help."

Wolforce's smiled. He reached into a back pocket and removed a small picture. He showed it to Ratcliff.

"My, my," Radcliff responded, barely audible. His tongue flicked the edge of his mouth.

"One like this is a real bargain at fifty thousand dollars. However, this particular one is not available."

"You know my wife," said Radcliff. "She works in her family's business. She is away a lot, travels. Uh, would such a girl be available, you know what I mean?" Little beads of perspiration formed on Ratcliff's upper lip.

"Look, these girls are … Well, how do I say this? They are in no position to protest or resist, if you understand what I am saying."

"But they are illegal. What if I was caught, you know, like with an undocumented person in my home? Well, in my position, my future, uh, you know, it would be rather embarrassing."

"If they weren't illegal, you wouldn't be able to do with them what you have in mind. Papers can be arranged," Wolforce explained. "They look authentic, and if they prove not to be, well, you hired her in good faith. Understand? And don't forget there is going to be some resolution of this illegal issue that will enable people like her to stay here, especially if they have a job and no other legal problems."

Ratcliff nodded. He remained subdued while he gazed at the photograph. "I want her, Adrian. I must see her first."

"Fifty thousand," Wolforce said smiling. He paused. A worried expression gathered his face into a frown. "Oh, there is a problem. She has a baby. She wants to bring him here. Then look at her. Worth much more. I want five thousand before I do anything."

"A baby? I don't know."

"Think about that. Think how generous you will seem providing a woman a home and taking care of her and her baby along with your own kids. You are a generous man, Mallard. People will admire you."

"Don't worry about the money. Get the girl. What's her name?"

"Maria."

25

*M*orrison answered the phone on the third ring. *"It's me," Wolforce said. "I Met with Ratcliff. You need to know!"*

"Okay, same place?"

"Yeah, DeGrazia, tomorrow. Ten thirty in the morning, all right?"

"Perfect."

Morrison punched off, stood, and walked to the sliding glass doors and onto the patio before making his way to the far side of the pool. The moon was just creeping over the top of the rocky hill to the east. He turned and looked behind him toward a window on the second floor.

The light remained on in Maria's room. He had just spent nearly forty-five minutes with her. She would be up first tomorrow to prepare his breakfast. With Gretchen not home, she would enter his bedroom with a cup of coffee and the Wall Street Journal. Leisurely, he would read it there before having his breakfast in the formal dining room where he watched the morning news on CNN.

She was the third Mexican girl he had brought home, the prettiest and most compliant. She seemed to have taken to all of it, the sex, the household responsibilities, learning English, and driving. She seemed to enjoy learning. Still, she needed a driver's license. That was not a problem once he was sure she could pass the test. Most surprising, and certainly unusual, she did not sympathize with other illegals.

Now worth more than the three thousand he had invested by buying her from El Coyote, she was smarter, determined, and, interestingly, not concerned with legalities or moral inhibitions. Of course, he realized, she had little choice. He could turn her in anytime or sell her. What she lacked was power, and that is where he came in. He suspected her goal was status and wealth, or at least to be in its presence, and that could work to his advantage.

He had to make a decision soon. With previous girls, he had sold them after they had been with him for six months. Keeping them for much longer was risky. Once others suspected an illegal immigrant is in his home, an investigation might follow, leading to the discovery of his other activities, which meant lots of trouble. Because she had worked out so well, he was reluctant to put her into the trade, where she'd be swallowed up, hiding in the shadows and exploited by everyone. He had definitely decided not to return her to El Coyote.

Gretchen also liked her. They got along very well. Maria managed the household, almost eliminating the pressure on Gretchen, providing direction, ordering various services including maintenance, shopping for food, and overseeing the landscaping with Marco.

A narrow shadow slid across the pool and patio. He turned to find her standing at the sliding doors watching him, wearing the robe he had bought her. He smiled and returned.

"You wanted to speak to me?" she asked.

"Yes, please, sit down." He motioned toward a sofa.

"A white wine would be nice," she said. "That one we had the other night."

"Ah, the chardonnay. A nice choice, Maria."

He approached the bar, took two glasses, removed a bottle from the cooler beneath the bar, pulled the cork, and poured two glasses. Carefully holding the glasses, he walked to where she was seated on the wide leather couch.

Most of the furniture in the room consisted of oak or cedar, handcrafted in Mexico along with leather for the sofas and chairs. Beside the beauty of the wood, the scent of cedar and leather added to the room's warmth.

Bending down, he presented the glass to her. They touched glasses. "To you," he said, turned, and settled into a chair across from her before taking a sip. "Let's see, how long have you been with us?"

"Almost a year, I think."

"Doesn't seem that long. Your English is improving. Maybe this is a time to make a change."

Her eyes widened. "Where should I go?"

"You know I bought you!"

She nodded.

"I can sell you to someone else and get back my money, or if you wish, I can give you money and you can continue on your way. Also, I can place you in a group that hires out workers and laborers."

"I don't know what to do. My aunt said I can work with her at house cleaning in Tucson, do hotels and offices."

"What had you planned to do when you left Mexico?" Morrison asked.

"We were going to go to Tucson. Miguel would work with my uncle in gardening or construction. Then we'd send for Juanito."

"Who are those?"

"Miguel was my husband. Juanito is my son. He'll be two soon."

"Where are Miguel and Juanito?"

"Miguel's dead. Juanito is with Miguel's parents until I can get him."

"Where's home?"

"Las Flores, Sonora State. We lived in a family compound on a hacienda. I shall probably never see it again," she said without any outward emotion while watching him over the top of her glass as she sipped.

"How did Miguel die?"

"Killed by the man who took us across the border. They call that man El Coyote. He raped me. Miguel tried to stop him. El Coyote, he killed Miguel. El Coyote took me to a house and raped me again and again and again." Tears pooled at the bottom of her eyes. She blinked. Quickly, she wiped them away with the back of her hand and stiffened her jaw.

"I'm sorry that happened. I know of that man, El Coyote," Morrison noted.

"How?" Maria asked.

"He is a trafficker, a smuggler, a coyote boss and does things for a cartel."

Her expression did not change. Though she was beautiful, her eyes were cold like a rattlesnake's ... large, black, and indifferent.

She curled her legs up under her on the soft leather. They sat quietly sipping their wine. As she surveyed the room, her eyes settled on a large cedar breakfront with a display of thin, colorful pottery. She had seen it before many times, but now it captured her interest again.

At first, after she was delivered to Morrison's home, she was too frightened to pay attention to the furnishings. As time passed, she became more comfortable with his lifestyle and paid increased attention to the many objects in this home.

Observing her interest in the pottery, Morrison asked, "Are you interested in Mata Ortiz pottery?"

Frowning, she said, "I have not heard of it."

"These are the kind of things you should learn so you can become educated. We respect education here. Education or the appearance of education is part of this culture and a person's success. See, we have books here, and paintings, some by Mexican artists, some by European, and some by Americans."

"And some by your wife, no?" She got up and walked to a section of the wall where Gretchen's paintings were displayed. She sipped her drink and turned toward the pottery.

Morrison said, "She likes art, books, classical music. She told me she likes you. Marco helps you with English. Marco came to us ten years ago from

Mexico, like you. He manages a few of my outside projects, hires the workers, that kind of stuff."

"Yes. Sometimes we talk while he helps me with English."

"I know. He tells me. Let me show you this pottery."

They left their wine glasses on an oak coffee table near the display that was inlaid with a variety of small colorful square tiles. They walked to the cabinet. He reached behind a corner and turned on an interior light. He opened one of the cabinet doors and removed a slender pot with various intricately painted designs. He let her hold it.

"See how fine this is?" he noted.

She nodded.

"This pottery is made in a small pueblo called Mata Ortiz, which is how the pottery got its name. It's not far from Casa Grandes, Chihuahua State. The designs are painted on the pots by using human hair. That's why the lines are so thin and intricate. The clay comes from mountains not far from the pueblo. Each pot is formed by hand and fired over cow chips in open fires. Almost everyone in that pueblo is a potter. Some have become quite famous for the quality of their work. The pots are valuable." He pointed to several and mentioned names of the potters. "Pottery has made the pueblo rich."

"I am one of the few dealers who is trusted by the artists," he continued, "and I sell their work here. We will go to Tubac, and Gretchen can show you the way to tell original work from the fakes that are now entering the market. I also take orders from merchants to provide pots for their shops. Marco takes a van to buy the pots. Now that he is legal, he can freely cross back and forth without incident, except, of course, for paying the proper fees to Mexican border agents."

"This is beautiful and interesting," Maria said while carefully turning one in her hands and studying the design.

"If you turn it over, you can read the name of the artist."

She checked and carefully gave the pottery back to him. They returned to their seats and wine.

"You haven't told me why you wanted to talk to me," she said.

"Okay, then." He settled into his chair and smiled at her. "Do you like being here, this house, the work?"

"It is better than cleaning hotel rooms in Tucson."

"You are a smart girl, Maria."

A spark flashed in her eyes, the most excitement he had seen from her. Quickly, she looked down at her hands and curled them around the stem of her glass, which she tightly grasped as though afraid he might take it away.

When she looked up again, she asked, "What is it you want?"

"You know the place El Coyote took you? There were other girls there, were there not?"

"Yes, they were the same as me, there until they paid off the money. Except Marco brought me here. I now know you paid El Coyote for me."

"The other girls there, Maria, what do they do to pay off the money?"

Her face was stern. Her eyes were wide and staring straight into him. "They are whores. They make money on the streets. Many like me, taken there and held, all their money and backpacks taken away, and delivered to men for sex. Some came with children. Some of the little girls they are also delivered to men. Some did not return. I heard they are sold like me. So are small boys."

"There is still money you owe me, you know. I can't keep you here much longer without papers."

"Marco has papers. You can get me papers. I can manage this house for you."

He sat quietly watching her as they sipped their drinks.

She held his gaze, put her glass down, then sat stiffly, and stared into his eyes. "I want to bring Juanito here. Marco said children stay here now if they have parents. It's easier, and they are not sent back if the parents are already here."

He stood, holding his glass. He walked slowly toward the end of the room and stopped to look at the bookshelf. He turned and walked back to her, stopping in front of her chair as he looked beyond her to the pool outside.

"Would you like to stay here and manage the house, and when Gretchen is not here to accompany me to business events? That will pay off your debt to me. I will then pay you."

A flash sparked her eyes. She looked down at her hands and curled them around the wine glass, which she again tightly gripped as though still afraid he might take it away from her.

"I will have to think about this some more, talk to Gretchen," he noted. "She will be home tomorrow. I am picking her up at the airport."

Maria looked outside toward the pool and beyond to the shadowy mountains now dark in the distance. She turned and gazed around the room again, as if it were the first time that she'd seen it, as though she were taking ownership. She had seen similar furnishings at the hacienda in Las Flores: large piano, rugs, lamps, pictures and artwork, a pool, a view from the patio, and a Mercedes in the garage. Here she had her own bedroom and a bathroom larger than her entire casa in Las Flores, all the things that Miguel could never have provided her. Here in this place are most of the reasons she had wanted Miguel to bring her to America.

While Gretchen was away, they usually slept together. She turned to him and asked. "Does she not object to this ... I don't know what to call it, I guess, arrangement?"

He smiled at her. "Do you think she doesn't know about you and me?"

"I didn't think so."

"She knows. She has her own friends and interests. I have mine, and we work well together. We've had girls here before."

Maria raised her eyebrows and stared unflinchingly at him. "It is hard to believe a married woman would accept such an arrangement."

"We are not exactly married, not by a church anyway, but the relationship is like a marriage, including rings."

"I will make sure the house is nice. Someone is coming tomorrow morning to clean. I will make sure she does a good job for Gretchen."

"We will talk more about this. You need to think about it. Also, you will help Gretchen. You will get documents, including a Social Security card and soon a driver's license like Marco."

She leaned forward, set her glass on the coffee table, crossed her legs, and placed her hands in her lap. She looked him in the eyes and said, "Marco says he is still illegal. He says his papers are not valid. He says he has to be careful."

"That will be the same for you. Most are able to do well with those documents as long as they don't get into trouble. Maybe soon people like you and Marco will get amnesty and citizenship."

"Will you share me with other men?"

"No, Maria. I am not a pimp, and you are not a whore."

26

*T*he DeGrazia Gallery in the Sun, nestled in the foothills of the Catalina Mountains, was the location selected by Wolforce for a meeting with Morrison. He waited alone in the small adobe chapel the artist had built on approximately ten acres in the 1950s in honor of Father Kino and dedicated to Mexico's patron saint, the Virgin of Guadalupe. A gallery of DeGrazia's work and a gift shop occupied a nearby building.

Gretchen was fascinated by the artist's background and his work, which included internationally popular portraits of children adopted by UNICEF. She was a benefactor of the foundation. DeGrazia became famous after he burned some of his paintings in order to protest taxes.

"So, let's have it," Morrison said, sliding into a pew next to Wolforce.

"I'll make it quick. First, Ratcliff wants a girl. I suppose you are unwilling to give up Maria."

"You suppose correctly."

"You can supply another," Wolforce noted.

"Depends on the girl. If I locate another like Maria, then yes."

"That's what he wants. Okay?"

"Who is this Ratcliff?"

"He's a petty self-styled big shot who believes he should be the director of the Office of National Intelligence."

"I'll check it out and get back to you. What else?" Morrison looked at his watch.

"This is an important matter, Malcolm. If we gain an advantage over Ratcliff, given his position with people in the Office of the Director of National Intelligence, we'll get access to inside information from which we can significantly profit."

"You are talking about blackmail."

"Yes. Just think, the director of ODNI briefs the president every morning. The director's sources are the seventeen members of the so-called intelligence community. Ratcliff's particular expertise is drugs and human trafficking. He works for the deputy director. Mostly, he is bluster and bullshit. He likes to brag about his importance, and that merely makes him more vulnerable."

Wolforce stopped talking and looked at Morrison. He had Morrison's attention. "Imagine what a man in his position with a Washington socialite wife and family and prestige and unlimited political ambition would be *willing to disclose to prevent pictures and evidence that exposes his relationship with a beautiful, young, undocumented Mexican girl."*

"What makes you think he'd go for a girl even if he does have such an appetite?"

"For one thing, his wife. They run in a nanny circle. She does not have one for their kids. It was a marriage of convenience. She has family money and some role in the family business. Prestige is what Ratcliff was supposed to provide: access to memberships and important organizations and his position and friends in Washington, especially the president. She was to provide the money for the lifestyle he wanted. Not having a nanny is embarrassing for her, Ratcliff tells me. Would it not be a shame to let such a fish get away? Well worth our time to satisfy his appetite, don't you think?"

Morrison nodded.

"Also, Ratcliff was recently appointed chairman of the president's new Select Commission on Human and Drug Trafficking for the Arizona border sector. It and similar committees were created to award big local campaign donors who won't do much but will have some access to valuable information for anyone with the ability to exploit it. We gain even more advantage through his wife. You know, if he doesn't do as we want, we tell his wife. Not bad, right?"

"So, what does all this have to do with me?" Morrison asked

"Well, you can supply a girl to Ratcliff, for instance."

"I get that," Morrison replied. "But I think you have more things in mind."

"Okay, I'll explain further."

The door to the chapel, creaking on its hinges, noisily opened, the sound echoing within the building. Sunshine washed into the shadowy interior. Startling them, they turned and saw a woman who also noticed them. She poured holy water into the receptacle near the door and left.

Wolforce, noticeably irritated at the interruption, caught his breath before continuing. "Where was I? Oh, yes. A market exists for the kind of information an insider like Ratcliff can provide. Just for instance, an organization that maintains contacts with narco bosses, as well as Homeland Security and others outside government who don't want to draw attention to themselves can earn large fees from groups by providing intelligence. You'd be amazed at what a baggie of coke can get you and who hints around for it even in the sacred halls of the capital and even the White House."

"*I can just imagine,*" *said Morrison.*

"*Exactly, and who can provide money laundering for the narco? For instance, I have learned you are in the import/export business. I know you operate internationally in construction and development. I also know that you are suspected of trafficking but so far no evidence warranting charges, yet.*" *Wolforce smiled.*

Before Morrison reacted, Wolforce continued. "*I see a big financial opportunity for us if we combine our resources, exploit contacts, and take advantage of what we learn. As I am sure you already know, the money involved in trafficking is, well, overwhelming. Maybe even unlimited.*"

Morrison twisted in the pew and intently watched Wolforce.

"*What if there was a group of bankers, financiers, government insiders, and a couple of narco big shots who controlled a cartel who decided to invest in an international business of distributing illegal drugs and other merchandise?*" *Wolforce suggested.* "*Each person is an expert in his part of the scheme. These entrepreneurs would not be involved in the actual operations, of course. They'd be the secret board of directors of this transnational organization headquartered in Mexico, maintaining distance from the dirty work.*" *He cleared his throat and looked down at his nails.* "*Would you know anyone interested in such a venture?*"

"*Oh, while you think about that,*" *he added,* "*I have the name of a contact who knows about international customs failures, like when certain agents look the other way or where there are security weaknesses. If anyone is so inclined, they might find it easier to ship certain kinds of contraband overseas from Mexico with this man's help. This arrangement is especially suited to someone in the import/export business, such as you.*"

Morrison did not respond. Sending Gretchen to Europe to find such a connection was one reason for her recent trip. Eying Wolforce carefully, he slowly stood and walked to the front of the chapel, his footsteps on the tiles echoing, until he reached the candles, lit one, kneeled, and offered a short prayer.

Wolforce removed a phone from his pocket and looked at it. He did not look up until Morrison's returning footsteps stalled at the edge of the pew where he looked at his watch again before he slid next to Wolforce.

"*Couple of things,*" *Morrison said after Wolforce put away his phone.* "*I need to get to the airport, so I'll make it quick.*"

"Okay, I am listening."

"What is your role in this scheme? I will need to think it over. I know a person who might know how to get this man a girl. I will not be involved with the details or the transaction. Give me the information on your customs contact as a good faith gesture."

"I understand you need time, Morrison. However, there is some urgency. My role? I see my role as the facilitator and the link between the various parties." He reached into his pocket and withdrew a small red notebook, wrote a name, ripped out the paper, folded it in half, and extended the sheet toward Morrison.

Morrison took the paper, unfolded it, and looked back at Wolforce. "There is no phone number or address here. If I wanted to, how do I get in touch with him?"

Wolforce did not close the notebook. "I thought you might be interested. Know what I mean?"

"Oh, I see. Yes." Morrison reached into his pocket and removed an envelope containing five one-hundred-dollar bills.

Wolforce took the money. He wrote a phone number in the notebook and handed it to Morrison.

"What else, Wolforce?"

"Have you heard of a General Marcus?"

"No. The name means nothing to me," Morrison said. "Anything else? I have to get going."

"Yes. Ratcliff wants to set up a meeting with the president of Mexico and our president to tout what has been accomplished along the border. He wants to make a show of himself first, so he wants a photo op with the governor of Arizona and the governor of Sonora State."

"What's been done along the border?" Morrison questioned.

Wolforce shrugged his shoulders. "You know, new feelings of cooperation between our governments, a new era of understanding, diminished crossings, and so forth. The Mexican Institutional Revolutionary Party (PRI) is back in charge, as you are aware. He wants some speeches and coverage of a meeting somewhere down here: maybe Douglas, Nogales, Yuma, San Diego, and perhaps even El Paso. However, Ratcliff wants him in this sector somewhere, and then the next day a speech by the Mexican president before Congress."

"Sounds like a bunch of crap to me," said Morrison.

"Election coming up," Wolforce noted.

"And this has what to do with me exactly?"

"Just a thought, but think about your house."

"What? Are you crazy?"

"It's perfect. Think about it: large open area in the back surrounded by hills and mountains; space to hold a couple of reporters, camera people, and folks from the media; great views; casual but elegant; lots of parking; could even land a chopper or two nearby. You are in the middle of the controversial border region with opulent homes and families. You have room to get people in and out in a hurry, a mix of gringos and Latinos, and are not far from the border. It has everything he would like: casual, intimate but with grand vistas, and, you know, Southwest hospitality and atmosphere. Perfect!"

Shaking his head, Morrison stuttered. "I-I don't know about that. My house, I ... uh, we'll see."

Before Morrison could recover from the shock, Wolforce pushed harder. "Have you heard of a narco called El Caballo?"

"The horse? Can't say that I have."

"Lots of people are looking for him, especially me. If you hear anything of him, let me know."

Morrison was standing at the end of the pew and turned toward the door.

"One more thing," Wolforce said.

Morrison stopped and turned back to him.

"The directors of the art project want to meet you next Friday for lunch. Can you get away?"

"Okay," Morrison replied and stalked away.

"I still think Maria is the perfect choice for Ratcliff," Wolforce tossed after him.

"Forget about her!"

"*H*ow did it go?" *Morrison asked, kissing Gretchen on the cheek. "New perfume?"*

"*I thought you'd like it," she replied smiling.*

He had watched her on the monitor as she disembarked and walked with others from the arrival gate toward the luggage area. As a rule, pride was not a subject he dwelled upon; such vanity caused too many judgment mistakes. However, Gretchen was an exception, maybe his only exception. She wore a shapely beige business suit and high heels and was easily tagged a model, which was what she was when they had first met almost twenty years ago in Tampa.

Those were the early days when he received Colombian cocaine flown at midnight into a small airport in Pasco County, Florida. He stored it in his warehouse on the outskirts just off Interstate 75. He would then cut it and ship it to Chicago and Detroit.

The night the DEA raided the airport was a learning experience. Had he not been late for the drop, he would have been arrested, along with the pilot. He was with Gretchen that night and lost track of time. Never again had he allowed himself to be present with the merchandise. Possession and associates were the elements most likely to provide the evidence required to convict. He had stayed away from personal involvement and created a legitimate construction company by carefully investing cash he received from drug sales to traffickers who delivered the bricks to unknown out-of-state vendors.

Gretchen was an expert in laundering through a very successful import/ export business in Madrid. Her modeling bookings and interest in art allowed her to travel throughout Europe almost at will. With art and antiques, no questions were asked. Money exchangers and international banks made it easy to clean the cash. The porous international borders, including the Mexican and Canadian borders, enabled various vehicles to cross through border checkpoints. Even if a load of cash were discovered, the profitability of the drug trade made it merely a cost of doing business. Then he discovered real estate and construction businesses that required lots of cash, the perfect washing machine.

His conversation with Wolforce unsettled him. Wolforce's frequent reference to the word we introduced the uncomfortable idea that Wolforce implied they were partners. The consequences of an association with a man who provided information in exchange for money was the kind of man who would sell out his mother for a price. It was a mistake.

From an innocent gesture to support Gretchen's interest in supporting art, and maybe the temptation to make himself legitimate, Morrison had ignored his self-control and greedily bought into Wolforce's scheme, which he mistakenly thought an opportunity for more money. Inviting Wolforce into his home was a mistake; giving him his phone number, revealing his connection to human trafficking, and permitting Wolforce to have direct contact with him were all serious mistakes.

He knew of only one way to remedy the situation if it turned out Wolforce was a mistake. As usual, when he must confront a significant decision, he needed time to evaluate alternatives and methods. Right now, he must concentrate on Gretchen.

In the early days, she modeled clothes, perfume, lingerie, and swimsuits. She was well paid. Now she did mostly clothes for older women. However, to him, there seemed little difference between the older ones and the younger ones. She traveled to exotic places for photo shoots. What she did there was her business. She was still well paid, resourceful, and able to find contacts for their mutual business interests.

"I got a couple of paintings," she said as they met at the arrival gate and headed toward the luggage carousel. "They're shipped and should arrive in a couple of days, actually easier than expected."

A thump and discordant whirr drew their attention to the wall where the luggage dumped onto the carousel.

"My previous trip to Sicily resulted in finding a connection. I met with a trafficker in Messina yesterday, a busy place. He thinks that is the best location to receive product. Easy to get to Calabria and to the interior of Sicily with lots of small boats. We have to wait for the port selection. He needs to nail down a few more details involving storage and transportation for their distribution in southern Italy and North Africa without crossing into Hezbollah turf.

"You still have to select a source for the merchandise and work out a deal, the most important element of which is to settle on a supplier. That, along with intelligence relating to customs inspections, is now up to you."

Wolforce had provided a lead on a custom official, and his legitimate business gave him the indirect contact to the Sonora Cartel through, of all people, the governor of the Sonora State. If these two matters were essentially resolved, the transition into Italy should move forward without his involvement in Wolforce's scheme of blackmail, corrupting government officials, and secret directors. When you do everything yourself, you minimize the prospects of leaks, and better, you do not have to share profits, he reminded himself.

He watched the luggage move toward them. Finally, after the other travelers were mostly gone, he recognized her bags.

As he lifted them, she said, "That's not all." She pointed to three more.

"Damn. Glad I brought the Humvee."

After turning south onto Interstate 19, Gretchen turned in her seat, watching the desert slide past her window.

"I was at one of your favorite places earlier," Morrison said.

"Oh, really?" She looked at him. "Which one?"

"DeGrazia Gallery. Had a short meeting in the chapel."

"Yes, I love it there; the art, the museum, the talent, and the mystique of the man. Going to tell me about the meeting?"

"Nope."

"Not even who you met with?"

"That's right."

"I didn't think so."

They were passing the hill covered by a jungle of saguaros. On their right, just coming into view, were the towers of the Mission San Xavier del Bac, known as the White Dove of the Desert and founded in 1692 by Eusebio Francisco Kino, a famous Jesuit missionary known throughout the region as Father Kino.

"You can't help but marvel at the history," Gretchen said. "Here's a mission on the sacred land of the Tohono O'odham Indian nation."

"Yes, and ironically, the reservation is perhaps the largest human and drug trafficking area in the country."

"I wonder how much has really changed since 1692, since father Kino and the Anza trail." She watched the mission flash past.

"Well, I don't know about that either. What's really changed? People?" He was quiet. "No, people haven't changed."

Well," she said, challenging him, "at least the Apache no longer attack us."

"Now, it's the cartels doing the attacking," he replied. "And what do you care?"

"I don't."

They passed Tubac.

"By the way, I had a little talk with Maria. She's becoming interested in

culture. Her English is coming along. I am thinking about having her handle the household and assist with the various meetings. Every time I am involved directly, I am taking a big risk. She's smart. She can handle it."

"If she's as smart as you say, what is to keep her from disclosing our businesses if she is threatened by a competitor?" Gretchen asked.

"Her family and son."

"Her family and son? I don't understand what you mean." And then she did understand. "You wouldn't!"

He looked at her.

"You would," she said. "What did she say?"

"She just wanted to know if I'd share her with other men."

"And you said?"

"No!"

"What about women?"

He looked at her, smiled, and looked back at the road as they passed Elephant Head.

28

*M*orrison allowed Maria to use the Mercedes for her driver's test. For a couple of months, Marco had coached her, both in driving and legalities. Driving practice took place in the area of Rio Rico. Marco also accompanied her to the test, which proved easy for her. She drove back to the house where there was a small celebration. Afterward, Maria and Gretchen headed to Tubac for shopping and a lesson in pottery and art. For the time being, until Morrison was satisfied with her background and believed she could be trusted, either Gretchen or Marco would accompany her.

After they left, Morrison placed a long-distance call to Hermosillo. The governor's office answered. In Spanish, Morrison told the woman his name, gave her a phone number, and asked her to tell the governor he wanted to speak with him when it was convenient. Although she did not seem to recognize his name, she told him she would leave the message.

"I want to run a couple of names by you to see if they are familiar," Morrison said to the governor after they had spent a few moments in greeting. "First is Adrian Wolforce. Are you familiar with him?"

"Why, yes. He talked to my assistant about the meeting with your governor. I never met him personally, however. Is there a problem?"

"No, I met with him recently, and he mentioned you."

"In what way has he met me?" the governor questioned.

"He didn't say. Do you know anything else about him?"

"No, just the meeting thing."

"Okay, thanks. How about Ernesto Vargas?"

"He's secretary of the interior in the president's cabinet. What is this all about … these questions of those people, Mr. Morrison? It seems unusual."

"He has a big ranch in Las Flores?"

"Yes, of course. Very big ranch."

"Do you know of a Gutierrez family who lives on the Vargas ranch?"

"No. I would not know if they lived there." After a short pause, he cautiously replied, "I do recall the name Gutierrez was mentioned by Vargas to Alvera at a meeting at the hacienda before the bombing. I think Vargas was recommending someone of that name. This name is common. Why this puzzle? Should I know something about this?"

"Probably not important. Just want to verify information I received from Wolforce and an employee. If you get a chance, you might mention the name

Maria Gutierrez or Miguel Gutierrez to Vargas. I have learned to check out everyone carefully."

"That is wise. We cannot be too careful. I have been meaning to talk with you about the plans for a new plant here, like the Ford plant but smaller. Maybe we'll get a chance to talk at your place."

"My place?" Morrison questioned.

"Yes, of course," the governor noted. "Wolforce mentioned a PR event at your house in Rio Rico."

"I, uh, wasn't aware, um, well, okay, maybe so."

Morrison punched off the phone, stood motionless for a while, and then walked to the window gazing toward Elephant Head. He closed his fist, walked back to the desk near the computer, and hit the desk with a closed fist. "Bastard!"

Maria and Gretchen returned carrying various packages and started to display the contents in the family room.

"Even though the art festival was in February, we still got some nice things," Maria said as she set the pictures on the floor to lean against the sofa in a display.

The phone rang. Morrison grabbed it.

"He wants Maria," Wolforce growled on the other end of the line.

"What? Wait until I get to another room." He quickly looked at both women holding paintings and turned toward the den, leaving Maria and Gretchen standing in the middle of the room.

"I told you no way! I have plans. She stays here with me."

"I showed him her picture. He wants her. That's all there is to it."

"Are you crazy? It's not your decision. She stays."

"Actually," Wolforce interrupted, "I have several pictures of her and Gretchen shopping in Tubac. They are both rather attractive. These pictures, they were given to me by a man who stressed that they might be in danger. One of them is illegal, right?"

"What's this all about, Wolforce?" Morrison's stomach knotted. He felt his neck pulsing, and his chest tightened.

"She is illegal right, Morrison? Isn't that what you told me? You said you could get another and you could sell Maria. You actually gave me a price. Remember?"

There was silence.

"Morrison? You there?"

Still no response.

"I have a recording," Wolforce continued. "I record that kind of thing ... just to cover myself. I'm a lawyer, you know."

"And a son of a bitch!"

"Even worse than that some people say. Nevertheless, it is what it is, Morrison." His voice was no longer casual. "You should have kept a better eye on that little slut. She likes the idea. I am doing you a favor."

"How do you know she likes the idea?"

"She told me. I just happened to bump into her when you weren't home. We had a nice talk on the veranda. Your security was with you somewhere, she said. I told her about Ratcliff, mentioned he's a big shot who lives in Washington, DC, has a very rich wife, big house, travels to Europe, New York. She also travels a lot and needs a special assistant and a nanny.

"Maria seemed excited, especially when she learned she could bring Juanito to the United States to be with her. I have already cleared that with Ratcliff. Can't begin to tell you how appreciative she was, right there on the couch in your family room. She even said it was like a dream come true. And Morrison, you know what else?"

"What?"

"This is just perfect. She is even willing to keep in touch with me and pass along information she thinks we'd like to know. For a price, of course, a chip off the old block," he chuckled. "That's not all. Of course, she knows a lot of the details of how she got here, that you bought her from El Coyote and she's worked off her debt with you and about promising to get her forged documents to stay here and sleeping together.

"I let her know me and you are partners. She thinks this is all your idea, and she really appreciates what you have done for her. Don't be too hard on her. By the way, we discussed how to make the transfer. With plans coming together for the PR event at your place, Ratcliff thought we could pass her to him there. He anticipated having security and a private plane. He even agreed to take the kid and fly her down there to get him. Of course, you need to be discreet about it, but it makes sense with all the people and confusion and so on."

"Go to hell!" Morrison slammed down the phone. "Maria!" he yelled.

She and Gretchen arrived in seconds.

"Do you know Adrian Wolforce?" he demanded.

"Yes," they replied in unison and then turned and looked at each other. Gretchen said, "Short, balding, one of these pencil mustaches that sort of looks like they've spilled chocolate on their upper lip. Moist hands when he shakes, eyes that wonder all over your body. Yes, I've met him. I was with you. Don't you remember? Wants to set up that art project we are going to support. What's the matter with you?"

"He looked at Maria. You've met him?"

"Yes, here. Soon after I came here. He came to the door. I fixed him a drink. You two talked. I went outside as you taught me. He looks like she said."

"Is that the only time?"

"Here again, a couple of times. He told me of Mr. Ratcliff who wants me. Said you thought it a good idea. I am so happy you would do this for me. An important man in Washington DC. He'll take Juanito also."

Gretchen looked first at Morrison, then at Maria. "What is this?" she asked.

"Maria is going to live with an important man in Washington and be a nanny. She told Wolforce everything she knows about us. We are hosting a political event here. That is when she and her kid join Ratcliff. Isn't that right, Maria?" There was no mistaking the disappointment and bitterness in his voice.

Maria stiffened, turned, and walked toward the stairs. She stopped, looked back at them, and said, "I do what I must for me and Juanito. That is what's important to me." She was certain Miguel had died at the trophy tree. Living with the Ratcliffe family in America was the realization of what she had hoped to find by crossing the border into America. She could not let the opportunity escape.

29

*L*ibrary repairs were completed. Dust covered the table where El Anglo, Quique, their financial officer, and Miguel gathered. Miguel found a rag on the bar and wiped the table.

"No notes. If we have no records, there is no evidence of what we do here." Quique closed his notebook.

"I want to cover what is being done in the Tucson Plaza. First, to reiterate, we won't use names if we can help it. We can't tell what we don't know. That's the same for everyone else. You avoid personal contacts with everyone and work through others. That's very important." He turned to Miguel. "Where are we in Paraguay?"

"We have a wine store with a couple of rooms in a medical building. As you instructed, we have no direct phone contact with the office or files or papers relating to us. We ship South American wine to various dealers in Mexico. The man who runs it and is listed as the owner has never met us. We supply the money; he selects the wine, stores and displays it, and arranges commercial transportation to Mexico to retailers who are theoretically legitimate."

Quique said, "Our audit of the operation does not indicate the business makes a profit. I don't know where he gets the wine or how it gets to Mexico. I don't even know his name. We've never met. I don't believe he has any idea who we are. His relationship is with the general. Our business, other than the wine, is done by smartphone or at one of the bars or other locations."

"Where did you find this man to do this?"

"The general," Quique replied.

"He just volunteered such a person?"

"Not exactly. The man's wine business was failing. For some reason, the general wants the man to keep the store, which we will do. We will let him sell his wine and let him have his profits from the wine business. In effect, the wine store is the front for our activities. The general told us the authorities would not ask questions. He also helps us to launder money through a branch of a Mexican bank."

"How will that work?" El Anglo asked Quique.

"Well, since the man already had a banking relationship and since he will remain in business, we can use that business to launder some of our cash along with his own sales. The accounting gets a little complicated. I can deal with that. Our agreement includes our doing the accounting for the wine store.

"Regarding our business, for instance, the cash we get from business in

America, we drive across the border and deposit in one of the banks in Mexico. From there, I can transfer funds directly to a Swiss bank account for the general or for our own accounts in the Caymans. I can also transfer funds out of the Mexican bank to a bank in Paraguay for deposit to an account of the wine store. Thanks to the internet, I can make the transfers from here with a cell phone through a contact there."

"How is he paid?"

"He takes a cut off the top ... both ways."

"And how do you know he doesn't get more than the agreed amount?"

"I audit each transaction through copies and statements from the bank or visiting the bank. Not foolproof, but there are consequences if the cash doesn't balance to the bank's books or the wine store. Stealing from us is suicidal."

El Anglo asked, "Doesn't Mexico have a law against money laundering and restrict the size of transfers?"

"It's a porous enforcement," Quique responded. "There's plenty of dollars to keep everyone happy. We have a large payroll."

"Yes. I see the numbers. Okay, enough of this accounting stuff." El Anglo looked at Miguel.

"The general has kept his word and provided security." Miguel said.

"How so?"

"We are in a complex that has a number of retail outlets. There is hired local security. I don't trust them as far as I can spit. There are soldiers in uniform on the corners. In addition, a small army detachment is nearby and visible."

"And the brokers?"

"We have contacted two through a third party who arranges for product from growers. The processor arranges for the contractors to ship the product to a destination we select, and another gang meets the shipment. Either we make that arrangement ourselves, or the broker makes it."

El Anglo interrupted him. "We do not make arrangements that require us to directly participate in any kind of trafficking. Find someone you can trust."

"Okay, but at this point, I don't trust anyone."

"Maybe a family member. They are usually loyal," suggested Quique.

Continuing, Miguel said, "The distributor does the rest with the dealers and street venders. Supposedly, no one in that chain knows who anyone else is except for their own link."

Quique added, "And no one gets paid until their part of the chain is completed. Usually, each link is an independent contractor. Need to find a few enforcers for this end of the chain. It is a large problem to manage. We have to keep each link in line to prevent theft and losses and sales to other chains, or we will lose links."

"Who is providing the enforcers?"

"Well," Miguel said, "the general has volunteered to supply them. I am afraid he will take over and cut us out."

El Anglo looked at both Miguel and Quique. He sat quietly for a minute, seemingly in deep thought. He sat up in his seat. "All right, there's lots to consider. When is the first shipment?"

"I'm working on it." Miguel said. "It's a test."

"Okay. Let me know. I am not sure this is what we really want to do. I'll talk with the others," El Anglo said. "Now, before we discuss the rest, I must warn you that once our regular suppliers know we are competing with them, they will try to retaliate in some way, much as the Morales Cartel tried to come after us when we took over the Tucson Plaza." El Anglo paused then added, "Spiro Morales has sworn to kill you." He looked at Miguel. "I suggest you keep Isdel, that Zeta assassin, close by. Just remember there is no loyalty to anyone. Don't tell him anything!"

He looked at both, and they nodded. "Now, one final thing. I've heard from our contact in Venezuela. He is almost ready to send over that shipment we discussed when we were down there. This is top priority. I will let you know. They have a couple of dates."

"I have set the crossing up already," Miguel said. He adjusted his seat and looked intensely at El Anglo. "What have we found out about Maria?"

"There is word about a yellow Humvee spotted near the border in Tubac. Don't know if it is the one. I just heard that from your stash house leader, Manuel. Check with him."

30

"*Just heard: yellow Humvee observed in Tubac in front of an art gallery across the street from the coffee shop where one of my informants works,*" Sheriff Howard Desmond said over the phone to Nate Gonzales. "*Where are you? Had lunch yet? Just played a round of golf and headed to the dining room for lunch. Can you meet me there? I'm paying.*"

"*No! Have not heard,*" Nate noted. "*But if you are paying, I'm on my way. Just leaving Nogales. Almost there. See you in fifteen minutes.*"

They met in the lobby of the clubhouse and walked to the dining room to a table with a view of the golf course and the Santa Rita Mountains. They had been friends since college.

A server followed them, and when they sat, she unfolded their napkins and placed them on their laps. "*I'll be right back with water.*"

Settled, Desmond said, "*According to my source, two women left the gallery carrying paintings, entered the Humvee, and drove away. She didn't think to get the license plate but is pretty sure it was an Arizona plate. She doesn't know which direction the car went once it reached the interstate. Sorry, not much help. At least we know there is one around here, though it is probably not the only yellow Humvee in the area. How long you been looking for it, Nate?*"

"*Four or five months,*" Nate Gonzales replied. "*You all are quick. I just made a request for your help about two weeks ago, remember?*"

"*I have cars in the area plus other sources. Usually, we're not this lucky. I have to say; Humvees are rather popular around here, or were. Afraid I haven't really been much help. We'll keep it on a hot sheet and try to get a license number. Anything else you can tell me to narrow it down, like year or doors, dents, last seen, etc.?*"

"*A yellow, late-model Humvee was reported at a drop house picking up a girl. Big Mexican guy driving.*"

"*Okay, I'm getting the picture. You are looking for the big Mexican.*"

"*I'm looking for the girl.*"

"*Can you describe her?*"

"*Mexican, young, twentyish, pretty.*"

"*Yeah, well that sort of describes them all. My source said there were two women in the car. Could mean we're on the right track. The younger one was a passenger, Mexican, maybe early twenties, a looker. The older, late thirties or early forties, blonde. Both good looking, actually, nicely dressed, carrying a couple of paintings. Many leads there, expensive car, original artwork, probably has money. So, we will check out some of the wealthier locations between here and the border. You know, look in driveways, garages, parking lots, gas stations, and nice restaurants.*

"Everyone says when you see a late-model Humvee or fancy car near the border; it probably means narco. It is a good place to start: a house, Humvee, Mexican driver, girl picked up; two good-looking women, bound to be attracting attention somewhere. Of course, could mean nothing. Wealthy women shopping in Tubac is standard. They could be from anywhere. I'll ask the deputies to check out the residential areas."

Sheriff Desmond looked around the restaurant. Several people nodded to him. Located in an upscale area adjacent to the golf course surrounded by foothills dotted with comfortable homes, the restaurant was a hangout for local business people and frequently by the sheriff who was a member.

"Should have brought your clubs," Desmond said, gazing at the golf course like a man thirsting for a drink. "I bet we could get in a quick round."

Chuckling, Nate said, "Yeah, I'm sure the locals would be happy to see a wetback BP agent in uniform playing the course. Your phone would be ringing for the next week."

They finished eating, and the server arrived with the dessert menus.

"Okay, Nate, let's have it. I know you did not want to meet to talk just about a yellow Humvee or golf. We could have done that by phone. What's this really about?" Desmond looked at the server, patted his stomach, and said, "I'll have that chocolate thing there, and give one to my friend." He pointed to the dessert at a nearby table.

"You got it, Sheriff," she said with a nod and a smile and a wink."

"What's up? You got something cooking, right? Anything I should know about?" Desmond asked.

"Yes, I've got something going. Unfortunately, I don't know what. This is just a heads-up for now." Nate lowered his voice. "I am working on a corruption case. I don't know how far up it goes or where it starts or goes. I know there is a port of entry official at the Nogales crossing who is dirty. I don't know how dirty. I also got some people inside very deep." He paused, observing Desmond's reaction.

"You are not going to tell me who or anything else, are you?"

"Nope."

"You didn't say deep inside what."

"Nope, I didn't."

Their server returned, and Nate looked at the dessert. His eyes widened. "Awesome. You can't really eat all that."

"Watch me."

The chocolate oozed onto the plate and the chocolate aroma seemed to soak into the atmosphere. Desmond sunk his spoon into the cake and slowly lifted it, letting it linger before Nate's eyes.

"All this has something to do with the Humvee and the girl, right?" Desmond asked.

Nate nodded and changed the subject. "Do you have a representative at the Joint Intelligence meetings?"

"No." A scowl crossed the sheriff's face. "You are talking about those ultra-secret meetings that no one is supposed to know about? We call them the let's-pretend group. My department is local. So is the state. We are not allowed to participate. After all, we are only the ones who have to deal with this mess day in and day out. Those meetings are just for your big shot Feds. Why'd you ask?"

"We are not invited either. Does the name Wolforce mean anything to you?"

Desmond sat back in his chair as though trying to grasp hold of an elusive thought. "Only that he's some hush-hush guy from Homeland Security or something. Should he mean something to me? ... Wait!" He frowned and looked down at the table and then nodded his head and looked back at Nate. "I think I got a notice of some kind of shindig in Rio Rico, and it had that name on it. There was something else. Uh, not sure. Yes, did not seem important at the time. I'll check it out."

"He's our guy on the committee," Nate said. "Seems a very busy man, according to someone inside the group. Trying to get a handle on some names. Does he have business or other connections around here?"

"Want me to find out quietly?" Desmond asked. "I know you have a connection at state, which must mean this is too close to home for you to pursue with him. Did you check the internet? Google the name? Has more info there than the NSA."

"I take it this is to be kept quiet?"

"Yep."

31

*M*iguel and Daniel Lopez, the new ostensible wine store owner in Ciudad del Este, sat in a corner table in a restaurant that was located several storefronts from the office and storage facility that now technically belonged to Miguel under a fictitious name arranged by General Martinez. Minutes passed before they adjusted to the low light and selected a table in the middle. Isdel followed them and took a seat at the end of the bar where he had a view of the door and both men. The ambiance of beer, fish, and mildew added to the cramped atmosphere. The fans were broken.

Bodyguards sent by the general sat at a nearby table out of earshot. Lopez was also Miguel's contact with a dealer, a man only known as The Fixer who called himself Jones and claimed to have connections in Peru, Colombia, Paraguay, Panama, Sicily, and the United States.

"This is a wholesale deal for two million worth of heroin to test this operation," Miguel said to Lopez, confirming a previous conversation. "No names. Understand?"

"Whatever you say."

Miguel had not informed Lopez of his identity or affiliation with the Sonora Cartel. Lopez did know him by the name El Caballo, probably from the general. Miguel did not know what else the general had told Lopez. To his word, the general had provided security, assuming they were there to protect him and not kill him.

"That money includes your commission as we agreed," Miguel noted. "You understand?"

Lopez nodded and looked toward the bodyguards. "Yeah, I understand. Where is the money? I'll give it to Jones for the purchase."

"I'll wire it when I get back to Mexico. The general gets some first, and he will get the rest to the dealer for the processors. Someone will let you know. How does it get from here?"

"Not from here, from Peru, to Guayaquil Ecuador, by boat to Guaymas Mexico, and then trucked to your destination wherever that is," Lopez explained.

"Who are these people? How do I know when it arrives?"

"I have no idea who the people are. I only talk to the dealer. Each leg makes its own arrangements. Many groups compete for these services. Some are doubtless at these tables hoping for work." He waved his hand in a sweeping motion. "When he knows when the cargo arrives in Mexico, he calls me, and I will either call you or whoever you say."

"Here is a number." Miguel gave Lopez his satellite phone number. Lopez would notify the transporter he had arranged to meet the load in Guaymas and deliver it to the warehouse. "How long?"

"Maybe a month. Anything can happen — weather, arrest, boat sinks, truck breakdowns, hijacking, whatever you can imagine." Lopez glanced nervously around the restaurant and then at the bodyguards. "Those guys know what they are doing?"

"Sent by the general … who knows?"

"That's not very comforting. Competition just arrived and looking this way. May not be a good sign if they think I am dealing with you, know what I mean?"

"They don't know me."

"Yeah, well, they know me and what I do, and this is not a friendly game of soccer, the competition is not friendly. See those guys over there?" He nodded slightly toward the back corner. There were two grungy-looking men looking at him.

Miguel nodded.

"Americano. DEA checking you out."

"You sure?" Miguel asked.

"Probably already took our picture." Lopez smiled. A couple of missing teeth made his mouth look like a miniature cave. "Best we finish our drinks and leave quietly. Oh, by the way, in case you didn't know, the Chinese cartels have a synthetic meth product with a lot of promise, just in case you might be interested."

A bodyguard drove Miguel and Isdel to the airport in Ciudad del Este. As they waited for their flight, Isdel stood by Miguel while he followed up on El Anglo's information on the Hezbollah agents, calling Habib Gemayel using his satellite phone. Gemayel immediately answered. Miguel only said, "El Caballo." Gemayel gave him a date, time, and flight to meet the arrival of two men at the airport in Mexico. He called them "a package."

After spending a couple of nights with his family at the compound, Miguel drove north. While waiting in line at the Nogales POE, Miguel saw Walker talking with two ICE officers with a German shepherd standing behind a car parked in the inspection area. Border officers on both sides of the border accepted his documents, previously supplied by Filberto, and his passport without question. After driving an hour and a half, he parked at a McDonald's and saw Manuel sitting under an umbrella outside, munching on a Big Mac.

"You know Florio Rodriquez is the new Plaza honcho," Miguel informed Manual.

"I met him. He's from Las Flores like you, right?"

"He's the husband of Maria's cousin Inez who was killed at the same time as Ignacio."

"Yeah. I heard all about it." He slid the container of fries across the table. "Have some. Get a sandwich or something."

Miguel shook his head. "Not hungry. How did you hear this?"

"He told me. This guy likes to talk. You would think he is a big deal or something. Doesn't think much of you. Says you caused their deaths. Tighten his mouth, Miguel. Know what I mean? He will get us all in trouble. He does not have your back."

"All right, I will. What else is new? Anything on Maria?"

"I don't know for sure … maybe. Nate wants to meet. People watching you?" Manuel asked.

"I don't think so, but I don't get around much. I try to stay away from places and folks. When and where?"

"Same place as last time. He said you'd know."

Miguel nodded.

"Where you staying?"

Miguel pointed to a Holiday Inn a quarter mile down the road. "How do I contact him?"

"You don't. He'll call you."

"What if there is something urgent?"

"Use your satellite phone and call me. Your phone is monitored. It is telling them exactly where you are and listening to every word. Might want to turn it off in the latrine … or in bed, you know, with your wife or something."

Others turned to them as their laughter echoed off the golden arches.

32

*F*ifteen minutes passed before Miguel saw Florio Rodriquez drive into the parking garage. He was annoyed because he had emphasized to Florio the importance of being on time. "Snitches," he had said, "are skittish. If they think anything is wrong, they run. So be on time!"

Since the complaint from Manuel about Florio, he doubted whether selecting Florio for Tucson Plaza leader was the right decision. Being relatives, he thought he could count on Florio's loyalty. Nevertheless, he'd taken El Anglo's advice seriously. Narcos are fungible as dollars. Miguel had asked Isdel to arrange with one of the gangs in Tucson to provide security and follow Florio after he received the money. Another car was to follow him once he had crossed the border.

Miguel walked to Florio's car and opened the door. "I'll do the talking," Miguel said before Florio left the car. "Your job is to listen and follow instructions for delivering the money. If I want you to participate, I'll nod to you." He paused, waiting for a response. Not seeing one, he stepped back to give Florio room and said, "You got that?"

Florio shrugged, nodded, and slammed the car door. As they approached the elevator, Miguel said, "This gringo is a weasel. He even looks like one. This is the third time I've met with him."

Florio followed him to the lounge where Quique and Miguel had previously met with Walker. Miguel saw him at the same corner table. The meeting was to pay Walker for information and his monthly stipend and to collect one million dollars in cash that Florio was to deliver to Quique at the hacienda.

In addition, Miguel wanted to set up a diversion so he could smuggle the Hezbollah agents across the border and deliver them to a Tucson stash house.

"This is Florio," Miguel informed Walker. "He is the new plaza leader and your contact. He will also deal with the cash transfers."

"He doesn't have some kind of a funny name like El Caballo?" Walker asked and quickly turned to Florio and sneered as though inspecting a piece of tainted meat.

Despite an attempt to appear sophisticated, Florio resembled a pit bull with a muscular neck, thick jaws, and bulging eyes. Florio offered his hand. Walker shrugged and ignored the gesture, leaving Florio's hand flapping in the air like a seal. Walker nodded to a nearby server and then returned to his seat.

Florio dropped his hand, straightened to his full height, and then slowly slid into the seat facing Walker.

Walker looked at Florio and said, "Where'd you come from?"

"Me and Miguel are family. Come from the same place. Las Flores, Sonora. Ever hear of it?"

"No. I don't know Mexican places. Isn't that right, El Caballo? Or should I say, Miguel?" A broad smile spread across his face. "You have a last name, Florio? I don't need any of that Mexican four or five name stuff, just your regular last name will do."

"Forget it, Walker," Miguel growled. "What you got for us?"

A server interrupted. "What can I get you boys?"

"Dos Equis," Walker said. "Miguel here's paying." He pointed to Miguel.

When she left, Walker continued. "In a couple more days, I'll have a contact for you in Miami with a team of people who can load stuff on and off cargo ships in the Port of Miami. Tell your honcho this fits well with any Mexican supplier who might want to get stuff to Spain. You understand, amigo?"

Walker's condescension further antagonized Miguel, but he chose to ignore it for now. He needed Walker's cooperation. However, he knew Florio's disclosures were certain to have consequences.

"So, what are you saying?" Miguel questioned. "That we have to get it to Miami somehow and pay you to allow it through Nogales, and then you pay for the transportation to wherever?"

"I don't pay for nothing," said Walker. "You pay me just to keep my mouth shut."

"Where's our money?"

"If Florio here takes these keys and goes to the garage, he will find an SUV in parking space three on the third floor. In the back under the floor is your money in a special compartment. He can cross through Sasabe without trouble after he gets a call." He turned to Florio. "If you don't get a call by four, don't go. Just wait. What is your number?"

Florio looked to Miguel, who nodded.

After they went over the details again, Miguel said, "You remember the project I mentioned last time at Denny's?"

"Yes."

"Soon I will be in touch. You have the same phone number?"

"Yes."

"What's up?" Florio asked. "What are you talking about? What project?"

"*Time to go*," Miguel said. *He removed an envelope from inside his shirt and slid it to Walker who slipped it inside his own shirt.* "*We're done*," Miguel said, glaring at Florio.

"*I'll accompany both of you to the parking garage*," Walker offered. *He followed them to the third floor. A black Toyota was in space number three and started with the key Walker had given to Florio. Walker started to leave and then turned to Miguel.* "*I will expect your call.*"

"*And I am expecting that every penny of this million is in this trunk.*" *The garage was deserted, except for Isdel standing unseen nearby in the shadow of a post.*

When Florio and Miguel were alone, Miguel grabbed him and slammed him against the car. "*You have a big mouth. I will tell you this only once. You caused great harm tonight because you think you are a big shot. You talk out of turn and, you die! You understand? This is a matter of your life or Maria's. Believe me, there is no contest.*"

"*I am the plaza leader. I have to know what is going on.*"

"*I will tell you what you need to know! You were told never to use my name or to say where you are from or live. You remember that?*"

"*Well, yes, but I thought —*"

Miguel shut Florio's mouth with a violent slap across his face that echoed through the garage and knocked him backward against the car. Blood oozed from his mouth.

"*If you were not Inez's husband, I would kill you myself, right here. My goal is to find Maria. Not to babysit you.*"

"*Yes.*" *Florio said, wiping away the blood with his hand.* "*Inez is dead. My daughter is dead. You were there. You did nothing. He shoved Miguel, who grabbed Florio's arm and twisted it into a half nelson, turning Florio until his chin rested on the car's roof.*

He released Florio when he felt the man relax. "*Save it, Florio. You have a job to do now. Don't mess this up. I don't have time to tell you what it means to lose a million dollars.*"

Isdel waited until the SUV disappeared before walking to Miguel.

"*I have Florio's keys*," Miguel said. "*Here. Your man here can return it to the rental. I want Florio followed to the border. Check on your security from the border to the hacienda and let me know.*"

"*My brother is already watching for Florio to cross the border.*"

Miguel returned to the lounge, taking a seat at the far end of the bar where he had visibility of the room and ordered a beer. Miguel finished his beer and then nodded to Isdel, who was sitting at the other end of the bar. They took the elevator to the parking garage. They got out on the floor where they had left their car. Miguel noticed a muchacho standing in the shadows and started to reach for his weapon. Isdel grasped Miguel's wrist.

"He's one of mine. El Anglo told me to get more security. He and another will follow us to the border. Two others will follow us in Mexico."

33

*W*hen Wolforce booked the Center, he insisted the staff not have access to the guests other than the waiters and bartenders. A private entrance opened into a meeting room. Two waiters and a bartender served drinks.

The venue was no longer a working ranch, although, for effect, grazing cattle and horses were visible from the long driveway. The location displayed a sweeping backdrop toward the river and beyond to the base of the Santa Rita Mountains. A large strand of live oaks and mesquite trees created a sense of seclusion. Near the end of a gravel driveway, a traditional Spanish-style home appeared around a bend as though springing into view from nowhere.

Morrison arrived last and parked the Humvee next to a Mercedes. He walked through an elaborate doorway into a hallway leading to a large interior patio that opened to the sky. A bronze statue of Juan Bautista de Anza dominated the center of a pool containing floating flowers. Various doorways leading to interior rooms enclosed the patio.

Now a bed and breakfast, the kitchen maintained a reputation for serving outstanding meals along with providing discrete services and amenities. Many secrets, both legal and illegal, were discussed there; plans were devised and implemented from the comfortable leather furniture in the main room where the owner, Mavis Sanchez, personally led him.

She inherited the property from her parents. Once an active cattle ranch, the historic Anza Trail began there as an exploratory expedition in 1774 and reached all the way to the Presidio in California. The trail passed through the ranch following the Santa Cruz River. Like every trail that runs north or south from the border in both those early days and now, travelers share the path with others seeking new lives. When land taxes increased dramatically, ranching became uneconomical, and occasionally and reluctantly, Mavis sold a few acres to developers and builders. She hired the staff and lived with her husband in a secluded area near the river.

Moments after Morrison's arrival, five men, including Wolforce, were directed into a casual room where enticing pecan pralines, nuts, chocolates, fruit, and various cheese and cracker selections were displayed on a large oaken bar. According to a wall plaque, the bar was once a majestic one-hundred-year old oak tree at the river's edge.

While Wolforce provided first-name introductions, Mavis personally gathered wine and dinner orders. Other guests utilized the main dining room on the opposite side of the kitchen. Wolforce passed out a prospective brochure of *the charitable project and a proposed business plan. They finished their drinks and retired to the alcove. Mavis brought a second round of wines to match their individual dinner selections.*

As they gathered around him, Wolforce pointed to Morrison and said, "Malcolm Morrison is a new asset to our team. He is in the import/export business, as well as a builder-developer doing business in Arizona, Mexico, and South America."

"Actually," Morrison interrupted, "my wife owns the business and is contributing her own monies for this project, expecting to be appointed to the board."

Wolforce nodded. "That can certainly be done. Any objections? Okay, she will be CEO. However, Malcolm runs the place." Wolforce chuckled. He looked at Morrison, who shrugged. "Malcolm also has business connections with the governor of Sonora and the governor of Arizona." He paused. "Let's get started."

They found seats and settled in. Mavis brought a last round and walked out closing the door.

"We are meeting today to discuss using Malcom's property for our political purpose. That event is what we need to discuss. We cannot meet again except for formal director's meetings," Wolforce began.

Morrison squirmed, grasped the arms of his chair, stiffened, and gasped. Wolforce ignored him. Morrison did not understand the purpose of the meeting. Obviously, this organization had little or nothing to do with art. He was angry with himself for accepting Wolforce's demand he attend. It seemed a waste of time, except perhaps for the chance to meet a young banker named Robert who Wolforce advised might be interested in a money laundering scheme to launder drug money from the States to Europe or vice versa. The import/export business Gretchen was attempting to expand might provide an opportunity for such an operation in combination with smuggling drugs, art, and antiques.

That these people were to be the board of a so-called charitable organization seemed somehow perverted. Two young Mexicans Morrison had not noticed until now sat quietly alone. Wolforce had not introduced them.

Soon, Mavis brought dinner. When Mavis was out of earshot, Wolforce gestured to one of the Mexicans. "This man I am sure you do not know, but you may have heard of him."

They looked at the handsome well-dressed young man.

"Meet Spiro Morales, now capo of the Morales Group," Wolforce said with dutiful respect.

Spiro Morales stood.

"Gentlemen," Spiro began in excellent English, "since we don't personally know each other, let me begin by providing you with my background. I was born in San Antonio, Texas. My mother was illegal and pregnant and came to the US so I would be a US citizen. Then she returned to Mexico, leaving me with her naturalized parents. I was a decent student and soccer player. I was accepted and graduated from Harvard with a BA and attended Harvard Law where I served on the Harvard Law Review. I passed the bar exam first try. However, a background check revealed I was the son of a suspected Mexican drug lord. I was denied membership.

"I appreciate this opportunity to meet with you today. While we have never met, each of you does business with me because of my organization. This business has been lucrative for all of us. Mr. Morrison's participation in this organization will not only increase our ability to launder money and transport product to Europe, but he will also participate in development projects here and in Mexico. These projects usually are funded by foreign companies or governments seeking to do business or expand business in Mexico."

He looked at Morrison and continued to speak directly to him as though no one else was present.

"The governor of Sonora State is considering a new plant, which will likely be built by Morrison's company. We are all certainly aware of the potential construction of a wall along the border. Such projects generate dollars for subcontractors who must be approved by the state." Spiro smiled and the others nodded.

"I understand Mr. Wolforce has explained that the present US administration has declared that the border is now safe, something they seem pleased to boast about prior to the election. In addition, as you may know, a relatively new cartel has taken over some of our plazas and made claims that they will destroy us. One of their leaders, called El Caballo, assassinated my brothers."

He clenched his fists so tightly that his hands shook. The alcove remained silent while he turned around for his wine, inspected the glass, and swirled it before he took a sip.

"Not only is this new cartel determined to destroy us, but I think they *intend to create a narco state in Mexico. We can argue whether the violence on the border has, in fact, decreased or that illegal immigration has also diminished or whether a narco state is a viable alternative to our existing form of government. For us, such issues are primarily political and only matter in how they affect our business. What does matter is that we not allow the Sonora Cartel to control this territory. Like any business, we must grow if we are to survive.*

"If we are to continue to prosper, we need to recover what we have lost and destroy this festering Sonora cancer before it does us further damage." He stopped speaking and took a breath. He made eye contact with each man, as though evaluating each one by his facial expressions.

"My brothers and father believed the Sonora Cartel is indirectly supported by elements in the United States. They thought it not a coincidence their leader is an Anglo who has the support of a major benefactor."

Morrison interrupted. "Like what, for instance?"

"Money, for instance. They started from scratch several years ago without any apparent means of financing their operations. They were able to hire a few minor polleros to smuggle some undocumented migrants, and before long, they were taking more and more across the border. They began hijacking our mules in Arizona. They seemed to know where they were going to be. They suddenly had sophisticated weapons. These were all indications that someone was supplying them not only with intelligence but also with weapons and large amounts of cash and intel. From what I've learned, the leaders are wealthy Mexicans with large ranches, and political connections in the Mexican government."

"Yeah, connections all right, like the Bureau of Alcohol, Tobacco, Firearms, and Explosives, for instance. Remember Fast and the Furious?" Wolforce interjected. "You know where those guns went?"

"That's what the ATF wanted to find out," Morrison replied.

"They went to the Sonora Cartel to get them started in building a little army on their hacienda. The ATF could not simply give them away to Sonora ... too much of a paper trail. They let them walk out of Arizona. Some went to other Mexican groups to obscure the real destination," Wolforce continued. "This was set up by some group deep in the administration who wants to overthrow the Morales Cartel and the complicit Mexican government by the creation and support of an insurrection by the Sonora Cartel."

Spiro spoke up again. "There are some in your government who share this concern. Like you, they rely upon various compensation and favors indirectly from Wolforce."

He glanced at Wolforce and took a couple of swallows of his wine before continuing. "Violence serves an important function beyond killing enemies. It produces general fear. Killing a person may eliminate a nuisance, but more importantly, the act intimidates and frightens others and provides us with a blanket of power. I would much rather have someone fear me than simply kill them. Fear is dynamic. The more it is publicized, the more effective it becomes in spreading fear. Terrorism proves the point."

Their heads nodded like corks bobbing on water.

"What do Americans fear most beyond their individual safety?" Spiro asked the group.

The men were quiet, closely watching him.

"The victim does not have to wield political power, though should at least have perceived importance."

Outside, a lawnmower interrupted him. The afternoon sky had become increasingly overcast, spilling shadows over the alcove as evening quickly approached.

"Let's return to the other room," Wolforce said. "It's more comfortable."

"Okay," Spiro said once they had settled into new seats. "So, let's explain the plan."

The man with Spiro walked to him and said something. Spiro looked about the room and nodded. The man went to a phone on the mahogany bar. After turning it upside down, he unplugged the line from both the phone and the jack, coiled the line, and walked to the door. Opening it, he called Mavis, gave her the phone and the equipment, and continued searching the room. He then nodded to Spiro and went to a chair. Mavis left the room.

Spiro turned back to his audience and said, "We can never be too careful. He paused and slowly viewed his audience. "We want to create a spectacular event that will be blamed on the Sonora Cartel. I want them on the defensive." He paused. "Actually, I want them destroyed!"

Spiro took a couple of sips of his wine then smacked his lips. "Previously, we arranged for two Hezbollah assassins to enter the US. They were smuggled into the States by a couple of coyotes. That was a test. It worked without incident. They are undercover here. An event is to be held at Malcolm's home in Rio

Rico to celebrate Mexican and American cooperation in reducing violence and trafficking along the border. Malcolm will host the governor of Sonora, the governor of Arizona, and a deputy director of Homeland Security."

Spiro frowned and looked at Wolforce. "What's his name again?"

"Ratcliff."

"Right, that's our guy. We expect a few local dignitaries, plus a few folks from the media. It should make a nice venue. We should get great coverage. As I understand it, there is the backdrop of the Santa Rita Mountains, swimming pool, a perfect landing area for helicopters, parking space, and a balanced sprinkling of gringos and wetbacks. There will be some security, mostly local sheriff's deputies and whatever security the dignitaries may have.

"During the course of the event, which will be outside, weather permitting, these Hezbollah agents will attempt to assassinate the governors and the deputy director on television."

There was a loud gasp in the room. The men all looked at each other.

"Whether it is successful or not, the outrage of such a blatant attack on US territory will result in dramatically exposing the administration's false narrative. Ratcliff's assistant has publicly asserted that the border is not safe. Even if the deputy director is not killed, the point will have been made. The blame will rest entirely on the failure of the existing administration for misleading the public. The Sonora Cartel will be accused of working with Hezbollah to assassinate an American official."

"You make this sound so simple," Morrison said. "Just kill a couple of guys at my house like you are swatting pesky flies. You can't be serious."

Spiro looked at Wolforce, who intervened. "This really is quite simple, Malcolm. These men appear to be Mexican and can be easily smuggled into a mixed crowd. We are inviting other important Mexicans. The security will be light." He exchanged eye contact with Spiro. "Even if they are killed, who cares? They already know this is a suicide mission, martyrdom for the cause against the great Satan and an eternity with beautiful virgins. This is your consummate win-win situation." Wolforce chuckled.

Everyone in the room laughed, except Spiro and Morrison.

After the levity subsided, Morrison asked, "But what about the potential for collateral damage, a guest or someone else is injured?" He looked directly at Spiro. "This whole thing is bazaar." He shook his head as though trying to grasp whether the idea was even realistic. He glanced at the others who seemed spellbound by Spiro.

"Unlikely. The odds are against it. These men are professionals. However, the more violence, the greater the significance," Spiro said. He looked at Wolforce.

"This is not a discussion, Malcolm. It's decided. Perhaps if you are concerned about family or others, don't invite them. Send them shopping in Tubac or off to Disneyland or anywhere. This matter is too important an opportunity to let it slip by."

No one noticed several men gathering outside the room by the door leading to the patio. One man made a path. Another opened the door. Two men stepped in front of Spiro and escorted him to a waiting car. Morrison stumbled toward his Humvee, breathing heavily. The small Spiro entourage of four SUVs wedged past him. He followed them toward Nogales on the old highway.

When he turned off the highway at Rio Rico, he did not notice the car following him.

34

*M*iguel left before dawn, looking forward to meeting with Nate. He turned toward Whitehouse Canyon Road.

The pressure of leading a double life weighed upon him like an iron apron, a constant tug, draining his energy. Any minor mistake or misstatement might be fatal. He had learned that the best way to deal with the stress was to try to ignore the danger and take one step at a time, leaving the future to take care of itself. He felt like someone who, when lost in the desert, places one foot in front of the other in a deliberate and determined manner to minimize energy. Eventually, one finds an oasis.

Under present circumstances, he realized it might even be better that he had not yet found Maria. Bringing her into his situation would only increase complications. Being with him could be fatal for her. He continued to assume she remained alive. If he could just know for sure, he would at least know whether there was reason for hope. His only relief from the pressure was his short visits with his parents and Juanito in Las Flores.

Nate was the only contact he had come to believe was part of a normal world, except, of course, his family. Even with his family, there was stress. He did not want to think about the danger they were in just because he was a member of a transnational criminal organization. He knew his father would be proud of his undercover work, if he knew, but that only intensified the pressure. He knew he had placed his family in danger. What of his son?

How could he protect Juanito? If he found Maria, could they really become a family? If he did find her, then what? Their lives had changed. He tried not to imagine what her life had become.

The road took him toward Madera Canyon. From his previous visit, he considered the location a peacefully calming escape. Though the subjects he and Nate would discuss there were dreadful and his predicament was forced upon him by Nate, he nevertheless felt Nate was a soulmate. When everyone seems against you, there must be someone or something special to hang on to.

Miguel was unable to achieve a rational clarity for his conflicted feelings toward the Sonora Cartel. He felt remorse for his participation in their activities. Nevertheless, he admired El Anglo and respected Alverez. Maybe such an inexplicable attitude was the result of a rationalization that their objectives were honorable and the terrible means to achieve them therefore justifiable. Yet he still believed he had no acceptable alternative. As long as he still believed he would find Maria, his present course remained the only option.

He refused to dwell on all the contradictions that tormented him during weak moments. However, at bottom, he was determined not to let his confusion and misgivings matter. Like the desert, nothing was going to change. Only survival mattered. His goal must remain the same: find Maria, no matter what was required, regardless of how much each of them had changed.

He arrived at the picnic area and pulled into the same parking lot with the breathtaking view of the valley.

"Quite a view, is it not? I never tire of it up here," Nate said from behind him. "This is the place I end up at when I want to get away from everything down there." His arm swept through an arc over the valley.

Miguel turned. "Up here is a promise and a vision and a hope of a new world … an incredibly foreign and unimaginable place for a peon from a dusty compound in the Sonora Desert of Mexico. You think you have an idea what it might be like down there. Maybe it is hope for a decent life, but what you think is not even close."

"I've wondered if it is worth all the hardship of sneaking over here. Is it, Miguel?" Nate asked.

Miguel turned and looked at the mountain extending south, the same mountain range passing by his home, and below it was the same desert. Here is irrigation. There, except for the hacienda, water is scarce. Though the land is the same, the contrasts were stark. Somewhere farther south along this ridge he stood upon, were his family and his son.

He thought of the plight of migrants, suffering from the sheer physical effort of the miles of attempting to deal with the terrain. Now he knew about the exploitation and abuse from human predators along the route and the women who, like Maria, are raped for no other reason than there was no one to stop them. Not only do their coyotes rape them, but armed marauders claim rape is a tax for transit through their territory. Then there are the thousands of migrants kidnapped for ransom by predators and their needless slaughter by murderers just because they felt like killing. And for what? He wondered if Maria felt differently about America now.

He turned to Nate. "I am not really here yet. I am not part of this place. You can't be illegal and feel included. When and if I get legal, I'll let you know if it is worth it. For now, it seems to me the ancient ones are speaking."

"What are they telling you?"

"You deserted us. We will continue to make you pay."

The men were switching back and forth between English and Spanish. "You seem to be grasping the language well enough," Nate noted.

"Well, what else is there to do when you have time on your hands?"

They walked to a picnic table. "You weren't followed?"

"Didn't see anyone," Miguel assured him.

"What's new?"

"First, anything on Maria?" Miguel did not have much hope there would be any good news.

"We may have a lead on the Humvee. Don't know yet. Two yellow Humvees were spotted and are being checked out as we speak." Nate looked across the valley below them toward the next row of mountains to the west.

"What can you tell me about the call you got from Venezuela?"

"How do you know about that?"

"You still don't seem to understand. We monitor your calls and location from your phone. If you want anonymity, get a prepaid phone and dispose of it after you use it. Take the pieces out and throw them away."

Miguel turned away from Nate and watched a car moving along Old Nogales Highway, a mere speck weaving in and out of the pecan trees, like an ant following a pathway of crumbs. Finally, leaving the grove, it turned west toward Sahuarita.

Getting back to Venezuela, Miguel said, "Gemayel."

"And he is?"

"The middleman for the agents. I told you about him before. Gave me arrival time at the airport in Mexico City. I meet them there, and we go to the hacienda. I take them across at Nogales and onto the trophy tree just like before. Finally, to a new stash house in Tucson. I don't know where they go from there.

Nate asks, "Who will be the Coyote?"

Me, with Isdel, Joaquin and Emilio. We figure it will take us a couple of days, if we do not stop.

"From the beginning," Nate prompted.

"In Caracas with Quique, the financial guy, and El Anglo, we met with this Gemayel. El Anglo said they wanted us to take two men across the border to Arizona. They seemed to know each other already."

"El Anglo and this Gemayel?"

"Yes."

"Who is he?" Nate asked.

"No clue."

Nate wrote some notes in his tablet.

"Gemayel said he wanted me to do it since I had delivered the first two without any problems. El Anglo agreed."

"What did El Anglo say about the two men?"

"That they are Hezbollah like the first two. Quique, said we wanted to get into this business of getting important people across the border because it means more money. Also, I think we want to smuggle product there somehow."

"He said they were Hezbollah for sure?" Nate questioned.

"Yes."

"Are they are working for the Sonora Cartel?"

"No. El Anglo says our part is just to smuggle them into the country and get them to a stash house. Someone will pick them up there. Beyond that, we have no connection to them. El Anglo said we do not want to get involved with them, just to get them to America by walking them across the border like illegal aliens. If I think they will be arrested while they are with me or if they might be captured by hijackers, he wants me to kill them."

"That's murder, whether you do it or someone else does it."

"Who would know? Just two more dead guys in the desert," Miguel pointed out.

"You are writing all this down, Nate?"

"No, not all. Just the things I need to remember. Nothing about you except a personal code name.

"We'll be listening," Nate said, smiling.

They sat quietly for a few minutes.

"I have an idea. First, though, how do you keep these guys safe before you cross?" Nate asked.

"I control the plaza. Hawks will be watching for anything or anyone who might get in the way — on either side of the border."

"Like what?"

"Well, rogue bandits, police, soldiers, other coyotes. They have radios. I stopped with the phones. They will let us know."

"Easier for us to copy too," Nate said.

"I'll carry enough dollars for big payoffs. If that doesn't work, Isdel and his friends who will flank us and do whatever is required to keep us safe."

"Where'd you learn how to do this stuff?"

"Good teacher."

"Who?" Nate asked.

"El Anglo."

"Know who he is yet?"

"No," Miguel told him. "I'm guessing he was once US Special Ops or something like that. What's your idea?"

"How about we clear the road for you once you cross, including all the way to the stash house?"

"I don't want to know anything about it," said Miguel. "I got an idea too. I'm using Walker as a patsy to clear someone who is merely going through as a decoy. But I can put shit on him, and if Walker lets him through and doesn't check him out and catch him, then you call it a test of security or something like that."

"I still think Walker is our best lead to Maria," Nate replied. "You want him jacked up? I think he is small potatoes in this, and I still need for him to take us to the next level."

"If you take him, he'll squeal like a pig. He is going to sell me the name of a contact in Spain who can arrange a deal in Spain for receiving coke."

Nate picked up the binoculars he'd laid on the table earlier and slowly scanned the area beneath them. He handed them to Miguel and said, "Take a look. See if you know that car."

"No, don't think so."

The early morning remained still, lifeless. Even the birds seemed worn out. A light breeze was beginning to develop, creeping over the mountain from behind them from the east. As the front passed, Miguel watched as the leading edge tossed small debris into the air before it as it slid down the slope toward the valley.

Beside him, Nate asked, "What was your part in the assassination of the Morales clan?"

Miguel turned and gave the binoculars to Nate. "You knew about it?"

"You are El Caballo, are you not? Everyone says the Sonora Cartel did it, and El Caballo was the assassin. There's still another one, you know," Nate said. "Spiro, the youngest, and allegedly the most ruthless is still out there. He missed your festivities."

35

*J*ose finished his evening chores and walked toward the house. The night sky was unusually dark, as though the clouds had gathered in response to an invitation from a higher authority, enveloping the compound in a surreal shadow in which objects blended into each other. Usually one of the security guards stopped him for a short and friendly conversation before he locked up for the night. For some reason, none appeared.

A vehicle slowly approached from the direction of Las Flores. Since it was Friday night, some traffic was usual, with most of it from the cantina in Las Flores where men had doubtless celebrated with the winner of the horse race. Since Maverick and Miguel were no longer living at home, Jose felt no urge to attend. He rarely visited the cantina. The locals were dubious about the increasing number of strangers passing through Las Flores, many of them armed.

Instead of passing the compound, however, the car slowed and turned into the driveway and slowly approached the casa. Jose looked around for the guards.

They must have been busy behind the barn. Normally, they would have stopped a car before it got that close.

Jose rushed to intercept the car. It stopped. A single silhouette remained motionless behind the steering wheel. As Jose approached, the engine stopped. The interior light activated when the driver opened the door. Jose recognized Florio. Still, the guards did not appear.

"Welcome, Florio," Jose said. "What brings you out here on such a warm night?"

"Miguel asked me to tell you how well he is doing. I am working for him now, you know."

Jose nodded toward the casa. "She's just checking on Juanito. About to tuck him in. Why don't you come on inside?"

"Thanks, just for a minute."

Yolanda met them at the door and held it open for them. "Sit there," she said, pointing to the table. "I'll get Juanito."

Florio watched her disappear into a new room addition. A new overstuffed chair, probably Jose's, was in the corner. The new rocking chair on the other side of the room near the wall must be Yolanda's. There was now a wood floor, two new chairs at the table, and a shade for the single light bulb that hung from the ceiling. A few rugs, quilts, and in the kitchen pans, plates, towels, and food laid up as a precaution to provide subsidence in the event of a flash flood that might wash out the road.

Juanito appeared in the doorway and stopped, looking at Florio. Yolanda went to him. After picking him up, she returned and sat across from Florio at the table.

"Nice place," Florio said without looking around, concentrating on Jose. Florio glanced at his watch. "We hoped for a place like this once, some land, a horse or two. My dreams died when Inez and the baby were murdered. I cannot forget that day, coming home and finding them slaughtered like pigs. No one helped them. Miguel just walked away. To him, they were just bodies, pieces of meat. To me, they were everything."

"He told us. It was terrible," Yolanda said. She exchanged glances with Jose.

"I don't understand," Jose said. His smile vanished as he shifted toward the front edge of his chair.

While Florio's mouth formed a smile, his eyes and face remained plastic, molded as though it had cured too soon and was forever preserved. He ignored Yolanda and kept his gaze on Jose.

"You can't know what it is like unless you have lived it, seen it, realized the bodies are your family. Our little baby, covered with blood, his face gone. Blood on the counter, on the floor behind the bar, splattered on the wall. Every day it haunts me. The pain remains." He looked toward the window. "I see you have improved the property, a new barn. Miguel hangs out now with the big shots. There are even two guards here, right? Just to protect the big man's family? The boy is walking now, I see. I'll be sure and tell Miguel El Caballo Gutierrez … Now it's his turn to suffer."

Florio turned his head, following Jose's glance toward the wall where a rifle hung. Yolanda turned away and stood. She quickly walked to Juanito who was still standing in the doorway. She placed her body so her back was toward Florio, keeping Juanito on the opposite side away from Florio.

"Florio, what is this? What's going on here?" Jose said.

The door burst into splinters, and Yolanda screamed. Two men entered the house carrying automatic weapons. Jose died before he fell from the chair. Yolanda fell backward in the doorway holding Juanito.

Florio stood as the blood quickly pooled and began sloshing over his feet. He walked to Yolanda who was lying on her back still clasping Juanito. Florio *watched Juanito crying, bent down, removed Juanito from Yolanda's arms, and then handed him to El Coyote who held him at arm's length as though he had just pulled stinking garbage from a trash can.*

"Get me a damn towel!" El Coyote bellowed.

Florio rushed out of the room and returned with a towel. Except for Juanito's cries, the killing room was deadly silent.

"I know where we can sell him," El Coyote said. He handed Juanito back to Florio. El Coyote calmly removed his watch and placed it in the middle of the table.

The two men then tore away the remnants of the door and casually strolled toward the car.

Florio walked to the driver's side, stopped at the rear door, and opened it for El Coyote and Juanito.

"You drive," El Coyote said to Florio.

Spiro opened the passenger's side door. As he settled into his seat, he said, "And then there was one." Spiro nodded to El Coyote.

El Coyote handed Juanito to Spiro and shut the car door. As Florio turned to walk to the driver's side, El Coyote pulled the knife from his waist, grabbed Florio from behind, forced his knee into the small of Florio's back, and slit Florio's throat with such intensity he almost decapitated him. El Coyote bent down over Florio's body, wiped the knife on his clothes, and then secured the knife in the sheath. Spiro handed Juanito to El Coyote and turned on the engine.

After the car faded into the night, Rascal walked from the barn, entered the casa, sniffed at the bloody bodies, and lay down beside Jose.

36

*M*iguel drove all day and finally arrived at the hacienda after midnight. Just before nine o'clock the following morning, El Anglo entered his room. "Miguel, wake up. Now!"

When Miguel entered the library a few minutes later, Alvera and El Anglo stood. El Anglo poured a cup of coffee at the bar, moved toward them, and gave Miguel the coffee. "Sit down, Son," Alvera said.

"We have very bad news," El Anglo said, looking into Miguel's eyes. Miguel wondered why El Anglo was serving them instead of the maid. He looked around the room for her.

El Anglo closed the door and stood next to Miguel. "There is simply no way to say this," said Alvera.

Miguel looked from one to the other.

"Your parents are dead!" El Anglo told him.

They watched him carefully, prepared to assist him. He did not move, did not breathe. The silence could not have been louder.

"I ..." He stammered. "What? When?" He looked from one to the other. "Juanito?"

"Missing," El Anglo said.

"Last night sometime," Alvera said. "Bus arrived this morning to pick up your father. After waiting, the driver went to check and found them. He called Vargas who sent a man there right away. Vargas got a couple of security guys and went there himself. He called me."

"He is rarely late for the bus. Always telling me not to be late," Miguel mumbled, remembering the morning trips to the hacienda. He felt adrift, like he was elsewhere, far away from this reality where rarely something meaningful had entered his life. On those rare occasions when he was touched by happiness, it was taken away, like Maverick or Maria and now his parents and Juanito. Until now, he had not succumbed to despair. The desert seemed to be collecting a debt for something he had neglected or had done in the past ... something the spirits resented.

They found the body of Florio near your house, throat slit, almost decapitated.

"Also, two security men, behind the barn, throats slit," said Alvera.

"Throats slit? My parents ... throats slit too?"

El Anglo shook his head. "No. AK-47s, at least three of them, maybe also an AR-15. Emptied their magazines — 7.62, .223, and 5.56 casings all over *like spilled seedpods. Suggests three shooters. Probably one car involved. Two sets of tracks. One set drove into your driveway. Another set was a quarter mile east of the driveway, leading off the road and into a mesquite grove. Two sets of fresh footprints from there led to the compound, none returning. The vehicle must have dropped two off at the mesquite grove. They approached the casa on foot and then surprised and killed the security. The third one drove to the casa, where the driver got out.*

Miguel could not feel his hands. He saw them clasped in front of his knees. He looked at El Anglo. "This is all about me, isn't it?"

"Probably." El Anglo nodded. "Someone found out your name and knows where you live."

"Florio … Walker!" Miguel gasped.

"Let's go," El Anglo said and stood. "Alvera stays here."

Miguel was frozen. El Anglo grasped his shoulder, pulling him up. "Get your 16. Come on, let's go. Plane is waiting. We can talk on the plane."

"Ambush?" Miguel asked, stiffening his shoulders, now appearing all business and trying to control his emotions. "Could we be walking into something?"

"Doubt it. Area has been cleared. Army checked it out. Have not messed up the scene too much. Waiting for you."

During the short flight, Miguel told El Anglo about the meeting with Walker and Florio and that he had roughed up Florio. "Florio blamed me for the murders of his wife and daughter. He gave my name to Walker in front of me. He has to be the one. No one else knows. It had to be Florio, and then he gave it to Walker, and then Walker told …" His voice trailed off, and though his lips moved, the only sound was a moan.

The plane dipped low over the hacienda as El Anglo checked below. Then after wheeling around, the landing gear locked, wheels touched the packed sand runway and with desert dust spewing behind came to a noisy stop.

"Vargas is waiting for you," a security man said once they had disembarked.

Within an hour, they were standing at the smashed door to the casa. The bodies were gone, and the blood had dried into a brown stain covering most of the floor and the rug. The smell of death remained.

Without formality, Vargas called out to Miguel, who had remained in the doorway hesitating to enter. "Over here!" He stood by the table with his hands on his hips, a tense expression on his face.

When Miguel got to the table, Vargas removed a pen from his pocket. Miguel watched as Vargas leaned over the table, slid the pen through the band of a watch, and lifted it until it was level with Miguel's eyes.

"Look familiar?" Vargas asked, showing a gold watch to Miguel.

Miguel looked Vargas in the eye and then glanced at the watch. Vargas turned the watch over. "Maverick" the inscription read.

Miguel froze before gasping, "El Coyote." Miguel moaned and then slumped into Jose's heavily bloodstained chair. The room whirled dizzily around him.

Vargas said, "I gave this watch to Miguel when we delivered a horse to him here. The horse we named Maverick. The watch was one of a kind. I had commissioned several gold watches from the gold mine in which I have an interest. The nugget was processed by hand and then made into several watches. I had them engraved in Cuernavaca by a jewelry maker I know. He made several for me at the same time with different inscriptions." He pulled back his shirtsleeve and displayed a similar watch.

"Explain this," El Anglo said. "How did El Coyote get it? Take your time."

The events at the trophy tree passed through Miguel's mind. His hands trembled while he slowly turned the watch over. "We'd sit out there on the porch, watching the sunset, drinking, sometimes talking ..." He placed the watch on his wrist.

Miguel looked at them, stood up to gather himself, and turned to El Anglo. "At the trophy tree, a dirty clearing at the pickup spot that was our last stop after crossing the border, El Coyote took all our money and valuables. This included our jewelry, including watches.

"He was here! He planted it where he knew I would find it. He killed my parents. He killed Maria. How else did it get here! He kept it all this time just for something like this. Now he wants me. Don't you all see?"

"There were three shooters, we think," Vargas said. "Three different casings. Out here it's too far for anyone to hear."

Miguel said, "This is a sadistic statement of revenge from El Coyote ... a challenge to me to find him and the bait to go after him. Florio must have told him where to find me." He then told them of Maria's rape and their treatment. He explained being wounded and waking up on the floor at the stash house in Tucson to discover Maria was missing.

El Anglo walked out onto the back to the porch where Juanito and Jose had sat in the evening and then walked around the compound. He entered the barn where he saw a horse was in a stall. He returned to the house.

"I don't think this is the kind of planning by El Coyote. He is a remorseless killer, all right. This, however, they carefully planned in advance. It wasn't an opportunity killing. No, this is all about you, Miguel, and if I had to bet, I'd put my money on Spiro Morales as the planner. This is about revenge, payback, and repudiation of Sonora power, but mostly about himself. No, he had to do this, and I wouldn't be surprised if he wasn't here."

"Why didn't they also kill my son?"

"Children are sold or held for ransom. Motherless babies are usually killed. Just too much trouble. This is not the normal. There has to be a reason it was done this way, Miguel."

37

"We found the Humvee," said Sheriff Desmond into the phone to Nate.

"Hallelujah," Nate replied. "Where? What's the deal?"

"Remember how I said we were checking on two of them?"

"Yeah, I think we were trying to eat that huge dessert at the time. All I can remember is that I was going to explode. So, what's the story?"

"The two turned out to be the same one seen a couple of times. A deputy followed one leaving a resort. Got the tag number and called it in. He just happened to see it in a parking spot when he was having lunch with his wife. As we were chatting about it, sure enough, a guy comes out and gets into it. They follow him right to his house in Rio Rico. Registered to a Morrison who lives there. Swanky house, my guy says. Also, a Mercedes and a Porsche in the garage. You know what they say about cars and houses like that in that location."

"Yeah, big deal narco. This guy fit?" asked Nate.

"Got nothing on him. Don't know about the feds."

"Anyone on him, watching the house or anything?"

"No, can't spare the manpower. Oops," Desmond said, "got another call, got to go. I'll email you the address and what we got."

"To my home. Not the office."

"Roger." Desmond hung up.

Nate pushed back his chair and started to stand when a young woman walked into his office. "Sorry to bother you, but someone by the name of Ricky called. Said he needed to talk to you."

"Did he say where?" Nate asked.

"Said you'd know. Okay?"

"I've got to leave for a while. You got my private phone number?"

She shook her head.

He said, "Here it is." Nate wrote it down and left.

After a fifteen-minute walk, Nate entered a small gift shop. After casually looking at a couple of cards on the rack that stuck out above the others, he selected one with a small pencil mark near the top. He returned to his office. Opening the card, he read. "Miguel's family murdered. Perps unknown at this time."

Nate slid the card into the shredder, returned to his desk, placed his arms on the desktop, and laid his head on his arms.

Again, the phone rang. It was Sheriff Desmond. "I hold in my hand a security notice about a press shindig. Guess where."

"I give up already."

"Morrison's. It says he's an international developer. Built a factory in Ciudad Juarez, this says. A bigwig from Homeland Security is to meet with the governors of Sonora and Arizona to celebrate cross-border cooperation. Then they go to DC for a formal discussion with someone not defined in the administration. We are to provide security here. No Secret Service or other backup."

Nate dialed, listened for the clicking to stop, and then said, "We've found the Humvee, not the girl. His parents assassinated. Son missing. No details yet."

The line went silent. Finally, Marcus said, "Nate, I am sorry. This is not your fault. What do you need?"

"A couple more agents to keep tags on Walker, the customs agent. We need to know what he does, with whom he does it, and where he hangs out."

"Anything else, Nate?"

"Not at the moment, sir."

"Okay. I just got your report. Maybe give you a heads-up once I finish it. Oh, and I will get you a couple of folks from Davis-Monthan AFB; I think they have an AFOSI unit there. Don't tell them anything more than their assignments."

The highly publicized funeral for Miguel's parents took place in Las Flores at the church and the burial at the adjacent cemetery. Mourners spilled outside, and many were not able to find standing room at the grave site for the internment. Flowers and pictures adorned most of the grave sites. Vargas made the arrangements. Miguel took care of the flowers.

Las Flores was overwhelmed by a sea of mourners and the curious. Ernesto Vargas, Arturo Alvera, and the governor of Sonora State attended, which brought many others, including abundant security that included a contingency of police and military.

The funeral was a gathering of the poor and the wealthy, the powerful and the weak. Miguel recognized only a few people from Las Flores, plus some from the hacienda in Hermosillo. He doubted most of them even knew the names of his family. Miguel was numb to the service and the burial. He did not know the priest and later would not recall his words.

During the short flight back to Vargas's hacienda, El Anglo said, "The unusual attendance was perhaps an expression of a pathological descent into a world now overrun by opioids affecting everyone: rich and poor alike in societal chaos, which we seem unwilling to stop. We have experienced too much pain and lives lost."

Miguel just wanted to focus upon Jose, Yolanda, Juanito, and Maria. If only we had taken Father Michael's advice. "Go back to Las Flores!" None of this would have happened.

Without Maria and Juanito, the world had instantly become a solemn, lonely struggle for survival. Miguel believed he was doing what he had to do to remain alive to find them. He had to assume Maria and Juanito were alive in order to continue to justify the terrible things he was doing. If she remained in the area, surly, the notoriety and publicity surrounding the funeral would get her attention. Still, what could she do? He refused to accept that both Maria and Juanito were dead. He would have to see their remains just as he had seen his parents. The watch left on the table at their casa was again on his wrist … a constant reminder of his mission to destroy El Coyote.

38

*M*iguel and Isdel disembarked the Gulf Star at a VIP terminal in Mexico City and proceeded to the waiting area to meet the Hezbollah assassins. Because they had no luggage, the wait was short. The agents wore business suits, white shirts, and ties and were cleanly shaved. Had they not approached Miguel because of the sign he was holding, Miguel would have mistaken them for Mexican executives.

So far, their arrival was going as planned. Miguel believed he had already taken care of the necessary financial arrangements. Now, it was merely a matter of boarding the Gulf Star aircraft for the return flight to the hacienda. The difficult part was ahead in smuggling them across the border into Arizona.

Isdel and Miguel boarded the plane. Miguel started to climb the ramp when he heard a siren and then noticed a Mexican customs car rapidly approaching. A customs officer in a brown uniform and cap carrying what looked like a clipboard and a folder assertively stepped out of the car before it completely stopped.

"Sir, please stop. One minute." He motioned for Miguel to step down from the ramp and follow him back to the tail of the aircraft where they were out of sight. "We have orders to inspect this plane for contraband and will have to detain you here overnight while we check it out." He paused and looked at the plane. "Hmm, it is not as large as I thought. I can probably take care of this right now, and you can be on your way." He smiled broadly while turning his head back and forth, apparently evaluating the aircraft.

"I appreciate your consideration in this matter Sir," Miguel said. "We are in a bit of a hurry. Do you think this would cost more than five hundred dollars?"

"Well, sir, I think one thousand is the going rate for these kinds of transactions."

"Oh, yes, of course. I just happen to have that amount with me." Miguel reached into his pocket, removed one thousand dollars, and inserted it into the folder.

"Right, sir. You can tell the pilot to turn her on." The officer turned and entered the car.

During the flight, no conversation occurred among them, as ordered by El Anglo. When they arrived at the gate, a black SUV whisked them to the hacienda.

A meal was prepared for the traffickers, the crew, and served in a separate room off the kitchen. Miguel arranged for three shifts of security guards for twenty-four-hour protection and observation.

Vargas, El Anglo, and Miguel had dinner in the main dining room, and discussed the details of the crossing. Miguel had left his phone on so Nate could hear the conversation. They settled on a plan that in two days Miguel, Isdel, Emilio, and Joaquin would take the two assassins across the border near Nogales, along the walking trail previously used by Miguel, and deliver them to a new stash house in Tucson.

El Coyote and Pedro were finishing their first bottle of beer at a hotel bar awaiting instructions from the Morales Cartel. El Coyote received a call. After listening he turned to Pedro and said, "An informant inside the Sonora Cartel reports that El Caballo will take two men across the border near Nogales in two days. When El Caballo crosses the border into Arizona you are to notify the Morales Cartel. You and your crew are to then follow El Caballo through the desert until they reach a final destination. Then notify the Cartel again and receive further instructions.

Miguel's first thought was the time. Then he acknowledged to himself that he remained alive to face another day. At dawn, he, Isdel, Joaquin and Emilio expected to begin their journey from Hermosillo, Mexico, cross the border into Arizona, and deliver two assassins to Manual in Tucson. In a way, it reminded him of the morning he and Maria began their journey to America. Since then, he had grown into a person he barely recognized.

He questioned whether if knowing then what he now knew he would have left Mexico. He wondered if Maria had found her dream, and if it was worth the many people affected by her ambition. El Anglo's question regarding why Juanito's body was missing haunted him. Where are they? Where is Maria?

He tried to shove these thoughts aside to concentrate on the task ahead. Nevertheless, the visions of El Coyote and panties hanging from the branches signified the desperation of people willing to do anything to find a better life.

To him, El Coyote and the trophy tree symbolized evil. He wanted El Coyote dead even if he himself died in the process.

Miguel dressed as he had that first day, though now he did not have new shoes, and he did not have to ask what to do, for he was experienced and no longer naive. He knew what was out there. What he did not know was whether he really gave a damn, except for El Coyote and Maria and Juanito.

He took his time dressing. Finally, when he went outside, they were waiting for him. Three armored SUVs he had ordered were parked in a row. He entered the middle one with one assassin. Isdel rode in the last one with the other assassin. Isdel's brother Joaquin, was in the lead car with Emilio who had completed his sniper training. Each man carried an AR-16, a change of clothes, and knapsacks full of ammo, food, and water. In addition to the automatic rifles, each also carried a sidearm.

They waited at the border until midnight, and then crossed into Arizona passing through the same ranch property Miguel and Maria had passed through previously with EL Coyote and Pedro.

Because they did not stop at night, they were able to move fast and arrived quickly at the stash house in Tucson without incident. Nate was waiting for them. With the assassins secure in the stash house, Nate walked Miguel and Joaquin to the hotel next door. Joaquin remained outside as security. Nate then left with Isdel and Emilio.

In the shadows, Pedro watched the activity until Nate departed then called the Morales Cartel.

39

A knock at the door woke Miguel. Grasping his Glock, Miguel shouted, "Who's there?"

"Manuel. I have breakfast." Once inside, Manuel said, "We got lots to talk about, Miguel. While you were sojourning through the countryside, there were developments you need to know."

The quirky smile he gave Miguel seemed to settle him. He sucked down breakfast as though he had not eaten in several days, which was, in fact, the case.

"Nate arrested Walker at the Nogales POE. As you thought, he sang like a canary, even implicated you in money laundering.

"He also gave us the name of a person in Miami who traffics in drugs from Mexico to Sicily. We are keeping an eye on him. In addition, he gave us a narco connected to El Coyote who Walker said is a member of the Morales Group. He said he knew about the search for a yellow Humvee but didn't know any details about it."

Manuel walked to the window, pulled the curtains apart a few inches, wiped the pane enough to see through the smudges. In the alley below he saw Joaquin watching the hotel.

Where's Nate?" Miguel asked.

"Staying away. Being seen meeting with the likes of us is not a good idea. My contact with you is expected. Tomorrow I will take you to a new location."

"All right. What's Nate's plan?"

"We will get to that in a moment. First, I need to give you a heads-up, okay?"

Miguel nodded. Manuel moved to the bed and sat on the edge. Miguel nibbled at the food on the desk.

"Nate arrested a man named Morrison. He seemed relieved when Nate talked to him about his activities. This is big, Miguel. His home is the location of a political publicity stunt in which your Hezbollah agents were going to attempt the assassination of the governors of Arizona and Sonora State."

Miguel's mouth fell open. "What? You're kidding."

"The purpose of the assassination, believe it or not, and I still can't grasp it, is to do two things." Shaking his head, he looked at Miguel. "This is unreal. First, they want to demonstrate that border violence has not decreased despite the statements, assurances, and narrative of the administration. Second, to blame the Sonora Cartel for smuggling assassins into the US to kill the *governors. They think this accusation, especially when delivered by Ratcliff to his boss, will convince the NSC to recommend to the president the sanction of a surreptitious eradication of the leaders of the Sonora Cartel, which, of course, will give Morales sole control of the plazas."*

Manuel walked to the window again and peeked outside. He turned back to Miguel. "That's not all, Miguel. Get this. Spiro Morales, the mastermind of this plot, believes the attack will influence the appointment of this Ratcliff guy to the position of deputy director of national intelligence, after the expected reelection of the president."

Miguel just shook his head. He had no idea about American politics. The names, the positions, the various departments, and the alleged conspiracy meant nothing to him, but Manuel's excitement indicated this stuff was important. He just nodded his head when it seemed the appropriate response.

With a long sigh, Manuel continued. "Ratcliff is a big shot. Fortunately, we were able to squelch the event.

"Apparently, Morrison is a reluctant participant in this group who is tied to the Morales Cartel through Adrian Wolforce. Morrison intensely dislikes Wolforce. This Ratcliff has something to do with the distribution of Miranda funding by the State Department. He recommends specific projects in Mexico to the secretary of state.

"Ratcliff recommended Wolforce to be one of his assistants. Other than some rumors, we have nothing on Ratcliff or Wolforce that we can use. Morrison has a lawyer already. Seems assassination crosses some kind of line for him, while human trafficking does not. Anyway, he claims Wolforce is the group's facilitator.

"Here's what we think. They are a disgusting bunch who launder money for the Morales organization from narco and human trafficking, as well as from kidnapping and extortion. Wolforce apparently tips the group off to Mexican projects of interest; thus, their interest in Morrison, who is a major contractor. Nate thinks they are an arm of the Morales Cartel but cannot prove it. They desperately want to destroy the Sonora Cartel, their greatest competition. Incidentally, congratulations, Miguel. You and El Anglo are at the top of their hit list."

Miguel only partially heard Manuel. This nightmare will never end, he thought, realizing that not only was his family murdered, but he had willingly

298 | Dave Wilcox

smuggled foreigners into the United States to kill some governors. All of these lives and more were now on his hands.

Solemnly, Manuel walked to Miguel and grasped his shoulder. "Here is the good news, Miguel. Until just a few days ago, about the time you were saddling up to bring assassins here, and during most of the time since we first met at the stash house, Maria was at Morrison's home in Rio Rico, the very location where this assassination plot was to occur. El Coyote had sold her to Morrison. We have passed her every time we crossed in or out of Mexico through Nogales."

Miguel gasped and then coughed. "Yes, yes!" He punched the air. "I knew it. I knew they were alive. I knew I'd find her." He started to pace. "What's the next step? Where are they?"

Manuel placed his hand on Miguel's shoulder. "You need to know the rest of it. Wolforce arranged for her sale to Ratcliff who had agreed that Juanito would go to Washington with her. Ratcliff was to take possession of her and Juanito at the event at Morrison's. Obviously, Ratcliff couldn't take her while there, too risky. He has a wife and two small kids. Selling a young woman and her kid to Ratcliff while surrounded by media, well, not a good idea.

"Maria was to be the wife's helper and nanny at their Georgetown home. More importantly, she was to be Ratcliffe's mistress, as Morrison put it. Juanito was to be delivered to Maria at Morrisons, and then both were to be taken to the Tucson Airport for a charter flight to Washington, DC. Wolforce made the arrangements.

"El Coyote had told Maria you died at the trophy tree. She innocently disclosed your name and home to Morrison. He claimed he did not make any connection between her and the name El Caballo. Walker also disclosed the location of your home to El Coyote, thereby ending the quest to find El Caballo and his family.

"Spiro placed a one-hundred-thousand-dollar bounty on the head of El Caballo. That he wanted revenge for the assassination of his brothers is no secret. He wants you to suffer like him from the murder of your family. Of course, he must also save face."

"What of Florio? What's he got to do with this?" asked Miguel.

"Florio was assigned to the kill team because he was a family member who was known by your parents and could provide the team with access. According to Walker, after your meeting with Walker when you brought Florio to the Marriott, Walker somehow informed Spiro of the information about your *home and name. El Coyote then bought off Florio, trying to turn him into a snitch for Spiro. Florio was expendable. There was something about revenge for Florio setting up the ambush of Ignacio. We may never know about that."*

Miguel's heart was pounding so hard he was certain Manuel could hear it from across the room. "Where are Juanito and Maria?" he stammered.

"We don't know." Manuel took a deep breath. "They never showed up at the airport. Morrison says he paid a ransom for Juanito so Maria could take him with her as part of the deal with Ratcliff."

"Florio is dead. My parents are dead. They must have taken Juanito. Why would they ... of course ... as hostage to get to me. That's why they did not show up at the airport."

"That's what Nate thinks. He wants you to stay here until contacted. You are the bait. That way, if contacted, we will learn their next move and respond accordingly.

Miguel rose and began to walk around the edge of the room as Manuel resumed his post near the window and watched him.

"Miguel, stop. Listen to me. This won't be easy, but you have to listen. You must understand what has happened to her."

He looked at Manuel, remembering what Nate had said at the Cucaracha Restaurant and what he had learned about how women are treated by the cartels. He wondered what she did all this time at Morrison's. He returned to the edge of the bed and lowered his head into his hands.

"You have to know what has happened," Manuel said. "If you know, you can forgive. Without knowing, there can be no forgiveness, just endless suspicion and endless guilt. Think about it. Slowly, Manuel added, "What right do you have to judge her. What have you done to stay alive?"

Miguel looked at Manuel. "It's not the same," he answered. "All this was her idea. She wanted beautiful things and a life I could not provide her in Las Flores. Family was not enough for her. Yes, we were poor, very poor. If she had not wanted these things ... I thought we were happy."

The tears were just lurking, not far behind his eyes. He wanted to stop them before they appeared. He grew quiet and sat stiffly on the edge of the bed, listening to Manuel describe what life must have been for her. When he stopped speaking, both remained silent, listening to street noise.

Manuel's phone rang.

"Nate wants to see me," Manuel noted. I must return," he sighed. Nodding to Miguel he opened the door slowly, nodded again then disappeared.

After midnight, the room's phone rang. It was Joaquin's voice. "I'm downstairs. Someone here wants to see you. Let us in when we get up there. El Coyote has Juanito and Maria. He will kill them if we do not do exactly what they say. We will come up the stairs. No gun, Miguel, or they will kill them. This guy says to tell you his name is Pedro. Says you know him. I told him he is a dead man."

The phone went silent.

Miguel's room was on the top floor, requiring several minutes to reach him from the lobby. Miguel thought about concealing a weapon and killing them. Maybe it was a bluff. All he was sure about was that Pedro had all the cards. He knew they only wanted him. Juanito and Maria were hostages merely to get to him. Maybe they would make him watch as they killed them in front of him or do all three of them at the same time. He walked to the window and looked down to where Joaquin was stationed. He was not there. Miguel did not think they would kill them in the hotel, which meant that El Coyote was holding them somewhere else.

The worst thing that could happen was they would kill him. Would that be so bad? he wondered. Is there anything left to live for? He unlocked the door, removed the phone Nate had given him from the nightstand, punched the emergency number, and placed it in his pocket. He racked the Glock, released the safety, and gripped it, waiting.

Shuffling in the corridor drew close. He pressed his back against the wall next to the door, pointing the Glock at the ceiling in a double handgrip. He had never felt so calm. The noise in the hallway stopped, the doorknob slowly turned, and the door opened. Pedro shoved Joaquin into the doorway, a pistol at his head. Miguel saw his hands were bound by zip ties, his eyes and body language reflecting rage.

"We have them," snarled Pedro at Miguel. "Don't even think about it. You won't make it out this doorway, and they will die." He held a necklace in his hand and shoved it into Miguel's face.

Miguel recognized it as the necklace El Coyote had taken from Maria at the trophy tree. Several young men pointed handguns at him. He could not see how many others were in the hallway out of sight.

Pedro shifted his pistol from Joaquin and shoved it up and into Miguel's face. "Drop it!" he demanded.

A man picked up Miguel's weapon and put it in his pocket. Pedro shoved Miguel back into the room and up against the opposite wall. Four men held him there at gunpoint.

"Turn around, and face the wall!" Pedro ordered. "If he moves, shoot him!"

They did not seem to care about the noise, correctly believing their weapons canceled any interference. Pedro roughly searched Miguel. Finding Miguel's phone, he shoved it into his pocket and then searched the room. Finding cash, he wadded it up and stuffed it into the same pocket as the phone.

Miguel had the urge to take Pedro down hard. He gathered himself and then had second thoughts. Getting Pedro would do nothing to help Juanito or Maria. They would kill them for sure. This was between him and El Coyote. Wait for the chance, he said to himself. They will take me to him.

With Miguel's hands tied behind him, Pedro slugged him in the face and then in the stomach before trying to shove him out the door as the others watched. Miguel did not budge. Pedro, whose head barely reached Miguel's shoulders, grabbed the back of Miguel's collar, turned, and tried to shove Miguel toward the door. He almost fell as Miguel maintained his position. The young men started to giggle.

Pedro turned to them and yelled, "Get him out of here!"

Three men grabbed him and shoved him into the hall beside Joaquin. Pedro started for the stairs as the others shoved Miguel and Joaquin ahead of them. They noisily walked down the stairs, out a side door, and into the alley where several SUVs and a van waited with engines running. They pulled out of the alley and into the deserted streets. Shortly they stopped at the trailhead leading to the trophy tree.

While the shadows remained deep within the nearby gullies and crevices, the sun slowly began to crest the ridge to the east. They dragged Miguel and Joaquin from the cars.

Pedro removed two ropes from a car, tied slipknots in each, and dropped them over their heads like lassos, tightening them around their necks. A man held each one. They herded them like cattle along the trail for several miles to the trophy tree. El Coyote and several others waited in the clearing. Miguel and Joaquin's ankles were cuffed. They removed the ropes from their necks.

Pedro placed his foot in the small of each man's back and shoved them face-first to the ground.

"This I have saved just for you, El Caballo. Your head hanging from the trophy tree proclaims I am the best. I have not used this knife since I was at your stinking shack of a house. I am going to slit your throat and then take your headless body to Hermosillo and hang it from the bridge with a sign that reads, 'This is what happens to those who attack Morales.' Then they will pay me one hundred thousand American dollars. The narcocorrido musicians will write songs just about me." He pulled back Miguel's head and held the knife in the air so all those at the trophy tree saw it.

Suddenly, El Coyote's face erupted, splattering Miguel with tissue and blood. Eerily, there had been no sound except a splat. The people guarding Miguel looked at each other. Two fell to the ground. Two crawled through the garbage. Both were hit. Another died. One by one, those standing fell. One started to run but only made a few steps. Those remaining dropped their weapons and raised their hands, and the killing ceased.

A figure slowly rose from the brush near the crest of a small rise. At about ten degrees to the northwest of the first shooter a second shooter rose. Their camouflage clothing made them difficult to see amid the brush. Although the sun was behind both shooters, Miguel recognized Emilio, the boy who had saved Maria from falling off the Beast. The second shooter was Isdel; both were capable of such accurate shooting.

Seven young men in various positions were down in the center of the clearing beneath the trophy tree. Most of El Coyote's face was missing. Four others stood with their arms raised, including Pedro. El Coyote was sprawled next to Miguel. Because of the zip ties, Miguel and Joaquin were unable to stand. The firing ceased. An unnatural silence hung over the trophy tree. The panties dangling from branches did not move in the lifeless air.

A helicopter noisily appeared low over the clearing, churning dust. Panties waved in the breeze. It hovered over the scene and then moved away, landing nearby.

Miguel heard footsteps approaching from behind him. He tried to turn. Manuel, carrying a sniper's rifle with attached suppressor, reached into his pocket, removed a knife, opened it, cut the ties at Miguel and Joaquin's ankles and wrists, and helped them to their feet. Looking down, Miguel saw El Coyote's blood flowing onto his boots, and before stepping away, Miguel wiped them on El Coyote. He reached down, picked up the knife, and wiped it on El Coyote. He then cut a piece of cloth from El Coyote's shirt and wrapped the knife before putting it in his own pocket.

"They'll clean it all up," Manuel said to Miguel. "Let's get out of here."

"Where are we going?" Miguel asked.

"You will know soon enough."

40

*T*hey turned into a residential area of small homes with older cars and continued a couple of blocks before slowing and entering a driveway. Manuel unlocked the doors and then stepped out, motioning Miguel to remain in the car.

Manuel looked around the area. He nodded to Miguel. A man and a woman stepped out of the house and stood together on the stoop, watching them approach.

To Miguel, they seemed familiar. He gasped as he recognized Maria's aunt and uncle. Her uncle turned and opened the screen door and stepped aside. Standing in the shadow were Maria and Juanito.

Miguel's legs wobbled. Unable to catch his breath, he felt his knees buckling, and had Manuel not grabbed his elbow and wrapped his arm around Miguel's waist, he might have fallen.

"Maria," he said, choking.

Their faces were a portal through which flashbacks streamed: the compound in Las Flores, the corral, the houses they built, the evenings he shared with his father watching the sun slipping behind the mountains, his dog Rascal lying between them, Maverick trotting to him in response to his whistle, the Friday horse races. He relived Ignacio, Inez, and her baby in pools of blood; the attack at the hacienda and Filberto in pieces; beheadings at the killing house; and the carnage and the stain and odor of his parent's spilled blood on the floor in their casa.

As his knees gave way, Maria's uncle held him up from one side and Manuel on the other. Together, they helped him walk into the house and lowered him to the sofa.

Miguel took a deep breath, gathered himself, and stood. He turned to her. Her face flooded with tears, and they embraced.

She said, "They told me El Coyote killed you. I am so sorry, Miguel, so sorry. It's all my fault. If I had not wanted to leave Mexico, your parents, Ignacio, Inez, their baby, Florio … she sighed. None of this would have happened." She sobbed, shaking.

Once she calmed down, she said, "There are things I must tell you. Things have happened to me. You have to know, Miguel."

"We can talk later." He looked down at her. "There are things you must know about me also. We should be happy we are alive and together now." He knelt in front of Juanito.

"He's your daddy," she said.

Juanito reached for him, and Miguel picked him up and held him. He slowly walked around the room, thinking that the only importance to his life now was in this room … what he held. He set Juanito on the sofa and sat down himself so that Juanito was between him and Maria. When the time was right, he knew they had to talk about what had happened to each of them. He saw she had changed. An aura of sadness seemed to engulf her. What she must have gone through since they had last been together was a lot for both of them to try to overcome or accept. He wondered if it was worth it or even possible to recover what he thought they had before leaving Las Flores. What he had done and experienced had changed him as well, he acknowledged, remembering what Manuel had said. When they married, they were different people, unrecognizable now. Was it even possible to resume their lives without Jose and Yolanda? If it was possible, could they ever feel safe?

Miguel went to the door, stepped outside, and walked to Manuel who was leaning against the car talking to Maria's uncle, the scoped rifle lying on the hood near Manuel's hand.

"I need to speak to Manuel alone," he said. He felt vulnerable now standing in the open. An attack could come at any time.

Her uncle nodded and moved to the house, leaving them at the car.

Manuel looked down the street one way, and Miguel watched the opposite direction.

An unmarked car with opaque windows turned at the corner and slowly approached. Manuel placed his hand on the rifle and pulled it closer. At the driveway, the car turned in and stopped behind Manuel's SUV. Nate stepped out.

"I'll stay just a minute. Not good to be seen together with you two." To Miguel, he said, "Glad you made it." He turned to Manuel and said, "Nice job. Good shooting."

Manuel nodded.

Nate and Miguel shook hands.

"Like I said, El Caballo, we start with the lowest guy on the totem pole and let him take us to the top. That guy was you. Look where you've gotten to, Miguel."

Sure, Miguel thought to himself. Just look where I've gotten to: murderer, narco, snitch, and half of my family dead.

Miguel looked at Nate. "Couple of questions?"

"Sure."

"How did you know they would take us to the trophy tree?"

"Your phone, Miguel. We were monitoring it. Remember?"

He remembered. "You said it would follow my location. It wasn't with me. It was in Pedro's pocket. What if we weren't together?"

"We heard everything in your hotel room. We were also following a couple of your guys who were watching from the shadows outside. The group coming to get you was not exactly concerned who saw them, easy to follow. Also, a drone followed you from the hotel. A chopper brought Emilio and Isdel to the trophy tree before anyone arrived."

Manuel interrupted. "El Anglo authorized a few more guys, just in case. Thankfully, whoever led the group that captured you was an idiot. We flew over them and thought we'd given ourselves away. Apparently, they didn't notice us."

"How did Maria and Juanito end up here?" Miguel asked.

"Well, El Coyote took Juanito from the compound after your parents and Florio died. He knew Morrison needed Juanito so he could sell both to Wolforce. He also realized they were potential hostages for you. We got to Morrison first, and he told us when and where they were. They were to fly out of Tucson. We arrested Wolforce. The sheriff has him in custody for the FBI. We took Maria and Juanito to a detention center. She gave us the name of her aunt and uncle, and that was enough to track them down."

"What about papers? Are there not exceptions for this sort of thing like asylum or something?"

"And for you too," said Nate. "This was an important bust." Nate's phone rang with the tune of "La Cucaracha." He sheepishly smiled and answered. "Yes, sir. I will tell them. They are standing right here and safe."

Nate hung up and continued. "Vargas arranged for a private plane to pick up the three of you at Tucson International Airport. You must be there by ten tomorrow morning at the military section. They'll be expecting you. We'll meet you there to be sure everything is in order." He nodded to Manuel.

"You spoke to Alvera?" Miguel asked.

"No, my boss in Washington." He extended his hand to Miguel. "We shall talk again soon."

Miguel returned to the house. There were two bedrooms, a living room, a dining room, and a kitchen. If Maria stayed there with Juanito, they would be safer than in Las Flores, where she no longer had family.

He had achieved his goals. El Coyote was dead. Maria and Juanito were safe. There'd be no celebration. Somehow, they had survived in the desert of life.

Obviously, Nate was not simply going to forget him. He was deep inside the Sonora Cartel and the narco world. Could El Anglo or Spiro Morales simply let him walk?

Miguel knew this was only one battle won. Miguel remained El Caballo with a price on his head.